China's Relations with Arabia and the Gulf 1949–1999

This is the only comprehensive volume available on China's relations with countries of the Gulf and Arabian Peninsula, from the establishment of the People's Republic of China in 1949 to the end of the twentieth century.

Based on extensive original research, it looks at the relations between China and each of the countries of the region over the entire period. Using a neo-realist theory of international relations, the book provides a theoretical and practical analysis of the conduct of Chinese foreign policy. *China's Relations with Arabia and the Gulf 1949–1999* demostrates that two key factors have shaped China's foreign policy with the region: China's relations with the United States and the Soviet Union, and China's drive to increase its economic ties with the countries of the region, especially after becoming a net importer of oil in the early 1990s.

Mohamed Bin Huwaidin argues persuasively that the Gulf and Arabian Peninsula have in fact always been part of China's foreign policy agenda, and that the region has been a significant region for China both politically and economically. The book stresses that this region will continue to be key as China pushes towards achieving – and sustaining – new levels of economic modernization. Scholars working in International Relations, Asian Studies and Politics will find this volume a vital insight into modern Chinese foreign policy.

Mohamed Bin Huwaidin is Assistant Professor in Political Science at United Arab Emirates University.

Durham Modern Middle East and Islamic World Studies

1. **Economic Development in Saudi Arabia**
   Rodney Wilson with *Monica Malik*, *Abdullah Al Salamah* and *Ahmed Al Rajhi*

2. **Islam Encountering Globalisation**
   Edited by *Ali Mohammadi*

3. **China's Relations with Arabia and the Gulf 1949–1999**
   Mohamed Bin Huwaidin

China's Relations with Arabia and the Gulf 1949–1999

Mohamed Bin Huwaidin

LONDON AND NEW YORK

First published 2002
by Routledge
2 Park Square, Milton Park, Abingdon, Oxfordshire OX14 4RN

Simultaneously published in the USA and Canada
by Routledge
711 Third Avenue, New York, NY 10017

Routledge is an imprint of the Taylor & Francis Group

First issued in paperback 2011

© 2002 Mohamed Bin Huwaidin

Typeset in 10/12pt Times by Steven Gardiner Ltd

All rights reserved. No part of this book may be reprinted or
reproduced or utilized in any form or by any electronic,
mechanical, or other means, now known or hereafter
invented, including photocopying and recording, or in any
information storage or retrieval system, without permission in
writing from the publishers.

British Library Cataloguing in Publication Data
A catalogue record for this book is available from the British Library

Library of Congress Cataloging in Publication Data
Bin Huwaidin, Mohamed, 1969–
  China's relations with Arabia and the Gulf, 1949–1999 / Mohamed Bin Huwaidin.
    p. cm.
  Includes bibliographical references and index.

  1. China – Foreign relations – Arab countries. 2. Arab countries – Foreign
relations – China. 3. China – Foreign relations – 1949– I. Title.
DS777.8.B57 2002
327.51017′4927 – dc21   2002068012

ISBN 978-0-700-71730-9 (hbk)
ISBN 978-0-415-51537-5 (pbk)

To my father and mother who believed in me from the day I was born and share their sense of pride in me. They stayed in my mind throughout the time I worked to achieve my goal.

Contents

List of tables ix
Acknowledgements xi

PART I
Introduction 1

1 **General elements and literature review** 3

Focus and purpose of the study 3
Significance of the study 3
Why study China? 4
Literature survey 7
Chapter plan 18

PART II
China's foreign policy in a global context 21

2 **Theorizing China's foreign policy** 23

Internal factors 24
External factors 38
Conclusion 51

3 **China's relations with the United States, the Soviet Union, and Russia** 53

China's early interactions with the superpowers (1949–1954) 53
China and the changing of its foreign policy strategy (1955–1969) 56
China and the policy of leaning towards the United States (1970–1981) 63
China's independent foreign policy (1982–1990) 68

China's relations with the United States and Russia in the post-Cold War era (1991–1999) 74
Conclusion 90

PART III
China's foreign policy toward the Gulf and Arabian Peninsula region 93

4 China's perceptions of the Gulf and Arabian Peninsula region 95

Phase 1: China's early involvement in the region (1949–1970) 96
Phase 2: China's pragmatic foreign policy towards the region (1971–1989) 104
Phase 3: China's new interest in the region (1990–1999) 119
Oil 131
Conclusion 134

5 China's relations with Iraq, Iran, and Yemen 136

China and Iraq 136
China and Iran 153
China and Yemen 173
Conclusion 185

6 China's relations with the countries of the Gulf Co-operation Council 188

China and Kuwait 188
China and Oman 201
China and Saudi Arabia 213
China and the UAE 236
China and Qatar 250
China and Bahrain 256
Conclusion 260

PART IV
Conclusion 263

7 Summary, conclusions, and some remarks for future relations 265

Appendix 275
Bibliography 285
Index 303

Tables

2.1	China's participation in international organizations, 1960–1989	36
2.2	China's military expenditures official figures, 1976–1996	49
4.1	China's main arms customers by region, 1982–1986	115
4.2	China's main arms customers by region, 1987–1991	115
4.3	China's top arms customers, 1982–1986	116
4.4	China's top arms customers, 1987–1991	116
4.5	China's arms sales to Iran, 1981–1988	117
4.6	China's arms sales to Iraq, 1981–1988	118
4.7	China's arms sales to Iran, 1990–1997	128
4.8	China's production, consumption, export, and deficit of crude oil, 1991–1997	131
5.1	Iranian arms transfers by major suppliers, 1983–1997	169
6.1	Oman's exports of crude oil by country	211
6.2	Oman's main trading partners	212

Acknowledgements

Praise be to Allah, the Almighty God, without whose blessings this work could not have been accomplished.

Producing this academic work has been a very significant step in my life. I would like to express my great gratitude and thanks to all those who have helped and encouraged me while producing this work. First of all, my great thanks go to my parents whose blessings kept me encouraged and focused. Second, I am deeply grateful to Professor Anoushiravan Ehteshami of the Centre of Middle Eastern and Islamic Studies at University of Durham, for the perceptive remarks, useful guidance, and kindness he has given me over the period of conducting this study. I owe Professor Hassan Hamdan al-Kim of the Political Sciences Department at United Arab Emirates University and Professor Tim C. Niblock of University of Exeter a great deal for their encouragement and support. I would also like to express my gratitude to United Arab Emirates University, my sponsor, for offering me the opportunity to contribute in the development of my country and the field of my study. Sincere thanks are due to Ms Dulvadee Leewiraphan (Pook) who devoted some of her time and energy to help me produce the technical data required to produce this work.

May God bless them all!

Part I
Introduction

1 General elements and literature review

FOCUS AND PURPOSE OF THE STUDY

This book focuses on the foreign policy of one of the most important and influential states in today's international system, the People's Republic of China (PRC), and attempts to assess its relations with the Gulf and Arabian Peninsula region. The book identifies and explores different forces and variables that have impacted China's foreign policy behaviour towards the Gulf and Arabian Peninsula region from the time of the establishment of the PRC in October 1949 until the end of the twentieth century. Its purpose is to establish and develop a comprehensive understanding of China's foreign policy behaviour towards the countries of this region. Such an understanding is critical for analysts of China's foreign policy and policy makers, particularly in the Gulf and Arabian Peninsula region, to explain and even predict China's behaviour towards the region. The book also aims at filling an important gap in the study of China's foreign policy. Most of the current works on China's foreign policy towards the region deal with this area as part of the bigger picture of China's relations with either the Arab world or the Middle East. No other study has dealt comprehensively with the issues of China's foreign relations with the countries of the Gulf and Arabian Peninsula region. This work is the first comprehensive attempt at exploring China's relations with the region during and after the Cold War. It covers China's political, economic, and social interactions with Iraq, Iran, Yemen, Kuwait, Oman, Saudi Arabia, the United Arab Emirates, Qatar, and Bahrain.

SIGNIFICANCE OF THE STUDY

This work aims to overcome the shortcomings pertaining to the study of China's foreign policy towards the Gulf and Arabian Peninsula region. The literature on China's foreign relations with the countries of the region does not cover China's relations with all the countries of this area. Instead, it focuses on studying China's foreign relations with some of the countries of

4 *Introduction*

the region in the context of the implications for China's relations with the rest. Abidi's study (1982), for example, focuses on China's relations with Iran, leaving only a part of his study to the discussion of China's relations with the other Gulf countries. Other studies such as Yitzhak Shichor's (1979), John Calabrese's (1991), and Lillian Craig Harris's (1993) study China's foreign relations with the countries of the region in the context of China's foreign relations with the rest of the Middle East. Issues such as China's relations with Egypt and China's policy on the Palestine question are treated, along with China's relations with the United States and the Soviet Union, as the key issues in shaping China's foreign policy towards the countries of the Gulf and Arabian Peninsula region. This work, however, is an attempt to provide the first comprehensive study of China's foreign policy towards the region, covering China's interaction with all its countries during and after the Cold War.

WHY STUDY CHINA?

China's economic and strategic weight, at both the global and regional levels, forms one of the most prominent elements in today's international politics. China's importance reflects two significant factors. The first is the sustained growth of the Chinese economy since 1979 and its implications for China's long-term economic and strategic power. The second is the increased political muscle and military capability of China and its continued transfer of advanced military technology to many parts of the world.

Since 1979, China has embarked upon one of the most successful economic modernization programmes in the world. A programme that earned China a 9.3 per cent average annual growth rate of its Gross Domestic Product (GDP) between 1979 and 1993, and 11.8 per cent in 1994 and 9.8 per cent in 1996. Such growth was one of the highest in the world, particularly since the rest of the world experienced an average growth rate of just 2.6 per cent for the same period. China's GDP increased 3.76-fold in just 15 years (Fei-Ling Wang 1998: 68). The World Bank has estimated that China's economic output will reach $10 trillion by the middle of the twenty-first century; and it is expected that China will become the world's largest economy, in terms of GDP, by 2010 (Frolic 1997: 324). Today, China's dynamic economy attracts more foreign investments than any other country in the world, except the United States. The implications of the strong Chinese economy are said to be important for regional security. Gary Klintworth (1995) argues that the strong Chinese economy gives the Chinese a lucrative interest in the preservation of regional stability, which may account for Beijing's contribution to resolving Cambodia's civil war and keeping the 1994 Korean crisis from escalating (Klintworth 1995: 488). Stuart Harris (1995) indicates that the world wants a strong Chinese economy, to prevent the dangers of internal instability and to deepen its participation in the world economy, potentially making China a more responsible international actor and a lucrative economic partner with its neighbours. Harris, however, argues that a strong economy could also provide China with the basis for immense political power, which Beijing might use to force its own interests upon its neighbours (Harris 1995: 37). In either case, China's regional and global significance will be enhanced as the Chinese economy continues to grow in an impressive manner.

However, it is not only economic modernization that has created an important role for China in today's international system, but also China's increasing military capabilities and its continuing political and military cooperation with many countries in the world. China is not only a nuclear power but also a power possessing some of the world's most advanced military technologies and has military dominance over many of its Asian neighbours. It is working to enhance and increase its military capabilities by developing a modern tactical airforce, which includes the Russian Su-27, the FC-1 light fighter, the F-10 multi-role fighter, the advanced XXJ fighter, the F-8 IIM interceptor, and the FB-7 striker (Anselmo 1997: 324). It is also developing much more accurate ballistic and cruise missiles. In addition, China is increasing its naval offensive capability by purchasing two Russian Sovermeny-Class destroyers and four Russian Kilo-Class conventional submarines, as well as developing its own nuclear powered boats (Hynes n.d.). Such an increase in China's military capabilities has been coupled with a rise in Chinese military technology exports to many parts of the world including the Middle East. China has emerged as one of the world's major suppliers of military hardware. According to the Stockholm International Peace Research Institute (SIPRI) Yearbooks, China became the sixth leading supplier of major conventional weapons in the 1990s. The value of China's military exports was around US$4,357 million between 1992 and 1996 (*SIPRI* 1997: 268). China sees its military cooperation with countries such as Pakistan, Iran, Syria, Saudi Arabia, Iraq, and Libya (some of the Middle Eastern countries that China has provided with military technology), as both a source of hard currency and an opportunity for Beijing's foreign policy to score some political and strategic points. International concerns over Chinese military transfer is prompted not just by China becoming one of the leading arms exporters in the world, but by the type of country that China is providing weaponry technology to. Most of the countries that China is believed to have supplied arms technology to are countries perceived by the West as dangerous to regional and world stability and supportive of terrorist activities. This, therefore, has upgraded China's importance to the West as well. Its cooperation with the West in halting its military transfer to such countries is considered a vital Western interest.

China's geography, population, and political weight in the international arena have also contributed to increasing China's role in the international system. China is a vast country of 9.6 million square kilometres, next in size only to Russia and Canada. Its land borders total 22,800 kilometres and bound fifteen different countries. Across the seas to the east and the south-east are South Korea, Japan, the Philippines, Brunei, Malaysia, and Indonesia. Because of its military power, China has been able to secure and ensure stability in its border areas. Alastair Iain Johnston and Robert S. Ross (1999) argue that small neighbours, like South Korea, will reconcile to reduce the threat and benefit from cooperation; on the other hand, countries such as Japan and India might pursue an aggressive strategy in an attempt to balance against China (Johnston and Ross 1999: 283). Both Japan and India are countries that China has continued to have territorial and border disputes with. Not surprisingly, therefore, China's rising military power has triggered a similar response in these two countries to increase their own military capabilities. Japan began to expand its military spending and work, and has advocated implementation of a national missile defence theatre. India, on the other hand, started to build up its own military capability by becoming a nuclear power (Bracken 1999).

China is the world's most populous nation, where over 1.2 billion people, 22 per cent of the world's population, lives (excluding Taiwan, Hong Kong, and Macao) (Benewick and Donald 1999: 11–17). It is predicted that China's population will reach 1.63 billion by the year 2030 (including Hong Kong and Macao) (Brown 1995). The political weight of the large Chinese population is believed to be one of the most important factors to be felt not only in regional terms but also internationally. According to Lester Brown (1995), China's arable land will dwindle greatly in the process of industrialization. This will lead to a decrease in China's self-reliance in food supply, which, according to his calculation, will cause a worldwide food crisis in the coming century (Brown 1995). Scot Stevenson (1998) highlights this point by arguing that if the continuing growth of China's population is not matched by an increase in the welfare of the people, massive population movements from China to the neighbouring countries could threaten the region. This would clearly spell large political, economic, and social problems for the neighbouring countries, in particular, and for the security of the region, in general (Stevenson 1998; Goldstone 1995: 35–52). Some have even indicated that the continuing growth of China's population could force China to adopt a more aggressive policy and push towards the new territories and natural resources of Central Asia (Ehteshami 2000: 108). It is not surprising then to witness Japan, South Korea, Singapore, America, and South-East Asian countries pursuing an engaging economic policy with China. It can also be said that the sixty million wealthy, overseas, ethnic Chinese who occupy key economic positions in many South-East Asian countries also contribute to China's importance. Steven W. Mosher (2000) has highlighted the dangers to the Far East of China using its overseas ethnic population to re-establish its regional hegemony. To Mosher, the increased numbers and role of the ethnic Chinese populations in many countries of Asia could encourage China to redraw its borders and set new claims over new territories, and could also lead China to justify its intervention in the internal affairs of many countries of the region.

All of the above contributes to the widespread international certainty that current policies towards China should reflect long-term national and multi-lateral responses to the rise in Chinese influence and power. A constructive type of engagement has been adopted by many countries of the world in their relations with China. The goal of this strategy has been to make China's leaders more sensitive to regional and international security and political concerns through dialogue and peaceful discussion.

LITERATURE SURVEY

There is a wide range of literature examining and analysing different aspects of China's foreign policy. Two major schools of thought have dominated this study. One school has argued for the internal factor as the most dominant factor in shaping China's foreign policy. The other school has focused on China's rivalry with both the United States and the Soviet Union as its motivating factor. The latter argues that China's relations with both the United States and the Soviet Union have been the pre-eminent factors in shaping China's foreign policy towards the world. Since the former is discussed in greater detail in Chapter 2, the latter will be the focus here.

Some Chinese foreign policy strategies have been regarded by scholars as a natural result of Beijing's perception of its relations with Washington and Moscow. The 'two camps' theory and the 'leaning to one side' policy of the early 1950s, for instance, are both widely accepted to be products of China's perception of superpower behaviour during that period. Chun-tu Hsueh and Robert C. North (1977) argue that these two Chinese foreign policies had been derived from the policies of both the United States and the Soviet Union towards China in the 1950s. They believe that Washington's criticism of communist government in China and Washington's unprecedented support for the nationalist government in Taiwan pushed China towards adopting the two foreign policy strategies (Chun-tu Hsueh and North 1977: 49–53). Similar argument is also made by Michael H. Hunt (1996). Hunt indicates that Mao Zedong was flexible and opportunistic in his handling of China's foreign policy. Mao, according to Hunt, was willing to reach a deal with Washington before the adoption of these two foreign policies. However, it was American rigidity that prevented accommodation, which in the end led China to adopt the hostile foreign policies of leaning to one side and the two camps (Hunt 1996).

China's perception of its relations with the two superpowers was also reflected in the literature studying the changes in Chinese foreign policy in the late 1950s and early 1960s with the growing political and ideological disputes between Beijing and Moscow. As China began to look to Third

8 *Introduction*

World countries as potential allies in the struggle against imperialism, particularly following the Bandung Conference, China–Soviet relations started to deteriorate. Chen Jian and Yang Kuisong (1998) contribute the tension between the two countries to Khrushchev's secret speech of February 1956, in which he attacked Stalin's policy. According to them, China's foreign policy towards the world had shifted, following Khrushchev's attack on Stalin, from pursuing alignment with the Soviet Union towards challenging the Soviets throughout the Third World. Donald S. Zagoria (1962) contributes the differences between Beijing and Moscow to calculations of the risk involved in protecting and supporting local revolutionary movements. While Moscow accused the Chinese of minimizing the dangers of all-out nuclear war, the Chinese accused the Russians of exaggerating those dangers (Zagoria 1962). The result was the failure of the Chinese–Soviet alliance, which was marked by extensive border clashes and disputes (Doolin 1965). This development in Chinese–Soviet relations was perceived by many international analysts to have a profound impact on the direction of China's foreign policy. Peter van Ness (1970) argues that China, after the collapse of its alliance with the Soviet Union, began to use its support for revolutionary movements as an instrument of its foreign policy throughout the Third World; therefore, challenging the Soviet presence and influence there. Tai Sung An (1976) believes that the deterioration in China–Soviet relations urged Chinese foreign policy makers to adopt countermeasures to spoil Soviet efforts in Asia, Europe, Latin America, and Africa by seeking a 'united front'. The United States was not left out of this new Chinese foreign policy outlook. The shift in China's foreign policy towards Washington in the late 1960s and early 1970s was seen by many as part of both Beijing and Washington's efforts to undermine Soviet policy in Asia, Europe, and in other regions. Jonathan D. Pollack (1991) finds that the opening of China to the United States 'reflected longer-term strategic developments that directly affected Beijing's security calculation'. Among these developments was 'the increase in Soviet conventional and nuclear forces deployed in Asia that posed a direct threat to the security of China' (Pollack 1991). Such an analysis continued to dominate China's foreign policy towards the two powers in the 1970s (Pollack 1991: 402–7). With regard to China's relations with the United States, John W. Garver (1993) argues that the new Chinese policy originated in the ancient Chinese strategy of 'using barbarians to control barbarians'. According to Garver (1993a: 74–6), China was aiming to divide the superpowers by improving relations with the United States, then use the strength of the United States to offset that of the Soviet Union. Garver, in my opinion, is right when he indicates that China was aiming, by developing relations with the United States, to use Washington to undermine Moscow's policies throughout the world. Robert G. Sutter (1978a) sees China's need to use Chinese–American rapprochement to offset the Soviet pressure on China as the main factor that led Beijing to pursue a new foreign policy.

He argues that the outbreak of Sino-Soviet border clashes in late 1960s and the American pullback from Asia had motivated China to improve relations with the United States and its allies around the world. The Chinese, on one hand, saw the American pullback from Asia as solid evidence of Washington's interest in improved relations with Beijing and the abolishment of its containment policy. The change in China's foreign policy was evident in the adoption of a flexible policy towards Eastern Europe. The aim was to turn Soviet bloc discontent with Moscow to China's advantage. China also focused on strengthening its influence in key neighbouring countries and on blocking suspected Soviet initiatives there. In North Vietnam, China began to overlook its past differences with the North Vietnamese, adopting a more amicable attitude towards its communist neighbour. In North Korea, China continued its efforts to demonstrate its solidarity with Pyongyang (Sutter 1978a: 63–102). Harry Harding (1992: 162–9) talks about the rationale in continuing the strategic relationship between Beijing and Washington. He views Chinese–American strategic relations as an important counterweight to Soviet power in Asia, which could have helped promote the Soviet withdrawal from Afghanistan and the removal of Vietnamese forces from Cambodia. Jonathan D. Pollack (1984) argues that the continued improvement in Chinese–American relations at the end of the 1970s was based not only on Chinese anxieties about Soviet political and military encirclement, but also on the ascendance of Deng Xiaoping who was prepared to cement ties with the West. Deng was hoping to receive some vital assistance for China's modernization effort.

However, the literature on China's foreign policy in the 1980s started to play down the impact of China's relations with the United States and the Soviet Union on China's foreign policy. New variables, like modernization, have been seen as the dominant factors in determining China's foreign policy.[1] Yet, in the 1990s, another school of thought began to see China's foreign policy as being driven by its ambitions to emerge as a powerful state that will dominate regional and, to some extent, international affairs. Two main developments in China brought about a profusion of 'China threat' literature. First was the increase in China's military capability compared to East and South-East Asian countries and its continuing military cooperation with many unfriendly Third World countries to the West. Second was the rapid rise in China's economic power and the advanced technological investment by Western companies in China. The main assumption of the 'China threat' thesis could be traced to the general finding of Samuel P. Huntington (1996). In this and some other earlier works, Huntington underlines how Chinese civilization presented a challenge to Western

---

1 The impact of these variables is discussed in the next chapter.

civilization. He believes that in the post-Cold War era, the ideological conflict has been replaced by a conflict of civilizations, which has become the root of international conflicts and wars. He has also said that the primary adversary of Western civilization is Islam and Confucianism, which have formed a coalition challenging Western values, interests, and power. While Huntington's argument provoked a great deal of controversy among Chinese officials and intellectuals who criticized him 'for ignorance of and bias against Chinese culture', (Wang Zhongren 1997: 7–8) many Western scholars have adopted this argument in explaining China's foreign policy. The work of Richard Bernstein and Ross H. Munro, 'The coming conflict with America' (1997), illustrates this. Bernstein and Munro argue that the Chinese leadership since the late 1980s has taken an offensive national policy, which is contrary to American interests, and aims to replace the United States as the dominant power in Asia. China since then, according to Bernstein and Munro (1997: 18–32), has come to see Washington not as a strategic partner but as the chief obstacle to its own strategic ambitions. Therefore, it has worked to reduce American influence in Asia, to prevent Tokyo and Washington from containing China, to build up its military capability, and to expand its influence in the region's essential sea lanes. In a later work, Bernstein and Munro (1998) argue that China's policy towards the United States is focusing on using Washington to achieve China's goals; meanwhile, the United States policy towards China is not guided by a clear and firm sense of American national interests. In their opinion, the United States' military, economic, and political engagements with China are serving Beijing's national interests more than those of Washington. They encourage Washington to adopt a clear policy that outlines the need to prevent China from becoming the hostile hegemon that could interfere with the American pursuit of its interests in Asia (Bernstein and Munro 1998: 203–21). Edward Timperlake and William C. Triplett II (1998) agree with the above argument and indicate that China is the only foreign country currently targeting American cities for nuclear destruction. They criticize the Clinton administration for selling out America's national security by cooperating with Beijing militarily and allowing the Chinese government to influence American politics by raising campaign cash. In a later work, Timperlake and Triplett argue that China, armed with the most modern weapons of mass destruction, is the only regime in the world that poses a greater threat to global security. To Timperlake and Triplett, China is an expanding regional power poised to dominate the Pacific by challenging the United States and its allies in the region. The increasing capability of its military, the continuing supply of arms technology to 'terrorist countries', the growing Chinese forces in the South China Sea, and the continuing threat to Taiwan have been directed by China's foreign policy objective to dominate the region and get rid of American influence there (Timperlake and Triplett 1999). Steven W. Mosher (2000) goes further and claims that China is a hegemonic power aiming to dominate the world. Its appetite for domination, according to Mosher, is embedded in its long history, with its origin in the Qin dynasty; the hegemon's appetite for dominance grew century after century until, by the time of the Qing dynasty in the eighteenth century, China held control of a vast territory stretching from today's Siberia, southward along the Himalayas to the Indian Ocean, and eastward across Laos and Vietnam. China's dominance, however, declined in the nineteenth century when it came into conflict with Western powers. But, according to Mosher, China's hegemonic spirit reawakened after the communists seized control of the country and the new 'Mao dynasty' was created. Mosher believes that China's quest for domination will develop in three stages: first, China will begin by recovering Taiwan and then reclaim the small islands in the South China Sea; second, China will move towards establishing a strong influence in Siberia, Mongolia, and the Central Asian republics. Then, China will continue to assert its position in the Korean Peninsula and in the South-East Asian countries. Third, China will work to complete its regional domination by bringing the Philippines and Indonesia under its sway. It will neutralize India and extend its reach into the Middle East and Africa (Mosher 2000: 47–116).

To some extent, all of the above arguments about 'China's threat' and its foreign policy have some validity in them. China's foreign policy towards Asian countries has reflected China's interest in preventing the emergence of a dominant power in Asia. China carries a foreign policy that criticizes Japan's military development and its efforts to establish a national defence missile system, supports the communist regimes in North Korea and Laos, sells arms technology to Pakistan, uses military force to control the disputed territories in the South China Sea, works to establish political and economic influence in the Central Asia republics, and continues to criticize US support for the Taiwanese regime. All these foreign policy strategies suggest that China is hoping to achieve political and military influence for itself in the region. The assumption that China is increasing its efforts to challenge or undermine the American presence in Asia is not quite clear. Other than the US involvement in Taiwan, the Chinese leadership seems to have accepted the American presence in the region. The American military presence in Japan, for instance, is China's best way of keeping Japan from pushing to build a nuclear capability and, therefore, dominate the region as it did in the past. China also, at least, is not doing any harm to US efforts to bring a peaceful reunification of the Korean Peninsula. Therefore, China's foreign policy towards Asia might have been driven by China's ambition to dominate the region but its perceived challenge, by the above literature, to American interest in the region is not impressively accurate.

The literature on China's relations with the countries of the Middle East tend to study the origin and evolution of China's foreign policy towards these countries in the context of China's relations with the superpowers. This rivalry, mentioned earlier, between China and the two superpowers constitutes the basic background for the literature studying China's relations with the countries of the Middle East. Yitzhak Shichor is the first scholar to study in depth China's relations with the countries of the Middle East. His study discusses the evolution of China's foreign policy towards the Middle East in its first thirty-eight years of development. Shichor's (1979: 1) basic assumption is that the Middle East had always been important to China 'as a part of the general historical development of the world which affected and involved China's interests'. Shichor asserts that China's policy towards the Middle East had been a reflection of China's own perception of its relations with the United States and the Soviet Union and both superpowers' relations with each other. His division of his work to five subjects illustrates that China's policy towards the Middle East from 1949 to 1977 reflected China's relations with both the great powers. He argues in his first chapter that the origin of communist China's Middle East policy can be found in the early 1940s, long before the Bandung Conference or the establishment of the PRC. In his view, Chinese communist leaders realized in the early 1940s the strategic importance of the Middle East to the country's future. They believed that the domination of the Middle East by a hostile power, like Germany, would lead to the collapse of the British presence there, which would clear the way for the new dominant power to seek domination in Asia and therefore China. However, China remained isolated politically from the region. Despite Israel's recognition of the PRC in the early 1950s, diplomatic relations were not established between them. Shichor (1979: 9–22) contributes the absence of diplomatic relations between China and Israel at that time to the Israeli government's refusal to foster diplomatic relations with China. He, however, does not give a clear explanation as to why the Israeli government refused to establish diplomatic relations with the newly-established communist regime in China. His only explanation is directed towards the following Israeli official response: 'the Government had decided in principle to establish diplomatic relations with People's China, but nothing should be done in this direction until the situation in the Far East becomes clear' (Schichor 1979: 23). China's relations with the Arab countries in the mid-1950s began to draw more positive results, however. Despite the absence of diplomatic relations, economic and cultural relations were China's first tactic towards fostering relations with countries of the Middle East. This was coupled with China playing an important indirect role in producing the first major arms deal between Moscow and Cairo in 1955 (Schichor 1979: 41–2). In May 1956, Egypt became the first Middle Eastern country to establish diplomatic relations with China. Cairo's decision was said to be directed by Nasser's belief that China could play the role of an independent source of arms. Syria and Yemen followed suit in July and August 1956, respectively. Shichor sees China's policy towards the Middle East in the late 1950s as being directed towards the struggle against Western imperialism and to undermine its presence in the region. China's foreign policy became more militant. But, as China's ideological rhetoric found little sympathy in the Arab world, China

General elements and literature review 13

turned to support the 'people's war' idea in the most revolutionary areas of the Middle East (Schichor 1979: 97). But, as China's relations with the Soviet Union began to seriously deteriorate in the 1960s, China used the Middle East to wage its struggle against American imperialism and Soviet revisionism. Shichor says that China in the first half of the 1960s did almost everything it could to please the Arab governments in order to get rid of the American and the Soviet influence there. China, however, did not succeed. From 1966 onwards, China's foreign policy became more oriented towards national liberation movements that were still committed to the struggle against imperialism and, by implication, against Soviet revisionism as well. According to Shichor, China's perception of the Middle East changed in the 1970s as its perception of its relations with Washington and Moscow changed. China became more pragmatic in its relations with the countries of the Middle East, supporting most of their policies and abolishing its revolutionary propaganda (Schichor 1979: 145–88).

Like Shichor, John Calabrese has produced an insightful book on China–Middle East relations. His *China's Changing Relations with the Middle East* (1991) has mapped the changes and continuities in the first forty years of China's relations with the Middle East. Calabrese sees China's Middle East policy as reflecting the changes and shifts in Chinese foreign policy as a whole. Calabrese's discussion echoes Shichor's central thesis that China's Middle East policy can best be understood as a reaction to global events that were dominated by the superpowers, rather than to indigenous conflicts in the region. The book provides analysis of China's changing perceptions of, and relations with Egypt, Iran, Iraq, Syria, Saudi Arabia, Kuwait, Israel, and the PLO. Calabrese explores these relations in a chronological narrative format, describing China's foreign policy towards the Middle East in seven different development phases. Phase 1 is China's 'leaning to one side' policy of 1950–7. China's policy towards the region in this phase, according to Calabrese, was determined by China's hostility towards the United States and its strategic alignment with the Soviet Union. Therefore, China adopted a 'tactically flexible approach' in its relations with the countries of the Middle East in this phase. The most notable feature of this approach was the adoption of a more flexible and pragmatic tone, instead of showing a more ideological rigidity, during the Bandung meetings (Calabrese 1991: 7–14). In Phase 2, one becomes aware of the cost of militancy in China's Middle East policy from 1958 to 1965. Calabrese argues that China's dispute with the Soviet Union over the later 'weak' responses to Western intervention in the Middle East, namely in Lebanon and Jordan, during that period generated divergence between Beijing's and Moscow's policies in the region. While relations with Egypt stumbled upon difficulties, China moved to foster closer ties with the newly-established regime of Qasim in Iraq. But relations did not last long and China once again found itself isolated, except in its relations with the Palestinians, by advocating struggle against imperialism in the region. Calabrese concludes that China during this period did not achieve its goal of reducing Western predominance in the region. In Phase 3 (1966–8), China's foreign policy towards the region changes from advocating a united front with the countries of the region to narrowing the front to the liberation and revolutionary movements of the region, mainly the Palestine Liberation Organization (PLO) and the Dhofari rebels. He concludes that China was successful in building credit among them that could pay future dividends in the event of their victory; but, on the other hand, China failed to achieve a lasting influence in its relations with the PLO, and it further worsened its relations with the governments of the region. In Phase 4 (1969–71), he finds that China's perception of the Soviet threat to the region prompted China to begin adopting a more pragmatic foreign policy in its relations with the countries of the Middle East. In Phase 5 (1972–7), the new pragmatic foreign policy reaches its peak. During this period, China classified the Soviet Union as China's primary enemy. China believed that the balance between Washington and Moscow was in Moscow's favour. Therefore, China pushed for closer ties with Washington and the governments of the region. In Phase 6 (1978–81), modernization became the central objective of Chinese foreign policy and international stability became the essential prerequisite for its successful pursuit. For its oil and markets, the Middle East was part of China's modernization efforts. In the last phase (1982–9), Calabrese indicates that China's foreign policy in the Middle East was shaped by its general aim of carving an independent foreign policy, which meant paying close attention to the superpower rivalry without close alignment with them. China's main aim in the region in this phase was to compete with the Soviet Union for market and political influence. China's foreign policy concentrated its efforts on promoting and protecting its political and economic relations with the countries of the region. Calabrese's work is very useful for it provides a clear analysis of China–Middle Eastern relations in the first forty years of interactions. Calabrese's study, however, lacks details about many aspects of China's foreign policy towards the Middle East. Take, for example, the Front Liberation National of Algeria (FLNA); China supported the FLNA in its struggle for liberation from France. It also, unlike Moscow, recognized the provisional government of the Republic of Algeria in September 1958, and criticized Moscow's support for the French position to achieve a ceasefire in Algeria.[2] By 1960, China provided the Algerians with credit estimated at US$10 million for the purchase of military equipment and other supplies (Ogunsanwo 1974: 52–3). It also provided Algeria with economic assistance worth US$126.9 million, ranging from donations, loans, and small and large-scale industrial and social construc-

---

2 See Peking Review, No. 43, 25 October 1963, pp. 7–14, and Donald S. Zagoria (1962: 272–3).

tion projects between 1956 and 1977 (Bartke 1989: 37). All of this demonstrates that Algeria was an important part of China's foreign policy towards the region. Yet, both Shichor's and Calabrese's works do not discuss in any detail the objectives and implications of China's involvement in Algeria.

On the other hand, Calabrese's last phase could also be used to explain China's relations with the Middle East in the post-Cold War era. China's policy towards the region in the post-Cold War era is driven not by China's rivalry with Washington and Moscow but by China's efforts to increase its economic contacts with the Middle East and to establish political influence there. The Middle East presents China with a potential market for Chinese civilian and military goods. It is also a place where China could cooperate with a country like Israel in developing some advanced military technologies.

Hashim S. H. Behbehani's *China's Foreign Policy in the Arab World 1955–1975* (1981) presents three case-based analyses of China's foreign policy towards the Palestinian Resistance Movement (PRM), Popular Front for the Liberation of Oman (PFLO), and Kuwait. Like Shichor and Calabrese, Behbehani's work illustrates the changes that took place in China's policy towards the Arab world during the 1950s, the 1960s, and the 1970s. These changes were perceived to have been dictated by China's perception of the world, as a whole and its national interest at each stage, and not specifically by the conditions present in the case studies. His study is the only work that discusses in great detail the evolution and development of China's support for the Palestinian and other revolutionary movements in the Gulf, mainly in Oman, and the different variables involved in the development of China's relations with Kuwait. Based on these three cases, Behbehani argues that the changes that occurred in China's policy towards the Arab world in the period from 1955 to 1977 was a result of China's desire to fill a gap and achieve a leadership status in the Third World. Throughout the 1950s, China's foreign policy towards the Arab world followed the Soviet Union's policies in the region. In the 1960s, China began to compete with the Soviet Union for influence in the Third World. China's remedy for the Third World countries was to use armed struggle, which China itself followed in order to achieve independence. The PRM and PFLO provided a great opportunity for China to achieve its political and strategic goals in the region. According to Behbehani (1981), China provided the two movements with military aid and encouraged a 'people's war'. But China's changing policy in the early 1970s contributed to the withdrawal of support from the PFLO and directly led to the weakening of the movement. He emphasizes that the changes in China–PFLO relations were not due to the latter's failure on the ground. The PFLO consistently adhered to Chinese political and ideological lines, but China changed its policy toward gaining a foothold in the Gulf by dealing with existing regimes, which contributed to the abandonment of its support to the PFLO in favour of establishing relations with Iran and Kuwait. On the other side, China supported the

PRM and provided military assistance to Fatah. Yet, Behbehani argues that the changes in China's foreign policy in the 1970s did not lead to the decline in China's support for Fatah. He explains the decline in Chinese interest in the light of improved Soviet–Fatah relations in the 1970s. He makes the point that changes in China's policy towards both the PFLO and Fatah, and the effort towards improving relations with Kuwait, were brought about by changes in China's foreign policy towards the two superpowers, most specifically by adoption of its anti-Soviet policy.

Lillian Craig Harris's *China Considers the Middle East* (1993) discusses both traditional and modern Chinese relations with the Middle East, paying particular attention to the historical origins of that relationship. According to Harris, the historical contacts between China and the Middle East extend back two thousand years. China used the Middle East as both a barrier and bridge between it and Europe. Both sides enjoyed commercial benefits from the trade relations that were conducted through the Silk Road. The road also enhanced China's cultural relations with the Middle East. But, Harris argues that the breaching of the barrier between China and Europe by the Mongols, which had led to the European incursion, yielded a decline in China's relations with the Middle East. In the republic era (1912–49), China's relations with the Middle East were very limited. Trade relations reached their lowest level due to termination of the role that was played by the Silk Road. But, Islam provided the only significant medium of exchange with the Middle East. Harris then turns to discuss China's foreign relations with the Middle East in the post-1949 era. According to Harris, China's relations with the United States and the Soviet Union contributed to China's foreign policy interest in the Middle East. Harris argues that Bandung was the opportunity for China to rebuild bridges with the Middle East. It achieved some political gains, but on the whole failed to achieve its goal of presenting itself as a revolutionary model to the governments of the region. Instead, it moved towards supporting armed struggles in Algeria, South Yemen, Eritrea, Dhofar, and Palestine. The continuing deterioration in Chinese–Soviet relations in the 1970s brought China closer to the governments of the Middle East than at any other time previously. China used Islam and trade relations to foster closer ties with the countries of the Middle East. Harris (1993) argues that, in the 1980s, the Middle East had emerged as a major component in China's economic modernization. According to Harris (1993: 245), China's concerns in the post-Cold War era centred on the growing instability in both the Middle East and Central Asia. The Iraqi invasion of Kuwait put at risk China's valued economic relations in the region. China, therefore, adopted new foreign policy tactics in order to rebuild closer relations in the region. Strengthening ties with Iran and Pakistan, selling arms to the region, and establishing ties with Israel are some of the new Chinese tactics. Harris (1993: 266) concludes that 'China had won out over the Soviets in the Middle East' in the post-Cold War era. She sees China's place in the Middle

East and Central Asia to have been boosted by the disintegration of the Soviet Union. This argument, however, remained unclear. The disintegration of the Soviet Union did elevate China's role in Central Asia. China's efforts to establish ties with the new Central Asian states following the fall of the Soviet empire could be traced to China's hope to fill the power vacuum there. Yet, the disintegration of the Soviet Union did not enhance China's role in the Middle East. For one, Russian military cooperation with the countries of the Middle East and its arms sales in the 1990s were much higher than those of China. Even Moscow's involvement in the Middle East peace process is more noticeable than Beijing's. Thus, it is not clear how the disintegration of the Soviet Union affected China's position in the Middle East.

Abidi (1982) is the only work that focuses its attention on the relations between China and the countries of the Gulf and Arabian Peninsula region. Although much of Abidi's work focuses on Chinese–Iranian relations, China's relations with the other countries of the Gulf are also discussed. Abidi's study identifies the historical, international, and domestic forces that brought China and Iran into a logical partnership. The work includes informative chapters on Iran's recognition of China in the early 1970s and the relations before and during the Iranian revolution as well as the way the Chinese sought to maintain relations with the Islamic republic. Though not comprehensively, China's relations with Iraq, the Yemens, Kuwait, Oman, Saudi Arabia, the UAE, Qatar, and Bahrain have also been discussed. His justification for his focus on Iran stems from his understanding that Iran claimed more attention from China than any other littoral state of the Gulf. In addition to that, Iran's special position in the Gulf, because of its size, geo-strategic location, resources, and regime orientation, marked its importance in China's foreign policy. According to Abidi, the 1960s presented China with the first real opportunity to assess its policy in the region. Iran began to reassess its attitude towards China, and Kuwait gained independence. Yet, no breakthrough in the relations between China and the countries of the region emerged in the 1960s. This was mainly due to China's support for the revolutionary movements in the region. But the changes in China's perceptions of the superpowers in the late 1960s and early 1970s led China to foster political, economic, and social relations with Kuwait, Iran, and Oman. In the name of preserving stability in the region and preventing the Soviets from advancing there, China offered recognition unilaterally to Bahrain, Qatar, and the UAE.

All the above works on Chinese foreign policy towards the Middle East tend to study such relations in terms of the relations between China and the two superpowers. Yet the work edited by P. R. Kumaraswamy (1999) discusses China's relations with some of the countries of the Middle East in terms of China's quest for influence rather than challenging the two superpowers. Kumaraswamy's chapter in the book argues that China's recognition of Israel in 1992 was viewed by the Chinese leadership as a

18 *Introduction*

stepping stone to Western technology. He also argues that China is hoping that its defence cooperation with both Israel and its adversaries will give it the necessary political influence to play an active role in Middle East politics in the future. Meanwhile, William H. Haddad and Mary Foeldi-Hardy further this argument by indicating that China's relations with the Palestinians in the 1990s took a new turn from its old supportive policy of the Palestinians. China's interest in becoming a business partner to all the parties in the Middle East including Israel forced a readjustment in China's calculations about its relations with both the Palestinians and Israel. As a consequence, China has adopted a more neutral position, rather than supporting or leaning towards one side or the other (Haddad and Foeldi-Hardy). John Calabrese's article on China's relations with Iraq briefly reviews the evolution of China–Iraq relations. It concludes that China's policy towards Iraq reflects its overall foreign policy objectives. While rivalry with the two superpowers may have characterized China's policy towards Iraq in the first thirty years of interaction, China's policy towards Iraq in the 1980s and 1990s was a reflection of its modernization programme (Calabrese 1999: 52–67).

It is clear from the above that there is a growing body of literature on China's foreign policy towards the Middle East. Yet, there is no detailed study and analysis of the dynamics of relations between China and the countries of the Gulf and Arabian Peninsula region. With the exception of Abidi, all the others have only made fleeting references to China's relations with the Gulf and Arabian Peninsula region, and then only in the context of the overall discussion of China's Middle Eastern foreign policy. This study hopes to improve the analytical picture somewhat.

CHAPTER PLAN

The book is divided into four parts. We have just discussed Part I, which included a discussion of the conclusions of research into and literature on Chinese foreign policy, in general, and Chinese foreign policy towards the Middle East, in particular. Part II surveys China's foreign relations in a global context. It encompasses a chapter on international relations theory and its relevance to the study of China's foreign policy. Several theories and approaches of international relations are explored and discussed in Chapter 2, so as to assist the researcher in finding a suitable theoretical approach to apply to the study of China's foreign policy towards the Gulf and Arabian Peninsula region. As will be shown, the neo-realist theory of international relations, as developed by Waltz, has been chosen to be the principle guideline for the research. Neo-realism, as we will see, focuses on the external factor, rather than the internal one, as the important factor in determining states' foreign policies. Part II also includes a chapter studying

China's foreign policy towards the United States and the Soviet Union. Studying the relations between China and the two powers is essential for producing a strong understanding of how the external factor has affected China's foreign policy towards the Gulf and Arabian Peninsula region.

In the third part, we shall discuss China's foreign policy towards the Gulf and Arabian Peninsula region. Chapter 4 looks at China's foreign policy towards the region. I have divided China's involvement in the region into three main stages, and argued that China's policy towards the region in each stage has changed in accordance with the changes in China's relations with both the United States and the Soviet Union and China's drive to increase its economic, political, and military capabilities. Chapters 5 and 6 review China's bilateral political, economic, social, and cultural relations with each of the states of the Gulf and Arabian Peninsula region. We shall then draw these themes together in a final concluding chapter that assesses the international dimensions of China's foreign policy towards the region and its implications for both China and the countries of the region.

Part II
China's foreign policy in a global context

2 Theorizing China's foreign policy

The People's Republic of China's policies and its importance have led to a quantitative explosion of literature studying the different aspects of its foreign policy. Yet, there is still no single coherent theory in international relations that can explain and predict all aspects of China's foreign behaviour. Therefore, different theoretical approaches have been applied to explain and predict China's foreign behaviour, but none is able to give a consistent explanation that can be applied to the conduct of every Chinese foreign policy initiative and at any given time. Many theoretical frameworks have successfully been applied to explain and predict China's foreign policy regarding specific issues and situations, but they remain mostly one-sided explanatory approaches. They tend to explain China's foreign policy by looking either at the impact of the external factor or the internal factor in determining China's foreign behaviour. By doing so, they limit their explanations of China's foreign behaviour to one independent variable, and tend to some degree ignore the other variables.

Generally speaking, the lack of a 'grand' theory in the field of China's foreign relations and foreign policy can be, on one hand, seen as a result of a disciplinary shortage in the field of social sciences, which is described as being 'coloured by hidden normative and policy preference, an absence of conceptual clarity, and the repeated intrusion of policy makers' concerns and slogans into intellectual discourse' (Kim 1994: 402). On the other hand, the absence of a broad theory of China's foreign relations and policy can also be blamed on China's own behaviour and practices. Samuel S. Kim argues that ambiguity in China's foreign behaviour provides a major obstacle to theorizing about China's foreign policy, as theory requires 'the actor's behavioural consistency over time' (Kim 1994: 402).

Against this backdrop, this chapter seeks to address the different theoretical approaches to China's foreign policy in order to gain an understanding of China's foreign behaviour from different points of view. Our aim is to find a more useful theoretical approach to serve as a conceptual map that can help us make sense of China's foreign policy towards the Gulf and Arabian Peninsula region.

There are several schools of thought regarding China's foreign relations and policies. They tend to explain China's foreign behaviour as being directed by either internal or external factors. This chapter is going to survey these two most dominant schools in the literature of Chinese foreign policy.

INTERNAL FACTORS

The most dominant theoretical approaches to international relations that focus on internal factors as the prominent component of states' foreign policy are the state-level approach and pluralism. The state-level approach surveys the internal characteristics of a state and argues that a state's domestic characteristics have a greater influence on determination of its foreign policy than external factors (Bachman 1989: 32–4). Characteristics such as history and traditions, political system, leadership, and ideology are seen as the primary sources of a state's foreign policy (Roy 1998: 235–8). Scholars in international relations such as Morton A. Kaplan (1966: 13–25; 1976) and Richard N. Rosecrance (1963) acknowledge the importance of history and traditions in determining states' foreign behaviour. Some have highlighted the role of leadership in determining states' foreign policy. Margaret G. Hermann (1976: 327) has argued that the more authority the leader has over a nation's foreign policy machinery, the fewer people will be above him in the foreign policy bureaucracy to change his decisions; and the less well defined the policy makers' roles, the more likely the leader's personal characteristics will influence foreign policy. Others have turned to analyse states' political systems as the main determinant of their external behaviour. Gabriel Almond (1960), Almond and G. Bengham Powell, Jr (1966: ch. 2), Karl Deutsch (1964), and David Easton (1965a, b) have concerned themselves with the functions performed by the political system and the role it plays in shaping the foreign behaviour of a state.

The pluralist image of international relations is another approach to the study of domestic sources of foreign policy. One fundamental criticism of traditional realism, a school that dominated the field for some time, is its emphasis on the significance of internal factors in determining states' foreign policies. Unlike the realists, who argue that balance of power and the international system are the most important factors in determining foreign policy, pluralists believe in the role of different internal factors – mainly economic – in shaping states' foreign policies. Paul Viotti and Mark Kauppi (1993) summarized the assumptions of the pluralist image of international relations. They presented the following assumptions as the basic elements of the pluralist image of international relations:

Theorizing China's foreign policy 25

1   Unlike the realist image, the pluralist sees non-state actors as important entities who cannot be ignored in international relations. International and regional organizations play as important a role as states in international relations.
2   Unlike in the realist image, a state in the pluralist image is not a unitary actor, instead it comprises different actors such as individual bureaucracies, interest groups, and individuals who attempt to influence the making of foreign policy. Therefore, foreign policy decisions are not easily made, as the realist would think.
3   To pluralists, states are not rational actors as the realists would assume. To them, the foreign policy decision-making process is a complicated one and requires clashes, bargaining, and compromise between and among different actors.
4   To pluralists, it is not only the security issues, as the realist would argue, that play the dominant role in designing foreign policy. Pluralists see economic and social issues as important elements of foreign policy debates, besides the security issue (Viotti and Kauppi 1993: 78).

The pluralist image of international relations is associated with the work of many scholars, among them Wolfram F. Hanrieder. Hanrieder (1978) has argued that the realists' traditional distinction between domestic and international politics is breaking down, and that the result has been a 'domestication' of international politics, in which security issues have been diminished in salience and economic issues have gained a new significance. According to Hanrieder, the satisfaction of rising demands of citizens has become an important issue for any state's legitimacy; and such demands 'can be satisfied only by extensive commercial, monetary, and technological interactions on the international level.' Such interaction can be 'horizontal' (at the government-to-government level), 'lateral' (at the society-to-society level through subnational groups and organization), and 'interactive' (involving a great deal of integration, like the European Economic Community). All these levels are 'the structures through which governments perform a variety of functions' including the 'way in which state and society seek to arrange their domestic and foreign environment'. 'The choice of one structure over another is determined as much by internal ideological, institutional, and political orthodoxies as it is by external necessities.' Therefore, he concluded, 'the bulk of today's global political processes are of a kind that are typical of an approximate domestic political process, leading to the "domestication" of international politics', and that 'it is not a new type of international politics which is "dissolving" the traditional nation-state but a new nation-state which is "dissolving" traditional international politics' (Hanrieder 1978: 1276–87). G. John Ikenberry (1986: 53–77) looks at the interaction between domestic and international political economy and its effects on the state elites. He argues that state elites are engaged in the continuous process of adjustment between the demands of domestic and international activities, and do so by bargaining rather than competition. Chadwick F. Alger (1977: 277–93) stresses the major role that interest groups can play in the shaping of foreign as well as domestic policies. He believes that interdependence generates new types of policy issue and new participants in the foreign policy process, undermining the realist assumptions of the state being a unitary actor. Edward L. Morse (1970: 371–92) focuses on the impact of modernization on the formation of foreign policy. Modernization leads to an increasing level of interdependence among societies at the international level, leading to increasing priorities of domestic rather than external needs at the national level. He argues that the process of modernization has broken down the realist distinction between foreign and domestic policy, changed the balance between 'high' and 'low' politics in favour of the latter, and reduced the level of control that any state can exercise at the domestic or the international level. Robert Keohane and Joseph Nye, Samuel Hantington, and Charles Pentland all argue the importance of international and multinational organizations in world politics. Keohane and Nye (1974: 39–62) point to the role played by international organizations in providing a forum for national government officials to meet and form coalitions as well as open new channels for policy formation at the international level with officials of other states. They therefore contest the realist assumption that international organizations are only instruments of state policy. Huntington (1973: 333–68) emphasises multinational corporations as independent actors in world politics. Instead of being created by the nation-state, multinational or transnational organizations prosper through a process of bargaining and agreement with the nation-state. He argues that both are interrelated and that the existence of one requires the existence of the other. Pentland (1976: 631–56) extends the significance of international organizations in world politics to include: first, states use international organizations as instruments to pursue their own foreign policy objectives; second, states tend to use them to modify their behaviour; and, third, states can through them achieve a degree of autonomy and influence as political actors.

On the issue of theorizing China's foreign policy, many scholars have paid a great deal of attention to the impact of the internal factor in determining China's foreign behaviour. They tend to adopt the above arguments about the role of domestic factors and non-state actors in shaping China's foreign policy. They argue that different variables such as history, traditions, ideology, leadership, economy, national interest, political system, bureaucracy, intellectuals, and media play a key role in forming China's foreign behaviour. In order to survey the literature about the impact of these variables on China's foreign relations, we focus on the impact of the following main domestic components on China's foreign policy: history and traditions, ideology, leadership and political system, and modernization.

History and tradition

Those who have written on the impact of history and traditions on China's foreign policy argue that history and traditions are essential and central to an understanding of Chinese foreign behaviour. To them, the pre-1949 experience exercised a significant influence on China's post-1949 foreign policy. Among those who argue for definite continuities of the past in the present are Mark Mancall, Robert A. Scalapino, John Cranmer-Byng, Chih-yu Shih, and Rafe de Crespigny. Mancall (1963) looks at China's traditional world order and summarizes the Chinese assumptions of world order as follows:

1 China's world order was hierarchical, not egalitarian.
2 China's centrality in the world was a function of its civilization and virtue, particularly the virtue of the Chinese ruler.
3 No balance of power existed.
4 National power was a reflection of the natural virtue. Power was moral because it derived from the possession of virtue.
5 International society was the extension of internal society; no boundary existed since there was no nation-state. Boundary was defined in terms of cultural differences (Mancall 1963: 17–19).

The Chinese saw themselves at the centre of the world and as the source of all civilizations and cultures.[3] They regarded their country as the 'Middle Kingdom' or the centre of the world, with the Chinese emperor at the heart of everything as a universal ruler, and the 'uncivilized barbarian' nations at the peripheries (Frank 1967: 4). They regarded their civilization to be superior to any other nation's. And their rulers were designated with the mandate of heaven, as the sons of heaven, to govern the land from one dynasty to another (Chen 1972: 8). Foreign societies were ranked high or low in the hierarchy depending on how close they were to China culturally. In the Chinese perception of world order, territorial limitations were imprecise and the purpose of interactions between 'barbarians' and the Chinese was transformation of the former along the lines of the Chinese model.[4] 'Barbarians' – foreigners – could come to China to participate in the benefits of the Chinese civilization and learn from the achievements of the Chinese in spheres of natural and social sciences. Those who wished to come to China and learn to be civilized must accept Chinese culture and recognize

---

3 The Chinese did not differ in this respect from other great civilizations. The Greeks and the Romans saw themselves as the sole sources of all culture and civilizations as well.
4 For a comparison between the Chinese view of world order and European world order, see John W. Garver, *Foreign Relations of the People's Republic of China* (Englewood Cliffs, NJ: Prentice-Hall, 1993a).

the supreme authority of the emperor as mediator between heaven and earth by bringing tributes. The tributary system was established to enable the tributary state to trade with China and receive permission for their traders' power in China from the emperor (Fairbank and Teng 1972: 13). Thus, the tributary system was the means for conducting and establishing foreign relations with China. In order to deal with them, foreigners were required to send tribute missions periodically to the Chinese emperor. Such missions were perceived by the Chinese as recognition by the 'barbarians' of the emperor's superiority.

Mancall (1963: 21–2) states that the breakdown of the institutions of China's traditional world order, after the signing of the Treaty of Nanking on 27 August 1842 with the British, took place faster than erosion of the above assumptions on which the order itself was based. It is therefore, as he argues, possible that historically-rooted assumptions concerning the nature of international order, differing from that of both the West and Russia, may be a complicating factor in contemporary China's foreign relations. He specifies the influence of the past on China's foreign policy through the following levels:

1 A vivid sense of outrage directed at the Western imperialist powers that contributed to the erosion of China's traditional world order and influence.
2 A sense of China's primacy in its relations with its neighbouring countries marked by the signing of border agreements with Pakistan, Nepal, and Burma, which depended on China's goodwill for their validity.
3 Adoption of old techniques in contemporary Chinese diplomacy including the exchange of cultural missions, official visits, and 'using barbarians against barbarians' in its relations with both the United States and the Soviet Union (Mancall 1963: 23–6).

Scalapino (1962) further argues that China's old diplomatic techniques of receiving gifts has now been substituted by the exchange of dance and musical troops, official delegations, students and scholars, journalists, and civic leaders. Personalized diplomacy through cultural missions, Scalapino argues, is central to China's diplomacy as it was under the Ming Emperor. He also sees the influence of the past on China's foreign relations in the continuance of xenophobia in China's foreign relations, which led China to adopt a nationalist foreign policy in its relations with neighbouring Asian countries and the superpowers. China, according to Scalapino (1962: 262–77), is seeking to achieve the following three objectives: first, to define and defend its boundaries; second, to acquire a buffer system that gives it security in depth; and, finally, to exercise some degree of hegemony over the region with which it has primary contact. To him, China was

Theorizing China's foreign policy

showing a sense of primacy when marking its boundaries with the surrounding countries, gaining rather than making concessions.

In addition to the above arguments regarding the levels of influence that the past has had on China's foreign policy, its traditional assumption of hierarchy in world order has also left its mark. This was evident in China's own classification, in the 1950s, of the international system through its 'two camps theory' and in its 'three worlds theory' of the 1970s. Such classifications highlighted the hierarchical ranking of states in each theory.

Cranmer-Byng (1973) argues that, despite China being forced by powerful Western countries and Japan in the late nineteenth century to abandon its own 'well-tried methods and ideology for conducting relations with non-Chinese people', the method remained influential on many powerful Chinese leaders. Sun Yat-sen and Chiang Kai-shek in the 1920s and 1930s, respectively, maintained that China had to become strong so that it could once again play its traditional role in the world through the moral influence of Chinese culture. Mao's adoption of Marxism–Leninism was based on his beliefs of the possibility of world revolution in which China's example would be crucial. According to Cranmer-Byng, both versions of China's mission in the future coexisted after the establishment of the PRC and were nourished by strong feelings of nationalism and pride in China as an exemplar in 'cultural' values. He concluded:

> One essential quality, which both versions of this faith in China's special mission have in common, is their 'imprinted' belief in the relevance of Chinese cultural values and lifestyle as an inspiration to guide other peoples of the world in the future.
>
> (Cranmer-Byng 1973: 76–9)

Chih-yu Shih (1990) studies the effect of Chinese traditions and cultural norms such as Confucianism, Buddhism, and Taoism on China's foreign behaviour. He produces three different styles of leadership: the hierarchical style, the normalcy style, and the rebellion style. The hierarchical style refers to a leadership that seeks coercive incentives to demand mass support for certain moral principles, and emphasizes loyalty and organization. The normalcy style refers to a leadership that tries to 'reconcile national interests and individual citizens' self interest through materials incentives', and emphasizes rationality. The rebellion style refers to a leadership that encourages the masses to fight against the status quo. According to him, the adoption of a certain style depends on the leader's personality, personal experiences, and the situation. He finds that, before the Cultural Revolution, Mao Zedong adopted the hierarchical style, which tends to apply 'asymmetric norms' to diplomacy that advocate Confucianist ideas of control through punishment and reward, superiority and obedience. Liu Shaoqi, Zhou Enlai, and Deng Xiaoping adopted the normalcy style, which tends to apply 'symmetric norms' to diplomacy that advocate Confucian brotherhood, friendship, and to maintain them through compromise. After the Cultural Revolution, Mao adopted the rebellion style, which tends to apply the 'Yi norms' to diplomacy that advocate 'revolutionary brotherhood', and commitment to challenge the 'unjust' authority (Chih-yu Shih 1990: 80–190). Chih-yu Shih concludes that China's diplomacy 'reflects the world view held by Chinese leaders' and that the 'norms for inter-personal relationships are applied to understanding and the management of inter-state relationships' (Chih-yu Shih 1990: 190).

Crespigny (1995) states that the past has left its mark on contemporary Chinese foreign policy in terms of the following:

1   The old issue of Chinese rejection of foreign interference in its internal affairs is being carried out by the Chinese government in its foreign relations today.
2   The hierarchical nature of the traditional Chinese view of internal and international systems and their division of power within each system continues to play a key role in China's present interests in East and South-East Asia. Its policy towards this region is not only influenced by a sense of order but also by expectations of control and guidance, which stems from the old Chinese family hierarchical system in which the father and the elderly assume a superior role.
3   Official control by central government is another aspect of the influence of the past on China's contemporary foreign policy, as control has been viewed as an essential ingredient of the effort involved in keeping the country undivided (de Crespigny 1995: 42–3).

All the above arguments suggest that history and traditions have played a key role in influencing and shaping China's foreign behaviour.

Ideology

The writings on the role of ideology in China's foreign policy suggest that there are two stages in the development of the role of ideology. The first is the Mao Zedong period from 1949 to 1978, and the second is the post-Mao phase from 1979 to the present time. The role of ideology in China's foreign policy has been perceived in terms of this timescale. Ideology is seen to be the most dominant factor in shaping China's foreign policy during the first stage. Scholars and political analysts base their views of China's foreign policy on the teachings of Marxism–Leninism and Mao Zedong, as the ideological guidance behind foreign policy. Beijing's behaviour towards accepting Moscow's superiority in the 1950s, supporting solidarity in the Third World, advocating a new Third World policy in the 1960s, and shifting its alliance towards favouring closer ties with the United States in the 1970s have all been viewed as the logical result of China's conversion to

Marxism–Leninism and Mao Zedong thought. Among those who adopted this pattern are H. Arthur Steiner (1961: 394–402), Tang Tsou and Norton H. Halperin (1965: 80–104), Franz Schurmann (1968), Chieh Hsiung (1970), and Steven I. Levine (1994: 30–46). From the 1980s onwards, many scholars and analysts began to view a decline in the role played by ideology in China's foreign policy. They, therefore, see new doctrines such as nationalism, modernization, and national interest as the replacements for the old principles of Marxism–Leninism and Mao Zedong thought (Schram 1984: 417–61; Harding 1984: 177–208: Burger 1990; Dirlik and Meisner 1989; among many others).

Those who argue for the significance of ideology in China's foreign behaviour tend to focus on the influence of Marxism–Leninism and of Mao Zedong thought. Schurmann (1968: 19–33) distinguishes between the two forms of ideology in relation to their actions. He defined Marxism–Leninism as the 'pure ideology' and Mao's thought as the 'practical ideology'. To him, 'pure ideology' aims at shaping the thinking of the people, rather than producing immediate actions; and 'practical ideology' aims at producing action to implement certain policies. In this account, 'pure ideology' is a shared ideology among all communist parties of the world, but 'practical ideology' is something that varies from one party to another according to the circumstances of each country. According to him, 'pure ideology' played a key role in developing 'practical ideology' in China. Mao's world outlook was seen as a product of the impact of 'pure ideology' in China's foreign policy. Two main themes of Mao's thought were given substantial attention by analysts for their roles in shaping China's foreign policy. First is Lenin's (1908: 700–16) interpretation of imperialism, which had made a great impact on Mao's perception of the 'enemy' in international relations. James Chieh Hsiung stresses that Lenin's theory of imperialism filled an intellectual vacuum for many Chinese, including Mao himself, who found no explanation within their own traditions regarding exploitation (Hsiung 1970: 36–7). During the Chinese–Soviet alliance in the 1950s, Mao adhered to Lenin's imperialism, made imperialism the main slogan in China's propaganda war against the United States and the West, and viewed the world order in terms of two camps: the socialist camp headed by the Soviet Union and the capitalist or imperialist camp headed by the United States. The conflict between these two camps was the basic element that shaped the nature of China's foreign policy. Therefore, he saw the 'lean to one side' policy as the most reliable foreign policy strategy to achieve China's foreign policy goals in the 1950s:

> Internationally, we belong to the side of the anti-imperialist front headed by the Soviet Union, and so we can turn only to this side for genuine and friendly help, not to the side of the imperialist front.
> (Mao Zedong 1971: 313–14)

32 China's foreign policy in a global context

Another important aspect of the impact of Mao's thought on China's foreign policy was his thought on contradictions. According to this thought, in order for a society to develop towards the final objective – in China's case this is Communism – it had to advance through stages. In each stage, there are some 'primary' and 'secondary' contradictions embodying the struggle to achieve the advancement of society to the next stage. Resolving the contradictions of each stage would be the primary step in the development of societies (Mao Zedong 1971: 91–8). Such analysis is essential to explain the change in China's foreign policy from one period to another particularly in regard to its relations with both the United States and the Soviet Union. The deterioration of China's relations with the Soviet Union in the 1960s onwards, and its shifting policies towards the Third World and later on towards the United States could be explained by looking at this analysis. John W. Garver (1993a) explains Mao's thought on contradiction in political terms. He indicates that, at each stage of China's history, there has been a primary enemy stopping Chinese society from achieving its final objectives: the Japanese were the primary contradiction in the 1930s, the Chinese Nationalists in the 1940s, the United States in the 1950s and 1960s, and the Soviet Union in the 1970s. This means that China has to increase its efforts to solve the primary contradiction in each stage first, before it moves to the next one (Garver 1993a: 44–8).

Thus, the impact of ideology on China's foreign policy can be explained in the following terms:

1. Ideology had led China to adopt the 'lean to one side' policy following the proclamation of independence in 1949 and guided China's foreign policy to follow the Soviet line in its foreign relations. China, as a result, was isolated from the non-communist countries of the world, and ended up in total confrontation with the United States (Garver 1993a: 44–8).
2. Mao's thinking shifted China's foreign policy strategy from ignoring the countries of the Third World in the first half of the 1950s to engaging them in the second half of the 1950s and the 1960s. The announcement of the Five Principles of Peaceful Coexistence as the main elements of China's foreign relations with the countries of the Third World represented China's willingness to establish friendly relations with those countries in order to weaken the US strategic position mainly in Asia (Garver 1993a: 119).
3. Mao's revolutionary thinking played a key role in the 1960s throughout the Third World. China supported the idea of 'people's war', endorsing revolutions in a total of 23 countries in the world in 1965 'van Ness 1970: 132–48), and devoted substantial resources for military training, arms supply, and ideological teaching to revolutionaries throughout those countries (van Ness 1970: 114–16).
4. Mao's idea of contradiction helped China's foreign policy to adjust the shift in China's alliance from the Soviet Union towards rapprochement

with the United States in the 1970s. Moscow, rather than Washington, according to Mao, had become the primary contradiction – principal enemy – to Beijing. China, therefore, had to work first to eliminate the primary enemy even if that required an alignment with the secondary enemy.

Leadership and political structure

Some argue that leadership has also played a key role in shaping and determining China's foreign policy. David Bachman (1998) agrees with this argument and stresses that the Chinese Communist Party (CCP) leadership plays a critical role in conducting China's foreign policy. Mao, according to Bachman (1998: 37–41), was the 'undisputed' maker of China's foreign policy. He enjoyed complete authority over China's foreign policy, as foreign policy was his major intellectual and political concern. A. Doak Barnett (1985: 12) extends this argument and argues that Mao totally dominated foreign policy decisions up to the time of his death and that Deng Xiaoping took the final decisions on many foreign policy issues in the 1980s and 1990s. He indicates that Deng, up to the time of his death, remained the ultimate source of authority for making policy decisions in China – on foreign as well as domestic issues – even though he did not occupy the highest formal positions in the party or government. Most major decisions were taken by him and all had to be accepted by him. Barnett, however, distinguishes between Mao's method and Deng's method of foreign policy decision making. Mao's method was individualistic because he enjoyed complete authority, while Deng's method was based on building a coalition in support of his policy instead of imposing it on others (Barnett 1985: 16). Such a method is said to be carried out by the Jiang Zemin leadership as well.

Bachman (1994: 51) also argues that the characteristics of China's political structure – authoritarianism, highly-articulated nature, fragmentation, and bargaining – also shape China's external behaviour. All these characteristics of the political system 'affect foreign policy behaviour via co-ordination and control problems and competition among Chinese entities' and 'enable the state to pursue a largely mercantilist international policy'. He stresses this point by giving an example of the missile sales to Saudi Arabia. He indicates that high-ranked officials in the Chinese government and party made the decision to sell weapons, without even consulting the foreign ministry. Thus, the authoritarian nature of the system in China allows centralization of the decision-making process around a few high-ranking officials. Harry Harding (1987) believes that political reform in the post-Mao era has transformed some of the ideological features of the Chinese political system. He describes the system as a 'consultative authoritarian' regime, in which the party may consult with individuals and institutions from inside or outside the government in its determination of national policy. Harding (1987: 200) sees it as 'a significant departure from the totalitarianism of the recent past, but not a truly pluralistic, or even quasi-democratic, political system.' China, according to this analysis, still does not allow independent parties, autonomous media, and independent social and professional organizations to participate in the formation of national policy. Zhao Quansheng (1992: 162–4) demonstrates that the process of foreign policy making in China was transformed in the post-Mao era from its 'vertical authoritarianism' during Mao's leadership to 'horizontal authoritarianism' or 'collective authoritarianism' in the post-Mao era. The former was a one-man-dominated process based on a vertical command system; the latter involves several players participating in the foreign policy making process. An example of the post-Mao 'horizontal' or 'collective authoritarianism' is the adoption of the 'independent foreign policy' in 1982. Zhao Quansheng argues that the proclamation of the 'independent foreign policy' in China's relations with both the United States and the Soviet Union was a product of collective authoritarian compromise between Deng's line of foreign policy, which favours closer ties with Washington, and Chen Yun's (a powerful senior leader in the party) line, which favoured a conciliatory policy towards Moscow (for a review, see Baum 1980).

Economic modernization

China's Four Modernizations programme was launched as a result of the approval by the Third Plenum of the Eleventh National Party Congress Central Committee in December 1978. The modernization of agriculture, industry, national defence, and science and technology were to be carried forward to build 'socialism with Chinese characteristics' (Schram 1993). In order to carry the programme forward, adjustments to the country's foreign policy needed to be made. As a result, many of Mao's principles were postponed indefinitely. Mao's formula of 'solving war by war' was replaced by Deng's formula of 'solving war by peaceful means'.[5] An 'independent foreign policy' was adopted in September 1982. Its basic objectives have centred on creating a global environment favourable to China's reform efforts (Hu Yaobang 1982: 29–33). Trade, industrial, social, and military cooperation with Moscow began to increase after the introduction of the independent policy. China's economic modernization programme's aims are:

---

5   Deng (1994a: 59) said: 'There are many disputes in the world, and we have to find ways to solve them. Over the years I have been considering how those disputes could be solved by peaceful means, rather than by war'.

Theorizing China's foreign policy 35

1   To legitimize the authority of the CCP among the Chinese people by providing job opportunities for millions of Chinese workers.
2   To introduce new and more advanced technology through foreign investment in China.
3   To support the modernization of China's defence. Deng announced the importance of economic modernization for the modernization of defence at an enlarged meeting of the Military Commission of the Central Committee of the Communist Party on 4 June 1985:

> The four modernisations include the modernisation of defence. Without that modernisation there would be only three. But the four modernisations should be achieved in order of priority. Only when we have a good economic foundation will it be possible for us to modernise the army's equipment. So we must wait patiently for a few years. I am certain that by the end of the century we can surpass the goal of quadrupling the GNP. At that time only, when we are strong economically, we shall be able to spend more money on updating equipment.
> (Deng Xiaoping 1994a: 133)

Thomas W. Robinson (1994: 187–99) argues that, despite the long historical background of humiliation and domination by the West and Japan, China's modernization programme has changed the Chinese government's view of interdependence since it stresses investment, trade, technology transfer, and scientific exchange. China's new view of interdependence stresses mutual benefits. He sees the growth of China's foreign trade, the increase in foreign investment, and China's borrowing from foreign commercial and multilateral institutions as well as foreign countries as measures of China's economic interdependence. He also sees growing interdependent links in the field of science, security, politics, and culture. Another aspect of the impact of China's modernization on foreign policy is its membership and active participation in a number of multilateral economic institutions. William R. Feeney (1994: 226–45) argues that China's economic modernization programme made the Chinese government adopt an 'inclusive participatory approach' to the international economic system in order to gain access to foreign capital and expertise and other long-term economic benefits. In 1980, China joined the International Monetary Fund (IMF), the International Bank for Reconstruction and Development (IBRD) (the World Bank), and the International Finance Corporation (IFC). In 1983, China was granted observer status to the General Agreement on Tariff and Trade (GATT) – known today as the World Trade Organization; and, in 1986, it officially applied for full GATT membership, and joined the Asian Development Bank (ADB). China's behaviour towards international organizations has also changed in the post-Mao era. Samuel S. Kim (1994: 406) observes that China, by 1977, participated in twenty-one international

36 *China's foreign policy in a global context*

Table 2.1 China's participation in international organizations, 1960–89 (from Kim 1994: 406)

	1960	1966	1977	1984	1986	1987	1988	1989
IGO	2	1	21	29	32	35	37	37
INGO	30	58	71	355	403	504	574	677

intergovernmental organizations (IGOs) and seventy-one international non-governmental organizations (INGO). This however changed with the acceleration of China's modernization programme: its memberships increased to thirty-seven IGOs and 677 INGOs by 1989 (Table 2.1).

China's attitudes towards the United Nations has also shifted from viewing it as a dirty international organization manipulated by a few big powers to emphasizing the importance of the existence of the United Nations for world peace. China's Premier Zhao Ziyang, on the eve of the fortieth anniversary of the founding of the UN said:

> While it [UN] has made some serious mistakes, on the whole it has done much and has played an active part in safeguarding world peace, opposing armed aggression and occupation of one country by another, encouraging the restructuring of the inequitable international economic order, and promoting international economic and technological co-operation.
>
> (*Beijing Review* Vol.. 28, No. 42: 4–5, 21 October 1985)

China's stance on aid and investment has assumed a new understanding. China has changed since 1978 its international status from aid giver to aid recipient (Copper 1979). From 1979 to 1992, it received 752 loans from different bilateral and multilateral sources valued at $74.7 billion (Yabuki 1995: 162–3).[6] China changed its old argument of rejecting foreign investment in favour of encouraging foreign investment in its territory. Between 1985 and 1996, approximately $176 billion of foreign direct investment was made in China (EIU 1998: 52); and, between 1993 and 1997 China became the world's second largest recipient of foreign direct investment (Findlay and Watson 1997: 113).[7] China's involvement in the world capitalist market has increased its trade interdependency. Womack and Zhao (1994) argue

---

6 Between 1983 to 1991, China's cumulative loans were $50,446 million supplied by Japan 32.3%, World Bank 21.6%, France 11.1%, Great Britain 5%, Hong Kong and Macao 4.9%, Germany 4.6%, USA 3.1%, Canada 2.9%, and others 14.5% (Yabuki 1995: 162).
7 The single largest source of foreign investment was Hong Kong (over 50%), Taiwan (8.4%), Japan (8.0%), and the USA (7.9%) were distant second, third, and fourth, respectively. See EIU (1998: 52).

that China's dependence on a single trade partner declined from over 50 per cent in the 1950s to 37 per cent in the 1986–1990 period (Womack and Guangzhi Zhao 1994: 141). Its total trade share in GNP had risen greatly from 9.89 per cent in 1978 to 27.90 per cent in 1991 (Robinson 1994: 191–4).

Zhao Quansheng (1992: 163) argues that China's economic modernization programme and its policy of opening up to the outside play a key role in the transformation of the process of foreign policy making in China from its 'vertical authoritarianism' to 'horizontal' or 'collective authoritarianism'. The same argument is made by Harry Harding (1987: 200) who maintains that political reforms coinciding with economic reforms in China transformed the process of foreign policy making from an absolute authoritarian process to 'a consultative authoritarian' process. A. Doak Barnett (1985: 93) extends the argument by showing that the increasing salience of China's foreign economic relations enhanced the role of China's Ministry of Foreign Economic Relations and Trade (MFERT) in China's policy making process. According to him, the MFERT is 'the second most important ministry directly involved' in the conduct of foreign policy in China. Allen Whiting (1994: 258–9) argues that the policy of opening up to the outside and the subsequent dependence on foreign trade and technology, together with foreign loans, grants, and investments, have increased the role played by modernization in the determination of foreign policy. China's foreign policy has been adjusted to secure foreign investment, technology, aid, and funds into China. Guocang Huan (1992a: 87) indicates that China's need to balance between its economic open areas and other parts of China requires the Chinese government to adopt foreign policies that can encourage foreign investment and bring funds into those poorer areas.

Responding to the severe, yet temporary, economic sanctions against China imposed by the West and Japan after the Tiananmen Square event of 4 June 1989, the Chinese government understood that, in order to sustain its economic development, it had to keep its economic relations with the US, Japan, and the international and regional organizations in a good and peaceful manner. Despite its rejection of foreign pressure on its internal affairs, the Chinese government used every possible opportunity to convince the West to lift its sanctions. Deng, for example, emphasized the need for China to restore its relations with the US in discussions with the special envoy of President George Bush on 10 December 1989, and said:

> I hope that as a special envoy you will tell President Bush that there is a retired old man in China who is concerned about the improvement of Sino–US relations.
>
> (Deng Xiaoping 1994b: 338–9)

Western and Japanese economic pressure on China left its mark on China's foreign policy during the Kuwait Crisis. China supported all ten UN resolutions that ordered military and economic sanctions against Iraq and abstained on resolution 678, which permitted the use of force to compel an Iraqi withdrawal from Kuwait (Foot 1995a: 240). Such cooperative behaviour gained some economic and diplomatic rewards. Economic assistance and loans from the World Bank, IMF, ADB, UNDP, and others were resumed (Feeney 1994: 226–7). Diplomatic relations were established with South Korea in August 1992; China's relations with India were improved in a new peaceful manner, particularly after Indian Prime Minister Rajiv Gandhi's visit to China in December 1989;[8] China became more involved with the South-East Asian countries to enhance security and cooperation (Kim 1996: 263–305); Beijing–Moscow relations were improved by signing, during Russian President Boris Yeltsin's visit to Beijing in December 1992, accords with the Russian President ranging from the reduction of troops along their borders to granting of loans and economic and trade cooperation.[9] China's relations with the United States have also entered a new phase. US Secretary of Commerce Barbara Franklin visited Beijing in 1992 and economic cooperation talks started, for the first time since July 1989 (*Beijing Review* Vol. 35, No. 52).

In sum, China's foreign policy in the post-Mao era has been shaped, according to this approach, by China's drive for modernization. The foreign policy strategy of the Five Principles of Peaceful Coexistence has replaced the old foreign policy strategy of armed struggle and world revolution. The leadership of Deng and the post-Deng leadership have repeatedly emphasized the Five Principles – mutual respect for sovereignty and territorial integrity, mutual non-aggression, non-interference in each other's affairs, equality and mutual benefits, and peaceful coexistence – as the basis and guiding principles for not only good relations with other states but also as the basic guidelines for establishment of a new international political and economic order (Xie Yixian 1989: 12–17).

EXTERNAL FACTORS

One of the most popular theoretical approaches that focus on the impact of the outside world on a state's foreign policy in international relations is neo-realism: the focus of this section.[10]

---

8 For the joint press communiqué issued by the two governments at the end of Gandhi's visit to Beijing, see *Beijing Review*, vol. 32, no. 1, 2–8 January 1989, pp. 5–6.
9 For example, a memorandum of understanding was signed to establish a 100-kilometre demilitarized frontier zone, a measure Moscow resisted in the past. *Beijing Review*, vol. 35, no. 52, 28 December 1992, p. 4.
10 World system theory is another approach that focuses its attention on the impact of outside factors on a state's foreign policy. The world system theory of international relations goes

Neo-realism

The classical realist theory of international politics dominated the study of international relations during the first twenty-year period after the end of the Second World War. During that period, the United States and the Soviet Union emerged as the two major superpowers in the world and dominated world affairs; the Cold War determined the relationship between them. The birth of the bipolar international order and the Cold War, therefore, required a new way of thinking and dealing with international relations. The result was the realist theory of international politics, which shifted Western thinking on international relations away from Utopianism towards a resurgent realism, and from idealism to the elements of power. Nevertheless, another school of thought on international relations emerged in the 1970s after the oil crisis of 1973. Its focus was on cooperation and interdependence in international relations.[11] Its scholars define what they call 'the regimes' – namely, international and regional organizations – as the best way to achieve the good of all. During the same period, there had been not only a revival interest in realism and interdependence but also the emergence of a broadly-based neo-realism approach to the study of international relations. During and immediately after the Second World War, the tradition of power politics was regenerated and reinvigorated in the United States. John Herz, George Kennan, Walter Lippmann, and Hans Morgenthau articulate what Morgenthau called 'political realism' in contrast to the Utopianism or idealism in international politics. The works of E. H. Carr, Hans Morgenthau, George Kennan, Raymond Aron, Henry Kissinger, and Hadley Bull exemplify the realist tradition. They build their work on the philosophical outlooks of the work of Thucydides (400 BC), Niccolo Machiavelli (1469–1527), and Thomas Hobbes (1588–1679). This kind of philosophy is not only based on the realm of 'what is' rather than 'what ought to be', but also on the

---

back to the work of Karl Marx and Lenin. It was, however, developed by Immanuel Wallerstein. The core of Wallerstein's analysis is the world system, which he defines as 'a unit with a single division of labour and multiple culture systems'. He argues that the world system is 'the appropriate unit of analysis for the study of social behaviours' whether it is poverty in Africa, ethnic conflict in the Balkans, a state's foreign policy, or family life. According to him, the capitalist world economy constitutes the appropriate unit of analysis in the modern world. It is divided into core, periphery, and semi-periphery, which are linked together by unequal exchange and characterized by unequal development. In sum, the world system approach argues that, in order to understand the development of states' relations, we must keep our eye on the development of capitalism. We should, therefore, examine the world system, which is controlled by capitalism, in order to understand the fate of a particular country. Thus, a state's foreign policy is shaped and guided by the world system and not by any other factor. See for details Immanuel Wallerstein (1979; 1991).

11 See the previous section – internal factors – for details.

realm of 'what can be'.[12] The measures of human beings, according to this philosophy, are their ability to extend their language of power and interests rather than of ideals and norms.

The realist theory of international relations finds that the international system is based on the following assumptions:

- states are the key actors in international relations;
- states are unitary and rational actors (Daugherty and Pfaltzgraff 1990: 81);
- domestic politics can be clearly separated from foreign policy;
- international politics is a struggle for power in an anarchical international system;
- power is only defined in terms of military capability;
- there are gradations of capabilities among states (Viotti and Kauppi 1993: 81); and
- among the array of world issues, national security tops the list for states as a 'high politics' issue (Viotti and Kauppi 1993: 7, 36).

Having said this, realists rely heavily on the concept of power, rationality, and the balance of power. They characterize international politics as a struggle for power and statesmen as individuals who 'think and act in terms of interest defined as power' (Morenthau 1967: 5). Therefore, their focus on interests and power is central to their understanding of how nation states deal and interact with each other. Morgenthau (1967: 25) sees power not only as an instrument for the attainment of other ends in a competitive international system, but also as an end in itself. Due to the nature of human beings, realists assume that there is no essential harmony of interests among states. Instead, they argue that states often have conflicting national objectives, some of which may lead to war. Power to them is defined ultimately in military terms as recourse to force in war.

Realists suggest that governments act rationally, that they have consistent, ordered preferences, and that they calculate the costs and the benefits of all alternative policies in order to maximize their utility in light of both those preferences and their perceptions of the nature of reality. They recognize the problem of lack of information, but they assume that decision makers will try to achieve their best possible decision (Viotti and Kauppi 1993: 35–6). Furthermore, moral principles should not be applied to specific political action.[13] Realists' concepts of the balance of power refer to a

---

12 Niccolo Machiavelli (1950), for example, in *The Prince and the Discourses* suggested many strategies for the prince to adopt in order to enhance his sovereignty and maintain or regain the state's strength and independence.
13 Machiavelli (1950), for example, justifies, in his book *The Prince and the Discourses*, the use of immoral means to achieve a state's national ends.

Theorizing China's foreign policy 41

situation of equilibrium as well as to any situation in which a power struggle takes place (Morgenthau 1967: 161–3). Its aim is to maintain stability of the system by preventing the emergence of any dominant state (Daugherty and Pfaltzgraff 1990: 31). Stability, then, depends on the preservation of a power balance.

The neo-realist approach to international politics introduces and defines some key concepts of the classical realist theory differently in order to integrate the classical theory into contemporary politics. Neo-realism identifies with the writings of Kenneth Waltz, particularly his book *Theory of International Politics* (1979). The writings of Robert Gilpin, George Modelski, Charles Kindleberger, and John Mearsheimer also contribute to the development of the neo-realist school of international relations. Waltz's aim in writing his book was 'to examine theories of international politics' and 'construct a theory that remedies the defects of present theories' (Waltz 1979: 1). Thus, he discusses what theories are, what they are not, and how they are made. Theories, to Waltz, are collections or sets of law pertaining to a particular behaviour. They are different from laws in a way that theories are statements that explain laws. Waltz (1979: 6) argues that 'this meaning does not accord with usage in much of traditional political theory, which is concerned more with philosophic interpretation than with theoretical explanation'. He emphasizes that 'in order to get beyond the facts of observation ... we must grapple with the problem of explanation' (Waltz 1979: 6). Everyone can predict the sunrise and the sunset, as he explained, on the basis of empirical findings without benefit of theories explaining why the phenomena occurs. To form theory requires first simplifications that 'lay bare the essential elements in play and indicate the necessary relations of cause and interdependency or suggest where to look for them' (Waltz 1979: 10). Simplification requires isolation, abstraction, aggregation, and idealization. Second, theory also requires a set of common assumptions to make explanation possible (Waltz 1979: 10).

Waltz emphasises that a good theory of international politics must be systematic, since the way in which relationships among states are organized strongly affects governments' behaviours towards one another. A system, to him, consists of a set of interacting units exhibiting behavioural regularities and reaching identity over time. Thus, he rejects the 'reductionist' theories, and challenges the ideas of Morgenthau and Kissinger in believing that the preservation of peace and the maintenance of international stability depends on the attitudes and the internal characteristics of states. He also rejects Kissinger's argument of war and instability as a result of revolutionary states in the international system, and argues that Kissinger regards some states as war-like states. Waltz writes:

> In order to turn a system approach into a theory, one has to move from the usual vague identification of systemic forces and effects to their more precise specification, to say what units the system compromise, to

indicate the comparative weight of systemic and sub-systemic causes, and to show forces and effects change from one system to another.

(Waltz 1979: 40–1)

Thus, as he argues, we need to go beyond the description of the international system to identify its structure. To Waltz (1979: 72), 'system theories explain how the organisation of a realm acts as a constraining and disposing force on the interacting units within it.' They tell us about the forces the units are subjected to (Waltz 1979: 72). 'From them we can infer some things about the expected behaviour and fate of the unit' (Waltz 1979: 72). In other words, understanding the structure of the international system in Waltz's theory allows us to explain patterns of state behaviour, since a state determines its interests and strategies on the basis of calculations about its own position in the system. According to Waltz, we need first to understand the context of the action before we can understand the action itself. Since the structure of the international system shapes the political relations that take place between its members (states or units), it is important to know what Waltz means by 'structure'. Waltz (1979:81) defines structure as the way in which the parts are arranged and ordered: 'Structure is not a collection of political institutions but rather the arrangement of them.' Waltz defines structure in three ways:

1   by the ordering principles (hierarchical and anarchical) in which it is organized;
2   by specification of functions of formally differentiated parts; and
3   by the distribution of capabilities among the units themselves (Waltz 1979: 88–101).

Waltz argues that, since we live in an international system that is ordered by the principle of anarchy, we need not be concerned with the functions performed by the units, because they are functionally alike. There is no difference between units on the basis of their functions. Therefore, the key changes that we are to look for in international politics are changes in the distribution of capabilities between the system's units. As Waltz indicates:

> The structure of a system changes with the changes in the distribution of capabilities across the system's units ... and changes in structure change expectations about how the units of the system will behave and about the outcome their interactions will produce.
>
> (Waltz 1979: 97)

The most significant capabilities are those of the most powerful states. Small and large states differ from each other not by differences in the attributes and functions of the units but only by distinctions among them according to their capabilities.

Neo-realism accepts the basic assumption of realism about the state being the main international actor in world politics and the assumption that states are mainly concerned about their survival. However, cooperation is not something that is impossible to achieve in the anarchical international society. States cooperate with each other in order to increase or upgrade their own capabilities (Krasner 1985). Neo-realism explains a state's international organizational behaviour by arguing that states are using international organizations to maximize their global status and increase their access to multilateral aid, information, and technology while minimizing sovereignty-restricting conditionalities (Kim 1994: 29).

Waltz developed his theory of balance of power by using his understanding of international structure. To Waltz, a good theory will not only point to the importance of power and the balance of power, as Morgenthau assumed, but will account for the recurrent formation of balance of power in world politics, and can tell us how changing power configurations affect patterns of alignment and conflict in world politics (Waltz 1979: 102–28). From the anarchic nature of the international system and the assumption that states are 'unitary actors who, at a minimum, seek their own preservation and, at a maximum, drive for universal domination', Waltz (1979: 118) infers that balance of power must necessarily emerge. And, as states compete with each other in a competitive international system, 'they will imitate each other and become socialised to their system' (Waltz 1979: 128). As a result of the absence of a universal authority capable of prohibiting the use of force, 'the balance of power among states becomes a balance of all the capabilities, including physical force that states choose to use in pursuing their goals' (Waltz 1954: 206). According to Waltz (1979: 176–83), a system of two (bipolar) superpowers is more stable than a system of many (multipolar). Waltz sees the problem of miscalculation, by some or all of the great powers in the system of many, may threaten the stability of the system. He found that both the United States and the Soviet Union depended militarily mainly on themselves, and balanced each other by their own capabilities, which is more reliable and precise than the external balancing and the capabilities of allies. Thus, he rejects the classical realists' view of bipolar system as an unstable system.

Neo-realism argues that statesmen will try to use all the means available to them in order to achieve their national ends (Waltz 1979: 118). These means fall into two categories:

1 Internal efforts: move to increase economic capability, military strength, and develop clever strategies.
2 External efforts: move to strengthen and enlarge one's own alliance or to weaken and shrink an opposition one (Waltz 1979: 118).

Neo-realism accepts all the assumptions made by the classical realists including the concept of power. However, the concept of power in neo-realism is not defined only in terms of military power. Instead, neo-realism defines power according to a wide range of capabilities. Waltz (1979: 131) states:

> The economic, military, and other capabilities of nations can be sectored and separately weighted. States are not placed in the top rank because they excel *in one way or another*. Their rank depends on how they score on all of the following items: size of population and territory, resource endowment, economic capability, military strength, political stability and competence.

Therefore, the measurement of a state's power in the international system is not only restricted to its military capability, as the classical realists would argue, but also to its performance in several different capabilities. Such combined capabilities constitute a state's power in the international system. To neo-realism, combined capabilities is an important factor in providing the means of maintaining a state's autonomy in the face of force that others yield, permitting wider ranges of actions, and allowing wider margins of safety in dealing with the less powerful states (Waltz 1979: 194). To illustrate this argument, Waltz (1993: 44–79) later indicates that the lack of combined capabilities has led to the disintegration of the former Soviet Union and the possibility of newcomers to play the leading role in today's international system. Waltz (1993: 76) argues that in order for a state to rise to great power status, either through challenging a leading state or attempting to reverse a state's decline, it has to rely on economic, political, and military capabilities all together. Therefore, states should use all their capabilities 'to serve their interests' (Waltz 1979: 131).

The end of the Cold War and the disintegration of the Soviet Union in the neo-realist account threaten the bipolar status of the international system. Neo-realists have repeatedly emphasized since the end of the Cold War that the main actors in the international system would work through realignment and enhancement of their own capabilities to prevent the emergence of a unipolar system dominated by one state (Brown 1997: 108). According to this analysis, the shift from bipolarity towards unipolarity would mean the end of the anarchical system and the emergence of a hierarchical one.

Like many other theories in international politics, neo-realism has received plenty of criticism. Christine Sylvester (1994) has argued that, like many other international theories, neo-realism ignores women's roles in world politics. She emphasizes that neo-realism tends to argue that state craft should remain 'man craft' because men have ascribed to women qualities such as irrationality, intuition, and temptation. Richard Ashley (1986) argues that neo-realism is a static and conservative theory that portrays the structure of the international system as though there is only one structure, and its existence is independent of states rather than constructed by them. To him, neo-realism denies history as a process. 'All movement is confined within a closed field whose limits are defined by the pre-giving structure.' It denies men and women the practice of making their world. He said:

> Nowhere in neo-realist categories do we find room for the idea that men and women who are the subjects of theory can themselves theorise about their lives; are in fact engaged in a continuing struggle to shape and redefine their understanding of themselves, their circumstances, their agencies of collective action, and the very categories of social existence; do indeed orient their practices in light of their understandings; and, thanks to all of this, do give form and motion to the open-ended process by which the material conditions of their practices are made, reproduced, and transformed. Neo-realist structuralism cannot allow this to be so.
> (Ashley 1986: 291)

Robert Cox (1986) describes neo-realism as being a problem-solving theory that 'takes the world as it finds it, with the prevailing social and power relationships and institutions into which they are organised, as the given framework for action.' Its aim, according to Cox (1986: 208), 'is to make these relationships and institutions work smoothly by dealing effectively with the particular source of trouble'. According to this analysis, neo-realism does not question the institutions as a whole, but seeks to 'solve the problems arising in various parts of a whole complex in order to smooth the functioning of the whole' (Cox 1986: 209). Therefore, neo-realism to Cox is a theory that accepts the prevailing order and does not account for change in world order. John Ruggie (1986: 131–55) has argued against neo-realism and claimed that it cannot explain change and it must incorporate other variables – such as 'dynamic density' – to do this.

Neo-realism and China's foreign policy

Neo-realism, as we have seen above, would argue that a state's foreign policy in the international system is not nearly as complicated as observers make it sound, that all foreign policy behaviour can be explained and even determined by the structure of the international system. According to this school, a state's national interests in an anarchical international system can be defined as securing its survival by increasing its economic, military, and political capabilities in order to balance its power. Therefore, balance of power becomes an important principle in guiding the relations between states. To neo-realists, the balance of power is not so much imposed by statesmen on events, as the classical realists would argue, as it is imposed by events on statesmen (Waltz 1954: 209). The Chinese leadership seems to function within the neo-realist's assumption of national interest (survival) and deploys every effort to increase its economic, military, and political capabilities in the international system. Since its establishment, the PRC has given the issue of security high priority among all of its short-, medium-, and long-range objectives in its foreign policy. The PRC has demonstrated its willingness to use military force and involve in military conflicts against any external threat to China's territorial security. This was evident in the Korean Peninsula where China militarily challenged American troops in the early 1950s, in its 1962 war with India where Chinese troops penetrated Indian territory and voluntarily withdrew later, in its border clashes with the Soviet Union in 1969 where many Chinese soldiers lost their lives, in its move to seize the Paracel (Xisha) Islands from Vietnam in 1974 in a brief naval battle, in its short war against Vietnam in 1978 when the latter invaded Cambodia to overthrow the pro-Beijing regime of Pol Pot, and in its frequent military confrontations with the naval forces of the Philippines over Mischief Reef, disputed between the two countries throughout the 1980s and 1990s. The PRC has also demonstrated its seriousness to use force and any other means to protect the communist party and China's territory from any internal threat. The Chinese government's reaction to the Tiananmen Square demonstrations of May 1989, its continued policy of arresting local human rights activists and prohibiting any opposition group to the rules and norms set by the CCP to work in China, and its continued belligerent rhetoric against Taiwan and its minorities indicate its basic policy towards internal threats. China's cooperation with other states is also centred on achieving its own national interest. Harvey W. Nelson (1981: 200–1) and Donald W. Klein (1989: 144) argue that China's changing alliances from the Soviet Union to the United States and its political and military supports for Third World countries are guided by China's self-interest to achieve its foreign policy objectives rather than promoting cooperation.

The post-Mao leadership has adopted the neo-realist's concept of power as capabilities. During the Cold War, the Maoist leadership saw power merely in military terms as the most dominant force in the international system and the relations among nations. The result was an increase in China's military capabilities by, first, allying itself either with the Soviet Union to balance the power of the United States (1949–1959) or with the United States to balance the power of the Soviet Union (1970–1982); second, developing its own military capabilities, and promoting its objectives in the Third World through economic aid (for details, see Copper 1979). Towards the twilight of the 1970s, the Chinese leadership started to shift its understanding of the concept of power towards the neo-realist's concept of capabilities. The proximity to the neo-realist's concept of power by the Chinese government is evident in China's Four Modernizations programme: the modernization of agriculture, industry, national defence, and science and technology. In order for China to achieve superpower capabilities, the Chinese leadership has understood the significance of scoring well in all of these areas. Deng Xiaoping asserted in 1985 the importance of new capabilities to constitute power in the international system and stated:

> We should ... recognise that the new revolution in science and technology all over the world is developing vigorously and that economic strength, science and technology play an outstanding role in world wide competition. Neither the United States and the Soviet Union, nor the other developed countries, nor the developing countries can afford to ignore this.
>
> (Deng Xiaoping 1994a: 132)

Since then, China has embarked upon a foreign policy that would achieve a rapid increase in China's political, economic, and military capabilities relative to those of the main regional and international powers.

The structures of the international system have affected China's concept of balance of power. In the bipolar international system, China was forced to balance its power with those of the two major superpowers by allying itself with either power. With the changes in the structure of the international system after the end of the Cold War, China was obligated to upgrade its capabilities or yield new ones in order to prevent the transformation of the international system to a system dominated by a hostile country. This was evident in its efforts to increase its cooperation with developed countries and Russia in order to create a common consent against the domination of the United States in world affairs, and in its efforts to work against the establishment of any form of strategic military alignment between a 'hostile' state and the countries of South and South-East Asia. For instance, China has argued against trying to create a formal security regime in the region to parallel the organization for security and cooperation in Europe; it has also campaigned against the US promotion of theatre missile defence to ensure the security of Taiwan, Japan, and all other US allies in the region (Cambone 1997: 66–84). China, as Deng argued in 1990, should not belittle its importance in the multipolar world, instead it should be counted as one of the major poles in the post-Cold War international system (Deng Xiaoping 1994a: 341). As a result, China has made every effort to speed up its Four Modernizations programme by getting involved in more economic and technological cooperation with developing countries and military cooperation with Russia and some other countries like Israel. The Four Modernizations programme is an effort to modernize China's economic and military capabilities. The Chinese government believe that, in order for China to compete with the main actors in the international system, it should, first of all, abandon much of its old rhetoric and, second, adopt new policies that can achieve a leading role for China in world affairs. Thus, as mentioned in the previous section, China adopted the 'open up to the outside' policy, which has aimed at achieving a strong economy through cooperation and accepting foreign investment. Its involvement in international economic norms in the post-Cold War era reflects neo-realist thinking. Denny Roy (1998: 229) and Thomas J. Christensen (1996: 37–51) argue that China's cooperation in international and regional organizations is not governed by its commitment to the principle of political and economic integration between nations, but by the fact that China saw no other means of readdressing its economic weaknesses. Therefore, by adopting the 'open up to the outside' policy, the Chinese government has aimed at achieving a short-term and a long-term objective. The Chinese government's short-term objective was based on its willingness to achieve political stability inside China by creating more job opportunities for the Chinese. Its long-term objective, however, has been to achieve superpower capabilities that can allow China to assume a leading role in world affairs in general and Asian affairs in particular.

China's drive towards modernizing its economy coincided with efforts to modernize its military capability. As previously mentioned, the Chinese leadership has also aimed at strengthening its military capability and modernizing its forces through achieving a strong economy. Despite the reduction in military spending in favour of more funding to modernize the economy during the 1980s, defence modernization had not witnessed major setbacks. The Chinese defence and security specialists began in the mid-1980s to emphasize a new Chinese defence strategy. The new strategy viewed world conflict in terms of the inevitability of the old assumption of a global nuclear war to the possibility of more limited and regional wars (Shulong Chu 1994: 177–8). Thus, superpowers' influence is reduced and the potential for local and regional wars are increased with the emergence of many regional powers (Lin Qinggong 1992: 26–7). The massive military action against Iraq and the collapse of the Soviet Union demonstrated the need for China's military determination to possess a modernized force capable of defending China against any internal and external threat. New and modern war conditions, that were demonstrated by the West in the Gulf against Iraq, articulated the need for China to modernize its own military strategy. Such a new perspective of international conflict has left its mark on the Chinese defence budget. For the first time since the 1970s, official Chinese military expenditure had increased continuously between 1990 and 1996 despite the fall in global military spending since 1992 (see Table 2.2; for an analysis of China's defence budget increase, see Ball *et al.* 1994: 441–8). It is important to note that the estimated figures of China's military expenditure are two to four times higher than the official figures (Ball *et al.* 1994: 441–8). The broad range of the Chinese People's Liberation Army's (PLA) commercial economic activities, its covert programmes, and the higher inflation figure make it very hard for analysts to know exactly what China's military spending actually is. China's defence modernization programme has also shifted China's focus towards building quality arms rather than quantity,

Table 2.2 China's military expenditure, official figures, 1976–1996

Year	Current values (yuan, billions)	Constant (US$, billions)	Percentage of share of gross domestic product
1976	13.4	7.0	5.0
1977	14.9	7.6	5.6
1978	16.8	8.5	5.6
1979	22.3	11.1	6.6
1980	19.3	9.0	5.3
1981	16.8	7.6	4.3
1982	17.6	7.8	4.1
1983	17.7	7.7	3.7
1984	18.1	7.6	3.2
1985	19.1	7.2	2.7
1986	20.1	7.1	2.4
1987	21.0	6.8	2.3
1988	22.0	5.5	1.5
1989	25.0	5.4	1.6
1990	29.0	6.1	1.6
1991	33.0	6.7	1.6
1992	38.0	7.2	1.6
1993	43.0	7.1	1.4
1994	55.0	7.5	1.4
1995	63.0	7.4	1.6
1996	75.0	8.2	1.6

Numbers from 1976 to 1987 are based on 1988 prices. Numbers from 1988 to 1996 are based on 1990 prices. Sources *SIPRI* (1991: 157), (1997: 196–203).

raising the level of education of the PLA officer corps, replacing elderly officers by younger men, decreasing military participation in politics, and reducing headquarters staff and ground, air, and naval forces (Henley 1988: 100–7). To raise the level of its armed forces, China has moved far from strategies and military operations, associated with 'people's war', to military exercises conducted under nuclear conditions.[14] Modernization also means developing a more sophisticated nuclear capability. China's nuclear capability is estimated to contain about 400 warheads structured in short, medium, long and intercontinental ranges of land-based missiles, bombers, and submarine-launched missiles (*SIPRI* 1997: 401). In 1997, China deployed the Dong Feng-31 (DF-31) (Dong Feng means 'East Wind'), a land-based intercontinental missile with a range of 8,000 km and ability to carry one 200–300-kt warhead (*SIPRI* 1997: 401). It is also developing the 12,000-km range ICBM DF-41, which is scheduled for deployment around 2010,

---

14 In late 1982, the Chinese military conducted exercises in the northern part of China using stimulated tactical nuclear weapons. See Paul H. B. Godwin (1986: 1–3) and, for a good discussion about this topic, see Richard Fieldhouse (1991: 37–42).

50 *China's foreign policy in a global context*

and the 8,000-km range Julang-2 (Great Wave), known to NATO as CSS-N-4, as a submarine-launched ballistic missile to be available in the late 1990s (*SIPRI* 1997: 401). China has worked to gain foreign technology to modernize its military capabilities by purchasing the Sukhio-27 (Su-27) fighter bomber from Russia in 1992 (equivalent to an American F-15) and increasing its military cooperation with Russia through signing a five-year military cooperation accord in 1993 (for Chinese–Russian military cooperation, see Bin Yu 1993: 302–16). Under another agreement, Russia agreed to sell production rights to China to assemble and produce Su-27s in China. Reports indicated that China concluded in 1997 a new military agreement with Russia that included the purchase of two Sovremenny-class guided missile destroyers equipped with SS-N-22 submarine anti-ship cruise missiles (ASCMs) with a range of 100 km. China has also received assistance from Israel in developing the American F-16-equivalent and the American–Israeli-built Lavi-equivalent J-10 fighter-bomber (Fulghum 1995a: 26–7, 1995: 44–5). Many official and unofficial Western reports have concluded that Israel has supplied assistance to China in air defence, air-to-air missiles, upgraded Chinese combat aircraft, and improved Chinese tanks (Gill and Taeho Kim 1995: 81–6). Israeli transfers of military-related technology to China since 1982 is estimated to be valued at US$2–3 billion (Gill and Taeho Kim 1995: 83). In 1997, China signed an agreement with Israel in which the latter would install a radar system on the Russian Ilyushin Il-76 aircraft, which was secretly transferred to Israel from Russia.[15] The development of the J-10, the purchase of the Su-27, and the efforts to own an early-warning spy plane are considered essential steps in strengthening China's air power. China has also gradually upgraded many of its Chinese-made weapon systems by acquiring more advanced technology from countries like France, Germany, Italy, Canada, the United States (see Footnote 15, *Ibid.*: 73–80 and Ngok Lee 1989) and South Africa.[16] Its acquisition of some 100 Patriot-like S-300 surface-to-air missiles from Russia indicates that China is either upgrading its air system defence or starting a new missile defence effort (Denoon and Frieman 1996: 425). In line with the PLA's new defence strategy, China has acquired in 1994 the Russian Kilo-class submarine to safeguard its territorial waters in the South China Sea and to add new submarine technology to its own submarine programme (Gill and Taeho Kim 1995: 60–3).

All the above shows that China has adopted a neo-realist understanding

---

15 Due to US pressure on Israel, the agreement remained unimplemented. See report by Israeli newspaper *Ha'aretz* on 2 November 1999; BBC, *Summary of World Broadcasts* (hereafter SWB), MEW/0614, WME, 9 November 1999, p. 9; and BBC, *SWB*, MEW/0615 WME, 16 November 1999, p. 7.
16 China signed in February 1997 an arms deal with South Africa for the Chinese purchase of South African military equipment worth about 1 billion rands, BBC, *Summary of World Broadcasts* (hereafter SWB), *FE/2834*, 4 February 1997, p. G/1.

to speed up its economic and military modernization through its Four Modernizations programme in order to ensure the survival and security of the PRC and its communist party leadership.

The Chinese understanding of the concept of balance of power is also neo-realist. Neo-realists would argue that the balance of power is imposed by events on statesmen rather than by statesmen on events. In the case of the PRC, events such as American military involvement in Korea, Soviet military movements along the Ussuri River, Soviet penetration around the world, disintegration of the Soviet Union, the massive American victory against Iraq during the Second Gulf War and the rapid increase in oil consumption in China all have determined the patterns in which China balances its power with the different actors in the international system. Due to such events, China has shifted its strategy from strengthening its military capability to building combined capability, and from the inevitability of a global nuclear conflict to developing a new understanding based on more advanced and limited regional conflicts. Another neo-realist assessment in China's foreign policy is the fact that the CCP leadership has always used the concept of power not as an end in itself, as the classical realist would argue, but as a means to achieve other ends. Domestically, power in terms of capabilities is very helpful in maintaining security and political stability. By strengthening its economy and preserving internal political stability, the CCP is going to rule without a strong opposition. Internationally, power in terms of combined capability is important to enhance China's international status, and enable it to achieve more influence in international affairs.[17]

CONCLUSION

From the above discussion, we find that the study of China's foreign policy is based on two assumptions. The first is that theorizing China's foreign behaviour is not something that can simply be explained by a single theoretical approach or model. Many aspects of China's foreign behaviour can be looked at differently through different theoretical perspectives. The second assumption is that the two factors (internal and external) are the most used frameworks by scholars and researchers in explaining China's foreign policy. Such focus paralleled a few studies that used a combination of both factors in studying China's foreign policy behaviour. Therefore, the author believes that the neo-realist explanation of international relations is

---

17 Robert Gilpin, a leading neo-realist, emphasizes this point by arguing that economic, military, and technological capabilities present the means for states to pursue not only wealth and economic gain but also political power in world affairs. See Robert Gilpin (1981).

the most useful framework for the purpose of this work. Based on all the previous assumptions, he finds that China's foreign policy behaviour towards the Gulf and Arabian Peninsula region is largely consistent with the neo-realist theoretical approach of international relations (the external factor). China's perceptions and relations with both the United States and the Soviet Union, on the one hand, and China's drive towards increasing its economic, political, and military capabilities, on the other, are the most dominant factors in shaping China's foreign policy towards the Gulf and Arabian Peninsula region. Thus, the earlier discussions on the external factor, namely the neo-realist assumptions of foreign policy, will serve as our guide for the study of China's foreign policy towards the Gulf and Arabian Peninsula region. The author's argument throughout this book can be summarized in the following manner:

- China's foreign policy behaviour towards the Gulf and the Arabian Peninsula region from October 1949 to 1999 had been guided by China's perception of, and relations with, both the United States and the Soviet Union, and China's drive to upgrade its economic, political, and military capabilities. These two factors had formulated a platform for the Chinese government's policy behaviour towards the Gulf and Peninsula countries during this period.

In order for the author to carry this argument forward, he will first survey China's relations with both the United States and the Soviet Union so as to capture a clearer understanding of the effects of these relations on China's policy towards the Gulf and Peninsula region. This subject will be addressed in the next chapter.

3 China's relations with the United States, the Soviet Union, and Russia

As shown in Chapter 2, the study of China's foreign policy behaviour has witnessed different theoretical approaches by scholars and researchers. Since we argue that China's foreign policy towards the Gulf and Arabian Peninsula region depends on China's relations with both the United States and the Soviet Union, this chapter is going to discuss China's foreign relations with both powers. China's relations with both superpowers and the superpowers' interactions with each other, along with its view of the world are the keys to understanding China's policy towards the Gulf and Peninsula region. And since China's relations with both the United States and the Soviet Union have changed, China's involvement in the Gulf and Peninsula region has also changed with time. The change reflects China's overall analysis of the international system and its relations with the main actors in it. China's relations with both powers will be discussed here chronologically.

CHINA'S EARLY INTERACTIONS WITH THE SUPERPOWERS (1949–1954)

China–superpowers relations have evolved throughout different stages since the establishment of the PRC in 1949. Marxism–Leninism and Mao Zedong's thought played a profound role in China's relations with both superpowers during the first three decades of their interactions. Mao Zedong's perception of the 'enemy' and his theory of contradictions[1] brought the PRC's leadership to view the Soviet Union as China's most trusted partner in the 1950s, and as China's most dangerous enemy in the 1970s. It also brought them to engage in a hostile relationship with the Unites States in the 1950s, and in strategic alignment in the 1970s. In addition to ideology, history – another component of China's foreign policy

---

1 See the ideology section in the previous chapter for further details.

discussed in the previous chapter – had also guided China's views and relations with both superpowers. Mindful of the past century of humiliation and foreign domination, the CCP's leadership was very careful not to view the Americans positively. The CCP's leadership criticized the China Aid Act, which was approved by the US Congress on 2 April, 1948, to provide military and economic assistance to the national government in Taiwan (Gupta 1869: 212). The CCP's leadership considered the act as a policy that contributed to the extension of the civil war; without it, the nationalist government would have surrendered a long time ago and all China would have unified under the leadership of the CCP (Garson 1994: 24). Mao Zedong saw the United States as the 'primary enemy' that contradicted the newly-established communist state in China in its early days. In order for the PRC to advance further, according to Mao's theory of contradictions, it had to resolve its principle contradiction, the United States, first before advancing to the next stage. As a result, the Soviet Union was viewed by the CCP's leadership as the best available alternative to ally itself with, in order to exploit the Americans, maintain its security, and achieve its national goals of restoring its lost territories. This policy resulted in creation of the Chinese–Soviet alliance on 14 February, 1950 with the signing of:

1 a treaty of friendship, alliance, and mutual assistance that bounded the two sides to assist one another against Japan or any state aiding Japan in aggression;[2]
2 an agreement providing that after the signing of a peace treaty with Japan, and not later than 1952, the Soviet Union would transfer, free of charge, all its rights in Manchuria to China and withdraw its troops from the Port Arthur (Lushun) naval base; and
3 an agreement on the granting of long-term credit to the amount of $300 million to China.

Recognizing the weakness and vulnerability of its regime, particularly in developing modern industry and administrating large urban areas, the Chinese government looked to the Soviet experience and assistance to fulfil its needs. It adopted the Soviet economic model in its first five-year plan in 1953. By the first half of the 1950s, more than half of China's annual foreign trade was with the Soviet Union (Clubb 1971: 392). Throughout the

---

2 The treaty concluded that: (1) the PRC and the USSR should 'take all necessary measures ... for the purpose of preventing repetition of aggression and violation of peace on the part of Japan, directly or indirectly, in the act of aggression; (2) either side should not take part in 'any coalition or action or measures directed against the other'; (3) both would consult each other in regard to 'all important international problems affecting the common interests' of both countries; and (4) both should not interfere in each others internal affairs. For the text, see Grant F. Rhode and Reid E. Whitlock (1980: 15–16).

1950s, more than 100,000 Soviet technical specialists and advisors went to China to train and supervise Chinese personnel; and, during the first plan period, over 7,000 Chinese were trained in Soviet enterprises and about 10,000 Chinese scientists were trained by the Soviet Academy of Science (Barnett 1977: 28). The Chinese also adopted the Soviet methods of agriculture and received Soviet assistance in the field (Mayer 1962: 118–21). The Soviet Union provided training programmes for Chinese pilots and soldiers (Mayer 1962: 59–64). Some writers recount that, during the Korean War, the Soviet Union supplied China with military assistance to the value of US $2,000 million, including about 1,000 MiG-15 aircraft, aid to war industries in Manchuria, and to China's transport system (Day 1985: 3). The Soviets dispatched 1,000 to 25,000 Soviet experts (in 1952 for the Chinese airforce and navy, and 5,000 to 10,000 for the Chinese army in 1953 (Hsu 1990: 661). Nonetheless, the Chinese were required to pay for the military supplies they received from the Soviet Union during the Korean War (Barnett 1977: 30). PRC-USSR collaboration was advanced by Moscow's offer to China and other communist countries in January 1955 to extend the Soviet's scientific and technological assistance regarding utilization of atomic energy for peaceful uses (Clubb 1971: 408). Walter C. Clemens Jr (1968: 32) argues that by the late 1950s the Soviet Union had delivered short- and medium-range missiles to China. Even the death of Stalin in March 1953 did not slow down the PRC–USSR relationship. Instead, there was a substantial increase in economic and technological cooperation between the two countries, which allowed the relationship to reach its highest level of friendship and cooperation between 1953 and 1956. This period was highlighted by Nikita Khrushchev's visit to Beijing in 1954 during which he agreed to help build 156 production enterprises in China (Hsu 1990: 661).

Unlike the close PRC–USSR relationship, the PRC–US relationship in this period was extremely hostile. This relationship was marked mainly by US involvement in the Korean Peninsula and its policy in Asia. With the outbreak of the Korean War, US President Harry S. Truman, who was prior to the war unwilling to challenge the Chinese communists over Taiwan, declared on 27 June, 1950 that a communist attack on the island would be viewed as a threat to US interest in Asia. He, therefore, sent the US Seventh Fleet into the Taiwan Strait to block any attempt by China to seize Taiwan (Purifoy 1976). The Chinese government referred to the American action as an American 'occupation' of Taiwan (Hinton 1976: 16). As a consequence, the United States became China's primary enemy leading the 'imperialist camp' against the 'socialist camp'. The conflict between the two camps to the CCP's leadership would lead to a victory for the socialists.[3] Meanwhile,

---

3 For more details see the previous chapter.

a 'united front' with the socialist camp was a desirable strategy for the CCP leadership to defeat US imperialism. As a result, the PRC–US relationship was severely constrained in the 1950s. The two sides engaged in a bloody conflict in Korea, dangerous crises in the Taiwan Strait, and an intense war in Vietnam. While the United States viewed China as a Soviet agent trying to promote the communization of Asia, China viewed the United States as an imperialist power seeking to dominate and exploit Third World countries. As a result, the United States waged an extensive campaign to isolate and contain China. This policy was marked by the following:

1. The US negative perception of the Sino-Soviet alliance and the belief that any communist victory anywhere was a threat to the United States (Jervis 1980: 584).
2. The rapid increases in the US defence budget to maintain troops in Korea and to strengthen US naval forces in Asia.
3. The establishment of US military bases, bilateral and multilateral alliances, and military and economic aid programmes with the friendly states in Asia. These included bilateral defence treaties with Japan and the Philippines in 1952, Taiwan in December 1954. By 1954, the United States had organized two alliance systems: the Australian–New Zealand–United States alliance in 1951 and the South East Asia Treaty Organization (SEATO).
4. An increase in US commitment to the security of Eastern European countries against any Soviet attack by militarizing NATO.
5. An increase in US efforts to prevent China from developing external contacts, gaining recognition in the UN, and conducting state-to-state diplomatic and trade relations with the rest of the world.

The CCP's leadership viewed this US containment policy as aggressive and a threat to China's security. Therefore, along with increasing its ties with the Soviet Union in the first half of the 1950s, China began in the second half of the 1950s to woo, for the first time, the non-communist states of Asia and Africa. China's foreign policy strategy was shifted from continuing its hostile propaganda against the non-communist states of the Third World towards attempting to win their sympathy and create an international united front against US policies. This foreign policy strategy reached its peak around the time of the Bandung conference in 1955.

CHINA AND THE CHANGING OF ITS FOREIGN POLICY STRATEGY (1955–1969)

China's foreign policy towards the superpowers started to change in the second half of the 1950s. This movement was reflected by the change in China's view of the Soviet Union after its adoption of Khrushchev's new policy of peaceful coexistence with the United States. Khrushchev introduced this policy at the Twentieth Congress of the Soviet Communist Party on 14–15 February, 1956. His new policy stemmed from the following arguments:

1   that the establishment of friendly relations with the capitalist nations based on the 'five principles of peaceful coexistence' would be of great importance for world peace;
2   rejection of Lenin's theory that war is inevitable as long as capitalism exists – he argued that wars could be prevented through social and political forces; and
3   unlike Beijing, Moscow believed in the peaceful transformation of capitalist countries to socialism (for a discussion of Krushchev's report, see Wolfe 1957; Avtorkhanov 1956: 3–19; Achminov 1956: 20–9).

Khrushchev's new foreign policy contrasted Mao's thought of advocating struggle for resolving contradiction, namely against the United States and the capitalist camp. The Chinese feared that Khrushchev's new policy and his attack on Stalin at the Twentienth Congress would weaken the unity of the Communist Bloc in its struggle against the capitalist world. In an attempt to pull the Soviet leadership away from its policy of peaceful coexistence with the West, Mao travelled to Moscow during its celebration of the fortieth anniversary of the Bolshevik Revolution in November 1957. During his visit, Mao made his remark on 'the East Wind is prevailing over the West Wind.' Mao's assessment was that the socialist camp headed by the Soviet Union, with its development of a hydrogen bomb in 1953, ICBM capability, and technological advancement with the placement of the first earth satellite into orbit in 1957, had become technologically stronger than the imperialist camp headed by the United States. His remarks were directed towards the argument that the Soviet Union should share its technological advantage with the rest of the socialist countries and advance the cause of communism throughout the world even at the risk of nuclear war (for a discussion, see Floyd 1963: 48–60; Zagoria 1962: 160–5; Gittings 1968: 79–84). However, the Soviet leadership did not favour the Chinese strategy. They viewed it as unprofitable to Soviet interests and believed that it could lead to vast destruction. By 1957, the CCP leadership became convinced that the Soviet leadership was not willing to challenge militarily the imperialist camp, nor was it prepared to transfer its technology to the task of turning the PRC into a major military and economic power. Therefore, despite Soviet disapproval, the CCP leadership decided in February 1958 to use China's own energy to build and develop its economy over the next three years through the Great Leap Forward. The Great Leap Forward was marked by a general turning away from the Soviet Union. The Soviet model in military training was abandoned, and China's previous method of relying for its industrial development on large industrial complexes built with Soviet aid was cancelled and replaced with a policy of constructing hundreds of thousands of small- and medium-sized plants all over the country (Quested 1984: 122). The divergence in China–Soviet relations escalated in 1958 after the following:

1. The CCP leadership was distressed at Khrushchev's 'soft' response to the Western landings in the Middle East, Lebanon, and Jordan, in the summer of 1958. While the Chinese advocated the use of force against the Western military action, the Soviets adopted a political approach to solve the situation and accepted the Western proposal for emergency summit meetings within the framework of the UN Security Council (Zagoria 1962; 195–9; Gittings 1968: 89–92).
2. The CCP leadership was disappointed at the value of their alliance with the Soviet Union during China's military attack on Quemoy Island in August–October 1958 in an attempt to seize Taiwan. During the crisis, the Soviet Union limited its support to issuing a statement of warning; and, not until the crisis had passed the danger point, did Khrushchev threaten the use nuclear weapons in the event of a nuclear attack on China. Other than that the Chinese received no Soviet military assistance to enable them to recover the island (Gittings 1968: 200–17). The crisis demonstrated to the Chinese that the Soviet Union was not prepared to give China the support it desired.

Despite the signing of several agreements between the PRC and the USSR in 1958 and 1959,[4] the Chinese–Soviet relationship continued to spiral downwards from 1959 troubled by disagreement over the following issues:

1. the Soviet refusal in mid-1959 to supply China with a sample of an atomic bomb and technical data related to its manufacture (Gittings 1968: 102–9);
2. the Soviet declaration of neutrality between China and India in their border clashes in August 1959, and its continuing economic and military assistance to India including the transfer of eight four-engine troop transports in 1961, and helicopters and MiG-21 jet fighters in 1962 (Barnett 1977: 46; for the nature of the conflict, see Lu 1986);

---

4 This included the signing of a protocol to govern their scientific and technical collaboration on 4 July 1958; the signing of an agreement on 8 August 1958 for providing Soviet aid to China in designing and installing industrial plan; and the signing of an agreement on 7 February 1959 to supply China with equipment, materials, technical assistance, and training programmes.

3   Khrushchev's visit to Washington in September 1959 and his appeal for a peaceful coexistence and universal disarmament;
4   the establishment of friendly relations between the Soviet Union and Yugoslavia in May/October 1962;
5   The Cuban Crisis of October 1962;
6   The Soviet Union signing of nuclear test-ban treaty on 25 July 1963 with the United States and the UK in Moscow (Whiting 1987: 521; Clubb 1971: 469).

In April 1960, the Chinese government made public for the first time its ideological differences with the Soviet Communist Party. An article written in Red Flag (16 April 1960) titled 'Long Live Leninism!' warned against the idea that the nature of imperialism had changed in any way since Lenin's time and contrasted Khrushchev's views of peaceful coexistence and his argument on the inevitability of war (*Peking Review*, No. 17, 1960). Furthermore, despite the attempts to resolve differences within the communist movement during the Bucharest Conference of 20–26 June 1960, Peng Zhen, head of the Chinese delegation to the Conference, contested in his speech Khrushchev's argument that war was no longer inevitable. Peng declared that 'as long as imperialism exists there will always be the danger of war'.[5] The Soviets criticized the Chinese position in a letter sent to the CCP. The Chinese replied by criticizing the Soviet party position in ignoring Stalin's policies and putting forward a new policy without previously consulting the other communist parties (Day 1985: 20–1; Gittings 1968: 123–8). Since then, the Chinese government began to refer to the Soviet government as 'revisionist'. In July 1960, the Soviet specialists started to depart from China because of the 'mistreatment and disregard to their expertise' as the Soviet reported (Clubb 1971: 445–6). In 1962 and 1963, the PRC–USSR conflicts escalated further over nuclear arms control agreements. On 31 July 1963, the CCP issued a strongly-worded statement denouncing the test-ban treaty agreement. The statement said:

> This treaty signed in Moscow is a big fraud to fool the people of the world. It runs diametrically counter to the wishes of the peace-loving people of the world. The people of the world demand a genuine peace; this treaty provides them with a fake peace.
>
> (Gittings 1968: 187)

---

5   'Quarterly chronicle and documentation', The China Quarterly, No. 3, July–September 1960, pp. 114–5; and Edward Crankshaw (1965): 97–110).

On behalf of the Chinese government, Premier Zhou Enlai sent a letter to the leaders of all states on 2 August 1963 proposing a world conference of heads of governments to discuss the matter.[6]

By 1963, the Chinese leadership became convinced that the nature of the threat had fundamentally changed towards both the 'imperialist power' of the United States and the 'revisionist government' of the Soviet Union. Many attempts to bring about a measure of reconciliation between the two sides were rejected by the Chinese party including several proposals for a world communist conference and a united front to aid North Vietnam (Day 1985: 47–59). The PRC boycotted a number of communist conferences in Moscow. Challenging the Soviets, the Chinese carried their own aid programmes to revolutionary movements in Asia, Africa, and Latin America.[7] It also sought to influence Third World countries through promoting the second Afro-Asian Solidarity Conference to be held without the presence of the Soviet Union (Neuhauser 1968). The Chinese stressed the need for an international united front against both superpowers. Lin Biao's *Peking Review* (No. 36: 9–30) article 'Long live the victory of people war' on 3 September 1965 criticized Khrushchev's view that the Soviet line of peaceful coexistence and peaceful competition would lead to 'a world without wars'. It argued that 'the general line of the Khrushchev revisionists is nothing other than the demand that all the oppressed peoples and nations and all the countries which have won independence should lay down their arms and place themselves at the mercy of the US imperialists and their lackeys who are armed to the teeth', the article went to say that 'to win the struggle against US imperialism and carry people's wars to victory, the Marxist–Leninists and revolutionary people throughout the world must resolutely oppose Khrushchev revisionism'.

The CCP, temporarily and for the first time, proved willing to readjust its view of the Soviet Union after the removal of Khrushchev on 14 October 1964. The CCP congratulated Leonid Brezhnev and hoped that the new leader would bring the Soviet Communist Party closer to the Chinese Communist party. Zhou Enlai made a state visit to Moscow on 5–13 November 1964 for the celebration of the anniversary of the Bolshevik Revolution.[8] A day after Zhou's arrival, Brezhnev made a public speech in which he stated that Moscow would continue its foreign policy laid down by Khrushchev. This declaration along with their differences on how to resolve

---

6   *China Reconstructs*, Vol. 12, No. 10, October 1963, p. 1.
7   For example, the PRC provided North Vietnam with MiG-17 jet fighters and trained Vietnamese pilots in China; it also granted Tanzania with credit of $42 million, and Pakistan with a long-term interest-free loan of $60 million in 1964. See Whiting (1987: 529–36).
8   'Quarterly chronicle and documentation', The China Quarterly, No. 21, January–March 1965, pp. 208–9.

the Vietnam war[9] led the Chinese to criticize the Soviet Union's new leadership directly for the first time since the dismissal of Khrushchev. An editorial published in *Peking Review* (No. 25: 5–10) on 18 June 1965 declared that the Soviet Union's new leaders 'have not departed from the essence, namely of Khrushchev's revisionism, splittism, great power chauvinism, and Soviet–US cooperation for the domination of the world'.

With the introduction of the Cultural Revolution, at the Eleventh Plenary Session of the Chinese Party's Central Committee held on 1–12 August 1966, the PRC isolated itself diplomatically, economically, and socially from the outside world. Thomas Robinson (1991: 219–20) argues that, despite its isolationism, China's foreign policy during the Cultural Revolution was in line with its overall previous foreign policy. Following the session, the Chinese party's central committee adopted, on 12 August a communiqué that reaffirmed the Party's hostility to Soviet 'revisionism', and its refusal to cooperate with the Soviet Union on the Vietnamese question.[10] During the Cultural Revolution, the PRC had expressed its displeasure at Soviet policies through allowing huge demonstrations to be staged in front of the Soviet embassy in Beijing (Robinson 1991: 236–7). At the same time, officials on each side made their countries' displeasure at the other side's policies very obvious. For instance, at the celebrations of the seventeenth anniversary of the PRC on 3 October 1966, the Soviet representatives left the ceremony when Lin Biao criticized the Soviet party for cooperating with 'imperialism' against the Vietnamese people. The Chinese acted similarly during the celebrations of the anniversary of the Russian Revolution in Moscow when the Soviets criticized Chinese policies in Vietnam (Day 1985: 75).

Several factors had played a major role in changing the nature of the PRC–USSR dispute in the 1960s from being an ideological one to a political and strategic one. First, the Soviet invasion of Czechoslovakia on 20 August 1968 followed by the Brezhnev Doctrine frightened the CCP leadership. Zhou Enlai, in a speech at Rumania's National Day reception in the Rumanian embassy in Beijing on 23 August, delineated his government's stand on the Soviet action. Zhou said that:

> The Chinese government and people strongly condemn the Soviet revisionist leading clique and its followers for their crime of aggression and firmly support the Czechoslovak people in their heroic struggle of resistance to Soviet military occupation.
>
> (*Peking Review*, No. 4, 23 August 1968: 3)

---

9 The Soviet Union made repeated efforts to bring about negotiated settlement to the war; the Chinese consistently opposed any suggestion of compromise to settle the Vietnam War. See Orbis, Summer 1965, pp. 9–2.
10 For the text of the communiqué, see *Peking Review*, No. 34, 19 August 1966, pp. 4–8.

62 China's foreign policy in a global context

The Chinese government's support for the Czech government came despite their displeasure at the Czech communist party leader's (Alexander Dubček) political programme. The CCP leadership, also, refused to accept the Soviet contention that Moscow had the right to intervene in any country where socialism might be threatened. Its initial response was a massive propaganda campaign against the Brezhnev Doctrine (see Rea 1975: 22–30; Rea and Yawsoon Sim n.d.: 1–10). Second, the border clashes between the PRC and the USSR in March 1969 along the Ussuri River brought China to view the Soviet Union as the principle threat to its survival and national goals. The Chinese started another massive anti-Soviet propaganda campaign featuring nationwide demonstrations and criticism of the 'aggressive nature of the Soviet revisionism and Social imperialism',[11] meaning that they were socialists who were behaving like an imperialist power. Third, the rapid expansion of Soviet power and influence in Asia compared to the decline of American power in Asia with the beginning of its withdrawal from Vietnam in 1969. Between 1966 to 1969, this expansion was evidenced in the Soviet Union increasing aid to North Vietnam. The Soviets, also, began, in 1968, to make efforts to improve Soviet ties with the non-communist countries of South-East Asia. Plus, Moscow improved its bilateral economic and political relations with Singapore in January 1968, Indonesia in August 1969, and Malaysia and Australia in September 1969. In April 1969, the Soviet foreign minister visited Burma, Laos, Cambodia, and Japan (Garver 1982: 9), while, in May 1969, the Soviet president visited the People's Republic of Mongolia and the People's Democratic Republic of Korea (Garver 1982: 10). The Soviets also worked towards strengthening its naval power in the Pacific and Indian Oceans. In 1968, Soviet warships visited India for the first time, patrolled the Indian Ocean, and paid visits to ports along the East African Coast, the Arabian Gulf, the Red Sea, the South China Sea, and the Philippine Sea (Garver 1982: 26–8). Finally, the Chinese perceived the collaboration between Washington and Moscow in the area of nuclear weaponry as anti-China. The Chinese feared the two superpowers' cooperation in concluding the nuclear test-ban treaty in August 1963, the non-proliferation treaty in July 1968, the development of anti-China anti-ballistic missile (ABM) systems in 1967, and the beginning of the strategic arms limitation talks (SALT) in November 1969 (Garver 1993a: 72). They believed that all of these efforts were strategies to balance the superpowers' nuclear capabilities and to prevent either the United States or the USSR retaliating on China's behalf in the event of a nuclear attack on China by either side.[12] Therefore, all these four factors upgraded the nature of the

11 See *Peking Review*, No. 10, 7 March 1969, p. 4 and pp. 5–11.
12 See, for instance, Chiao Kuan-hua's speech at the UN General Assembly on 13 November 1972, printed in *Peking Review*, No. 46, 17 November 1972, pp. 5–6 and pp. 7–9.

PRC–USSR dispute from being merely ideological to include political and strategic dimensions.

CHINA AND THE POLICY OF LEANING TOWARDS THE UNITED STATES (1970–1981)

China's fear of Soviet Union efforts to contain China continued throughout the 1970s. As a result, the CCP leadership took action to adjust its foreign policy in a way that could prevent the Soviets from succeeding in isolating and containing China. The Chinese first continued their anti-Soviet propaganda. They repeatedly described the Soviet Union as 'hegemonic' by which they meant that Moscow would try to expand its military, economic, and political influence on the world stage at the expense of the sovereignty of other countries. An article published in *Peking Review* in 1970 presented China's view concerning the international nature of the Soviet system. The article stated that:

> The Soviet revisionists ... have turned a number of East European countries and the Mongolian People's Republic into their colonies and dependencies ... attempted to occupy more Chinese territory ... stretched their arms out to Southeast Asia, the Middle East, Africa and even Latin America and sent their fleets to the Mediterranean, the Indian Ocean, the Pacific and the Atlantic in their attempt to set up a vast Soviet revisionist empire spanning Europe, Asia, Africa and Latin America.
>
> (*Peking Review*, No. 17, 24 April 1970: 5–15)

Thus, the CCP leadership was persuaded to tilt towards a strategic alignment with the United States. The Nixon administration's decision to reduce its involvement in Asia made the Chinese perceive the United States as no longer a threat to China (Harding 1972: 37). The US initiative to ease travel and trade restrictions with China in July and December 1969, the termination of the regular two-destroyer patrol in the Taiwan Strait in November 1969, and the US announcement that all nuclear weapons on Okinawa would be removed by 1970 showed the Chinese that the Americans were willing to start a new era of relationship with them.[13] Despite a short break in the improvement of the PRC–USA relationship, because of the US and South Vietnamese invasion of Cambodia in May 1970, Mao Zedong at the Second Plenum of the Ninth Central Committee meeting in

---

13 'China–US policy since 1945', *Congressional Quarterly* (Washington, DC: Congressional Quarterly Inc., 1980), pp. 6–8.

64 *China's foreign policy in a global context*

August–September 1970 gave his support for rapprochement with the United States (Garver 1982: 135)

The Chinese government's initiatives to get closer to the United States were presented in April 1971 when an American table tennis team and a high-level American envoy were invited to visit China (Garver 1982: 39). After many direct and indirect talks, Beijing welcomed, secretly, in July 1971, Henry Kissinger, Nixon's national security advisor, to China.[14] In February 1972, US President Richard Nixon visited Beijing, after which the two sides issued the Shanghai Communiqué on 27 February. The Taiwan issue remained the main obstacle. However, the Chinese leaders saw that the Soviet Union had become a threat to the point that working with the United States through a strategic alignment against the Soviets was, at least for the time being, more important than the dispute over Taiwan. In the communiqué, both sides agreed that there was to be further progress towards 'normalization' and to maintain contact with each other. The Chinese continued opposing any form of separation of Taiwan from China, and requested the withdrawal of American troops from the island and the reunification with the 'motherland'. The Americans, who shared with the Chinese the need for one China, made their military withdrawal conditional on China's continued commitment to a peaceful resolution to the Taiwan question. Most importantly, the two sides agreed that 'neither should seek hegemony in the Asia–Pacific region and each is opposed to the efforts by any other country or group of countries to establish such hegemony' (for the text of the communiqué, see Harding 1972: 373–7) This initiative was directed mainly against Soviet attempts to control the region. Henry Kissinger in a talk with Chairman Mao Zedong and Chinese Vice-Premier Deng Xiaoping, during his visit to Beijing in October 1975, summed up US interest in China by saying that 'In terms of strategy we are trying to contain Soviet expansionism, and this is why in strategy China has priority for us' (Burr 1999: 392–3). However, US commitment to the security of the Nationalist regime in the Republic of China, and the PRC's insistence on severing the US relationship with the island continued to prevent the establishment of full diplomatic relations between Beijing and Washington. The need for continuing contacts between the two countries led them to agree, in 1973, to establish a liaison office. PRC–USA relations continued to improve after the signing of the Shanghai Communiqué. The volume of their trade rose from US\$5 million in 1971 to US\$95.9 million in 1972, then US\$805.1 million in 1973, and US\$933.8 million in 1974 (Hinton 1976: 54). By 1973, the United States had become China's second largest trading partner.

---

14 The visit took place due to the efforts of the Romanian President Nicolae Ceauşescu and Pakistani President Mohamed Yahya Khan.

Despite the slowdown in the China–US relationship during Gerald Ford's presidency,[15] the Chinese government was very much concerned about declining US power in Asia with the closing down of its bases in Thailand and its inability to support its allies in Cambodia and South Vietnam. They were worried about the possible shift in global balance of power to the Soviet advantage (Garver 1993a: 85–6). At the same time, the Chinese were worried about President Jimmy Carter's policy of avoiding close ties with the Chinese, for fear of angering the Soviets.[16] The rising Soviet threat with its support for Cuban intervention in Angola in 1975 and in Ethiopia in 1976 and 1978, Soviet unwillingness to accept deep cuts in its strategic arms, Soviet support for the Vietnamese initiative in Cambodia, and their growing modern weaponry along China's northern border had led the new Chinese leadership of Deng Xiaoping to adopt a more pragmatic policy towards the United States and to view the Americans as an important strategic partner in an international alignment against Soviet expansionism. Meanwhile, Carter shared the Chinese fear of Soviet expansionism and started to tilt towards Zbigniew Brzezinski's, Carter's National Security Advisor, view of containing the Soviets through establishing close ties with the Chinese. As the perceived Soviet threat was rising, both the United States and China agreed to establish diplomatic relations in December 1978. Washington met Beijing's three conditions for normalization:

1. withdrawal of all US military forces from Taiwan;
2. elimination of diplomatic relations with Taiwan; and
3. termination of the US–Taiwan mutual security treaty of 1954 (Garver 1993a: 91).

At the same time, the Chinese accepted Washington's conditions that the United States would:

1. continue to provide Taiwan with defensive military equipment;
2. maintain extensive unofficial relations with Taiwan;
3. terminate its defence treaty with Taipei after one year's notice;
4. keep in force all other treaties and agreements with Taiwan; and

---

15 Gerald Ford, who replaced Nixon, was not willing to make any important concession on the USA–PRC relationship.
16 Carter's policy was encouraged by Carter's Secretary of State Cyrus Vance who argued against establishing close ties with China because it would harm US relations with the USSR. On the other hand, Carter's National Security Advisor Zbigniew Brzezinski argued for establishment of ties with China in order for the United States to contain the Soviet threat. President Carter, who succeeded President Ford in January 1977, preferred Vance's argument during his early years in office. For the Vance–Brzezinski's debate, see Harry Harding (1972: 67–77).

5 make a unilateral statement calling for a peaceful settlement of the Taiwan issue and that the Chinese would not contest such a statement (Harding 1972: 77).

The Chinese government accepted the American conditions because of the importance of preventing a further shift of the global balance of power in Moscow's favour. The two sides issued, on the evening of 15 December 1978 in the United States and on the following morning in China, the agreement on the normalization. In a joint communiqué, the United States 'acknowledged' that Taiwan is part of China (Harding 1972: 81). Yet, after the signing of the normalization agreement, the Chinese government was disappointed over President Carter's reaction to the following developments:

1 The Chinese invasion of Vietnam on 17 February 1979 and Carter's call, on the following day, for immediate withdrawal of the Chinese troops. The Chinese government felt betrayed by Carter's reaction, as he had showed no opposition to China's plan to invade Vietnam during Deng Xiaoping's visit to the United States in early 1979 (Copper 1992: 46–7).
2 Modification to the content of the Taiwan Relation Act (TRA) by the US Congress, in which the United States would be responsible for maintaining the security of Taiwan against any foreign threat (for the text of the TRA, see Footnote 13: 343–5), and President Carter's approval of the act (Copper 1992: 67–9).

Nonetheless, the Soviet invasion of Afghanistan in December 1979 renewed the significance of the PRC–US strategic relationship. Cooperation between China and the United States rose substantially after the event and many Chinese and American officials visited Washington and Beijing. The PRC allowed the Americans to establish electronic listening stations in China to monitor Soviet nuclear missile tests.[17] Both sides, also, collaborated in extending their support to the anti-Soviet Afghan resistance group, the mujahideen, and Pakistan (Garver 1993a: 92). The Americans granted the Chinese the most-favoured-nation status on 24 January 1980. On the same day, the US Department of Defence announced that the United States would sell selected military equipment to China (see Footnote 13: 264). Meanwhile, China terminated its ties with revolutionary communist parties in the Third World and supported the US military presence abroad to contain Soviet expansionism (Harding 1992: 93–4).

In addition to China's continuing efforts to improve its relations with the United States as a direct counterweight to Soviet expansionism in Asia and

---

17 *The New York Times*, 3 January 1980; and 20 January 1980, p. A1.

elsewhere, the Chinese continued their anti-Soviet propaganda. The CCP leadership began to play down the direct Soviet military threat to China and emphasized instead that the direct Soviet military threat was in the direction of Europe, the Middle East, the United States, and Japan.[18] Such propaganda reached its peak when the Soviets invaded Afghanistan.[19] The Soviet Union was described by the Chinese as an 'aggressive and expansionist power'. In addition, the Chinese government persuaded active diplomacy throughout Asia to restrict Soviet influence and promote a united front. Deng Xiaoping visited Japan in October 1978 marking the first visit of a top-ranking Chinese leader to Japan.[20] This was followed by Prime Minister and CCP Chairman Hua Guofeng's visit to Japan in May 1979 and July 1980.[21] In August 1978, a Chinese–Japanese treaty of peace and friendship was signed to oppose Soviet hegemony.[22] In the same month, Hua Guofeng visited Romania, Yugoslavia, and Iran, respectively.[23] He also paid visits to France, Italy, West Germany, and Britain in October and November 1979 as the first top-ranking PRC leader to visit Western Europe.[24] Deng Xiaoping paid an official state visit to Burma in January 1978[25] and Nepal in February 1978.[26] In all these trips, Chinese officials worked to strengthen anti-Soviet unity. China, also, had improved its relations with India and diplomatic relations had been restored at the ambassadorial level in 1976 (Garver 1991: 55–85). China gave strong verbal support to the Association of South-East Asian Nations (ASEAN). It supported President Anwar al-Sadat of Egypt in his efforts for rapprochement with the United States after the October War of 1973, and in his visit to Jerusalem in November 1977. The Chinese government was satisfied with the Egyptian government after the abolishment of its friendship treaty with the Soviet Union. After the signing of the Soviet–Vietnamese Treaty in November 1978, and following the Vietnamese invasion of Cambodia in

---

18 See, for instance, *Peking Review*, No. 3, 17 January 1975, pp. 6–8; *Peking Review*, No. 5, 31 January 1975, pp. 16–18; and *Peking Review*, No. 16, 16 April 1975, p. 17.
19 See *Beijing Review* (formerly known as *Peking Review*), No. 1, 7 January 1980, p. 3 and pp. 10–11; *Beijing Review*, No. 2, 14 January 1980, pp. 9–12; *Beijing Review*, No. 3, 21 January 1980, pp. 10–12; and *Beijing Review*, No. 4, 28 January 1980, pp. 9–10 and pp. 15–26.
20 'Quarterly chronicle and documentation', *The China Quarterly*, No. 77, March 1979, pp. 190–3.
21 *Beijing Review*, No. 29, 21 July 1980, pp. 7–8; see also 'Quarterly chronicle and documentation', *The China Quarterly*, No. 84, December 1980, p. 817–18.
22 *Peking Review*, No. 33, 18 August 1978, pp. 6–10.
23 *Peking Review*, No. 34, 25 August 1978, pp. 6–15; *Peking Review*, No. 35, 1 September 1978, pp. 4–15; and *Peking Review*, No. 36, 8 September 1978, pp. 5–9.
24 *Beijing Review*, No. 43, 26 October 1979, pp. 8–14; *Beijing Review*, No. 44, 2 November 1979, pp. 8–14; and *Beijing Review*, No. 45, 9 November 1979, pp. 8–14.
25 *Peking Review*, Vol. 21, No. 5, 3 February 1978, p. 3.
26 *Peking Review*, Vol. 21, No. 6, 10 February 1978, pp. 4–5.

December (for the Soviet–Vietnamese strategic relationship, see Zagoria 1989: 167–213), China terminated its aid programme to Vietnam and started to provide non-communist countries of Asia and Africa with the same amount of aid as given to communist countries (Copper 1979: 1–3).

In short, China's foreign policy toward both superpowers during this period was a reflection of China's fear of Soviet expansionism throughout the world. The Chinese government felt the need to adjust its foreign policy strategy in accordance with its new understanding of the threat to China's security and interests. The most important adjustment was the adoption of a new pragmatic policy towards the United States. The United States, which was seen as the primary enemy of communist China in the 1950s, had become China's most important strategic partner to counter Soviet expansionism. As a result, different foreign policy strategies had been adopted by the Chinese government to suit China's new foreign policy objectives during this period.

CHINA'S INDEPENDENT FOREIGN POLICY (1982–1990)

In the early 1980s, several major developments influenced the Chinese government to recraft its foreign policy towards the two superpowers and adopt its independent foreign policy. In terms of China's relations with the Soviet Union, the logic of China's modernization programme required a peaceful international environment. The Chinese government saw limited détente, or rapprochement, with the Soviet Union as a significant step that would allow China to concentrate its limited resources on its Four Modernizations programme. Meanwhile, the Chinese government perceived the policies of limited détente with the Soviet Union as an effective way of managing Chinese–Soviet conflicts and securing stability in their relations with the Soviets (Chi Su 1984: 245–7). In addition, the deterioration of the Soviet–American relationship and the rapid increase in the military build-up by the two superpowers, as well as the deterioration in China's relations with the United States in the early 1980s, encouraged the Chinese government to strike a more independent posture in its foreign policy towards the United States and the Soviet Union. The PRC's 'independent foreign policy' was launched at the Twelfth CCP Congress in September 1982 to allow China to attain a greater degree of manoeuvrability within the Chinese–American–Soviet triangle relationship and to avoid China being drawn into conflicts between the two superpowers (Chi Su 1984: 246). At this time, the Chinese government began to emphasize that it would not allow any superpower to use it as a 'card' against the other power (Legrold 1993: 65–88). In terms of China's relations with the United States, there was a slowdown in the relationship in the early 1980s. Ronald Reagan's pro-Taiwan stand annoyed the Chinese government. Although it approved Reagan's aggressive anti-Soviet stance, the Chinese government criticized the flow of US arms to Taiwan. It called upon Reagan's administration to reduce the supply of arms gradually and to set a date for termination of all arms sales to Taiwan (Garson 1994: 172). The Reagan administration understood the importance of China as a valuable counterweight to the Soviet Union. As a result, the two sides issued a joint communiqué on 17 August 1982 to 'reduce gradually' the US sale of arms to Taiwan and that arms sales to Taiwan would not 'exceed, either in qualitative or in quantitative terms, the level of those supplied in recent years since the establishment of diplomatic relations between the two countries' (for the text, see Harding 1972: 383–5). However, while the Chinese government reaffirmed support for peaceful reunification, the US government refused to accept Beijing's demand for a fixed date for the termination of its arms sales to Taiwan. The Chinese government saw no need to ally itself with the Americans against the Soviets, since the Americans were engaging in a huge military build-up. Therefore, it adopted a foreign policy of independence from the two superpowers that would allow it to benefit from both powers without engaging itself with one against the other.

On the other side, the Soviet fear of a possible strategic partnership between the United States and China led the Soviet government to woo the Chinese, especially at a time when Beijing was unhappy with the Reagan administration's earlier stand on the Taiwan issue. In March 1982 and prior to China's adoption of the independent foreign policy, Secretary General Leonid Brezhnev delivered a speech in Tashkent in which he appealed to the Chinese by affirming that the Soviets 'have not denied ... the existence of a socialist system in China', and that they 'have fully recognized ... the PRC's sovereignty over Taiwan island' (Day 1985: 175–6).

Following the adoption of China's independent foreign policy, China's relations with both superpowers improved significantly. Several talks and social and educational contacts took place between the Chinese and the Soviets (Medveded 1986: 156–68: Mills 1986: 535–57). However, their effectiveness in resolving outstanding issues was very limited as China continued to insist on the removal of the three obstacles to better relationship:

1 the withdrawal of Soviet troops from Afghanistan;
2 the reduction of Soviet troops along the Chinese–Russian border; and
3 the withdrawal of Vietnam from Cambodia.

After low bilateral trade in the 1970s,[27] PRC–USSR trade volume rose from approximately US$50 million in 1980 to US$363 million in 1982 and US$750 million in 1983 then US$1,327 million in 1984 (Chi Su 1993: 51). Yet, the most important development in PRC–USSR rapprochement began with the rise of Mikhail Gorbachev and the proclamation of new thinking in

---

27 The volume of trade between the two countries declined steadily from US$2.1 billion in 1959, to US$47.2 million in 1970. See S. H. Chou (1984: 261–4).

Soviet foreign policy. Gorbachev's speech in Valdivostok on 28 July 1986 was important to the Chinese as it addressed two of the three main obstacles to the PRC–USSR normalization process that the previous Soviet regimes were not willing to discuss and make concessions. Gorbachev announced that the Soviet Union would soon withdraw troops from Afghanistan, and that the Soviets were prepared to discuss reduction of its force level along the border (Ellison 1993: 93–119). Although PRC–USSR relations then began to take a positive turn towards peaceful collaboration on solving the three obstacles, Beijing remained cautious and sceptical and demanded the removal of the three obstacles.[28] In February 1988, Soviet Defence Minister Dimitrii Yazor announced that the Soviet Union would withdraw a large number of its troops from Chinese–Soviet border areas (Chi Su 1993: 55). Concerning Afghanistan, Gorbachev announced in March 1988 that Soviet troops would be withdrawn from Afghanistan starting on 15 May 1988 and issued a ten-month period for the complete withdrawal.[29] Then, in a speech at the UN General Assembly on 7 December 1988, Gorbachev announced that the Soviet Union would unilaterally reduce the Soviet force by 500,000 men, approximately 200,000 troops from Asia, with a substantial reduction of conventional weapons in two years.[30] In December 1988, Vietnam announced that it would withdraw 18,000 of its 120,000 troops from Cambodia; and, in April the following year, Hanoi declared its intention to withdraw all its troops from Cambodia by September (Chi Su 1993: 56). Therefore, the pull-out of Soviet troops from Afghanistan, the reduction of Soviet troops along its frontier with China, and Gorbachev's efforts to speed up Vietnam's withdrawal from Cambodia set the stage for the May 1989 summit meeting between Deng and Gorbachev.[31] Despite the summit not reaching a border agreement, full diplomatic relations had been restored and troops along the frontiers had been reduced.[32] The meeting was significant to both sides. It helped Gorbachev enhance his image as a man of peace and pragmatism, especially in East Asia, a region of growing political and economic interest to Moscow.[33] For Beijing, the Soviet withdrawal from Afghanistan, the continued reduction of Soviet troops along the border, and the continued progress in Soviet efforts to encourage

28 The Chinese were worried that any Soviet troop reduction along their frontier would be more than offset by modern Soviet weapons and the increased number of Soviet SS-20 missiles backing the troops that remained: *Business Week*, No. 2960, 18 August 1986, p. 55.
29 *The Current Digest of the Soviet Press*, Vol. XL, No. 6, 9 March 1988, pp. 1–4.
30 *The Current Digest of the Soviet Press*, Vol. XL, No. 49, 4 January 1989, pp. 1–7.
31 See *The Economist*, Vol. 311, No. 7602, 13 May 1989, pp. 13–14.
32 During the meeting, Gorbachev announced that the Soviet Union would withdraw 120,000 soldiers from their border with China by the end of 1990. See Andrew Bilski and Louise Doder (1989: 35).
33 *U.S. News & World Report*, Vol. 106, No. 19, 15 May 1989, pp. 30–2.

Hanoi to pull out of Cambodia meant that China succeeded in keeping the Soviets from establishing hegemony across Asia.[34] Since the May summit, PRC–USSR relations had improved, and Chinese Premier Li Peng paid an official visit to Moscow between 23 and 26 April of 1990. His visit was the first by a prominent Chinese leader to the Soviet Union in twenty-six years since Zhou Enlai's visit in 1964. During the visit the two sides signed six agreements.[35] Economic relations between the two accelerated with trade volume reaching US$3.8 billion in 1989, a 20 per cent increase over the previous year.[36]

Despite the slowdown in PRC–USA relations in the first half of the 1980s, the relations witnessed the most productive era of cooperation in the second half of the decade. Economic relations, military cooperation, and educational exchange increased rapidly between the two countries. Economically, the United States had become a very important partner for China's economic development. By 1989, bilateral trade between China and the United States accounted for 16 per cent of China's total trade compared with 11 per cent by 1985 and 8 per cent in 1979. Their trade volume rose from US$2.3 billion in 1979 to US$7.7 billion in 1985 and to US$17.8 billion in 1989, with China enjoying significant trade surpluses since 1986.[37] US investment in China rose from US$18 million in 1983 to US$751 million in 1985 and reached US$1.6 billion by the end of 1988 (see Footnote 27: 368). Numerous high-level visits by officials of both sides had helped the development of military cooperation between China and the United States. By June 1989, the PRC acquired military equipment from the United States, including twenty-four S-70c Black Hawk helicopters, LM 2500 gas turbine engines for ships, coastal defence radar, and communication equipment. The PRC–USA military cooperation had increased in the areas of anti-tank, artillery, air defence, and surface ship anti-submarine warfare (Ross 1990: 94). The value of US arms sales to the PRC rose from US$8 million in 1984, when China was first made eligible for the US foreign military sales programme, to US$106 million in 1989 (Foot 1995: 236). The United States became a critical partner for China's military modernization,

---

34 *Business Week*, No. 3057, 20 June 1988, p. 67.
35 These include: (1) an agreement on long-term cooperation and a development programme of economy, science, and technology; (2) an agreement on cooperation toward peaceful use of studies of space; (3) an agreement on mutual reduction of military forces in border areas and guiding principles of enhancing trust in the military field; (4) an agreement on consultation between the two foreign ministers; (5) agreement on governmental credit for daily-use commodities provided by China to the Soviet Union; and (6) an agreement on construction of a nuclear power plant in China and a Soviet loan to China. See *Beijing Review*, Vol. 33, No. 19, 7–13 May 1990, pp. 7–9.
36 *Beijing Review*, Vol. 33, No. 36, 3–9 September 1990, pp. 12–16.
37 In the first half of the 1980s, the United States enjoyed a favourable trade balance of approximately US$8 billion in its trade with the PRC. See Harry Harding (1992: 364).

particularly after the Chinese government's decision to change the orientation of its strategic doctrine from the inevitability of a global war to the possibility of local and regional conflicts. Educational exchange visits multiplied with some 75,000 Chinese students and scholars receiving visas to enter the United States between 1979 and 1989 (Harding 1994: 379). Thus, economic relations, military cooperation, and educational exchanges had replaced in the second half of the 1980s the traditional PRC–US strategic alignment of the 1970s and early 1980s.

In addition to the existing issue of Taiwan, several new issues had dominated the development of China–US relations during the second half of the 1980s. Most importantly, China's assistance to some Third World countries in developing nuclear programmes and its sales of Silkworms to Iran and CSS-2 intermediate-range ballistic missiles, capable of reaching Israel, to Saudi Arabia, bothered the United States. The United States suspended the liberalization of controls on the export of advanced technology to China, but relaxed it in August 1988 after receiving assurance that China had stopped the delivery of Silkworms to Iran (Harding 1992: 187). The Americans were also bothered by China's military cooperation with Israel, particularly in the transferral of Western military technology by Israel to China. This was mainly because of the transfer of such technology to Pakistan and Iran by China (Timperlake and Triplett 1998: 1–4). Another issue concerned trade and investment barriers to American firms. US traders and investors were faced with high tariffs, restriction and control, standard and certification requirements, import licensing requirements, and import quotas imposed by the Chinese government. The increasing trade imbalance with China had also dominated the focus of China–US relations during the second half of the 1980s. According to the US Department of Commerce, US imports from China increased from US$3.5 billion by 1985 to nearly US$15 billion by 1991. From 1987 to 1991, US imports from China had grown at an annual rate of 35 per cent and about five times as fast as overall US import growth, while US exports to China had expanded by about 11 per cent annually during the same period (Orr 1991–2: 47–54). China's trade surplus with the United States rose from US$1.7 billion in 1986 to US$3.5 billion in 1988 and left the United States with a trade deficit of US$126 billion by 1988 (Harding 1992: 190). Despite US discontent about its trade deficit with China, no major decision was adopted to restrict the flow of Chinese exports to the United States.[38] Protection of US intellectual

---

38 The US government adopted, in July 1984, new regulations redefining the country of origin of imported clothing. Chinese products that were sent to Hong Kong for modification would be sent to the United States as under China's quota not Hong Kong's as it was before. The US Congress in 1985 considered a bill to reduce the current import quotas for textiles, but President Reagan vetoed it.

property had also been another issue that dominated the relations between the two countries. US efforts to get China to comply with the USA–PRC Bilateral Trade Agreement of 1979, which initiated the protection of copyright, patents, and trademarks, did not achieve a fully satisfactory result from the Chinese (Lardy 1994: 79).

Unlike PRC–USA relations, PRC–USSR relations were not harmed by suppression of the student demonstrations by the Chinese government in Tiananmen Square on 4 June 1989. Gorbachev did not want to sever Moscow's relationship with Beijing or to offend the CCP. So, the Soviet government issued a declaration on 7 June, in which it described what had happened as 'internal affairs' of China (Lukin 1991: 121). By early August, however, it became clear to Gorbachev that the Soviet position contrasted with that of Western official and public opinion, which he was seeking to woo. Gorbachev continued to avoid direct official criticism of the policies of the Chinese government, stressing instead the need for dialogue. He stated his government's position by saying:

> We are in favour of the most acute problems being solved through political dialogue between the authorities and the people. That is our belief. Such is the method we have chosen for ourselves. But a people solves its problem on its own. This is our principal and, I believe, irreversible position.
>
> (Lukin 1991: 124)

Premier Li Peng visited Moscow; then a military delegation, led by the Central Military Commission Vice-Chairman Liu Huaging, paid an official visit for two weeks in May 1990 to discuss the Chinese purchase of Soviet military technology (Faust and others 1995: 111). In the following month, a Soviet army delegation headed by Rear Admiral Valdimir Khuzhokov, head of the foreign relations department of the Soviet defence ministry, visited Beijing for the first time in thirty years (Dittmer 1994: 101). At the same time, economic relations and educational exchanges continued. China–Soviet trade volume had increased from US$3.8 billion in 1989 to US$5.3 billion in 1990 and to more than US$6 billion in 1991. Between 1988 and 1990, China sent more than 1,300 Chinese postgraduate students to study in the Soviet Union, while the Soviet Union sent more than 800 students to China (Dittmer 1994: 101–2). On the other hand, the Chinese military crackdown of the demonstrations in Tiananmen Square severed the US relationship with the Chinese government. The Bush administration imposed, on 5 and 20 June 1989, a series of sanctions against China. These included:

1   the suspension of all government-to-government sales and commercial exports of weapons including export, manufacturing, and technological assistance licenses;

74 *China's foreign policy in a global context*

2   the suspension of high-level US and Chinese exchanges;
3   the freezing of new loans to China by multilateral development banks;
4   the extension of stays for Chinese students in the United States (Williams 1989: 27–30).

The Chinese government was divided on how to respond to the American actions against it. The hardliners called for retaliation and strengthening of China's ties with the Soviet Union and Third World countries opposed to the United States. In contrast, the pragmatists encouraged the Chinese leadership to maintain its foreign policy, re-establish stability within China, and stress China's dissatisfaction to the US reaction without severing links with the Americans (Harding 1992: 235–9). The Chinese leadership adopted the pragmatist view. It announced that 'what is happening in China is China's internal affair', and that the 'Chinese government is completely capable of quelling the current rebellion in Beijing'. It further said that the Chinese government will continue implementing its policy of reform, opening up towards the world and its independent policy.[39] Several Chinese official statements, including a statement by Deng Xiaoping, emphasized China's willingness to restore relations with the United States.[40]

CHINA'S RELATIONS WITH THE UNITED STATES AND RUSSIA IN THE POST-COLD WAR ERA (1991–1999)

The Chinese government and its communist party watched the collapse of one socialist regime after another in Eastern Europe with alarm. Publicly, the Chinese leadership avoided criticizing Soviet policy. Privately, however, the Chinese leadership blamed Gorbachev's 'misguided reform' as the reason for the collapse of socialism in Eastern Europe (Garver 1993b: 1–5). They had issued, since the fall of 1989, a number of documents for internal circulation criticizing Gorbachev and Russian President Boris Yeltsin, in addition the post-communist leaderships in Eastern Europe (Guocang Huan 1992b: 254). In another reaction, the CCP leadership had tried to woo the hardliners in the Communist Party of the Soviet Union. Several meetings had taken place between high-level Chinese officials and Soviet hardliners. This included a visit by Anatoliy Lukyanov, a leading opponent of Gorbachev's policies, to Beijing in September 1989; a visit by Ivan Polozkov, Yeltsin's hardline opponent, to Beijing in June 1991;[41] a

---

39 *Beijing Review*, Vol. 32, No. 24–5, 12–25 June 1989, pp. 235–8.
40 For examples, see Chapter 2, p. 37.
41 Polozkov's visit was announced shortly after Yeltsin's election victory as President of Russia and was timed to coincide with Yeltsin's visit to Washington. See John Garver (1993b: 5–6).

China's relations with the United States, the Soviet Union and Russia 75

meeting between Jiang Zemin and Soviet Vice-President Yanayev, later a key figure in the August coup;[42] a visit by Deputy General Secretary of the Communist Party of the Soviet Union Vladimir Ivashko, a hardliner, to Beijing in February–March 1991;[43] and a visit by PLA Chief of Staff Chi Haotian to Moscow a week before the August coup, where it was reported that, in his meeting with Soviet Defence Minister Dimitri Yazov, the Chinese military leader had emphasized his country's adherence to the principle of non-interference in Soviet internal affairs in the event of any internal attempt to change the leadership (Garver 1993b: 12–13). When the coup began, on 19 August, to overthrow Gorbachev and restore socialism in the Soviet Union, Chinese news coverage was generally sympathetic and supportive of the attempt (Garver 1993b: 12–14). But, when the coup collapsed, the Chinese leaders gradually switched their support toward Gorbachev. To them, Gorbachev was the best available alternative to counter Yeltsin's liberalization reform. As the Soviet Union disintegrated after the coup attempt, the Chinese responded quickly to the new development. A day after Gorbachev resigned as President of the Soviet Union, China announced, on 27 December 1991, its recognition of the Russian Federation, Ukraine, Byelorussia, Kazakhstan, Uzbekistan, Tajikistan, Kyrgyzstan, Turkmenistan, Georgia, Armenia, Azerbaijan, and Moldova.[44]

For the Chinese leadership, the disintegration of the Soviet Union into several newly-independent republics had both positive and negative consequences. The development had the following positive repercussions for China:

1 Neither Beijing nor Moscow viewed the other as a security threat.
2 Russia had become China's most valuable source of military technology including the transfer of Su-27 jet fighter technology to China and the recruit of several hundred Soviet scientists to work on China's military development programme (Guocang Huan 1992b: 254).
3 The Russian Republic had reduced the size of its armed forces and destroyed some of its nuclear weapons, and Kazakhstan had committed itself to reducing the number of its nuclear weapons.

---

42 Jiang Zemin met with Yanayev during his April visit to Moscow, while Yeltsin's request for a meeting with Jiang Zemin was denied. See Lowell Dittmer (1994: 103).
43 During the meeting, China offered the Soviets credit worth about US$700 million to be made up of Chinese foodstuffs to go along with the earlier credit of US$334 million for purchases of Chinese light industrial goods. See *Beijing Review*, Vol. 34, No. 10, 11–17 March 1991, p. 8.
44 See *Beijing Review*, Vol. 35, No. 1, 6–12 January 1992, p. 6. China recognized all the newly independent states and established diplomatic relations with them to prevent any diplomatic ties between the newly independent states and Taiwan.

76 *China's foreign policy in a global context*

4 Russia had cut off its economic and military aid to India and Vietnam, and had encouraged them to improve their relations with the PRC.
5 Russia was no longer competing with Beijing for greater influence in the Korean Peninsula (Meyer 1992: 757–72).
6 China's modernization programme had proved a more successful reform programme than Gorbachev's political and economic reforms, particularly for those in China concerned with the unity of the PRC as a unitary political and cultural entity.
7 Economically, Central Asia's new states presented potential markets for Chinese exports.[45] The region also emerged as a cheap source for raw materials, and an important bridge for Chinese exports to the Middle East and Europe.
8 China's development model had become something to which many leaders of the new republics, like Karimov of Uzbekistan, aspire. For China, this meant that its expertise became valuable to the implementation of development programmes in the new republics (Munro 1994: 234).

The disintegration of the Soviet Union had negative repercussions that led the Chinese leadership to worry over the following points:

1 An increase of political instability in the new independent republics could lead to foreign intervention from Muslim countries, which would impact on China's large Muslim population in its western provinces (Segal 1992: 848–54).
2 There was a possibility for a regional arms race with Russia, selling advanced weapons for hard currency.
3 A possible Russian–American collaboration against China's international interests (Garver 1993b: 19–20). To the Chinese a united Soviet Union is more likely to remain independent of the Western alliance system than disintegrated Soviet states in much need of US economic and financial assistance (Garver 1993c: 60–80).
4 The Chinese leadership was also worried that the United States and the West would turn their attention to China as the next target after the Soviet Union. Deng Xiaoping described the effect of the breakdown of communism on China by saying that 'everyone should be clear under present international circumstance all enemy strength will be directed

---

45 For instance, it was reported that half of Kazakhstan's consumer imports in 1992 came from China, in 1994 some 25 per cent of Kyrgyzstan's official trade was with China, and China's trade with Tajikistan rose from US$2.7 million in 1992 to US$4.4 million in 1993. See Ross H. Munro (1994): 230–3; and Martha Brill Olcott (1996): 82 and 109.

against China and will use every sort of pretext to create new difficulties and pressures for us'.[46]

Despite the continuing strain in PRC relations with the United States following the Tiananmen event, the US government worked to limit the damage to its relationship with China. President George Bush said: 'I do not want to see a total break in this relationship [USA–PRC] and I will not encourage a total break in the relationship'.[47] He, therefore, did not withdraw the US ambassador from Beijing and secretly sent his National Security Advisor Brent Scowcroft and Deputy Secretary of State Lawrence Eagleburger to Beijing to meet with Chinese leaders including Deng Xiaoping (Harding 1992: 228). In July, he permitted the sale of four Boeing 757 commercial aircraft to China (Harding 1992: 228). Despite many US legislators proposing that the administration should consider China's human rights record before it issued the required certification for renewing the most-favoured-nation status (MFN), President Bush extended the MFN unconditionally to China in 1990. Bush also renewed China's MFN in 1991 with only a promise to use diplomatic tools to address US concerns in China (this policy is known as 'Bush's constructive engagement policy'). Bush's policy was driven by his administration's belief that, after the collapse of the communist regimes of Eastern Europe and the Soviet Union, the wind of liberalization would move towards China. Therefore, the US government should engage China increasingly in the world's economy and should seek to ensure China's economic modernization did not collapse (Sutter 1996: 74–5). It was through engagement that Bush's administration believed that political changes would take place in China.[48] Bush expressed his policy by saying:

> The most compelling reason to renew MFN and remain engaged in China is not economic, it's not strategic, but moral. It is right to export the ideals of freedom and democracy to China ... it is wrong to isolate China if we hope to influence China.
>
> (*New York Times*, 28 May 1991: A1)

Following Bush, President Bill Clinton adopted the policy of engagement. Like Bush, Clinton renewed China's MFN status every year since becoming President of the United States. Most importantly, President Clinton on 26

---

46 *Zhengming*, No. 151, 1 May 1990, p. 7.
47 *Congressional Quarterly*, Vol. 47, 10 June 1989, p. 1426.
48 Other schools of thought dealing with the issue of US policy toward China criticize Bush's policy of constructive engagement and argued for either an 'unconditional engagement' or a 'conditional engagement' in US relations with China. For more details on the different arguments, see James Shinn (ed.) (1996); Richard Bernstein and Ross H. Munro (1998).

78 *China's foreign policy in a global context*

May 1994 announced that no longer would the future renewals of the MFN be linked to human rights conditions in China.[49] The Chinese government, which earlier criticized Clinton's negative views of China during his campaign for presidency and his promises to push the issue of China's human rights by using the MFN card against China, welcomed Clinton's decision to delink the two issues. President Clinton's engagement policy sought:

1   constructive Chinese participation in the UN Security Council and in the resolution of regional conflicts to enhance global security;
2   active participation by China in multilateral non-proliferation regimes;
3   economic and trade relations with China that meet US economic interests;
4   respect for internationally-recognized standards of human rights; and
5   chinese cooperation on global environmental issues.[50]

Since the Tiananmen Square massacre of June 1989, the following issues have dominated the development of PRC–USA relations:

1   Issues of human rights including political prisoners, freedom for Tibet, treatment of Chinese dissidents, China's birth control law, and treatment of Chinese intellectuals have dominated the relationship since June 1989. The US governments of Bush and Clinton (until May 1994 in Clinton Administration) had attempted every time to use the MFN status as a political instrument against China's human rights record. Furthermore, when Clinton detached the MFN status from the human rights record, he stressed the importance of bringing up the issues of human rights in every official meeting with the Chinese.
2   Trade issues have moved to the centre of USA–PRC relations. The driving force is the growing US deficit in its trade with China. From 1984 to 1994, US annual exports to China rose from US$3 billion to US$8.8 billion. Meanwhile, China's exports to the United States increased from US$3.1 billion to almost US$38 billion. This left the United States with a US$29.2 billion trade deficit with the PRC (Brahm 1996: 100). According to the US estimate, the trade deficit in 1996 was about US$39.5 billion, exceeded only by the US bilateral trade deficit with Japan (see Footnote 40: 2). The deficit stimulated demands

---

49   Many have argued that the economic significance of China to the United States led the US government to delink the renewal of MFN status to human rights issue. See David S. Cloud (1994: 1372).
50   'US–China Relations', on www.state.gov/www/regions/eap/fs-us-china-relations.html, p. 1.

in the United States that China improve its intellectual property protections[51] and liberalize access to its domestic market;

3 PRC's transfer of advanced missiles to Third World countries has also dominated the development of US relations with the PRC. The CIA reported that the PRC had delivered, in 1991 and 1993, Chinese M-11 missile components and technology to Pakistan (Waller 1997: 58). The United States responded by imposing military and trade sanctions on China. In 1994, however, the sanctions were lifted after receiving assurances from the Chinese government to curb missile sales to other countries. The Bush and Clinton administrations were also concerned over reported Chinese sales of missiles, missile components, and missile fuel to Iran, Syria, Saudi Arabia, Algeria, and Iraq (Sutter 1996: 108–10). The CIA reported that by 1996 China had delivered to Pakistan more than thirty ready-to-launch M-11s (Waller 1997: 58).

4 The Taiwan issue has always been a point of contention in the PRC–USA relationship. The Chinese leaders were annoyed in 1992 by the US decision to sell 150 F-16 fighters, twelve advanced anti-submarine helicopters, and other technology to Taiwan. The PRC viewed the sales as a violation of the 1982 PRC–USA communiqué on Taiwan in which the United States stated that it 'does not seek to carry out a long-term policy of arms sales to Taiwan', and that its arms sales to the island 'will not exceed ... the level of those supplied in recent years ... and that it intends to reduce gradually its sales of arms to Taiwan, leading over a period of time to a final resolution' (for types of arms sales to Taiwan, see Hickey 1994: 77–9; Lasater 1995: 195–7). The Chinese government protested at the US arms sales, and linked its policy on missile sales to Pakistan and other countries with the US decision to sell Taiwan the F-16s (Garver 1997: 36). The US decision on 22 May 1995 to allow President Lee Teng-hui of Taiwan to visit the United States unofficially sparked tensions in the PRC–USA relationship. Due to President Lee's policies to drive Taiwan away from the idea of unification with the mainland as a subordinative special administration region under a central government in Beijing and his democratization process led the Chinese government to view his visit as an attempt to establish international recognition for independence (Sutter 1996: 13–66). As a result, China responded by suspending arms control talks, cancelled the forthcoming visit of the Chinese Defence Minister, Chi Haotian, to the United States, recalled its ambassador in Washington for consultation, and delayed the United States for several months in its efforts to replace its ambassador to China (van Kemenade

---

51 US losses from China's violation of intellectual property rights were estimated to be more than US$800 million in 1993. See Nicholas R. Lardy (1996): 72–3.

1997: 47). In addition to that, China conducted, in July 1995, missile and live-fire tests in several areas around Taiwan (Sutter 1996: 74). This led to the March 1996 military face-off between the United States and China in the Taiwan Strait. The United States deployed two aircraft-carrier battle groups to the vicinity of Taiwan to protect the island from the massive Chinese military exercise, which was designed to intimidate the first presidential election in Taiwan (Sutter 1996: 96–110; Garver 1997).

In the post-Cold War era, China tried to benefit from its relations with both the United States and Russia. It continued to advance its economic and technological cooperation with the United States. This was obvious in its efforts to cooperate with the UN and the West in restoring Kuwait's independence by voting for all UN Security Council resolutions on Kuwait and abstaining from Resolution 678, which called for the use of force to liberate Kuwait. The Chinese government calculated that the economic and technological benefits of its abstention would be much more significant than if it vetoed the resolution. In its relation with Russia, China worked to limit the possible direct and indirect threat to its security from the newly-independent republics. In addition to the previously-mentioned Chinese efforts to build a good relationship with Russia, relations between China and the newly-independent republics developed rapidly after the Chinese government recognition of the new central Asian states. Kazakhstan's Prime Minister Tereshchenko paid a five-day official visit to Beijing in February 1992. Eight agreements were signed including agreements on the movement of citizens along the border, on China providing commodity loans, and on establishing economic, trade, and scientific cooperation.[52] In March 1992, President Islam Karimov of Uzbekistan visited Beijing and both sides signed fourteen bilateral agreements (Munro 1994: 234). Kyrgyzstan's President Askar Akayev paid an official five-day visit to China in May during which economic and cultural agreements were signed, and a free trade zone was established along the border (Munro 1994: 232). In November, Turkmenistan's President Supramurad Niyazov visited Beijing and signed eight cooperation agreements and a joint communiqué. In April 1994, Chinese Prime Minister Li Peng paid an official visit to four central Asian states – Uzbekistan, Turkmenistan, Kyrgyzstan, and Kazakhstan – and Mongolia. To reduce the perceived threat from China in the region, Li Peng laid down China's basic principles toward the region and emphasized that 'China will never seek hegemony or power politics even when it becomes more advanced and prosperous in the future. Instead China will always maintain equal and

---

52 *Beijing Review*, Vol. 35, No. 10, 9–15 March 1992, p. 9.

friendly relations with its neighbours'.[53] By 1996, China had reached agreements on setting boundaries and related issues with the four major central Asian states bordering it – Russia, Tajikistan, Kyrgyzstan, and Kazakhstan. This includes the 26 April 1996 agreement on confidence building in the military field in the border area. In this agreement, they agreed to mutual non-use of force or threat of force against one another, establish regulations for conducting military exercises along the borders, and mutual force reduction in the border areas (Mulvenon 1997: 114–20).

In the second half of the 1990s, China–US relations seemed to have gathered momentum. US Vice-President Al Gore visited Beijing in March 1997, followed by the Speaker of the House Newt Gingrich who visited Beijing a month later. President Jiang Zemin paid an official state visit to the United States from 26 October to 3 November 1997. It was the first visit by the President of China to the United States in 12 years. In June 1998, Clinton visited Beijing as the first American president to visit China in a decade. Premier Zhu Rongi visited Washington in April 1999 to smooth the way for China's entry to the World Trade Organization (WTO) (Gilley and Crispin 1999: 12–14). However, all these visits did not produce a dramatic change in China–US relations. Instead, relations witnessed a setback throughout the second half of the 1990s. The following issues have contributed to the souring of relations between the two countries in the second half of the 1990s.

The human rights issue

US officials have continued in their meetings with Chinese officials to discuss China's human right records and the continued arrests and trials of Chinese pro-democracy movements leaders and advocators as well as political activists in China,[54] in addition to the arrest of followers of religious groups like the Falun Gong. US officials, including President Clinton, continued to meet with the Dalai Lama, which has always angered the Chinese government. In response to American pressure, China issued its own report on the dire human rights situation in the United States, which was portrayed as an 'abyss of racial discrimination' with a manipulated press, low voter turnouts for elections and rampant crime (Spaeth 1999: 1). China also voiced strong resentment at the US government decision to allow

---

53 *Beijing Review*, Vol. 37, No. 18, 2–8 May 1994, pp. 18–19.
54 For example, the US government criticized the Chinese government arrests on 7 July and 21–22 July 1998 of pro-democracy activists, and the arrest of Xu Wenli, Qin Yongmin and other political activists on 11 and 30 November 1998. The US State Department issued in December 1998, its annual human rights report sharply criticizing China. See *Time*, 24 May 1999, pp. 40–1.

the Dalai Lama to visit the United States in November 1998. A Foreign Ministry spokesman said:

> China demands that the United States adhere to its stance of recognising Tibet as a part of China and of not supporting the 'independence of Tibet', and that it immediately puts a halt to its erroneous acts of interference in China's internal affairs concerning the Tibet issue.
> (*Beijing Review*, Vol. 42, No. 35, 30 August 1999: 7)

The security issue

China criticized the US Senate's decision in July 1998 to authorize the sale of American arms to Taiwan worth US$550 million.[55] China also criticized the passing of a bill in March 1999 by both US houses for the establishment of the National Missile Defence (NMD) to go along with the Theatre Missile Defence (TMD) system, which is scheduled to be voted on in June 2000.[56] The TMD is designed to neutralize a strike on US forces or their allies by destroying incoming enemy missiles (Wolf 1999: 26). Suspecting that expansion of this may be the ultimate target, China blasted the programme. A Chinese Foreign Ministry Spokesman said that the TMD:

> Does not conform with the trend of the time, is not conducive to work toward arms control and reduction and will produce an extensive and negative effect on global and regional strategic balance and stability in the 21st century. China is gravely concerned about this.
> (*Beijing Review*, Vol. 42, No. 25, 21 June 1999: 9)

China is also concerned about the US plan to draw Japan under the TMD umbrella. Japan's cooperation in the system, according to the Chinese perspective:

> Will greatly enhance the overall offensive and defensive level of the US–Japan military alliance, thus promoting Japan to violate the guarantee inscribed in its no-war constitution restricting it to a limited military capability for defence only, and expand once again into a military power.
> (*Beijing Review*, Vol. 42, No. 25, 21 June 1999: 9)

---

55 *Beijing Review*, Vol. 42, No. 33, 16 August 1999, p. 5.
56 See *Beijing Review*, Vol. 42, No. 25, 21 June 1999, p. 9.

China was even more alarmed at the inclusion of Taiwan into the future shield. A Foreign Ministry spokesman said:

> Any country providing Taiwan, a province of China, with any weaponry system including the TMD will seriously encroach upon China's sovereignty and territorial integrity and will firmly be opposed by the Chinese people. The Chinese side demands that the US side observes the three Sino-US joint communiqués and relevant promises and will not proliferate the TMD and its related technology to Taiwan in any form.
> (*Beijing Review*, Vol. 42, No. 25, 21 June 1999: 9)

On 20 August 1999, The Chinese Foreign Ministry also strongly condemned Taiwanese President Lee's remarks stressing the importance of the TMD for Taiwan and saying that the system 'not only meets the needs of the current situation, but is also in line with the long-term interests of the country'. The Chinese reaction to this remark was presented by a Chinese Foreign Ministry spokesman saying:

> The Taiwan authorities must understand that splitting the country and seeking independence for Taiwan is a dead end and, even with the TMD, such attempts are doomed to failure.
> (*Beijing Review*, Vol. 42, No. 36, 6 September 1999: 7)

China expressed its strong opposition to NATO's military operations in Yugoslavia in March 1999. The Chinese Foreign Ministry emphasized that 'the issue of Kosovo is an internal affair of Yugoslavia and should be settled by the relevant Yugoslav parties'; and that 'all countries should respect Yugoslavia's sovereignty and territorial integrity'. The spokesman said, 'The Chinese government strongly demands that NATO should immediately stop its military strikes against Yugoslavia, calling on the international community and Yugoslavia's relevant parties to make joint efforts to calm the tense situation, resolve crisis and restore peace in the Balkan region as early as possible'.[57]

China's opposition stems from fear for its own security. Regardless of the friendly relations between Beijing and Belgrade, China itself is in fact faced with the local question of separatist tendencies and struggles in Tibet, Xinjiang, and Taiwan. Therefore, NATO's US-led interference in Kosovo, which was never authorized by the UN Security Council, worried China about the integrity of its own national independence given China's potential internal regional instability. The Chinese government believed that, under

---

57 *Beijing Review*, Vol. 42, No. 15, 12–18 April 1999, p. 12.

such conditions, the independence of individual states would be adversely redefined and, within NATO, the United States would be able to impose destructive wars on countries that obstruct its interests. Their concern is so serious that the idea of forming a preventive force composed of China, Russia, India, and Iran against NATO is gaining Chinese support.[58] The Chinese press interpreted the NATO US-led operations in Yugoslavia as an attempt to establish NATO (US) control of Europe and the World. An article by Li Bian in *Beijing Review* entitled 'NATO changes international laws' argued that the end of the Cold War meant the collapse of America's leading role in the European Atlantic strategy and the loss of control over the security situation in Europe and the rest of the world. Therefore, US-led military action against Yugoslavia, according to the article, was intended both to 'maintain its hegemony in the world' and to 'see if its "new strategic concept" will work in the coming century'. The article continued:

> By examining NATO's military intervention in international affairs, the tolerance of the United Nations or countries like Russia and the degree of unity among members of NATO, the United States is trying to expand its defence sphere and strengthen NATO's military function in order to serve US interests around the world.
> (*Beijing Review*, Vol. 42, No. 17, 26 April–2 May 1999: 7)

Another article in *Fortnightly Review* called NATO's action an imperialist act aimed at US domination of the world. It said:

> NATO's raids on Yugoslavia, in the name of 'humanitarianism', are an out-and-out imperialist action. It is obvious that the attention of the United States and other Western powers is actually to do with the strategic significance of the Balkan Peninsula, which is considered as important as oil in the Middle East and the Panama Canal. Yugoslavia blocks the eastward expansion of NATO. It was only a question of time before NATO would want to eliminate this blockage. Thus, the Kosovo issue has been an excuse for NATO.
> (Ban Yue Tan 1999: 27)

China–US relations reached their lowest point since 1972 after US bombers launched an attack, and destroyed the Chinese embassy in Belgrade, Yugoslavia in May 1999. Three Chinese correspondents were killed during the attack. Immediately after, the Chinese government issued a statement to the US government protesting the action:

---

58 BBC, *SWB FE/3500*, 5 April 1999, p. A/4.

The action is a gross violation of Chinese sovereignty and tramples on the Vienna convention on diplomatic relations and the basic norms of international relations. This is a rare event in diplomatic history. The Chinese government and people express their utmost indignation and severe condemnation of this barbaric act and lodge the strongest protest against it. US-led NATO should bear full responsibility for anything arising there from.

(*Beijing Review*, Vol. 42, No. 21, 24 May 1999: 9)

In addition to large public demonstrations with the approval of local public security organised in cities like Beijing, Shanghai, Guangzhou, and Chengdu, where the US embassy and US consulates are located, President Jiang Zemin refused to take President Clinton's phone call to apologize about the 'mistaken' action by the United States.[59] The Chinese government postponed high-level military contact between the Chinese armed forces and the United States, as well as consultation with the United States in the fields of proliferation prevention, arms control, and international security. China also suspended its dialogue with the United States in the sphere of human rights.[60]

Allegations

China–US relations have also been affected by allegations that China's has attempted to influence American politicians through campaign finance, and that China has spied and stolen US military technology. In May 1999, a select committee of the US House of Representatives published the Cox Report on US National Security and Military Commercial Concerns with the PRC. The report is a little over 700 pages long and it argues that China is building the political, economic, and military leverage to push the United States out of Asia and the Pacific Basin, and put American cities at risk. The report found that China has stolen design information on the Americans' most advanced thermonuclear weapons since the early 1970s, including information on every currently-deployed thermonuclear warhead in the American ballistic missile arsenal, classified design information for an enhanced radiation weapon, and classified information on US W-88, W-87, W-78, W-76, W-70, W-62, and W-56 warheads. The report also found that China stole US missile and space technology that could improve Chinese military and intelligence capabilities. According to the report, China has acquired US technology by using espionage techniques, controlled commercial entities, and a network of individuals and organizations

---

59 *Time*, Vol. 153, No. 20, 24 May 1999, pp. 40–1.
60 *Beijing Review*, Vol. 42, No. 21, 24 May 1999, p. 11.

that engage in scientific, business, and academic activities. Therefore, the report concluded that communist China might pose an even greater threat to the United States than the Soviet Union did (deGraffenreid 1999). The Chinese government rejected the Cox Report's findings and called it a scheme by anti-China politicians in the United States. Zhao Qizheng, Minister in Charge of the Information Office of the State Council, said:

> The Chinese government and People are strongly indignant over this groundless attack that fabricates facts and confuses black and white. This is a great slander against the Chinese nation and is typical racial prejudice ... China has never 'stolen' secrets from the US nuclear weapon laboratory ... This is another adverse current against China among the series of anti-China events created by some people in the US over recent years. Their purpose is to divert public attention, fan anti-China feelings, defame China's image and try to hold back Sino-US relations so as to stop China's development. This attempt is doomed to fail.
>
> (*Beijing Review*, Vol. 42, No. 24, 14 June 1999: 9–11)

The three issues discussed above presented obstacles to the promotion of better relations between China and the United States in most of the second half of the 1990s. However, by the end of the century and particularly in November 1999, China–US relations began to gather some positive momentum. Despite their disagreement over the above issues, on 15 November 1999 the two sides reached an agreement that 'will help accelerate the process of China's accession to the WTO and the development of China–US economic cooperation and trade relations'.[61] According to the agreement, China has agreed to open its markets in industries ranging from banking and insurance to telecommunication and Internet sectors. The agreement cuts duties on a wide range of products, gives foreign companies the right to distribute their goods within China and allows foreign automobile manufacturers to provide car financing. The agreement also allows for increased imports of foreign films on a revenue-sharing basis (Lawrence and Holland 1999: 80–4).

While China's relations with the United States were riddled with difficulties in the second half of the 1990s, China's relations with Russia were characterized by common understanding and mutual agreements over many international issues. Russian Defence Minister Igor Nikolayevich Rodionov's visit to Beijing in April 1997 resulted in a 'long-term strategic partnership', according to the visiting official. His visit was to promote military and technological cooperation between the two countries and, more

---

61 See *Beijing Review*, Vol. 42, No. 47, 22 November 1999, pp. 4–5.

importantly, to discuss NATO's 'eastward expansion' policy. Rodionov said that Moscow 'appreciates the fact that China shares Russia's concerns over the eastward expansion of NATO'.[62] President Jiang Zemin visited Moscow in April 1997 for a two-day state visit, which articulated the development of a 'strategic partnership of equality and mutual trust' orientated towards the twenty-first century. On 23 April, the two sides issued a joint statement on international issues that called for:

1. the promotion of 'multipolarization' of the world as well as a new international order;
2. the respect of every country to choose the way in which it developed, with no country seeking hegemony;
3. the drive towards establishing a new and universally-applicable concept of security in which the Cold War mentality should be abandoned and 'bloc politics' should be opposed;
4. the strengthening of the role of the UN to promote peace in the world; and
5. the entitlement of the developing countries, as well as the non-aligned movement, to take their rightful place in a new international world order on an equal basis with other countries.[63]

On 24 April during President Jiang Zemin's visit to Moscow, the two countries along with Kazakhstan, Kyrgyzstan, and Tajikistan signed an agreement for the mutual reduction of military forces in border areas. Jiang described the agreement as having 'major political and military significance' and said that it:

> Offers a security model different from the Cold War mentality in safeguarding peace, security and stability in the Asia Pacific region and the world at large, thereby opening up a useful way for the enhancement of mutual trust among states.
> (BBC, *SWB FE/2902*, 25 April 1997: G/1)

The two countries also signed a contract in May on the drafting of a detailed design for a nuclear power station to be constructed in Jiangsu province. Russia also started the construction of the second stage of a gas centrifuge uranium-enrichment plant.[64] A joint project for gas supply from Siberia to Shanghai was also signed.[65] On 29 September 1997, China and Russia

---

62 BBC, *SWB FE/2895*, 17 April 1997, p. G/4).
63 BBC, *SWB FE/2901*, 24 April 1997, pp. G/1–2.
64 BBC, *SWB FE/2902*, 25 April 1997, p. G/7.
65 BBC, *SWB FE/2903*, 26 April 1997, p. G/3.

agreed to regulate border trade jointly. The measure was said to resolve the problems of unfair competition and trade monopoly.[66] Russian President Boris Yeltsin visited Beijing for a two-day state visit in November 1997. Yeltsin's meeting with Jiang Zemin took place within just ten days of Jiang's meeting with Clinton in Washington. The two presidents signed a joint declaration stating that all questions related to the demarcation of the eastern section of the Chinese–Russian border had been settled. The meeting called for international relations to be conducted on the basis of multipolarity, mutual respect, and equity of right for all. It also called for greater bilateral cooperation in the spheres of energy, outer space, transportation and communication, banking and insurance, and for enhancing military ties.[67] Chi Haotian, China's Defence Minister, visited Moscow in January 1998.[68] Premier Li Peng visited Moscow in February 1998.[69] In July 1998, Russian Foreign Minister Yevgeniy Primakov visited Beijing.[70]

All of these highly-ranked visits by officials from both countries have helped the development of relations between the two countries and brought both sides closer on many international issues. Two main factors could be discussed here to explain why the two countries have devoted greater effort to foster political contacts between officials from the two countries in this period:

1 Both countries were worried about NATO's 'eastward expansion' policy. Their meetings, therefore, could be designed to reach understanding on this issue or even to foster an alliance to counter NATO's policy (Black 2000: 130–3). This was evident in China's and Russia's identical reactions to the NATO operation in Yugoslavia.
2 China has always wanted to secure its border areas with Russia and the newly independent Central Asian Republics. So, these meetings could be directed toward settling China's unsettled border disputes with Russia and ensuring the security of its border areas.

These two issues seemed to have been ranked as a top priority in China's relations with Russia. This is evident in the recurrence of these two issues in the meetings between Chinese and Russian officials. It is also evident in China's continued efforts to eliminate deterioration in China–Russia relations. President Jiang ensured Yeltsin that China's commitment to developing ties with Russia was not 'makeshift' and would not be harmed

66 BBC, *SWB FE/3038*, 1 October 1997, p. G/3.
67 BBC, *SWB FE/3073*, 11 November 1997, pp. G/2–3.
68 BBC, *SWB FE/31333*, 24 January 1998, p. G/3.
69 BBC, *SWB FE/3156*, 20 February 1998, p. G/1.
70 BBC, *SWB FE/3287*, 24 July 1998, p. G/1.

China's relations with the United States, the Soviet Union and Russia 89

by 'any temporary incident'.[71] Even when a Russian patrol boat in the Bering Sea fired on a Chinese fishing vessel killing two Chinese in May 1998, the Chinese government and people did not react strongly and as violently as when US bombers attacked its embassy in Belgrade. The Chinese official reaction was limited to expressing regret over the incident.[72] While relations with the United States continued to deteriorate further, China–Russia relations have continued to improve. President Yeltsin visited Beijing in December 1999 and signed with the Chinese president a joint communiqué in which they:

- Called for international disputes to be settled peacefully through the UN, respecting the sovereignty and territorial integrity of all countries.
- Condemned attempts to amend the 1972 Anti-Ballistic Missile Treaty (ABM) and the proposed plan to build an anti-missile defence system in violation of the treaty.
- Warned that any attempt to extend the TMD to protect Taiwan would cause instability in Asia and was firmly opposed.
- Expressed regret that the United States had not ratified the Comprehensive Nuclear Test Ban Treaty.
- Expressed a commitment to nuclear non-proliferation, prevention of a space arms race, and banning of chemical weapons.
- Warned that any country undermining the current disarmament framework would have to bear full responsibility.
- Warned that 'negative momentum' in international relations was growing. They condemned the 'unipolar world' and 'single model of culture, value concepts, and ideology' being promoted by the West, which they said was undermining the UN and replacing international law with 'power politics'.
- Rejected the concept that 'human rights are superior to sovereignty': the justification used by NATO for military intervention in Kosovo and the reason for strong Western condemnation of Russia's offensive in Chechnya.
- Demanded China and Russia's entry to the WTO on terms that would ensure their 'equal status in the world trade system'.
- Promised to work together to combat 'international terrorism, religious extremism, and ethnic separatism' as well as international cross-border crime.
- Called for a foreign ministers' meeting of China, Russia, Kazakhstan, Kyrgyzstan, and Tajikistan in order to foster closer cooperation.[73]

---

71 BBC, *SWB FE/2902*, 25 April 1997, p. G/1.
72 BBC, *SWB FE/3240*, 30 May 1998, p. G/1.
73 *China Daily*, Hong Kong Edition, Vol. 3, No. 61, 11 December 1999, p. 1.

90 *China's foreign policy in a global context*

They agreed on the need for a multipolar world and refuted US efforts to solely 'dictate how the world should live, work and play'.[74] They exchanged support for each other's handling of territorial problems. Yeltsin reiterated the Russian government's consistent adherence to its principled stance on the Taiwan issue. Jiang, in turn, reaffirmed China's support for Russia's move in suppressing the Chechen separatist group and said that the Chechen war is Moscow's internal affair and rejected the West criticism of Moscow's action.[75] They also agreed to work together to develop further their strategic cooperative partnership.[76]

Thus, China–Russia relations found new interests in the 1990s. Rajan Menon (1997: 101–25) noted that the days of Chinese–Russian animosity are over. Their substantial political, economic, and military ties in the 1990s are not bound by an alliance as was the case in the early days. Today, Chinese–Russian relations are based on a calculation of self-interest and desire for leverage vis-à-vis third parties such as the United States, Japan, or India.

CONCLUSION

In this chapter, the argument has been that the Chinese government's view of the United States and the Soviet Union/Russia, and its perception of the threat to China's security and interests, had largely determined China's relations with both superpowers. Its relations with both powers have developed through different stages. At each stage, China's foreign policy strategies have been adjusted to suit the changes in its foreign policy objectives. During China's early interaction with the superpowers from 1949 to 1954, China's objective was to protect and sustain its new status as an independent and sovereign state under Chinese Communist Party control. So, all of China's foreign policy strategies were conducted towards achieving such an objective. The Chinese leadership found the policy of leaning towards the Soviet Union as their best option to achieve their objectives. The Chinese leadership viewed the United States as its primary enemy, who was trying to contradict China's progress to the next stage, as it did throughout the history of Western domination of China. By 1955, China's relations with both powers, particularly the Soviet Union, started to take a new turn. This time China's view of the Soviet Union began to change after the adoption in the Soviet government of Khrushchev's new policy of peaceful coexistence with the United States. China, therefore, adopted

---

74 *China Daily*, Hong Kong Edition, Vol. 3, No. 60, 10 December 1999, p. 1.
75 *China Daily*, Hong Kong Edition, Vol. 3, No. 61, 11 December 1999, p. 1.
76 *China Daily*, Hong Kong Edition, Vol. 3, No. 60, 10 December, p. 1.

several new foreign policy strategies in order to promote unity in the communist bloc to counter the capitalist bloc led by the United States. China's relations with the Soviet Union continued to spiral downwards and both parties severed their political, economic, ideological, and strategic relationship by the end of the 1960s. This disintegration of China's relationship with the Soviet Union escalated throughout the 1970s. China's ideological perception of 'the enemy' expanded to include the Soviet Union. After several developments, discussed earlier, the Soviet Union had become China's primary enemy, replacing the United States as the most dangerous threat not only to China's security but also to world security and stability. Therefore, China adopted foreign policy strategies aimed at containing Soviet efforts to contain China and dominate the world. The most significant strategy being their willingness to sympathize with US policy in Asia, in particular, and the rest of the world, in general. Disregarding past allegiances, China leaned toward Washington, to counter Moscow, in a strategic, political, economic partnership. This partnership continued between China and the United States throughout the 1980s. But, in the 1980s, China began to realize the importance of balancing its relationships with both the United States and the Soviet Union. China's independent foreign policy was aimed at achieving such a balance. The Chinese believed that a better relationship with the Soviet Union could help China express its dissatisfaction with the United States' continued military support of the nationalist regime in Taiwan. Further, it would allow China to concentrate its limited resources on its modernization programme by reducing tension between the two sides. This policy achieved its aims by the end of the 1980s. In the post-Cold War era, China's relations with the United States and Russia entered a new phase. Despite its unhappiness over the disintegration of the Soviet Union, the Chinese government had no choice but to work with the new governments in Central Asia. China's foreign policy objective at this time was to establish good political, economic relationships with the new states in Central Asia. This objective was driven by China's need to prevent establishing any political relationship between Taiwan and the newly-established states in Central Asia. It was also driven by its efforts to reduce tension along the border areas and to take every possible opportunity to benefit economically from the new republics. Russia was important to China because it was the only place China could obtain more advanced and sophisticated weapons. In terms of China's relations with the United States, the United States remained a very important source of capital and technology. So, the Chinese worked to improve their relationship with the Americans but at the same time remained unchanged on Taiwan.

Thus, China's relations with both the United States and the Soviet Union, later Russia, had been a changeable relationship. This change was a reflection of China's views and perceptions of its relations with both powers and of relations between the two powers themselves.

Part III
China's foreign policy toward the Gulf and Arabian Peninsula region

4 China's perceptions of the Gulf and Arabian Peninsula region

In the previous chapter, we discussed China's policy towards both the United States and the Soviet Union (and Russia). We argued that China's relations with the two powers were dominated by the change in China's own perceptions of its relations with both powers. In the Maoist era, China carried out every possible policy to undermine the influence of either or both superpowers. In the post-Maoist era, China's policies have transformed to reflect its own perception of change of power in the international system. Different foreign policy tactics and strategies have been carried out by the Chinese to suit the changes in the international system and to foster the achievement of China's own foreign policy objectives. Changes in China's relations with both Washington and Moscow have been coupled with internal change. China, who enjoyed a substantial level of economic growth in the 1990s, had found itself in need of independent international suppliers of energy and sources of investments and financial assistance. Thus, China's foreign policy towards the Gulf and Arabian Peninsula region could be explained in terms of the following two factors: first, China's perceptions of and relations with the United States and the Soviet Union; and, second, China's drive to increase its economic capabilities by ensuring the supply of oil to its own thirsty economy.

In order to explore this argument, China's involvement in the Gulf and Arabian Peninsula region will be divided into three main phases. In each of these phases, China's motives, objectives, and tactics have changed according to the changes in China's relations with both the United States and the Soviet Union and to its efforts to increase its economic and political capabilities. These phases are:

1   China's early involvement in the region (1949–1970);
2   China's pragmatic foreign policy towards the region (1971–1989);
3   China's economic interests in the Gulf region (1990–1999).

This Chapter therefore will examine all these three phases in the development of China's relations with the Gulf and Arabian Peninsula region.

PHASE 1: CHINA'S EARLY INVOLVEMENT IN THE REGION (1949–1970)

When the PRC was established in late 1949, its founders' main concern was to ensure the survival of the newly-established communist state as an independent political entity. This aim was the focus of the CCP leadership particularly after the United States' invasion of North Korea, under the flag of the UN, less than a year after the establishment of the PRC. Chinese troops entered the Korean Peninsula to prevent American troops from invading the fragile new communist regime in China and protect its friendly regime in North Korea. On the other hand, the United States was increasing its efforts to arm and protect the Nationalist regime in Taiwan and intensifying its campaign to isolate China politically and economically throughout East and South-East Asia. So, the CCP leadership found itself with no alternative but to ally itself with the Soviet Union against the United States. China's foreign policy in the Gulf and Arabian Peninsula region, during most of this period, reflected its 'lean to one side' policy, in favour of the Soviet Union. Against this background, China's interest in the Gulf region, mainly prior to the Bandung Conference of 1955, was very limited. East Asia instead captured most, if not all, of China's foreign policy attention. Almost all China's news coverage in the early 1950s revolved around developments in East and South-East Asia. Issues like the US and the West's involvement in the Korean Peninsula, US close ties with Japan, US efforts to strengthen its alliance in East and South-East Asia, and the Chinese–Soviet alliance were the main focuses of China's foreign policy. Despite China's 'Intermediate Zone' analytical classification of the Gulf and Arabian Peninsula region – that is, being in-between the capitalist camp, headed by the United States, and the socialist camp, headed by the Soviet Union – the Chinese always associated the region with the capitalist camp rather than the socialist camp. They described the governments of the region as 'puppets' in the hands of the West. China's association of the Gulf and Arabian Peninsula region with the West was due to the following two reasons:

1. The Gulf region was either under British colonial rule or ruled by reactionary monarchs closely allied to the West. Thus, the Chinese believed that the Western grip on them was strong enough to influence the direction of their foreign policy in favour of the West.
2. Some Gulf regimes such as Iran and Iraq condemned China as the aggressor in the Korean War and supported the US action in Korea.

Thus, the Chinese saw themselves unable to penetrate the region. Even when they had tried to exploit what they had believed to be some signs of anti-Western activities in the region, the Chinese shortly came to realize that they were wrong. Signs such as the nationalization of the oil industry in Iran, the Saudi and Yemeni abstention from voting on the UN General Assembly Resolution 498 6V on 1 February 1951 to condemn China as an aggressor in Korea, and the Saudi and Yemeni abstention from the US-sponsored resolution to postpone consideration of any proposal to exclude Taiwan from the UN on 25 October 1952 elevated China's hope that the region was beginning to take some anti-West stands. The Chinese welcomed all these developments. But the events that transpired fell short of their expectations. This disappointment was marked by Iran and Iraq, two of the major independent Gulf states, engaging themselves in a security alliance with the United States and Great Britain under the Baghdad Pact of 1954. Even more disappointing to the Chinese government was that the possibility of establishing political relations with the states of the Gulf and Arabian Peninsula region appeared impossible. The region maintained political and economic relations with Taiwan and did not support the exclusion of Taiwan from the UN in favour of China. The four independent states of Iran, Iraq, Saudi Arabia, and the Sultanate of Muscat and Oman refused to recognize China. In addition to the above, China's isolation from the Gulf and Arabian Peninsula region was also due to the following reasons:

1   China's own classification of the world into two camps and its insistence on favouring the Soviet Union, as the main insurance for independence of all Third World countries, distanced China from the British-controlled Gulf region. The failure to acknowledge any third way limited China's ability to exploit those states of the world that maintained close relations with the capitalist camp, including the countries of the Gulf.
2   The independent Gulf states' impression of China during that early stage was centred around their fear of the atheistic communist ideology. China's hope for assimilation of all ethnic minorities into one national identity led to the harsh treatment of the Muslim population in China in the early 1950s. This, subsequently, added to the unfavourable sentiment towards China in the region.
3   China's recognition of Israel and its efforts to establish diplomatic relations with Tel Aviv convinced the states of the Gulf and Arabian Peninsula region to maintain their relations with the Nationalist regime in Taiwan and reject the establishment of political relations with the communist regime in China.

In parallel with the lack of political relations, China's trade relations with the countries of the region in the early 1950s was also limited. Between 1950 and 1955, China's total trade volume with the countries of the region (namely Iran, Iraq, Kuwait, Oman, Saudi Arabia, and Yemen) amounted to only US$1.7 million. Chinese imports constituted over 75 per cent of that total. This volume of Chinese trade with the Gulf and Arabian Peninsula region accounted for less than 0.5 per cent of China's world trade volume. More importantly, it was less than 2 per cent of China's total trade with the Arab non-Gulf countries of the Middle East and Africa (Editorial Board 1984: 817–71). These numbers suggest that China's economic relations with the Gulf region were marginal.

In sum, China's isolation from the region in the first half of the 1950s had both political and economic consequences. Politically, China failed to gain any recognition from the governments of the region who favoured the Nationalist government in Taiwan over the Communist government in Beijing. Economically, China failed to establish an adequate trade relationship with the Gulf and Arabian Peninsula region.

China's interest in the Gulf region transformed in the mid-1950s, however. This shift was a reflection of changes in China's own interests. During this time, the Chinese began to lean towards wooing the countries of the Third World. Unlike the past, the Chinese believed that improving relations with the vast majority of the Third World countries, including the Gulf and Arabian Peninsula states, could mean a tremendous blow to the West. The Chinese government found a great opportunity to interact at a high level, and for the first time, with the countries of Asia and Africa at the Bandung Conference. The Gulf and Arabian Peninsula countries were part of such development. The region was represented by official delegations from Iran, Iraq, Saudi Arabia, and Yemen. The Chinese delegation to the conference sought to exploit this opportunity, to show the participants that China was part of them, shared the same experiences with them, and that they should not fear it, but work with it. In his speech at the conference, Premier Zhou Enlai, head of the Chinese delegation to the conference, stated:

> In the interest of defending world peace, we Asian and African countries, which are more or less under similar circumstances, should be the first to co-operate with one another in a friendly manner and put peaceful coexistence into practice. The discord and separation created among the Asian and African countries by colonial rule in the past should no longer be there. We Asian and African countries should respect one another, and eliminate any suspicion and fear which may exist between us.
>
> (*People's China*, 16 May 1955: 10)

Following Bandung, China accelerated its efforts to establish cultural, economic, and political ties with the Gulf countries. Culturally, China succeeded in persuading Saudi Arabia to accept Chinese pilgrims on the *hajj*. Between 1956 and 1959, China sent six different cultural delegations to Iraq, Saudi Arabia, and Yemen. Economically, the volume of China's trade with the Gulf and Arabian Peninsula region also rose dramatically to a total of US$34 million between 1956 and 1960.[1] Chinese exports to the region constituted over 80 per cent of that total (Editorial Board 1984: 817–71). Yet, the most important development in China–Gulf relations following Bandung was the establishment of diplomatic relations between China and the Yemen Arab Republic (YAR) in August 1956. The establishment of political relations with the YAR marked China's first diplomatic recognition by a Gulf and Arabian Peninsula country, and third by any Arab country after Egypt in May 1956 and Syria in July 1956. China's efforts to establish relations with the Gulf countries and the Arab countries in the Middle East and Africa were driven by China's worry about US efforts to 'drag' more Arab countries into the Baghdad Pact. The *People's Daily*, a Chinese official paper, published an article on 14 March 1956, which stated:

> The United States and Britain [are] doing all they can to split and create antagonism among the Middle and Near Eastern countries; they are in a mid summer madness, oppressing and threatening these countries, hoping to smother the movement for national independence. With this end in view the British and American colonialists are making a great effort to cajole or jockey more countries into the Baghdad Pact.
> (Republished in *People's China*, 1 April 1956: 44–5)

Importantly, the establishment of diplomatic relations between China and Egypt had helped the Chinese to foster their efforts in the Gulf and Arabian Peninsula region. It was through the Chinese embassy in Cairo that the YAR recognized the PRC. A few days before the Yemeni recognition of China, the Yemeni Premier Amir al-Badr met with the Chairman of the Chinese Islamic Association, Burhan Shahidin in Cairo (Schichor 1979: 44–5). This meeting is believed to have pushed the Yemeni decision to recognize the PRC. It was also through the Chinese embassy in Cairo that China first contacted the Omani revolutionary group (Behbehani 1981: 166–7). It is also important to note that China exploited Islam as a foreign policy tool to build political contacts with the region. China's toleration of Muslim activities following the Bandung meetings and its encouragement for Chinese Muslim leaders to make contact with the Muslim countries of the Middle East is a clear indication that China hoped to use Islam as a stepping stone to reach the Arab world (more detailed analysis of this issue will be discussed in the China–Saudi Arabia section, Chapter 6). In March 1958, the YAR became the first Gulf or Arab country to sign a treaty of friendship and to establish diplomatic relations with the PRC. China offered Yemen an interest-free loan of 70 million Swiss Francs and

---

1 Despite this increase in China–Gulf trade volume, the Gulf's share of total Chinese world trade volume remained less than half of 1 per cent.

increased its economic assistance to the country (Calabrese 1991: 13). China's involvement in Yemen was simplified by the role played by the Soviet there. China's assistance to Yemen was based on Sino-Soviet efforts to seize the opportunity from the Americans and the British and prevent them from succeeding in that country.

The Iraqi revolution of July 1958 presented China with another opportunity to further its relations with the countries of the Gulf. Abd-al-Karim Qasim's regime was at first a victory for the Chinese. The Chinese welcomed Qasim's detachment of Iraq from the Baghdad Pact. They were also satisfied with Qasim's tolerance of Iraqi communists, while, however, Jamal Abdul Nasser was suppressing Arab communists in Egypt and Syria. More important was the establishment of diplomatic relations between China and Iraq, just a few days after the proclamation of the new republic in Iraq. Iraq became the second Gulf state, after Yemen, to establish diplomatic relations with Beijing. All of these successes for China following Bandung suggest that:

1   China successfully broke the US economic embargo by establishing trade relations with Asian and African countries, including the countries of the region, following Bandung;
2   China also successfully broke its political isolation by getting involved with the countries of the Third World; and
3   China succeeded in rivalling Taiwan's presence in the Arab world by establishing diplomatic, economic, and cultural relations with Egypt, Syria, Yemen, Morocco, Iraq, and Sudan.

By the end of the 1950s, the Sino-Soviet alliance began to deteriorate. The Chinese started to regard the Gulf and Arabian Peninsula region as an arena of Chinese–Soviet rivalry as well as a stage to wage a campaign against Western imperialism (Calabrese 1990: 862–76). China's foreign policy, therefore, took upon itself the duty to challenge both Moscow and the West in the region. As a result of their political and ideological disputes, the Sino-Soviet convergence of interests began first in Yemen. China began to challenge Soviet aid to Yemen by providing massive assistance of its own to YAR. Then, China offered political and moral support to Imam Ghalib's movement against the Sultan and the British in Oman (Behbehani 1981: 164–75). It also extended political support to the Iraqi government's efforts, in the early 1960s, to take control of the direction of its oil exports from the British, the Americans, and the French.[2] China also worked towards holding a second Bandung meeting without the participation of the Soviet Union. Yet, its failure to convince the Arab countries to do this, its

2   See *Beijing Review*, Vol. 5, No. 8, 23 February 1962, p. 22.

disappointment over Nasser and Qasim's harsh treatments of Arab communists, and its unsuccessful attempt to pursue the 'people's war' throughout the Arab World following the June 1967 war, caused China to restrict its interest in the Middle East to those countries that appeared to have revolutionary potential. While its relations with Egypt and Syria were severed, China looked to the Gulf region as a potential revolutionary region. South Yemen and Oman captured most of China's interest in the region. Unlike the Soviet Union, who sought to maintain government-to-government ties, China moved towards supporting the anti-Western imperialism struggle in South Yemen and the guerrilla war in Dhofar.

South Yemen

Prior to the independence of the People's Republic of South Yemen (PRSY) on 30 November 1967 (later the People's Democratic Republic of Yemen – PDRY), China supported the proclamation of the YAR in September 1962 and the inclusion of Aden, which was under British control. This support was guided by China's hope that Yemen could present a great opportunity to wage the struggle against the West, particularly after launching of the National Liberation Front of Occupied South Yemen's (NLF) guerrilla resistance in October 1963, four months after its foundation. China criticized the British-sponsored 'Constitutional Conference' for Aden held in London. The Chinese described the conference as a 'new trick of the British colonialists to maintain their position' in South Yemen. The British were aiming, as pointed out in the *Renmin Ribao*, 7 September 1962, at:

> Strengthening their domination over the Arab East, and bringing the region, from the south part of the Arabian Peninsula to central and East Africa, under their control; and therefore, they would be able to suppress the national liberation movements there.
> (Republished in *Beijing Review*, Vol. 5, No. 37, 14 September 1962: 20)

At a banquet in the Great Hall of the People in honour of the visiting YAR President Abdullah al Sallal, Chairman Liu Shaoqi paid tribute to the people of Yemen for their struggle to 'oppose imperialism and to win and safeguard their national independence'. Liu declared that China 'support[s] the people of Aden, South Yemen and Oman in their struggles against colonialism in demanding the dismantling of all foreign military bases'.[3] After the last British forces left Aden on 30 November 1967, the NFL

---

3 *Beijing Review*, Vol. 6, No. 23, 5 June 1964, p. 5.

assumed power and declared the birth of the PRSY. China welcomed this development and contributed this victory to Mao's philosophy:

> Paying attention to the study of Chairman Mao's great military thinking on guerrilla warfare, they [Yemeni people in the south] smashed the British raids and blockade and using flexible tactics wiped out large numbers of the enemy.
> (*Beijing Review*, Vol. 10, No. 50, 8 December 1967: 36)

After its recognition of the PRSY, China offered financial, economic, and military aid to the new republic (Halliday 1990: 219). From 1968 onward, the PRSY, or the PDRY (1970), became a major focus for competition between China and the Soviet Union as both supplied military and economic aid. China's support for the PDRY can be explained by the following reasons:

1 China wanted to undermine the presence of the British in the South;
2 the independence of South Yemen could present China with an outstanding opportunity to impose its own presence and influence in the region, particularly after the breakdown of diplomatic relations between the PRSY and the United States;
3 South Yemen's foreign policy programme was favourable to China, particularly its support for the liberation movements in the Gulf and the Third World and its identification with the socialist camp; and
4 South Yemen's successful armed struggle could set a good example for the rest of the Gulf and could convince them that independence can be achieved in this way.

The Dhofari rebellion

Hashim Behbehani (1981: 164–75) traced China's relations with the liberation movement in Oman to China's first initiatives in the Arab World after the Bandung Conference. Its involvement with the movement began as early as Sino-Egyptian contacts in the 1950s. It was through the Imamate Office and the Chinese embassy in Cairo that the two sides contacted each other for the first time. Imam Ghalib Bin Ali's movement's aim to wage the struggle against the Sultan of Oman and the British, who were aiding the Sultan, captured China's attention (Behbehani 1981: 164–75). The Chinese committee for Afro-Asian solidarity, in a message to Imam Ghalib on Omani Day on 18 July 1962, expressed its deep respect for the Omani people and resolute support for their 'protracted and valiant resistance to British imperialist aggression'. The message described the Omani people's armed struggle for national independence against the 'British occupationists' as 'wholly just'.[4] This political support was also matched with military assistance. As early as 1957, the Chinese offered military aid to the Imamate movement through its envoy in Egypt (Behbahani 1981: 165). Even though the Chinese offer was rejected by the Imamate, the Chinese presented themselves successfully as a potential arms supplier to the movement. China–Imamate contacts through their offices in Cairo played a major role in planning for Salih bin Isa's, Deputy Imam of Oman, visit to Beijing from 29 January to 20 February 1959, in response to an invitation from the Chinese Islamic Association. During his stay in Beijing, Salih met Mao and Zhou. China's support for the Omani struggle was reaffirmed during these meetings and also in a China–UAR joint communiqué on December 1963, during Zhou's visit to Cairo.[5]

As a result of increasing Chinese support for the theory of 'people's war', particularly after Lin Biao's speech 'Long Live the Victory of People's War!' in September 1965, China worked to improve its relations with the Dhofar Liberation Front (DLF). The DLF launched its armed struggle in June 1965 against the rule of the Sultan of Oman, Said bin Taimur. In June 1967, the DLF's first delegation visited Beijing in response to an invitation by the Chinese People's Institute for Foreign Affairs. It was headed by Ahmad al-Ghsani, a member of the DLF Council. The Chinese promised to provide the DLF with light armaments, US$35,000, and Mao's writings and Marxist literature (Behbehani 1981: 176). Subsequently, following the Hirmin Conference of September 1968, the DLF's name was changed to the Popular Front for the Liberation of the Occupied Arabian Gulf (PFLOAG). This change was reflected by broadening of the movement's aim to extend the revolution from Dhofar to Kuwait. The change of aim and name was made after the British announcement in January 1968 of its intention to withdraw its armed forces from the Gulf region by the end of 1971. China supported the PFLOAG's armed struggle strategy to defeat 'imperialism and its lackeys' in the Gulf region (Behbehani 1981: 145). Several other delegations were sent by the PFLOAG to China. The Chinese provided the PFLOAG with finance, food, and medical and military assistance. The Chinese embassy in Aden played a major role in transferring Chinese aid to the rebels in Oman. But whether Chinese personnel ever served in Dhofar is still unclear. Since its establishment in 1969 in Aden, the New China News Agency (NCNA) reported frequently on the PFLOAG's military operations in Oman.[6]

4 *Beijing Review*, Vol. 5, No. 30, 27 July 1962, p. 20.
5 *Beijing Review*, Vol. 6, 52, 27 December 1963, pp. 9–11.
6 See, among many, BBC, *SWB*, Part 3, 12 June 1970, p. A4; BBC, *SWB*, Part 3, 17 June 1970, p. A4; BBC, *SWB*, Part 3, 17 July 1970, p. A4; BBC, *SWB*, Part 3, 22 July 1970, p. A4; BBC, *SWB*, Part 3, 30 July 1970, p. A4; and BBC, *SWB*, Part 3, 1 June 1971, p. A4.

China's objective in providing political, economic, and military support to the PFLOAG was mainly driven by the following:

1 China wanted to find a foothold for itself in the Gulf and Arabian Peninsula region, particularly as its relations with many countries of the Arab World such as Egypt and Iraq became strained;
2 China was hoping to advance revolutionary changes throughout the Gulf region;
3 the Chinese hoped to encourage the PFLOAG to adopt the Chinese model of revolution and accommodate Marxist ideology in order to set an example to revolutionary movements in the rest of the world;
4 China sought to undermine the Western presence and influence in the region;
5 China wanted to prevent the Soviet Union from taking the initiative towards the movement, and, therefore, ensuring China's isolation from the Gulf.
6 China wanted to ensure the independence of the newly established PDRY and prevent any possible British–Omani invasion of South Yemen via Dhofar. Thus, Dhofar was used as a buffer zone between Oman and South Yemen by both China and South Yemen.

PHASE 2: CHINA'S PRAGMATIC FOREIGN POLICY TOWARDS THE REGION (1971–1989)

By 1971, several developments had taken place and had forced the Chinese government to readjust its world outlook: the Soviet Union invaded Czechoslovakia, the Brezhnev Doctrine was announced, and the Sino-Soviet border arms clashes and hostilities escalated. All these developments forced the Chinese leadership to reconsider the Soviet Union as China's principal enemy and the world's most dangerous source of instability. China's foreign policy aim then shifted towards building an extensive front of resistance to Soviet penetration in the Third World. China's interest in the Gulf and Arabian Peninsula region was reflected by this pattern of foreign policy. The Chinese leadership was afraid that the Soviet Union might succeed in persuading some Gulf States to join the Soviet-proposed Asian collective security system, which would enhance Soviet advancement in the Indian Ocean and would benefit the Soviet strategy of encirclement of China. In addition, the Chinese government was worried that the Soviet Union was attempting to refill the 'power vacuum' in the Gulf region following the British withdrawal. Thus, the Chinese initiated both a shift towards accepting US policy in the Gulf and Arabian Peninsula region and a move to cultivate amicable relations with the independent states of the region. Fear of Soviet Union advancement in the Gulf and Arabian Peninsula region led the Chinese government to consolidate its relations with Kuwait and Iran, particularly after the signing in August 1971 and April 1972 of the Soviet–Indian and the Soviet–Iraqi treaties of friendship and cooperation, respectively. China's moves toward these two Gulf states were motivated by its desire to create a balance against Iraq and, therefore, the Soviet Union penetration in the region (Schichor 1979: 171–2). From the other side, the Soviet Union supported the idea that the affairs of the Gulf region should be managed by the states of the Gulf themselves and without any foreign interference, namely American or Chinese. However, the Soviets were worried about the close relationship between the United States and Iran, since the latter was given the green light to play a supervisory and protectionist role in the region by the Americans. The Soviets were particularly concerned about the Americans gaining influence in the Gulf region through the unprecedented armament of Iran.

China sought to prevent the Soviet Union from filling the power vacuum in the Gulf region. Chi Pengfei, China's Foreign Minister, supported Iran's foreign policy position on the issue of Gulf security. In a speech on 14 June 1973 in Tehran, Chi stated:

> At present, the situation in the Persian Gulf is arousing general concern. The intensified expansion, infiltration, and rivalry by certain Big Powers are gravely menacing the peace and security of this part of the world. Iran is an important country in the Persian Gulf and you have every reason to feel uneasy at this situation. We have consistently held that the affairs of a given country must be managed by the country itself, and the affairs of a given region must be managed by the countries and peoples of that region, and the world affairs must be jointly managed by all countries. Iran and some other Persian Gulf countries held that the affairs of this region should be jointly managed by the Persian Gulf countries and brook no outside interference. This is a just position and we express our firm support for it.
>
> (Cited partly in Peking Review, Vol. 16, No. 25, 22 June 1973: 3–5; Abidi 1982: 113)

China's position on the issue of Gulf security was intended to achieve the following two major foreign policy objectives in the region:

1 by supporting the principle of non-interference in the Gulf's affairs by outsiders, the Chinese aimed to keep the Soviet Union from establishing influence or presence in the region.[7]

---

7 The Chinese saw the Soviets increasing their efforts to stretch their 'claws of aggression into the Persian Gulf where they were trying their utmost to grab oil resources and strategic points'. See *Peking Review*, No. 37, 14 September 1973, pp. 17–18.

2 by stating and supporting the position that the affairs of the region should be jointly managed by the Gulf countries, China aimed to project a favourable image of itself for the future among certain Gulf States (namely Saudi Arabia and Oman).

Significantly, this period was the most productive period in China's relations with the countries of the region. During this period, China succeeded in establishing diplomatic relations with Kuwait in March 1971, Iran in August 1971, and Oman in May 1978. Kuwait, Iran, and Oman were motivated to establish diplomatic relations with China by their common fear of Soviet Union expansionist efforts in the Gulf region, mainly through Iraq, South Yemen, and Afghanistan (Shichor 1979: 173). China shared the Kuwait, Tehran, and Muscat fear of Moscow penetration in the region. This was evident in China's decision to terminate its support of the revolutionary movements in the region in favour of good ties with the governments of the region. To some extent, China's new policy was also motivated by Beijing's effort to counter the Taiwan presence in the region and to open new markets for its goods. China also continued its aid programmes to North and South Yemen. China's fear of the Soviet presence in both North and South Yemen intensified its interest in these two Arabian Peninsula countries. The Chinese believed that, if the Soviet Union established itself in the Horn of Africa, it would enhance its ability to move into southern Africa and the Arabian Peninsula. Thus, China welcomed the YAR's decision to expel Soviet military advisors and the YAR's efforts to modernize its armed forces through Saudi Arabia and the West (Creekman 1979: 73–81). The Chinese also launched a campaign of polemics warning of Soviet expansionism and Third World domination after the PDRY granted the Soviets the use of naval facilities (Creekman 1979: 78).

One of the most significant aspects of China's modified foreign policy towards the Gulf region during this phase was its termination of political and military support for national liberation movements in the region. The Chinese believed that the increasing Soviet influence in South Yemen and Iraq could only be matched through establishing good ties with the governments of the Gulf and Arabian Peninsula region. China's continued support for the PFLOAG presented an obstacle in China's efforts to achieve diplomatic relations with the countries in the region. Therefore, since 1971, the Chinese gradually began to cease their support for the PFLOAG. China even supported measures taken by countries in the region against the PFLOAG activities. For example, when Chi Pengfei visited Iran in June 1973, he supported Iran's decision to send troops to aid the Sultan of Oman against the PFLOAG and gave assurances that China had no ties with revolutionary groups in the Gulf region (Creekman 1979: 115–17). By ceasing its support for the PFLOAG, China hoped to cultivate a good relationship with Kuwait, which supported the Sultan of Oman against the

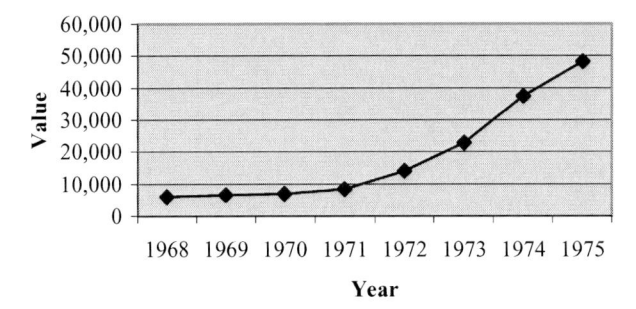

Figure 4.1. Value of China's trade with the Gulf and Arabian Peninsula region 1968–75 (in US$10,000). Source: Editorial Board (1984): 817–71.

insurgents. Thus, China's turn to the governments of the Gulf and Arabian Peninsula region was initiated by its fear of the massive Soviet naval build-up in and around the region. Hua Guofeng's Political Report to the Eleventh National Congress of the CCP in August 1977 stated:

> The Soviet Union has massed its troops in Eastern Europe and at the same time accelerated its plunder of strategic resources and its scramble for strategic basis in Africa and the Middle East in an attempt to encircle Europe from the flanks by seizing the Persian Gulf in the east, thrusting round the Cape of Good Hope in the south and blocking the main navigation routes of the Atlantic Ocean in the west.
> (*Peking Review*, No. 35, 26 August 1977: 40–1)

Besides its success in establishing political relations with North Yemen, South Yemen, Iraq, Kuwait, Iran, and Oman, China improved its economic relations with the countries of the Gulf and Arabian Peninsula region. As shown in Figure 4.1, China's trade volume with the Gulf countries increased dramatically after 1971. It jumped from US$59.37 million in 1968 to US$140.27 million in 1972, and to US$483 million in 1975. This increase in the trade volume with the Gulf and Arabian Peninsula countries was not limited to those Gulf states with which China had diplomatic relations. China's trade volume with Bahrain, Oman, Qatar, Saudi Arabia, and the UAE also increased substantially in the early 1970s, although these states had no diplomatic relations with China at that time. According to the *Almanac of China's Foreign Economic Relations and Trade* (Editorial Board 1984), China's trade volume with those five Gulf states jumped from US$14.41 million in 1969 to US$27.20 million in 1972, and to US$100.95 million in 1975.

China also began to approve of US policy in the Middle East, and particularly in the Gulf and Arabian Peninsula region. The Soviet Union dominated most of China–US discussions in the 1970s. In a memorandum to President Nixon in March 1973, Henry Kissinger, Assistant to the US President for National Security Affairs, summed up his meetings with Mao and Zhou in February 1973:

> In literally every region of the world the Chinese see the Soviet hand at play ... Mao and Zhou urged us to counter the Russians everywhere, to work closely with our allies in Europe and Japan, and to take more positive action to prevent the Soviets filling vacuums or spreading their influence in an area like the Middle East, Persian Gulf, Near East, south Asia and Indian Ocean.
>
> (Burr 1999: 112)

In a meeting with Kissinger, now Secretary of State, in November 1973, Mao Zedong emphasized that his country 'welcome[s] the US putting the Soviet Union on the spot' so 'that the Soviet Union cannot control the Middle East' (Burr 1999: 187–8).

By the mid-1970s, China completely ended its support to the rebels in the Gulf; and, in March 1976, the front collapsed, which ended the rebellion (Yodfat 1977: 10). In 1975, Kuwait dispatched its first ambassador to Beijing. China also improved its relations with Iraq. The renewal of Chinese interest in Iraq from 1975 onward was prompted by the decline of Iraqi dependence on the Soviet Union and the improvement of relations between Iraq and Iran. China extended its construction activity to Iraq, while Baghdad became an alternative supplier of sulphur to China (Calabrese 1990: 869). Despite the unmatchable Soviet aid to both Yemens, China continued its economic aid to both countries (Creekman 1979: 77).

The Soviet threat remained high during the era of Deng Xiaoping. His leadership was faced with an 'expansionist' Soviet power that, in its opinion, was increasing its influence in South Yemen and moving towards the Gulf and Arabian Peninsula region through Afghanistan. To the Chinese government, containing Soviet influence in the Gulf and Arabian Peninsula region could be achieved by adopting a foreign policy that favours the following:

1   a *de facto* entente with the United States;
2   maintain its political relations with the countries of the Gulf and Arabian Peninsula region; and
3   increase its economic ties with the countries of the region.

This policy was accompanied with Chinese support of the mujahideen resistance group in Afghanistan through Pakistan. It also maintained economic and political relations with PDRY, where the Soviet Union was enjoying a large influence. China watched carefully the developments in the

Gulf region with the coming of the Islamic regime in Iran and the outbreak of the Iran–Iraq war.

Revolution in Iran

The Islamic revolution in Iran caught the Chinese leadership by surprise. They did not know what to expect out of the new Republic. China, who had enjoyed a promising relationship with the Shah, was worried that the new Islamic regime's anti-US stand could favour the Soviet Union over the United States and, therefore, present the Soviets with another foothold in the region. Ayatollah Khomeini's regime of revolutionary militancy worried the Chinese that the stability of the Gulf states, which China had improved ties with, could be threatened. At the same time, the Chinese saw Moscow on the offensive and Washington on the defensive in the region. An article in *Beijing Review* criticized the Soviet strategy toward the new regime in Iran as follows:

> The Soviet Union, which shares 1,800 kilometres of border with Iran, has always dreamed of bringing Iran under its control and seizing the Persian Gulf as an outlet. The recent upheaval provided Moscow with an opportunity to meddle in Iran's internal affairs. Moscow took advantage of the tensions in Iran to vigorously support the pro-Soviet forces it had fostered, to fan up workers' strikes, and to instigate armed clashes, thus aggravating the situation. Meanwhile, at the bidding of the Kremlin, pro-Soviet Iranians who had been living in the Soviet Union and Eastern Europe clandestinely returned to Iran and infiltrated various factions and groups which stood opposed to the Shah. Immediately after the Iranian Provisional Government was formed, the Soviet press played up the role of the pro-Soviet forces and called for ensuring complete freedom for all organisations so that the pro-Soviet forces could maintain their legal status and seize political power at an opportune moment.

The article went on to remind the United States that:

> For a long time, Iran has been the military pillar of the US policy to contain the Soviet Union's southward expansion and ensure the safety of the West's oil routes. In addition, the United States imports 900,000 barrels of Iranian oil per day, which accounts for 10 per cent of its imported oil. If Washington wants to protect its vested interest in Iran, it has to resist Moscow's expansion.
>
> (*Beijing Review*, Vol. 22.1, No. 15, 13 April 1979: 19–20)

These concerns were elevated by the Khomeini regime's tense actions against the United States. The seizing of over sixty American hostages from the US embassy in Tehran, the banning of oil exports to the United States, and the banning of US aircraft or ships from entering Iran's territorial air or waters could only mean, to the Chinese, that Iran was moving towards the Soviet Union.

In light of these developments, China became concerned about how to preserve its relationship with Iran without harming its relations with the United States. To the Chinese, it was obvious that the United States was the only force that they could rely on to counter Soviet expansionist efforts in the Gulf. However, they did not want to be pictured as the enemy in the eye of the Khomeini regime. Thus, they exploited every possible opportunity that they could in order to engender a good relationship with Iran, and to prevent the Soviets from establishing influence on Iran's new regime. This was encouraged by what the Chinese perceived to be some anti-Soviet signs in Iran. First, the Chinese welcomed Khomeini's opposition to Moscow's intervention in Iran's internal affairs and his demand to stop such intervention.[8] Second, the Chinese also welcomed Khomeini's refusal to accept a Soviet offer of military aid to Iran.[9] Lastly, the Chinese applauded Tehran's execution of a Soviet diplomat for espionage.[10] As a result of these indications, China did not vote on the United Nations Security Council resolution for economic sanctions against Iran on 13 January 1980.[11] Chen Chu, China's representative to the UN, argued that:

> We [the Chinese government] stand for the implementation of the provisions of Security Council resolutions calling on Iran to release immediately the Americans being held as hostages in Iran ... The application of economic sanctions against Iran may not necessarily lead to the relaxation of tension and the release of hostages ... Therefore, we appeal to the parties concerned to exercise restraint, avoid taking any action that may aggravate existing contradictions and refrain from blocking any channels that may lead to the release of hostages through consultation and mediation.
> (Cited in *Beijing Review*, Vol. 23.1, No. 3, 21 January 1980: 11–12)

The Chinese also repeatedly stressed their hope that the United States and Iran would peacefully resolve their differences and emphasized that the break of the relationship between the two countries was not in the interest of either side. Commentary in *Renmin Ribao*, 13 April 1980, stated:

---

8 See *Beijing Review*, Vol. 22.1, No. 25, 22 June 1979, p. 27.
9 See *Beijing Review*, Vol. 23.1, No. 4, 28 January 1980, pp. 11–12.
10 See *Beijing Review*, Vol. 23.2, No. 29, 21 July 1980, pp. 9–10.
11 The Soviet Union vetoed the Resolution.

It is necessary to be vigilant as the Soviet Union is quite pleased by the unfortunate situation and is setting its propaganda machinery into motion in an all-out effort to widen the US–Iranian split for its own purpose.

(Cited in *Beijing Review*, Vol. 23.1, No. 16, 21 April 1980: 11)

All these Chinese concerns were elevated by the continuing presence of the Soviet Union in Afghanistan. In the Chinese view, the Soviet Union was engaged in a 'southward drive' to win control over the Gulf and Arabian Peninsula region and the important sea routes in Asia and Africa. The Vietnamese military occupation of Cambodia was also linked to the Soviet strategy of the 'southdrive'.[12] Therefore, from the Chinese perspective, the Soviet invasion of Afghanistan had made the Gulf region more salient. However, lacking sufficient economic, military, and political influence in the region, China had no alternative but to rely heavily on:

1 creating propaganda against the Soviet Union intervention in Afghanistan and its threat to the security of the Gulf region; and
2 supporting the Americans to act with greater authority in the region against the Soviet Union policies in the Gulf region, in particular, and the Middle East, in general (Yahuda 1981: 109).

The Iran–Iraq war

On 22 September 1980, Iraqi forces entered Iran and began a large-scale war against Iran. At first, Iraqi advances into Iran were marked by some military success. But, by the end of the year, the Iraqi forces stopped their advance and waited for Khomeini's regime to fall and for the opposition to grow. This did not happen. By the end of 1981, the Iraqi forces retreated after they were unable to achieve their political aim, and this time Iranian forces accelerated into Iraq in an attempt, as many have argued, to overthrow Saddam Hussain's regime and to establish a Shi'ite Islamic republic in Iraq. The war began to threaten the flow of oil from the region. This was marked by the tanker war in late 1983, Iran's threat to close the Strait of Hormuz, and the reflagging of Kuwaiti oil ships. Prior to Iran's acceptance of a ceasefire under United Nation Resolution 598, several military clashes took place between the Iranian and the American forces in the Gulf.

China's first official reaction to the eruption of the Iran–Iraq war was presented in China's Premier Zhao Ziyang's statement on 23 September 1980. Zhao stated that Iran and Iraq are both friendly countries to China. He said:

---

12 *Beijing Review*, Vol. 23.1, No. 4, 28 January 1980, pp. 15–19.

We are very much concerned about the recent armed conflicts between them ... We hope that they will settle their disputes peacefully through negotiations, guard against superpower interference and prevent the situation from worsening. This is not only in the interests of the people of Iran and Iraq but also conducive to peace and stability in the area.
(Cited in *Beijing Review*, No. 39, 29 September 1980: 5)

Their fear always revolved around the Soviet Union. The Chinese repeatedly argued that the continuation of the war in the Gulf region served the interest of the Soviet Union. They argued that: The Soviet Union can use this war to advance its southward strategy by taking advantage of its geographical proximity and relations with the two belligerents. By stout manoeuvres in both camps it can make its influence felt to bring long term goals nearer.
(Cited in *Beijing Review*, No. 44, 3 November 1980: 10–11)

Throughout the war, China's foreign policy was clearly guided by the following two main objectives:

1   preventing Moscow from gaining benefits out of the war;
2   preventing the war from spreading to the other Gulf states.

In order to achieve these two foreign policy objectives, China had adopted an official policy of neutrality. Early in the war, China recognized the limitation of the US influence on Iran and feared that Iran might turn to the Soviet Union. As a result, the Chinese decided not to leave Iran isolated, which might easily force it into the Soviet hands. Instead, China refused to support the UN-imposed arms embargo against Iran, following the passing of UN Resolution 598 (Hunter 1990: 161). China's decision was influenced by its fear that the Soviet Union could gain a foothold in Iran, particularly after some reports had argued that, despite no direct Soviet arms reached Iran in 1981 and 1982, Soviet advisors were involved in training the Revolutionary Guard and in organizing Iran's Intelligence Services (Chubin 1982: 122–52). In addition to its refusal to support the UN effort to impose an arms embargo on Iran, China continued its propaganda against the Soviet Union. China accused the Soviet Union of being behind the war and argued that the Soviets sought to exploit the conflict to their own interests (Yahuda 1981: 104). The Chinese held that the Soviet Union wanted the war to continue, providing it did not lead to a direct confrontation with the United States and Western Europe.[13] Thus, the Chinese repeatedly called on the two sides to solve their problems peacefully and to bring to an end the war that, according to the Chinese, neither Iran

---

13 See *Beijing Review*, No. 44, 3 November 1980, pp. 10–11.

nor Iraq was benefiting from. They even argued that the continuation of the war was helping their common enemy, Israel, by diverting the world's attention from focusing on Israeli policies against the Palestinians to the Iran–Iraqi war.[14] More importantly, the Chinese encouraged the rapprochement of relations between the United States and Iran as the best for the security of the Gulf and Arabian Peninsula region and for containing the Soviet Union.

China's second foreign policy objective was related to the Chinese government's concern about the stability of the region. China supported US efforts to prevent the war from spreading to the neighbouring Gulf states, with whom China had good economic and political relations. The official Chinese paper, *Renmin Ribao*, said that the war between Iran and Iraq:

> Is a war of mutual slaughter between brothers in which both sides suffer. If this war is further internationalised, it will no longer be confined to two countries but will spread to the entire Gulf region. More and more countries will then be involved until this region is drawn into the whirlpool of the superpowers' global contention. This will then constitute a serious threat to peace in the Middle East region and the world as a whole. If the situation develops to such extent, both Iran and Iraq will become pawns in the chess game which the superpowers are playing and will become victims of the superpowers' contention.
> (*FBIS-CHI-84-101*, 23 May 1984: 11)

China, who declined Kuwait's request to hire Chinese ships or have Kuwaiti oil tankers registered with Chinese authorities, pursued an 'active mediation' between Iran and Iraq. Unlike all other UN Security Council permanent members, China's good relations with both Iran and Iraq and its refusal to get involved in the acute oil tanker escorting war created a special position for China in its mediation efforts. China was the first UN Security Council member to send a special envoy to Iran following the UN Security Council adoption on 20 July 1987 of Resolution 598, which called on Iran and Iraq to cease fire and start talks to seek peaceful settlement of their disputes. Qi Huaiyuan, China's special envoy and deputy foreign minister, visited Tehran on 25th August 1987.[15] In all their meetings with the Iranian and the Iraqi officials, Chinese officials had always urged the two sides to cease fighting and seek peaceful negotiations.

---

14 See, for example, *Beijing Review*, No. 49, 8 December 1980, p. 12.
15 *FBIS-CHI-87-166*, 27 August 1987, pp. 3–4 (*FBIS* stands for Foreign Broadcast Information System).

114 *China's foreign policy toward the Gulf and Arabian Peninsula region*

It was the superpowers' presence in the Gulf and Peninsula region and involvement in the conflict that inspired the Chinese government to pursue its 'active mediation' between Iran and Iraq. China believed that the continuation of the war was the main obstacle to limiting the big powers' presence and involvement in the region. Therefore, the Chinese continued their call for the parties to solve their differences peacefully. However, China opposed the military involvement of the big powers in the region and did not agree that they should send their planes and warships to the region, even for the purpose of escorting ships. To the Chinese, the superpowers' involvement was mainly 'to seek military hegemony in the region and would only add more trouble to that region as well as make the situation more tense'.[16] When an Iran Airlines passenger plane flying over the southern part of the Gulf was brought down by US Navy forces in the Gulf on 3 July 1988, the Chinese government, through its media, criticized the action. It emphasized that its analysis of the superpowers' involvement in the region was correct. It believed that the airline incident 'underlined the urgency for the removal of big powers' military meddling' from the region 'and for the peaceful settlement between the warring nations' (see Footnote 16: 14). When Iran announced on 8 July 1988 its acceptance of UN Security Council Resolution 598, China welcomed the Iranian decision and sent its deputy foreign minister to Tehran for talks with Iranian officials on the post-ceasefire negotiations.[17] Following the ceasefire, China continued to reaffirm its position to support the mediation efforts of the UN General Secretary and to provide the 'best possible' cooperation for his work.[18]

China's arms sales to the region in the 1980s

Meanwhile, China sought to benefit from the US and Soviet preference for a stalemate rather than a decisive victory, by exploiting the war to its own economic and political advantages. The eruption and continuation of the war had made the Gulf and Arabian Peninsula region China's top arms customer in the 1980s. As shown in Table 4.1, China's arms exports to the Gulf and Arabian Peninsula region from 1982 to 1986 accounted for almost 70 per cent of China's total arms transfer to the world. Furthermore, the region's share of China's total arms from sales from 1987 to 1991 reached 77 per cent (see Table 4.2).

Iran and Iraq became the major recipients of Chinese arms not only in the Gulf region but also in the world; these two countries accounted for

---

16 See *FBIS-CHI-88-128*, 5 July 1988, pp. 13–14.
17 *FBIS-CHI-88-158*, 16 August 1988, p. 18.
18 The remark was made by Premier Zhao in a meeting with the visiting Iranian foreign minister Velayati in December 1988. See *FBIS-CHI-88-245*, 21 December 1988, p. 17.

Table 4.1 China's main arms customers by region, 1982–1996 (US$ million) (source: ACDA 1987: 127–30)

Region	Value	Share of China's total arms sales (%)
The Gulf and Arabian Peninsula region	4,505	69.85
The Arab Countries of the Middle East and Africa	1,135	17.5
South Asia	380	6.0
East Asia	285	4.5
Africa	135	2.0
East Europe	10	0.15
Total	*6,450*	*100*

Table 4.2 China's main arms customers by region, 1987–1991 (US$ million) (source: ACDA 1991: 131–4)

Region	Value	Share of China's total arms sales (%)
The Gulf and Arabian Peninsula region	7,320	77.0
The Arab Countries of the Middle East and Africa	265	2.8
South Asia	880	9.24
East Asia	720	7.5
Africa	300	3.15
North America	30	0.31
Total	*9,515*	*100*

about 70 per cent of China's total arms sales from 1982 to 1986 and 45 per cent from 1987 to 1991. This made China the fifth-largest seller of military equipment in the world.

As shown in Tables 4.2, 4.3, and 4.4, China's arms transfers to the Gulf and Arabian Peninsula region continued to dominate China's total arms transfer by 1991. While Iran and Iraq remained China's major arms customers in the region, Saudi Arabia had emerged as China's new primary arms customer in the Gulf region by the end of the 1980s. This was mainly due to China's estimated $3–3.5 billion deal with Saudi Arabia in 1987 to sell about thirty-six Dong Feng-3 (East Wind-3), known to NATO as CSS-2,

Table 4.3 China's top arms customers, 1982–1986 (US$ million) (source: ACDA 1987: 127–30)

Country	Value	Rank
Iraq	3,300	1
Iran	1,200	2
Egypt	625	3
Libya	320	4

Table 4.4 China's top arms customers, 1987–1991 (US$ million) (source: ACDA 1991: 130–4)

Country	Value	Rank
Saudi Arabia	3,000	1
Iran	2,600	2
Iraq	1,700	3
Pakistan	600	4

intermediate-range ballistic missiles (IRBMs), with ranges of 2,800 km.[19] During the Iran–Iraq war, China, despite its denial of any official arms sales to either side in the war, had sold Iran and Iraq fighters, bombers, artillery, armoured vehicles, and other military equipment worth $11–12 billion (Schichor 1988: 320–9). During the war, China was Iran's largest single arms supplier. For Iran, the low cost of Chinese weapons made China an attractive selling point. For China, Iran presented a great economic opportunity to gain some hard currency to support China's drive for economic and military modernization; politically, it was an irresistible opportunity to establish a friendly relationship with the Islamic regime in Iran, thus creating an importance for itself in the region. China and Iran signed a secret nuclear cooperation agreement, under which many Iranian nuclear engineers were trained by Chinese experts in nuclear reactor design and research (Timperlake and Triplett 1999: 100). They also signed their first large arms deal in 1984, in which China would transfer F-6 fighters, Type-59 tanks, field artillery and shells, multiple rocket launchers, and surface-to-air missiles worth $1.6 billion.[20] Another deal was signed in 1986

---

19 About this deal see, among many, *The Independent*, 2 May 1988, p. 12; *Far Eastern Economic Review*, 2 June 1988, pp. 26–7; and Congressional Research Service, 'Chinese Missile and Nuclear Proliferation: Issues for Congress', on *http://www.fas.org/spp/starwars/crs/92-056-1.htm*
20 *Business Week*, 29 December 1986, p. 47.

Table 4.5 China's arms sales to Iran, 1981–1988 (source: *SIPRI* 1989: 252)

No. ordered	Weapon designation	Weapon description	Year of order	Year(s) of deliveries	No. delivered	Comments
–	F-6	Fighter	1981	1986–8	30	Possibly via North Korea
60	F-7	Fighter	1986	1986–8	60	Chinese version of the Soviet MiG 21
–	T-59	MBT (Main Battle Tank)	1986	1987–8	240	–
–	Type-501	APC (Armoured Personnel Carrier)	1986	1986–8	300	
–	Type-63 (107 mm)	MRL	1982	1983–8	900	
–	Hai-Ying-2L	Anti-ship missile	1986	1987–8	8	Coast, ship, and air launched versions
–	Hai-Ying-2	Anti-ship missile	1986	1987–8	124	NATO designation: Silkworm
–	Hong Jian-73	Anti-tank missile	1982	1982–8	6,500	
–	Hong Ying-5	Portable SAM (Surface-to-air Missile)	1985	1985–8	600	
–	PL-2A	AAM (Air-to-air Missile)	1986	1986–8	540	Arming F-6 and F-7 fighters
–	PL-7	AAM	1986	1986–8	360	Arming F-7 fighters

in which China transferred F-7 fighters, more Type-59 tanks, and Hai-Ying-2 (Silkworm) anti-ship missiles to Iran for $1.5 billion (see Schichor 1988: 323 and Table 4.5).

In January 1990, China and Iran signed a ten-year 'military technology transfer agreement'. Edward Timperlake and William Triplett II (1999: 100) argue that under this agreement Chinese nuclear specialists began to appear at the Qazvin Nuclear Research Centre west of Tehran, and later at Karaj, another location where the Chinese were believed to have supplied nuclear assistance.

Table 4.6 China's arms sales to Iraq, 1981–1988 (source: *SIPRI* 1989: 252)

No. ordered	Weapon designation	Weapon description	Year of order	Year(s) of deliveries	No. delivered	Comments
4	B-6	Bomber	1987	1988	4	–
–	T-59	MBT	1981	1982–8	700	–
–	T-69	MBT	1982	1983–8	600	1,000–2,000 ordered in early 1980s
–	Type-531	APC	1981	1982–8	650	–
–	Type-59/1 (130 mm)	Towed gun	1981	1982–8	720	–
–	C-601	AshM (Anti-ship Missile)	1987	1988	128	–
–	Hai Ying-2	ShShM/ShShM	1986	–	–	Arming Osa-2 class FACs

In its pursuit of economic and political leverages, China also sold jet fighters, tanks, artillery, and missiles to Iraq (see Table 4.6). Some have reported that China helped Iraq build sophisticated magnets for stabilizing uranium-enrichment centrifuges.[21] Iraq reportedly sought Chinese assistance after failing to obtain the specific magnets from British sources. Others have argued that from 1984 to 1986 China conducted a feasibility study on building a clandestine nuclear reactor for Iraq (CRS 1996: 12).

In summary, during this phase, China's foreign policy towards the Gulf and Arabian Peninsula region remained close to China's relations with both Washington and Moscow. Beijing's fear of Moscow penetration in the Gulf and Arabian Peninsula region led China to foster closer ties with Washington's allies in the region. It also prompted the Chinese government to abandon its support for the revolutionary groups. China's foreign policy, therefore, succeeded during the 1970s in establishing diplomatic relations with Kuwait, Iran, and Oman. Despite the proclamation of the independent foreign policy in 1982, China's foreign policy towards the region continued to stress the potential of a Soviet manoeuvre to dominate the region, particularly since Moscow troops remained in Afghanistan. Thus, China stressed time and time again the need to solve the Iran–Iraq war peacefully so that the Soviets would not have an opportunity to exploit either side in the war for their own advantage. While Washington was supporting Iraq, China felt the need to back Iran to prevent Tehran from moving towards alignment with Moscow. China, therefore, provided a substantial amount of military assistance to Iran throughout its war with Iraq, and focused most of

---

21 *The Washington Times*, 14 December 1989.

its attention in the region towards generating more political and economic ties with Iran, at the same time keeping good relations with Iraq. This period also witnessed China pushing further for political ties with the remaining countries of the region, with which it had no diplomatic relations – namely Saudi Arabia, the UAE, Qatar, and Bahrain. China only succeeded in establishing diplomatic relations with the UAE in November 1984, Qatar in July 1988, and Bahrain in April 1989, but not Saudi Arabia.

However, China increased its military and economic cooperation with the Kingdom in the 1980s. Its objective was to eliminate Taiwan politically from the region. The Kingdom during this period had recognized Taiwan as the legitimate representative of China and had established diplomatic relations with it. The Kingdom was one of the three most prominent states that Taiwan enjoyed diplomatic relations with – the others being South Korea and South Africa. Therefore, China's rapid military and economic relations in the second half of the 1980s were driven by China's hope to score some political gains against Taiwan in the region. This policy achieved its objective in the early 1990s when the Kingdom decided that the political and strategic importance of China was greater than that of Taiwan, which had led to the establishment of diplomatic relations with Beijing and abolishment of its formal relations with Taipei.

PHASE 3: CHINA'S NEW INTEREST IN THE REGION (1990–1999)

During the 1990s, several important developments had taken place in and around the Gulf and Arabian Peninsula region that influenced China's foreign policy toward the region. The real, direct, Chinese-perceived Soviet threat to the region was illuminated following the withdrawal of Soviet troops from Afghanistan. The Gulf Crisis erupted. And China had become a net importer of oil for the first time in its 43-year history. During this phase, China began to establish long-term cooperation with the countries of the region in order to meet its own current and future needs for oil. It cooperated with Tehran's efforts to break the deadlock of American political and economic sanctions against Iran. It repeatedly called for the peaceful resolution of regional disputes. It also continued to upgrade its military cooperation with Iran, despite Washington opposition, to a level where Beijing could remain an influential and dependable supplier of arms to the region. Thus, China's Gulf foreign policy, during this period, can be defined in terms of China's needs to increase its capabilities and achieve its Four Modernizations programme. China's need for a long-term independent supplier of energy to sustain its high level of economic growth characterized China's relations with the countries of the Gulf and Arabian Peninsula region during this period.

The Kuwait crisis

The Kuwait crisis erupted as a result of Iraq's invasion and occupation of Kuwait on 2 August 1990. Worldwide condemnations of Iraq followed the Iraqi action. A series of resolutions requiring Iraq's immediate and unconditional withdrawal from Kuwait and calling for economic sanctions against Iraq were adopted by the UN Security Council. Several efforts had been made by the Arab countries and the international community to bring about a peaceful solution to the crisis and avoid a disastrous war in the region. Meanwhile, the United States began its 'Operation Desert Shield' on 7 August 1990 sending troops to the Gulf region. Iraq, however, refused to implement the Security Council resolutions or to accept a peaceful resolution. Subsequently, this led to adoption and implementation of UN Security Council Resolution 678, which authorized member states 'to use all necessary means', including military force, to uphold and implement the Security Council's previous resolutions unless Iraq withdrew its forces from Kuwait on or before 15 January 1991. Iraq continued to refuse to withdraw its troops from Kuwait (for more information, see Freedman and Krash 1993; Danspeckgruber and Tripp 1996). As a result, a coalition led by the United States began a massive air offensive on Iraqi troops in Kuwait and Iraq, followed by moving ground troops into Kuwait (for more information, see Bin Sultan and Seale 1995). This forced Iraqi troops to move out of Kuwait, so restoring Kuwait's independence, sovereignty, and legitimate government. Following the liberation of Kuwait, the UN has maintained sanctions against Iraq and worked on limiting its military capability.

To China, both Iraq and Kuwait were important states in the Gulf region for the following reasons:

1   China's drive for implementing its modernization programme required a stable world, including the Gulf and Arabian Peninsula region. China depended heavily on the strength of Western and Asian economies for its own economic modernization including foreign capital and technology. Not yet a major importer of Gulf oil, China was concerned about the impact of the crisis on the supply and demand of oil and, therefore, the subsequent impact on China's economy.
2   Prior to the crisis, China saw a substantial increase in its trade relations with the countries of the Gulf and Arabian Peninsula region. In 1989, 26 per cent of its total volume with the region came from its trade relations with Kuwait and Iraq. Kuwait was the third-largest trade partner with China, after Saudi Arabia and the UAE, respectively, in the region. China's trade volume with the Gulf and Arabian Peninsula countries reached US$5,074 million between 1985 and 1989, Kuwait accounting for US$719 million (IMF 1990: 135) Most notably, China's trade volume with Kuwait showed an increase in almost every year since 1985. Plus, China's exports to both Kuwait and Iraq exceeded its

imports from the two Gulf states, which provided the Chinese with much needed hard currency.
3   Iraq was a source of investment to many Chinese companies and a source of income to many Chinese workers who profited from the process of reconstructing Iraq's infrastructures that were destroyed during the eight-year war with Iran. Yitzhak Schichor (1991: 81–2) noted that Iraq's share of China's labour exports surpassed 50 per cent reaching $678 million by 1987. China also supplied Iraq with construction services amounting to more than $1 billion between 1976 and 1987 (see also Freedman and Karsh 1993: 140, who estimate that by August 1990 there were 5,000 Chinese working in Iraq).
4   Iraq, as mentioned in the previous section, was one of China's top arms customer in the world during the 1980s, which provided China with much needed hard currency to modernize its economy and military.
5   Kuwait was also a source of income for over 7,700 Chinese construction workers for contracted projects, where the value of labour service contracts with Kuwait reached US$500 million prior to the crisis.[22] Kuwait was also a source of soft loans for many of China's development projects. From 1982 to 1989, the Kuwait Fund for Arab Economic Development provided China with US$310 million in soft loans for the construction of thirteen projects in different provinces (Schichor 1992: 95–7).

China's official reaction to the crisis was presented in Premier Li Peng's report to the Fifteenthth Session of the Standard Committee of the Seventh National People's Congress on 28 August 1990. Li stated that China is firmly opposed to Iraq's invasion and annexation of Kuwait and to the military involvement of 'big powers'. He emphasized that China maintains that the disputes between Iraq and Kuwait should be resolved by peaceful means within the Arab countries, utilizing the UN mediation role to its fullest.[23] This position reflected China's foreign policy principles that state-to-state relations should be based on the Five Principles of Peaceful Coexistence, and that differences between states should be solved peacefully instead of resorting to force. Thus, the Chinese government opposed the Iraqi action against Kuwait and urged for peaceful restoration of Kuwait's independence, sovereignty, territorial integrity, and legitimate government. The Chinese government assured the visiting Kuwaiti Emir Jaber al-Ahmed al-Sabah, in late December 1990, that China would never change its 'principled stand' against the Iraqi invasion and occupation of Kuwait.[24]

22   *Beijing Review*, No. 37, 10–16 September 1990, pp. 10–11.
23   *Beijing Review*, No. 37, 10–16 September 1990, p. 7.
24   *Beijing Review*, No. 1, 7–13 January 1991, pp. 11–12.

China supported all the UN Security Council resolutions on Iraq except Resolution 678, from which it abstained, that legitimized the use of force against Iraqi troops in Kuwait. The Chinese government's behaviour in supporting, or at least not opposing, the UN Security Council's resolutions on the crisis can be explained in terms of the following points:

1. The Gulf crisis provided the Chinese government with a unique opportunity to rehabilitate its international image and lift the economic and political sanctions that were imposed following its suppression of the student demonstrations in Tiananmen Square in June 1989. Most importantly, China used the crisis as a useful gesture to improve its bilateral relationship with the United States, which was harmed after Tiananmen. Thus, foreign investment, capital, and technology, mainly from the West and Japan, were China's primary needs to continue its modernization programme. The Chinese government saw foreign investment, capital, and technology as more important, in the short and long term, than losing US$2 billion in arms exports to Iraq.[25] Following its support or non-opposition to the Security Council resolutions, the United States resumed high-level meetings with China and lifted its economic sanctions, resulting in Europe, Japan, and South-East Asia following suit.
2. China, for the sake of its own modernization drive, was concerned about the damage that the crisis might do to international economic relations and its own future oil needs.
3. China was unwilling to harm its improving relations with those Gulf states that did not participate in the worldwide campaign to condemn the Chinese government action in Tiananmen Square or in its violation of other human rights. Therefore, to preserve and expand its relations with the Gulf states and to prevent any tilt by the Gulf states towards Taiwan, China had no other choice but to cooperate.[26]

Following the outbreak of the war in January 1991, the Chinese government continued to emphasize its opposition to the Iraqi invasion and demanded that Iraq withdraw from Kuwait immediately. At the same time, it continued to advocate the need for achieving a peaceful solution to the crisis through political and diplomatic means and avoiding the use of force. This Chinese policy stemmed from the following rationales:

25 *The Financial Times* (London), 2 November 1990, p. 4.
26 For example, China, despite its criticism of the US presence in the Gulf region, did not criticize Saudi Arabia's decision to allow US troops to enter and operate from its own territory.

1. China wanted to strengthen its position as a Third World advocate and distance itself from military defeat in the region. Its hope for a positive role to solve the crisis had led the Chinese government to: (a) receive Iraqi Deputy Premier Taha Yasin Ramadan on 6 September, and (b) dispatch the Chinese Foreign Minister to Iraq and other Arab capitals to explore the 'possibility of a peaceful solution of the worsening Gulf crisis'.[27]
2. A military victory by the US-led coalition forces against Saddam Hussain could threaten China's position as one of the leading arms suppliers to the Gulf region by establishing a predominant US-led security system in the region.
3. China has always been very sensitive about the issue of using force against a sovereign state. Its emphasis on the need for the Five Principles of Peaceful Coexistence, as the main principles to govern relations among nations, is driven largely by its concern over its own quest for Taiwan and its policies in many unstable regions inside its own territory. Therefore, this has always been part of China's international positions, due to its own ambitions.[28]

China's concern this time was also about the danger that the war could spill and expand beyond the Gulf and Arabian Peninsula region and reach the Middle East. This concern was stated in Premier Li Peng's statement:

> The Chinese government and people strongly appeal to all parties concerned to exercise a great restraint to prevent the escalation and expansion of war, so as to protect the people of the Middle East countries from a greater catastrophe and provide opportunities and favourable conditions for the international community to continue its search for a peaceful settlement to the conflict.
> (*Beijing Review*, No. 4, 28 January–3 February 1991: 7)

In its own effort to bring the crisis to an end peacefully and to keep itself involved in developments in the Gulf region, the Chinese government set out, on 24 February 1991 – the same day that ground troops started to move into Kuwait, a six-point proposal for a peaceful solution to the crisis. The proposal called for the following points:

1. Iraq should unconditionally withdraw its troops from Kuwait.
2. The parties involved should show a willingness for peace.

---

27 For Qian Qichen's, China's Foreign Minister, trip to the Middle East, see *Beijing Review*, No. 47, 19–25 November 1990, pp. 7 and 8.
28 See, for instance, Qian Qichen's statement in *Beijing Review*, No. 41, 8–14 October 1990, pp. 10–11.

3   The urgent task at this moment is to prevent the war from expanding and escalating and to create favourable conditions for peaceful efforts. All sides involved in the conflict should do their best to avoid any actions that cause an increase of personnel casualties and destruction of civilian installations.
4   Matters concerning the security of the Gulf region in the aftermath of the conflict should be consulted and solved primarily by the regional countries. Foreign troops should withdraw from the region, and Arab and Islamic countries should play a more important role.
5   As for the Middle East issue, there can never be a real and lasting peace in the Middle East and the Gulf region as long as the conflict between the Arab countries and Israel remains unsolved. The international community should focus its full attention on this issue.
6   The above five issues may not be linked with each other, but they can be dealt with one after another. However, all these issues should be given equal consideration and attention.[29]

This Chinese proposal and other Chinese efforts to resolve the crisis peacefully illustrates the point that China was concerned about military activities in the Gulf region and the continuing US-led attack on Iraq. That is why China welcomed the suspension of allied operations against Iraq in March 1991.[30] Following the Iraqi troop withdrawal from Kuwait and the suspension of military operations by the West, China's policy toward the new arrangements was addressed by the Chinese Assistant Foreign Minister Yang Fuchang. Yang emphasized his country's position by arguing that the Gulf's affairs must be dealt with mainly by the countries in the region through dialogue. He stressed that the independence, sovereignty, and security of the Gulf States' territories must be respected and that interference in the internal affairs of the Gulf States must be rejected. He added that the arrangements issue must be dealt with by the Gulf States themselves, adding that the Security Council could play a positive role regarding this issue. He expressed China's support for the Gulf States in 'bolstering their unity and strengthening themselves to maintain peace and stability' in the region. He also expressed China's understanding and respect for the defence measures the Gulf States have taken for their security arrangements.[31]

In short, China's cooperation with the international norms during and after the Kuwait crisis suggests that China is interested in the stability of the region, in order to protect its own modernization. It signifies Chinese

29   *Beijing Review*, Vol. 34, No. 9, 4–10 March 1991, p. 4.
30   BBC, *SWB, Part 3: Far East*, 4 March 1991, p. A4/1.
31   *FBIS-CHI-91-122*, 25 June 1991, p. 15.

acceptance of the principle that development is unachievable in a climate of instability, in one of the world's most important regions. Stability of the Gulf and Arabian Peninsula region is vital to China's drive to modernize its economy, and therefore sustain or increase its capabilities relative to others. Unlike the past, China's actions in the 1990s were not preoccupied with its criticism of the American presence in the region. Instead, its focus shifted toward maintaining stability in the region and the prevention of domination of the region by a hostile country.

Market for Chinese military goods

China, like other weapon producers, needed to sell arms as a way of generating a higher scale economy, thus helping to subsidize some costs associated with running an indigenous defence industry, and to stay influential in the region against the other big powers. The termination of the Iran–Iraq war, the end of the Cold War, and the high-tech weapons systems demonstration in Operation Desert Storm all combined to decrease demand for China's lower-technology weaponry, in a region where China generated a large amount of profit in the 1980s. Russia's advanced technology weaponry attracted China's major arms buyers in the Gulf, namely Iran. China's arms supplies to Iran from 1987 to 1991 exceeded those of Russia by US$500 million. However, from 1991 to 1995, Russia's arms supplies to Iran increased substantially to reach US$3,300 million, and China's arms supplies to Iran dropped to US$1,365 million (ACDA 1991: 133; 1993: 141; 1996: 153). Therefore, in order for China to compete against the Russians and others for markets for its military industry in the Gulf region, it had to upgrade its service to cooperate with the buyers in the development of high-level weaponry despite US opposition. This was very important for China in order to compete for markets, to continue its presence in the region as an influential power and to create friendly relations with the countries of the region to ensure the spread of their crude oil to China. China's position on the arms sales issue to the Gulf region was presented by the Chinese delegation (to a conference on arms control in the Middle East) held by the five permanent members of the UN Security Council in Paris on 9 July 1991. The Chinese delegation stressed that China 'has all along adopted a responsible and prudent attitude towards international arms trade and complied with the following principles: (1) the sales should be helpful to the justified defence capacity of the countries concerned; (2) the sales should not be harmful to peace, security and stability in the region; and (3) no arms trade should be used to interfere in the internal affairs of other countries'. The delegation added that 'if all countries concerned stop selling weapons to the Middle East region, China will

126 *China's foreign policy toward the Gulf and Arabian Peninsula region*

have no difficulty to do likewise'.[32] As we will see, China, reportedly, continued to sell arms and military technology to the region.

Missile technology sales to Iran

Reports indicate that China continued in the early 1990s to assist Iran's HY-2 anti-ship missile programme and assisted an Iranian missile production facility near Isfahan, capable of producing the HY-2 missile (Gill 1999: 121–3). *Sawt al-Kuwayt* reported in November 1992 that Iran had signed an agreement with China in the same month, under which it would sell Beijing over 100 Iraqi military aircraft in return for Chinese technological equipment.[33] In 1996, US media reported that China supplied C-802 anti-ship cruise missiles to Iran, with a range of 120 km carrying a 165-kg warhead (Gertz 1996a: A12). It is reported that China's Precision Machinery Import–Export Corporation had sold and delivered about 40 of the C-802's, China's 'top-of-the-line' anti-ship cruise missile, to Iran by March 1996, plus Hudong fast attack boats to carry them.[34] The United States was concerned about the transfer of the C-802's to Iran because:

1   the missiles were considered to be a threat to US ships in the Gulf; and
2   the missiles were built with assistance from the United States, which created a continued debate in the US government over the transfer of US technology to a hostile power via China.

The CIA reported delivery of a Chinese missile guidance system and computerized machine tools to Iran in 1994 and 1995, which, according to the report, could improve the accuracy of Iran's Scuds and enable it to develop more of its own (Sciolino 1995a: 1). *The Washington Times*, 21 November 1996, cited another CIA report, which claimed that China agreed in August to sell gyroscopes, accelerometers, and test equipment to Iran's Defence Industries Organization that could be used to build and test components for missile guidance. Besides this, it was reported that China helped Iran in building the Semnan launch and missile test range in 1990, and assisted Iran in two missile tests at Semnan in 1991. It was also reported that, despite the fact China did not provide complete M-9 or M-11 missile system to Iran, it helped Iran in building a Silkworm and M9 plant near Isfahan and providing technologies and assistance, as well as providing a Silkworm anti-ship cruise missile to Iran in 1992 (Gill 1999: 125–7). China

---

32 BBC, *SWB, Part 3: Far East/1124*, 15 July 1991, p. A4/1.
33 *FBIS-NES-92-223*, 18 November 1992, p. 49.
34 The first shipment of the missile was delivered in July 1995 (see Gertz 1996a: A12).

delivered twenty CSS-8 ballistic surface-to-surface missiles (M-7) to Iran in 1994 (Table 4.7), with a range of 150 km.[35] China is believed to be assisting Iran with the technology to produce the solid-propellant unguided Mushak-120, with a range of 130 km carrying a and 500-kg warhead, and the longer range version, the Mushak-160, with a range of 160 km carrying a and 500-kg warhead, as well as the 200-km Mushak-200.[36]

China's nuclear cooperation with Iran

During President Rafsanjani's visit to Beijing in September 1992, China and Iran reached an agreement on nuclear energy cooperation. China reportedly agreed to build two 300-MW nuclear reactors in about ten years in Iran (Kan 1997: 33). This deal, however, remained on hold. Others reported that the China Nuclear Energy Industry Corporation has agreed to sell Iran a facility to convert uranium ore into uranium hexaflouride gas,[37] which can be enriched to the weapons-grade level (Landay 1996: 1). It was also reported that China has agreed to sell Iran a 25–30-MW reactor, which is an ideal size for making a small number of nuclear weapons per year.[38] *The Washington Times* reported that Chinese technicians had built an electromagnetic isotope separation system for enriching uranium at the Karaj nuclear research facility.[39] In 1993–4, the Institute of Plasma Physics of the Chinese Academy of Science transferred nuclear fusion research to the Azad University in Tehran.[40] It was reported by the CIA in 1997 that 'China is a key supplier of nuclear technology to Iran', exporting more than US$60 million worth annually. It was also said that a number of Chinese nuclear experts had worked at Iranian nuclear facilities in 1997.[41] Both the Chinese and the Iranian officials insisted that these items could be used only for peaceful purposes.

35 See the US rely on China's export promises?' in *Risk*, May 1996, p. 9; and Sciolino 1995b: A1.
36 FAS Intelligence Resource Program, 'Missile proliferation – Iran', on *http://www.fas.org/irp/threat/missile/iran.htm*, p. 2; and Gertz 1997.
37 The hexaflouride plant is essential to enrich uranium for use in atomic bombs; such bombs are easier to make than those fuelled by plutonium because uranium is easier to work with.
38 1997 Congressional Hearings, 'Special Weapons, Nuclear, Chemical, Biological and Missile', on *http://www.fas.org/spp/starwars/congress/1997-h/s970410m.htm*, p. 3.
39 *Washington Times*, 25 September 1995, p. A.1. In April 1996, the US Defence Department confirmed that the Iranians had purchased an electronic isotope separation unit from China. See *http://www.fas.org/spp/starwars/crs/980717CRSWeapons.htm*
40 1997 Congressional Hearings, on *http://www.fas.org/spp/starwars/congress/1997-h/s971008m.htm*, p. 4.
41 Congressional Record, 'China's Proliferation Activity', on *http://www.fas.org/spp/starwars/congress/1998/s980313a.htm*

Table 4.7 China's arms sales to Iran, 1990–1997

No. ordered	Weapon designation	Weapon description	Year of order	Year(s) of orders	No. delivered	Comments
8	HQ-2B SAMS	SAM system surface-to-air missile	1989	1990–3	8	Coastal air defence batteries
96	HQ-2B	SAM	1989	1990–3	96	For 8 HQ-2B SAMS
75	F-7M Airguard	Fighter	1991	1993–4	50	
10	ESR-1	Surveillance Rader	1992	1994–6	10	For 10 Hudong-Class fast-attack craft
10	Rice Lamp	Fire control radar	1992	1994–6	10	For 10 Hudong-Class fast-attack craft
10	Hudong Class	FAC(M) (fast-attack craft)	1992	1994–6	10	–
–	C-802	ShShM	1992	1995–6	80	For 10 Hudong-Class FAC(M)s
7	C-801/802 ShShMS	ShShM System	1995	1996–7	2	For refit of 7 Combattante-2-Type (Kaman-Class) FAC
80	C-802/ Css-N-8 Saccade	ShShM	1995	1996–7	16	For 10 refitted Combattante-2-Type (Kaman-Class) FAC

Source: *SIPRI* 1992: 338; *SIPRI* 1994: 526; *SIPRI* 1995: 526; *SIPRI* 1996: 502; *SIPRI* 1997: 311; and *SIPRI* 1998: 339.

China's chemical and biological sales to Iran

In March of 1996, *The Washington Post* reported that Chinese companies were providing Iran with complete factories suited for making chemical weapons (Smith 1996: A26). The *Washington Times* cited a CIA report claiming China, in the summer of 1996, delivered nearly 400 metric tons of chemicals, including carbon sulphide 'used' in the production of nerve agents, to Iran (Gertz 1996b: A1). Between 1993 and 1996, there had been several reports indicating that China was providing precursor agents, along with technical assistance on chemical weapons development, to Iran. China was also suspected by US intelligence sources of selling Iran a complete weapons factory to manufacture chemical weapons (Gertz 1996c). *The Washington Times* reported that a US intelligence report stated China Nanjing Chemical and Industrial Group completed, in June 1997, a plant in Iran for making glass-lined equipment used in producing chemical weapons.[42] *The Washington Post* reported that US intelligence learned, through intercepted communication in 1997, of negotiations between a Chinese state-run company and Iranian officials for the sale to Iran of hydrofluoric acid, which is used to refine uranium to weapons grade.[43] *The Washington Post* also reported similar negotiations in January 1998 between the China Nuclear Energy Industry Corporation and Iran's Isfahan Nuclear Research Centre to provide a 'lifelong supply' of hundreds of tons of anhydrous fluoride (AHF), or hydrofluoric acid. It said that the AHF chemical could be used to produce uranium hexafluoride used in uranium-conversion facilities.[44] Despite the Chinese government's repeated assurance to the US government that it stopped the sale of AHF to Iran, some have argued that the Chinese government is using such a statement to deny its involvement with Iran and deceive the American government. The London *Daily Telegraph* of 24 May 1998 reported a Chinese sale to Iran of 500 tons of phosphorus pentasulphide, which is useful for production of nerve agents.[45]

Other possible sales

The Observer, 28 April 1991, reported that China shipped arms to Iraq through Iraq's office in Jordan. China denied the report and called it 'totally groundless'.[46] Later, an Iraqi Kurdish opposition group alleged, in April 1994, that China was supplying Iraq with chemical weapons through a 'neighbouring' third country. According to this allegation, the 'Kurdish police intercepted two trucks carrying 19 tonnes of sodium phosphate used to make chemical weapons'. According to the allegation, the truck drivers admitted they were trying to smuggle the chemicals through Kurdish-controlled northern Iraq to regions controlled by the Iraqi central government.[47] Western intelligent reports have also argued that China has aided

---

42 *http://www.fas.org/spp/starwars/crs/980717/CRSWeapons.htm*
43 *http://www.fas.org/news/iran/1998/980313-iran.htm*
44 *http://www.fas.org/spp/starwars/crs/980717/CRSWeapons.htm*
45 Ibid.
46 BBC, *SWB, Part 3: Far East/1060*, 1 May 1991, p. A4/1.
47 *FBIS-NES-94-084*, 2 May 1994, p. 63.

Iraq's military establishments in countries like Algeria and Mauritania with advanced nuclear and chemical weapon technology (Timperlake and Triplett 1999: 85–95). According to another report, published in *The Sunday Times* of 7 August 1994, Saudi Arabia tried to buy experimental nuclear reactors from China as part of a secret twenty-year programme to become a nuclear power.[48]

It is very obvious that, following the UN arms embargo on Iraq – China's major arms customer along with Iran in the 1980s – and after the GCC (Gulf Cooperation Council) states dependence on US protection in the region, China found itself unable to compete against the United States for military markets in the Gulf region except in Iran. Iran's political and economic isolation from the United States presented the Chinese with the only viable arms customer in the region for China's military sales. Therefore, China's military sales and cooperation with Iran has dominated China's military sales programme to the Gulf and Arabian Peninsula region. This can be explained by the following points:

1   China viewed Iran as a potential counterbalance to the influence of any hostile power in the region.
2   China needed to develop a good relationship with Iran in order to prevent Russia from gaining influence in that country.
3   Iran is a major source of energy needed for China's current and future economic development.
4   China may have feared the influence that Iran could exert on China's 20 million Muslims who live in the Western provinces and hoped to prevent Iran from supporting that minority faction in a bid for autonomy. In addition, China sees Iran's support for the opposition group in Afghanistan as an important tool for keeping Taliban away from pursuing an intensive support for the Chinese Muslim quest for independence.
5   China needed to keep its military cooperation with Iran and any other Gulf country as a 'wild card' in dealing with US support and assistance to Taiwan.
6   China was interested in Iran for its geopolitical importance. Iran could be used as a bridge connecting central Asian oil to China, and as a gateway for Gulf oil reaching China.
7   China needed to generate profits in order to keep its military modernization programme going.

---

48   For more details, see *The Sunday Times* (London), 7 August 1994; or *FBIS-NES-94-154*, 10 August 1994, pp. 27–8.

Table 4.8 China's production, consumption, export, and deficit of crude oil, 1991–1997 (thousand bbl./day) (sources: OPEC 1998: 84, 86, 76; 1993: 84, 86, 76)

	1991	1992	1993	1994	1995	1996	1997
Production	2,804.6	2,814.5	2,910.9	2,974.7	2,996.2	3,173.2	3,252.4
Consumption	2,368.5	2,561.9	2,962.5	3,040.8	3,218.2	3,542.4	3,963.5
Export	452.8	429.8	391.2	373.2	377.9	406.6	397.7
Deficit	−16.7	−177.2	−442.8	−439.3	−599.9	−775.8	−1,108.8

From the Iranian perspective, Iran needed every possible supplier of more advanced weapons in order to modernize its own military capability. China, along with Russia, was the only available supplier of advanced military technology and weapons of mass destruction that was willing to provide and cooperate with Iran in the purchase and development of such weapons for hard currency and influence. Plus, China was the cheapest supplier of arms and military technology that Iran could find.

OIL

In the 1980s, arms sales to the Gulf countries dominated China's interaction with the Gulf region. In the 1990s, however, China's increasing demand for oil readjusted its interest in the Gulf region. China's former status as a net oil exporter was now changed to that of a net importer. In 1993, for the first time in over twenty-five years, Chinese imports of oil exceeded exports by around 10 million tonnes, which marked China's new status as a net importer of oil.[49] China began importing crude oil in 1988, but its imports increased substantially in 1993. The deficit between China's own production of oil contrasted with its consumption and export of oil (see Table 4.8).

China's economic growth is the highest among Asian countries at 8 to 9 per cent from 1992 to 2000 and expected to be one of the highest at 7 per cent from 2000 to 2010. As a result, China's energy demand is expected to increase. China, which only has about 2.4 per cent of the world's total oil and gas reserves, believes its future sources of energy supplies are going to be a significant factor in its continued ability to sustain a high level of economic growth. China's net external requirement for oil imports is expected to rise from the level of 600,000 barrels per day in 1995 and 1996, to 1 million by 2000, 3 million by 2010, and 7 million by 2015 (Calder 1996: 58). It is estimated that by 2020 about 90 per cent of China's oil will have to come from the region (Kemp 1998–9:138). This rise is due to the expanding gap

---

49 *Petroleum Times Energy Report*, Vol. 14, No. 20, 14 October 1994, p. 7.

between China's domestic oil production and demand for oil (see Koyama 1997: 45–63).

Thus, the Chinese government began to realize the importance of oil for China's economic development. As a result, the Gulf and Peninsula region continued to assume a great degree of importance to China. In addition to that, the Gulf's large oil reserves and the relatively low development and production costs shifted China's interest from South-East Asian producers to the Gulf region (Calabrese 1998: 356). In 1994, the Gulf region supplied about 40 per cent of China's crude oil imports. This share rose to around 60 per cent in 1997, and was expected to reach 77 per cent in 2000, and 92 per cent in 2005.[50] Li Yizhong, executive Vice-President of China Petrochemical Corporation (SINOPEC) told China's news agency Xinhua that in the past most of China's import of oil came from South-East Asian oil producers, but now China is focusing its interest on the Gulf, whose oil was marked by a large, proven reserve and low-sulphur character. He added that 'the Middle East countries, particularly the Gulf States will be the potential key sources of China's crude oil import'.[51]

Therefore, China tried to reach agreements with the Gulf and Arabian Peninsula countries to increase its imports of oil from them and to secure a long-term relationship with the oil-producing countries of the Gulf region. In May 1995, China reached an agreement with Iran to triple its oil imports to reach 60,000 barrels per day, in which Iran would earn more than US$400 million a year.[52] It was expected that Iran would increase its oil exports to China to around 70,000 barrels per day in 1997, 100,000 barrels per day in 1998, and to nearly 200,000 barrels per day in 2000.[53] China also reached an agreement with the Omani government to increase Oman's crude supplies to China from less than 20,000 barrels per day in 1995, to 100,000 barrels per day in 1996. Later, Oman's crude oil supplies to China jumped to about 230,000 barrels per day in 1997, enabling China to replace Japan as the primary importer of Omani crude.[54] Saudi Arabia's ARAMCO signed an agreement with the China Petrochemical Corporation in October 1997 to increase Saudi crude supplies to China from its current level of around 30,000 barrels per day to over 60,000 barrels per day.[55]

---

50 These numbers are according to a study conducted by Kang Wu and Fereidun Fesharaki from the East–West centre in Honolulu and quoted in *Oil & Gas Journal*, Vol. 93, No. 35, 28 August 1995, p. 105.
51 *FBIS-CHI-94-209*, 28 October 1994, pp. 89.
52 'China Said to Triple Oil Imports from Iran', in *New York Times Current Events Edition*, 31 May 1995, p. D15.
53 'China Turns to Gulf for Crude, Praises UAE's Marine Progress', in *http://www.uaeinteract.com/newsreport/19970612.htm*, p. 2.
54 *Ibid.*
55 *Ibid.*

China's interest in the Gulf and Arabian Peninsula region was not only confined to its purchases of crude oil, but also included joint oil exploration and development. Since it was suggested that China's oil sector needs $180 billion in investment for increasing refining capacity and expanding oil exploration, prospecting, and production operations, China had been paying great attention to encouraging governments and private companies from the Gulf region to invest in China's oil and gas sectors.[56]

This demonstrates China's interest in the region was reality. Its interest in Gulf oil has even influenced many of its policy decisions toward Gulf countries, particularly Iran and Iraq, which contain 20 per cent of the world proven oil reserves. China's arms and technology supplies to Iran and its continued cooperation with Iran in military fields, despite US opposition, could well be attributed to the fact that China needed Iranian oil to improve or sustain its economic development at levels that enabled China to feed and support 1.2 billion people in its own territory. With regards to Iraq, China called on the UN several times to lift or ease its sanctions against Iraq.[57] China was interested in promoting cooperation with Iraq in the oil, irrigation, transportation, communication, industrial, and commercial fields.[58] The real consequences of China's concern over its future oil supplies will be visible in the event of any future US-led effort designed to contain or pressure major oil suppliers in the Gulf region including Iran and Iraq, which China is unlikely to support. However, if an overwhelming international consensus existed supporting such action, China might prefer to move towards abstaining from voting in the UN Security Council, but it is still unlikely that it would actively support such an action. During the Gulf crisis, China had no other alternative but to support the UN Security Council resolutions on Iraq. But, it has remained unsupportive of the military actions against Iraq during and after the crisis. This can be understood largely in terms of China's interest in Gulf oil. China's need of energy from the Gulf region and Peninsula has also influenced China's decision to follow the line set by the UN, and fully supported by the GCC countries, regarding resolutions on the arms and economic embargo against Iraq. Except for a very few reports, China has not broken the UN embargo against Iraq since the mid-1990s.

56 It is said that China's energy market needs US$1,000 billion in investement over the next two decades. See *OAPEC Bulletin*, Vol. 21, Nos 8–9, August/September 1995, pp. 12–13.
57 See, for instance, *FBIS-NES-94-066*, 6 April 1994, p. 17; *FBIS-NES-95-045*, 3 March 1995, p. 16; and *FBIS-NES-95-070*, 12 April 1995, pp. 53–4.
58 *FBIS-NES-95-075*, 19 April 1995, pp. 34–5.

CONCLUSION

In this chapter, we have discussed China's foreign policy toward the Gulf and Arabian Peninsula region by dividing China's interactions with the region into three main phases. In Phase 1, China's early involvement in the Gulf and Arabian Peninsula region was started only after the Bandung Conference. After the conference, China had tried to establish relations with the countries of the region that had participated in the conference. But, its ability to do so was limited due to the existing strong ties between most of the Gulf countries and the West, especially Great Britain and the United States, as well as to the Gulf countries' early unfavourable perceptions of China. Therefore, China found it easier for itself to influence the region through supporting the idea of armed struggle throughout the region. Its support for the liberation movements in the Gulf region stemmed from China's ideological principle to defeat Western imperialism and its lackeys in the region. As a result, China did not, during this period, enjoy good relations with the governments of the Gulf and Arabian Peninsula countries. Thus, its support for armed struggle through the liberation movements in South Yemen and Oman limited China's ability to pursue good ties with the countries of the Gulf.

In Phase 2, China's fear of the Soviet Union had influenced China's decision to shift its foreign policy objectives in the Gulf region away from supporting the armed struggle and the liberation movements and towards establishing political and economic ties with the countries of the Gulf region. Once China had begun suspending its support for the liberation movements in the region, the doors started to open for China to establish diplomatic relations with some of the Gulf countries. This was marked by the establishment of diplomatic relations with Kuwait and Iran in the early 1970s and Oman in the late 1970s. China, during this period, started to become closer than ever before to Kuwait and Iran in perceiving the growing influence of the Soviet Union in and around the Gulf and Arabian Peninsula region, particularly in Iraq and later in Afghanistan, and its impact on the security of the region. China continued to push for isolating Moscow from the region by encouraging both Iran and Iraq to settle their disputes peacefully and by providing available military assistance to Iran as an alternative to Moscow. China enjoyed its first substantial profits from the situation in the Gulf region following the outbreak of the Iran–Iraq war where China accumulated economic and political assets. China's diplomatic relations with the Gulf and Arabian Peninsula countries increased to include establishing diplomatic relationships with Oman, the UAE, Qatar, and Bahrain. In addition, China, during this period, made itself very attractive to Saudi Arabia by showing its willingness to supply the Kingdom with advanced weapons.

In Phase 3, China's interest in the Gulf and Arabian Peninsula region was motivated by China's drive to increase its economic capabilities, particularly after becoming a net oil importer. As a result, the Gulf's oil attracted China's foreign policy makers. They became willing to cooperate with some of the countries of the region in the military field to secure the supply of crude oil to China, generate hard currency by selling advanced military technology, and expand their trade relations with the region. Therefore, during this phase, China sought to use every possible means to upgrade its relations with the countries of the Gulf and Arabian Peninsula region and to promote better economic and political ties with the region. In short, it was the Chinese economic need that prompted China's interest in the region in the 1990s. Oil and market were China's main interests. China wanted to secure long-term independent suppliers of oil in order to meet the continued rise in China's oil consumption. China also saw the region as a place where it could generate hard currency by selling military equipment and technology and increase the volume of its commercial exports. Therefore, in the Chinese perspective, the Gulf's oil and market are essential for China to stay a strong competitor in today's world economy and sustain the well-being of over 1.2 billion Chinese. In sum, China's foreign policy towards the Gulf region throughout the three phases has been influenced by China's interactions and relations with the United States and the Soviet Union, and its drive to increase or sustain its economic and political capabilities by fostering better ties with the countries of the region.

5 China's relations with Iraq, Iran, and Yemen

In the previous chapter, we discussed China's foreign policy toward the Gulf and Arabian Peninsula region in general. We concluded that China's foreign policy toward the Gulf region was a reflection of its relations with the United States and the Soviet Union and China's drive to increase its economic capabilities by deepening its economic and political ties with the countries of the region. In the following two chapters, we are going to survey China's relations with each of the Gulf and Arabian Peninsula countries and discuss the different variables that influenced China's foreign policy toward them. We will argue here that China's foreign policy toward each country of the region has been a reflection of China's overall foreign policy in the Gulf and Arabian Peninsula region. It is true that China, at certain periods, gave some countries of the Gulf region more attention than others, but this was largely a product of its overall foreign policy towards the Gulf and Arabian Peninsula region. Some countries of the region, at certain times, were seen by the Chinese government as closer to China's view of both superpowers than others. Therefore, the Chinese government would pay more attention to those countries to establish good ties with and try, as much as it could, to pull them away from the influence of either power. On the whole, China might have used different strategies to get closer to the countries of the Gulf region, but its relations with each country in the region had been a reflection of China's overall foreign policy toward the whole Gulf and Arabian Peninsula region. In this chapter, we are going to examine China's bilateral relations with Iraq, Iran, and Yemen. Chapter 6 will examine China's relations with the member countries of the Gulf Cooperation Council.

CHINA AND IRAQ

Chinese–Iraqi relations in the early days (1949–1957)

When the PRC was established in late 1949, Iraq and all Arab League members maintained their diplomatic relations with the Nationalist regime, which had made Taiwan its new headquarters, as the legitimate sole representative of all China. Iraq voted with the Arab League members in August 1950 to recognize the Nationalist government in Taiwan, rather than the Communist government on the mainland as the legitimate sole representative of all China. Iraq, despite the abstention of many Arab countries, voted on 1 February 1951 in favour of the United Nations General Assembly Resolution 498 6V to condemn the PRC for aggression in Korea. In addition to that, Iraq, one of the major independent Gulf states at that time, was engaged in a security alliance with the United States and Great Britain under the Baghdad Pact of 1954. Therefore, politically, China had no chance to gain influence for itself in Iraq in order to prevent the West from succeeding in the Gulf region. Economically, the two sides had nothing to offer to each other. Their trade relations prior to 1955 were almost non-existent. Thus, recognizing its weakness to influence Iraq, the Chinese government classified the Iraqi regime as part of the capitalist camp 'controlled by Western imperialism'.

Following the Bandung Conference, the Chinese made attempts to improve their relations with the participants, including Iraq. In their account, the Third World was believed to have potential for the Chinese to wage an international struggle against the capitalist camp. However, following the conference, Egypt captured most of China's attention in the Arab World; and Iraq was not regarded as a potential ally in the struggle against the West. As a result, China–Iraq relations did not witness an immediate improvement. This slowdown in the development of China–Iraq relations, following the conference, was largely due to the continuing American and British presence and influence in Iraq, as a result of the Baghdad Pact. China, therefore, was unable to create good ties with Iraq because of the strong presence of the United States and Great Britain in that country.

China's changing relations with Iraq (1958–1959)

It was only in July 1958 that China's policy toward the Arab World, in particular, and the Third World, in general, began to view Iraq as a potential ally in the struggle against the West in the Arab World. This shift in China's foreign policy toward Iraq was due to the success of the July 1958 revolution in Iraq headed by General Abd-al-Karim Qasim against the royalist regime. China's immediate reaction to the development in Iraq was full support to Qasim. China's support to Qasim can be explained as the following:

1   China saw Qasim as a new revolutionary leader who could challenge Nasser for Arab World authority, particularly after the Chinese dissatisfaction with Nasser's harsh treatment of Arab communists in Egypt and Syria, with his neutralist policy between the two camps, and with his support for Tibetan nationalists.

2   Qasim's decision to withdraw Iraq from the Baghdad Pact was viewed by the Chinese as a strong Iraqi challenge to American and British authority in the Gulf region, in particular, and the Arab World, in general.
3   Unlike Nasser, Qasim, particularly from July 1958 to March 1959, gave the communists in Iraq some key positions in Iraqi public life. Although they were not represented in the principal political offices, the communists enjoyed some influence on Qasim during at that time (Powles 1991).
4   Unlike many Arab states, including Egypt, Iraq did not support the Tibetan nationalist revolt against the Chinese communist government in 1958 to 1959 (Harris 1993: 104).
5   To China, the Iraqi revolution represented an encouraging step toward the liberation of the entire region from Western domination.

Diplomatic relations between China and Iraq were established in August 1958, which marked China's fourth recognition by an Arab state since its establishment in 1949. Furthermore, China was eager to defend Qasim's regime verbally and launch its first harsh attack on Nasser when Egypt supported an unsuccessful coup attempt to overthrow Qasim in March 1959.[1]

New challenges in China–Iraq relations (1959–1974)

All the above reasons, plus China's need to use the region to undermine Soviet rapprochement with the West, marked China's willingness to support Qasim's regime in Iraq. However, political and economic relations began to develop slowly after March 1959. This was due to the following reasons:

1   China was accused by the Iraqi regime of being behind the communist-inspired rioting in the Iraqi cities of Mosul in March and Kirkuk in July 1959;
2   the Iraqi regime's persecution of communist party members following the Kirkuk riots angered China;
3   China was unhappy about the Iraqi delay in sending an ambassador to Beijing, who was appointed only in April 1960.

Despite all these developments, and as China began to perceive both the United States and the Soviet Union as the main threat to its own security and world stability, the Chinese government sought to maintain its support

---

1   China's criticized Nasser's policies toward Iraq and compared them to Chiang Kai-shek's anti-communist policies. See *Beijing Review*, No. 12, April 1957.

of the Iraqi government in order to limit a full separation between China and Iraq and, therefore, limit Western and Soviet influence in Iraq. This support included offering Iraq vehicles for civil defence; however, Baghdad ultimately favoured more generous American aid. The Chinese government also supported the Iraqi government's efforts to control the direction of Iraqi oil exports. An article in *Renmin Ribao* on 16 February 1962 stated that:

> The British, U.S, and French [are] seeking to use the Iraq Petroleum Company and other monopolies to keep their hold on the country's economy and prevent it from developing an independent national economy; and they [are] exerting pressure on Iraq to prevent it from enforcing its oil law against foreign monopolies.
> (Cited in *Peking Review*, Vol. 5, No. 8, 23 February 1962: 22)

Zhou Enlai, in his message of greetings to Qasim in July 1962, stressed that the growing friendly relations between China and Iraq were in conformity with the common desire of the Chinese and Iraqi peoples and were important in promoting solidarity between Asian and African nations as well as preserving world peace. He finished his message wishing the Iraqi people 'new success in their fighting against imperialism and old and new colonialism'.[2] Chinese Vice-Premier Chen Yi, speaking at the National Day reception given by the Iraqi Ambassador, reiterated that the 'Iraqi people's just struggle' to 'oppose imperialism and safeguard national independence would always have the support of the Chinese people'.[3] On 10 January 1963, China and Iraq signed an agreement to renew for another year the trade agreement that was signed between them in March 1960. Under the agreement, China would export various commodities including industrial equipment, electrical appliances, silk and cotton, steel and timber, while Iraq would export dates, crude oil, oil products, wool and other products.[4] As a result, trade volume between the two sides increased substantially from US$8.5 million in 1959 to US$17.61 million in 1963 (Editorial Board 1984: 840). Despite Iraqi governments, including the new Iraqi regime that China recognized on 12 February 1963,[5] continuing the suppression of Iraqi communists, China continued its efforts to establish close relations with the Iraqi government. This can be explained mainly in terms of China's willingness to offset the United States and the Soviet Union's influence in that country. However, by 1965, China had become frustrated with Iraq's

---

2 *Peking Review*, Vol. 5, No. 29, 20 July 1962, p. 21.
3 *Ibid.*
4 *Peking Review*, Vol. 6, No. 3, 18 January 1963, p. 20.
5 *Peking Review*, Vol. 6, No. 7, 15 February 1963, p. 19.

foreign policy and the Iraqi regime's continuing suppression of communists in Iraq. And, after the 1967 Arab–Israeli war, China became convinced that it would be problematic to work with the Iraqi government, who was dependent on the Soviet Union for political and technical support since the war, in waging the struggle against Western and social imperialism in the Gulf, in particular, and the Arab World, in general. Thus, national liberation movements captured most of China's attention in the Gulf region during most of the Cultural Revolution period.

In the late 1960s and early 1970s, China's world outlook had changed towards perceiving the Soviet Union as the main threat to China's security, in particular, and world stability, in general. In the Gulf and Arabian Peninsula region, the Chinese were afraid that the Soviet Union would be able to sway the region to join the Soviet-proposed Asian collective security system as a step towards filling the power vacuum in the region. Thus, China's interests in Iraq in the early 1970s were manifested around preventing the Soviets from succeeding in Iraq. So, China again tried to woo the Iraqi regime. This time, the Chinese government tried to avoid criticizing Iraq's foreign policy. Instead, it started to welcome some of Iraq's foreign policy positions including Iraqi opposition to a political settlement of the Arab–Israeli conflict and Iraq's support of extreme Palestinian organizations (Yodfat 1977: 10). This had paved the way for the signing of an agreement on economic and technical cooperation between China and Iraq on 21 June 1971. According to the agreement, China granted Iraq an interest-free loan of US$36 million (Bartke 1989: 73). But, all these signs of improvement in China–Iraq relations in 1970 and 1971 did not last long. The signing in April 1972 of a Soviet–Iraqi Friendship Treaty had led once again to a cooling-off in China's relations with Iraq. Then, China moved to consolidate its relations with two other countries in the Gulf region, Kuwait and Iran, who shared China's concern over Iraq's ties with the Soviet Union. It is important to note that the cooling-off of China–Iraq relations did not lead to a complete collapse in the relationship. This was mainly due to China's policy of keeping as many contacts as possible with the Iraqi government in order to prevent a total breakdown of relations. This strategy was aimed specifically toward preventing the possibility of total Iraqi dependence on the Soviet Union. China continued participation in Iraq's celebration of its national days. China also continued economic relations with Iraq; this was obvious in the continuing trade relations between the two countries and in the signing of a protocol with Baghdad in December 1972 for technical and economic cooperation between the two countries.[6]

---

6 Bartke 1989: 73; and BBC, *SWB FE 37161*, p. A4/1.

China's renewed interest in Iraq (1975–1979)

Prior to 1975, China's interest in Iraq, as a revolutionary state, declined rapidly after the signing of the Soviet–Iraqi Treaty of Friendship. A renewal in China's interest in Iraq followed the decline in Iraqi dependence on the Soviet Union from 1975 onward and the improvement of Iraq–Iran relations from March of that year. The Chinese government welcomed the signing of a joint communiqué in March 1975 between Iraq and Iran, in which the two sides agreed that 'the region must be made immune from any foreign interference'.[7]

This period witnessed improvement in economic relations between China and Iraq, and relaxation in their political relations. Economically, trade relations reached their highest point, in 1975, than ever before. The total trade in 1975 was 8.5 times larger than that of 1973, and almost US$60 million higher than that of 1974. In May 1975, China agreed to purchase more sulphur, dates, and chemical fertilizers from Iraq (Calabrese 1991: 90). An agreement was signed in 1978 between the two countries for the import to China of 100,000 tons of Iraq's sulphur.[8] China also worked in July 1975 on constructing the Mosul Bridge I, which opened to traffic in July 1980, linking the Baghdad–Mosul express highway with the international road from Mosul to Turkey, and connecting Mosul city on the west bank of the Tigris and its developing outskirts on the east bank (Bartke 1989: 75). In November 1976, China agreed to construct a sports hall in Baghdad as part of a new economic and technical cooperation agreement (Bartke 1989: 75). The Chinese also aided the building of a woollen washing and spinning mill in Kifri in July 1978 (Bartke 1989: 75, nothing more was heard of this project).18 In August 1978, China signed a protocol with Iraq on the construction of the Sherquat highway bridge on the Tigris in northern Iraq (Bertke 1989: 75, again nothing more was heard of this project). Politically, several official visits took place between the two sides. The most significant of them being the visit to Beijing by Iraqi Vice-President Muhyiddin Marouf in July 1975. China's Vice-Premier Deng Xiaoping, in his banquet speech, praised Iraq and welcomed the new Iraqi–Iranian consultation, and called upon all the Gulf countries to resolve their differences among themselves in order to prevent foreign intervention.[9]

The improvement in China's economic and political relations with Iraq during this period was a reflection of China's foreign policy. Prior to 1975, China had less chance to improve its ties with Iraq and, therefore, had no chance to influence the government of that country; this limitation was due

---

7 *Peking Review*, Vol. 18, No. 12, 21 March 1975, p. 29.
8 *Middle East Economic Survey*, Vol. 21, No. 33, 5 June 1978, p. 7.
9 *Peking Review*, Vol. 18, No. 28, 11 July 1975, pp. 8–9.

to the strong political and security engagement of Iraq with the Soviet Union. But, after the decline in Iraqi dependence on the Soviet Union and the new Iraqi–Iranian initiative, China found a great opportunity to establish new economic and political ties with Iraq without severing its ties with Kuwait and Iran, who shared China's fear of Soviet–Iraqi ties. To China, Soviet–Iraqi ties presented a great deal of insecurity concerning the Soviet penetration in the Gulf and Arabian Peninsula region. Thus, China was hoping for a cooling-off in Soviet–Iraq relationships in order to prevent the Soviet threat to the Gulf region. Once the decline in Soviet-Iraq relationships began to occur, China could not resist the opportunity to take charge in improving its ties with Iraq and encouraging the Iraqi government to work with the countries of the Gulf region to settle their disputes peacefully and without foreign, mainly Soviet, intervention.

Chinese–Iraqi relations in the 1980s

Because of its fear of Soviet intervention, China never wanted to see a war in the Gulf region, particularly a war that involved Iraq and Iran. To the Chinese government, a war between Iraq and Iran would make the two vulnerable to Soviet penetration. Thus, after the war broke out, China called on the Iraqi and Iranian governments to resolve their disputes peacefully through negotiation and avoid direct military confrontation.[10] China continued to argue the war was benefiting the Soviet Union and Israel instead of either Iraq or Iran.

China, who perceived some signs of decline in Iraq's dependence on the Soviet Union since 1975, did not want to see a return to the pre-1975 Iraqi–Soviet relationship. Resolutely, China adopted a neutral position towards Iraq and Iran during their war. Its neutral policy regarding Iraq was evident in China's political, economic, and military relations with Iraq. Politically, China focused its efforts on:

1   avoiding criticizing either side's military and political actions against the other;
2   stressing the need for a peaceful settlement of Iraq's disputes with Iran;
3   welcoming the improvement of Iraq's relations with other Arab countries;
4   praising the Iraqi leadership's opposition to hegemony and intervention by foreign powers in Iraq's internal affairs;
5   welcoming the Iraqi leadership's opposition to the Soviet invasion of Afghanistan;

10 *Beijing Review*, No. 35, 5 May 1980, pp. 11–12.

6 applauding the flexibility in Iraq's attitudes towards the United States;[11]
7 defending Iraq's 'legitimate right to develop nuclear technology for peaceful purposes', and criticizing the Israeli air attack on the Iraqi Tuweitha nuclear plant in 1981;[12] and
8 identifying the Soviet Union as the ultimate beneficiary of the continuing conflict between Iraq and Iran.[13]

On the economic front, several agreements were signed by the two sides. These included an agreement in 1980 for the import to China of Iraqi nitrogenous fertilizers worth US$46 million.[14] An agreement on economic and technical cooperation was signed on 8 May 1981 during Iraqi First Deputy Prime Minister Taha Yassin Ramadan's visit to Beijing, and a Chinese–Iraqi economic and technical cooperation committee was established to further joint construction, agriculture, and high industry ventures (Harris 1993: 223). An agreement in December 1985 was formed in which China would import, the next year, Iraqi phosphate, sulphur, palm dates, and other products, while Iraq would import Chinese textiles, light industrial products, metal ware, and mineral products. The agreement stipulated that China would continue to take part in Iraq's construction.[15] A five-year agreement for China–Iraq economic, technical, and trade cooperation was signed in 1986 during Chinese States Councillor Zhang Jinfu's visit to Baghdad (Xu Wei 1989: 12–13). Under the agreement, Chinese firms would contract projects for building irrigation and drainage facilities, highways, bridges, and railways in Iraq.[16] China also furthered its joint construction project with Iraq. Chinese technicians began, in May 1980, their preparations for construction of the Number 4 bridge (the Saddam Bridge) on the Tigris River at Mosul. This project was completed in August 1984. In July 1986, three China-contracted dams were completed on Shamiya. China worked on construction of the Kifil Shinafiya irrigation project in May 1984. In March 1985, China agreed to construct its first three residential buildings in Baghdad. The project was completed in January 1987 by China's State Construction Engineering Corporation (CSCEC) at a cost of about US$9.3 million.[17] China also agreed in August 1985 to rebuild the Dibis Dam about 40 km north of Kirkuk at a cost of US$10 million.[18] A

---

11 See *Beijing Review*, 8 September 1980, pp. 15–16.
12 *Beijing Review*, 25 August 1981, p. 12.
13 *Beijing Review*, No. 4, 25 January 1984, pp. 14–15.
14 The agreement was signed in Baghdad by representatives of the Chinese Import Corporation and the Iraqi State Organization for Export. See *Middle East Economic Survey*, Vol. 23, No. 45, 21 July 1980, p. 4.
15 *FBIS-CHI-86-083*, 30 April 1986, p. I3.
16 *FBIS-CHI-86-083*, p. I3.
17 *FBIS-CHI-87-009*, 14 January 1987, p. I2.
18 Bartke 1989: 74; and *FBIS-CHI-85*, 157, 14 August 1985, p. I1.

Chinese team finished, in November 1985, drilling three production wells in the al-Zubayr oilfield in southern Iraq.[19] Reportedly, there were 20,000 Chinese workers and technicians working in Iraq by April 1986. They belonged to eight Chinese firms that provided labour services or contracted projects in Iraq.[20]

In the 1980s, China–Iraq trade relations experienced a setback. The prolonged Iraq–Iran war put the once-strong Iraqi economy into decline (see Table A.1 in the appendix). In view of Iraq's wartime economy, China offered a two-year extension for Iraq to pay for Chinese exports so as to maintain China–Iraq trade and economic cooperation. Iraq, however, failed to repay China's trade loans on time, because it had run out of foreign exchange reserves during the Iraq–Iran war (Xu Wei 1989: 12–13).

Once the war was over, China was eager to participate in the post-war reconstruction of Iraq. Chinese Vice-Premier Tian Jiyun visited Iraq on 13 March 1989. His visit was said to encourage China's participation in Iraq's post-war reconstruction and to bring about the realization of peace between Iraq and Iran. He was the most senior official to visit Iraq since the two countries established relations in 1958.[21] In April 1989, the CSCEC completed the Hindiya barrage project, which started in October 1984. The project cost US$240 million and was one of the largest projects China had ever built in a foreign country. The large-scale engineering complex included the barrage, a navigation lock, a fish passage, six bridges, a 60-MW power station, and housing.[22] The CSCEC undertook another project to lay a 132-kV electricity cable in Baghdad, which was worth US$30.4 million. It also worked on the north Jazira irrigation scheme, which was worth a total of US$170 million.[23]

While China–Iraq trade relations witnessed a deceleration, their arms trade reached its highest point. China's arms sales to Iraq became the dominant moneymaker for China with Iraq in the 1980s. Between 1982 and 1986, Iraq became China's primary arms customer in the world with total imports of US$3,300 million (ACDA 1987: 127–30). Iraq, along with Iran, became China's largest arms recipients in the world receiving about 80 per cent of China's total arms sales. Despite their denial of selling arms to Iraq during the Iraq–Iran war, many have reported that China had sold to Iraq, from 1981 to 1988, four B-6 bombers, 700 T-59 main battle tanks, 600 T-69

---

19 The work was completed under a contract signed between the Chinese Petroleum Engineering Construction Corporation and Iraq National Oil Company. It was reported that Iraq had asked the Chinese side to send another team and extend the contract for one more year. See *Middle East Economic Survey*, Vol. 29, No. 9, 9 December 1985, p. A.9.
20 *FBIS-CHI-86-083*, p. 13.
21 *FBIS-CHI-89-048*, 14 March 1989, p. 10; and *FBIS-CHI-89-049*, 15 March 1989, p. 11.
22 *FBIS-CHI-89-083*, 2 May 1989, p. 5.
23 *Ibid*.

main battle tanks, 650 Type-531 armoured personnel carriers, 720 Type-59/1 130-mm towed guns, 128 C-601 anti-ship missiles, and an unspecified number of the Hai Ying-2 ship-to-ship missiles (SIPRI 1989: 252).

In summary, China's policy toward Iraq, during the Iran–Iraq war, consisted of engaging Iraq in a better relationship with China. Politically, economically, and militarily, China had sought to benefit from the situation in the Gulf by extending its political, economic, and military cooperation with Iraq. Its aim was to prevent, or at least limit, the possibility of Iraqi dependence on the Soviet Union.

China and Iraq during and after the Kuwait crisis (1990–1999)

It was the Iraqi military involvement in the war with Iran that limited the improvement of China's economic and, to some degree, political relations with Iraq. Thus, when the war with Iran was ended, China's hope for better economic and political relations with Iraq increased. Yet, the Iraqi invasion of Kuwait in August 1990, and the subsequent economic sanctions against China after the suppression of the pro-democracy student demonstrations of June 1989 in Tiananmen Square, limited China's ability to manoeuvre in favour of closer ties with the Iraqi regime. During the Gulf crisis, China supported all UN Security Council Resolutions on Iraq except Resolution 678, where it abstained from voting. China opposed the Iraqi invasion of Kuwait and called upon the Iraqi government to withdraw its troops from Kuwait and solve its disputes with the Kuwaiti government peacefully. This Chinese stand was presented to Iraqi officials during Wu Xueqian's, Chinese State Council Vice-Premier, visit to Baghdad in September 1990,[24] and in a written message from China's President Yang Shangkun delivered to Iraqi President Saddam Hussain by Chinese Foreign Minister Qian Qichen on 12 November 1990.[25] The Chinese government even presented its own six-point proposal for a peaceful solution to the crisis (see previous chapter).

Chinese action within the UN was limited to either abstaining from voting on certain resolutions on Iraq or denouncing some of them, but never to veto them. This policy was demonstrated clearly during China's support for all United Nations resolutions on Iraq. It never vetoed any resolutions on Iraq. It only abstained from voting on UN Security Council Resolution 678, which was adopted by the Security Council at its 2,963rd meeting on 29 November 1990, and clearly authorized member states to use all necessary means to restore Kuwait's sovereignty. It also abstained from voting on UN Security Council Resolution 688, which was adopted at the Security

---

24 *FBIS-NES-90-178*, 13 September 1990, pp. 27–8.
25 *FBIS-NES-90-220*, 14 November 1990, pp. 21–2.

Council's 2,982nd meeting on 5 April 1991, on Iraqi suppression of the Kurdish rebellion on the grounds that Iraq was practising its sovereignty within its own territory.[26] This Chinese policy of not opposing the UN resolutions on Iraq was directed mainly by China's desire to see the easing and lifting of Western and Japanese economic and technical sanctions against China and to prevent further political and economic instability in the Gulf region.

In the aftermath of Western military operations against Baghdad, China's relations with Iraq were limited by the UN sanctions against Iraq. The most significant Chinese loss in its relations with Iraq, following the war, had been the loss of an important arms buyer and an economic partner. China had supplied Iraq with billions of US dollars worth of arms in the 1980s, generating much needed hard currency to develop China's military capabilities. After UN military sanctions on Iraq, China found itself unable to redeem its status as one of the top arms sellers to Iraq. However, different reports have connected China with providing nuclear and technological assistance to Iraq through a third party (Jordan) or by providing such assistance to develop Iraqi-sponsored nuclear facilities in Algeria and Mauritania (Timperlake and Triplett 1999: 85–96). Economically, it was estimated that China's top four overseas construction companies had lost US$1.7 billion during the crisis. The China State Construction Engineering Corp. reported a loss of US$856 million, the China Road and Bridge Engineering Co. US$109 million, China International Water and Electricity Corp. US$30 million and China Metallurgical Construction Corp. over US$10 million (Lake 1991: 38). These losses comprised payments for completed projects, lost deposits in local banks, abandoned plants, and the costs of repatriating workers in both Iraq and Kuwait. The UN sanctions on Iraq had caused China's trade relations with Iraq to reach their lowest ever level (see Table A.1 in the Appendix). It had also prevented Chinese firms from extending their economic cooperation with Iraq.[27]

Chinese officials had repeatedly called upon the UN Security Council to lift or at least ease the sanctions imposed on Iraq. Their interest is for China to expand the scope of commercial, industrial, and oil cooperation with Iraq. Chinese Foreign Minister Qian Qichen, for example, publicly stated he was in favour of a 'gradual' removal of sanctions against Iraq. After talks in Beijing with Iraqi Foreign Minister Muhammad Sa'id al-Sahhaf on 2 March 1995, the Chinese Foreign Minister declared that 'the international community should objectively evaluate Iraqi implementations of resolutions of

---

26 BBC, *SWB*, Part 3, *FE/1043*, 11 April 1991, p. A4/1.
27 See United Nations Resolution 661 that was adopted by the Security Council at its 2,933rd meeting on 6 August 1990 and affirmed United Nations sanctions against Iraq.

the Security Council and consider the gradual lifting of sanctions imposed on Iraq. This Chinese position was reaffirmed during Iraqi Vice-President Taha Yasin Ramadan's visit to Beijing three months later.[28] A number of Chinese firms, reportedly, have already resumed their activities in order to implement contracts and agreements that have already been signed with the Iraqi side in the past. However, the Chinese want to be able to establish and implement new economic contracts and agreements with Iraq, particularly in the field of reconstructing Iraq's infrastructure, which has not been rebuilt since its destruction by allied forces during their attacks on Iraqi buildings, bridges, and highways.[29]

China, who reportedly has already signed a trade and economic cooperation agreement with Iraq that will take effect when Iraq's oil-for-food deal with the UN is settled, welcomed the memorandum of understanding reached by Iraq and the UN for the implementation of UN Resolution 986, oil for food.[30] It also supported the UN Security-General's proposal in February 1998 to increase the limit on Iraqi oil exports.[31] China had a great opportunity to supply Iraq with foodstuffs, medicine, and other commodities in accordance with the memorandum, which allows Iraq to sell US$2 billion worth of oil every six months to raise money to buy food and medicine.[32] Prior to the China–Iraq agreement, China had donated medicinal raw materials to Iraq valued at US$360,000 in 1995, and US$500,000 in April 1996. China also signed a production-sharing agreement with Iraq for the development of the al-Ahdab oil field in August 1996. This was the first agreement to be initiated by Iraq, who had been carrying out upstream talks with foreign firms during the past five years. The agreement was signed in Beijing by the Iraqi Oil Minister, Dr 'Amir Rashid, and senior officials of the China National Petroleum Corporation (CNPC). This agreement called for a four-year development plan. In the initial stage, the Chinese firm would undertake, outside Iraq, an analysis of seismic work already done in the field, while Iraqi firms would carry out the construction of infrastructural projects and drilling activities on behalf of the Chinese. CNPC would pay the Iraqi firms once the United Nations sanctions were lifted.[33] The two countries also signed a trade, economic, and technical cooperation agreement during the Iraqi Minister of Trade, Dr

---

28 *FBIS-NES-95-042*, 3 March 1995, p. 16; and China News Digest, *http://www.cnd.org/CND-Global/CND-Global.95.2nd/CND-Global.95-06-27.html*, p. 4.
29 *FBIS-NES-95-070*, 12 April 1995, pp. 53–4; and *Beijing Review*, Vol. 37, No. 4, 24–30 January 1994.
30 BBC, *SWB, FE/2622*, 27 May 1996, p. A/4.
31 BBC, *SWB, FE/3142*, 4 February 1998, p. G/1.
32 China News Digest, *http://www.cnd.org/CND-Global/CND-Global.96.3rd/CND-Global.96-08-06.html*, p. 2.
33 *Middle East Economic Survey*, Vol. 39, No. 61, 25 November 1996, p. A3.

Muhammad Mahdi's, visit to Beijing in August 1997. The agreement contained provisions related to developing and diversifying trade between China and Iraq, promoting economic and technical cooperation in various economic sectors, and launching training programmes for experts and technicians. This agreement replaces the 1981 agreement. In appreciation of friendly relations, the Chinese government offered the Iraqi government a grant of 5 million Chinese yuan.[34]

The Chinese government had expressed its concern and was critical of the US air attack on Iraq's military targets following Iraq's attack, on 31 August 1996, on positions of the Patriotic Union of Kurdistan in the north.[35] It had also reaffirmed its position that China does not favour the use of force in handling international affairs. A commentary in *Xinhua News Agency News Bulletin* by its reporter Wang Zizhen entitled 'Unjust Causes Find Scant Support' criticized the United States and Britain for 'unjust actions' against Iraq. It spoke against the US air raid on Iraq and criticized the British-drafted resolution to the UN to condemn Iraq for using force against the Kurds in the northern part of the country.[36] The Chinese representative to the UN opposed the draft resolution submitted by Britain and made it clear that his country opposes the US air attack on Iraq. China had continued to emphasize the need for respecting Iraq's sovereignty during Turkey's military action into northern Iraq to eliminate forces of the Kurdish Workers' Party. The Chinese Foreign Ministry called upon Turkey's government to immediately halt its 'military incursion' into Iraq and respect the sovereignty and territorial integrity of Iraq.[37]

On the issue of the Iraqi government dispute with the UN Special Commission (UNSCOM),[38] China had emphasized its opposition to the use of force, the threat of force, or any method that further aggravated tension; and it had always urged the relevant sides to exercize self-restraint and properly resolve the issue through dialogue and cooperation. As the Iraqi government dispute with UNSCOM escalated in December 1997–January 1998, as a result of the Iraqi side's refusal to allow the UNSCOM team to inspect what it called 'presidential' or 'sovereign' sites, the Chinese Foreign Ministry stated its position by saying:

---

34 BBC, *SWB*, *FE/2994*, 11 August 1997, p. G/5.
35 BBC, *SWB*, *FE/2708*, 4 September 1996, p. G/1.
36 BBC, *SWB*, *FE/2713*, 10 September 1996, p. G/1.
37 BBC, *SWB*, *FE/2924*, 21 May 1997, p. G/3.
38 UNSCOM was founded in April 1991 in accordance with the UN Security Council's Resolution 687, which declares that Iraq shall accept unconditionally, under international supervision, the 'destruction, removal or rendering harmless' of its weapons of mass destruction and ballistic missiles with a range over 150 km. Centre for Non-proliferation Studies, *http://cns.miis.edu/research/iraq/uns_chro.htm*, p. 1.

The UN Security Council's resolutions should be comprehensively and earnestly carried out; and Iraq should fully cooperate with UNSCOM and fully carry out its relevant obligations so that UNSCOM can accomplish the Security Council's mandate at an early date ... The legitimate concerns of Iraq, a sovereign state, should be respected. It is essential for UNSCOM to improve its operations, including the composition of the inspection team, which should as much as possible reflect the diversity of the UN, and should be composed of personnel from more countries.

(BBC, *SWB*, *FE/3127*, 17 January 1998: G/1)

In the Security Council, China expressed its opposition to the US plan to launch a military attack against Iraq following the tensions caused by arms inspections in Iraq. Premier Li Peng, while visiting Moscow in February 1998, issued, with the Russian leadership, a joint statement on the Iraqi situation that called for:

A peaceful settlement of the crisis that would ensure Iraq's full compliance with the appropriate resolutions of the UN Security Council and guarantee that Iraq's mass destruction weapon potential is eliminated, and which would open the way for lifting the sanctions against Iraq, first of all, the oil embargo.

(BBC, *SWB*, *FE/3155*, 19 February 1998: G/1)

The above statement shows that China's concern about Iraq is centred on three main points. The first point is the peaceful settlement of the dispute. China continued to stress the need to avoid the use of force and to bring about a political solution to the UN disputes with Iraq. The major force behind this policy stemmed from China's fear that international forces could be legitimized to use force against individual sovereign states like China, which has ambitions over Taiwan and territories in the South China Sea. The second point is the need to eliminate Iraq's weapons of mass destruction. This policy was motivated by two main factors: (1) China wanted to make its statement acceptable to Western governments, whose main concern was Iraq's weapons of mass destruction; and (2) China wanted to eliminate Iraq's potential threat to the security of the Gulf and Arabian Peninsula region, on which China had become largely dependent for its energy needs. The third point is the need to lift the sanctions, mainly the oil embargo, against Iraq. China's interest was mainly centred around Iraq's potential as a supplier of oil to China and a source of investment to Chinese oil companies willing to develop Iraq's oil industry.

China welcomed the signing of the memorandum of understanding between the UN Secretary-General Kofi Annan and the Iraqi government on 23 February 1998[39] in connection with settling the issue of arms inspections in Iraq,[40] and encouraged the Security Council to implement it as soon as possible. China also had joined Russia, France, and the Non-Alignment movement in opposing the draft resolution, put forward by Britain and Japan and supported by the United States, on the issue of the use of force against Iraq. The draft resolution stated if Iraq violates the agreement reached between Annan and the Iraqi government, it would face the severest consequences: military strikes. The Chinese representative along with the Russian and the French representatives expressed their resolute objections to this draft. However, they suggested that the resolution, instead, should include the following four points: first, the agreement signed between Annan and the Iraqi government should be clearly approved; second, the agreement should be implemented as soon as possible and not be delayed by man-made factors; third, if Iraq abides by the agreement it signed with Annan, there should be hope for lifting the sanctions on Iraq; and, fourth, opposition to the inclusion of the 'automatic authorisation on the use of force' clause in the resolution, and the UN Security Council should be the one to judge whether Iraq violates the agreement and whether to adopt any penalties.[41] Generally speaking, whenever the Iraqi government limit or suspend UNSCOM activities in Iraq, the Chinese government urge the Iraqi government to resume full cooperation with the UN, and also urge the relevant sides to avoid the threat or the use of force and properly resolve the issue through dialogue.[42]

When the United States, along with Great Britain, launched their military strikes against Iraq on 17 December 1998 following the UNSCOM unforced withdrawal from Iraq, the Chinese government condemned the US and UK air strikes and urged them to halt all their military actions immediately. The

---

39 The memorandum of understanding obligates Iraq to provide UNSCOM and the International Atomic Agency (IAA) immediate, unconditional, and unrestricted access for their inspections in Iraq. The UN reiterates the commitment of all member states to respect the sovereignty and territorial integrity of Iraq. The memorandum also includes a pledge by the commission to respect the legitimate concerns of Iraq relating to national security, sovereignty, and dignity. It further provides for the establishment of special procedures that would apply to initial and subsequent entries at the eight presidential sites. It finally provides for the appointment of a commissioner to head the special group established to oversee inspections of presidential sites. Centre for Non-proliferation Studies, http://cns.miis.edu/research/iraq/uns_chro.htm, pp. 7–8.
40 BBC, *SWB, FE/3159*, 24 February 1998, p. G/1.
41 BBC, *SWB, FE/3165*, 3 March 1998, p. G/1.
42 See, for example, China's reaction to the Iraqi government Suspension of the UNSCOM activities in October 1998. BBC, *SWB, FE/3386*, 17 November 1998, p. G/1.

Chinese criticized UNSCOM's unilateral decision to leave Iraq without consulting the Security Council.[43] They accused the United States and Great Britain of having no authorization by the UN Security Council and unilaterally using force against Iraq. The Chinese Foreign Ministry described the action as 'a violation of the UN charter and the international norms' (see Footnote 43: G/2). The Chinese media carried its criticism and condemnation of US military actions against Iraq. *Xinhua News Agency News Bulletin* described the air strikes against Iraq as constituting 'a serious threat to international peace and security'. It said that:

> The Clinton administration chose this moment to strike was out of consideration for its own predicament. Clinton was facing impeachment by the US House of Representatives on account of the sex scandal case. The Clinton administration could on the one hand shift the line of vision and on the other gain time for going all out to win over Republican congressmen who were still wavering.

The Shanghai daily, *Jiefang Ribao*, said on 18 December that:

> The latest US military action was carried out without the approval of the UN Security Council. While repeatedly accusing Iraq of failing to comply with the UN resolutions, Washington's own action has completely violated the UN charter and norms of international law. The conduct of the United States has set a very bad and extremely dangerous precedent.[44]

The Chinese Communist Party's newspaper, *Renmin Ribao*, stated in its 18 December issue:

> The use of force against Iraq by the United States has neither a just cause nor has a legal basis. The US action neither has the authorisation of the UN Security Council nor is based on the consensus and confirmation of the international community. The use of force on the US part under such circumstances is totally a unilateral action ... Relying on one's powerful military force to wantonly go to war against a weak country, and even use force to overthrow the legitimate government of a country is typical hegemony and power politics. The international community cannot accept this.
> (BBC, *SWB*, *FE/3415*, 21 December 1998: G/1)

---

43 BBC, *SWB*, *FE/3413*, 18 December 1998, p. G/1.
44 BBC, *SWB*, *FE/3414*, 19 December 1998, p. G/5.

152 *China's foreign policy toward the Gulf and Arabian Peninsula region*

The UN Security Council adopted, on 17 December 1999, Resolution 1284 on the Iraqi issue, with eleven voting for and four abstentions. The resolution ended UNSCOM and replaced it with the UN Monitoring, Verification and Inspection Commission (UNMOVIC). It offered partial suspension of sanctions in return for Baghdad's cooperation with a new set of arms inspectors.[45] China, along with Russia, France and Malaysia, abstained from voting on the resolution. China could have used the veto, but under heavy pressure from the United States, decided that abstention was the better part of valour. The Chinese government justified its abstention by arguing that Resolution 1284 does not satisfy the 'reasonable proposal' put forward by China and other countries in terms of setting in motion the mechanism for suspending sanctions against Iraq and other issues.[46] Moreover, one can argue that China's decision to abstain might have been motivated by the following factors:

1   China wanted to see, in the short term, a full suspension of sanctions imposed on Iraq by the UN Security Council including financial and trade restrictions, and, in the long run, military restrictions;
2   China desired to ensure a long-term stable supply of energy from Iraq in order to diversify its import of oil and also to get oil development contracts in Iraq;
3   China was eager to bring to an end to the US and British (continuing) interpretations of the related resolutions: to have the right to use military means to enforce Iraqi compliance.

Thus, China's foreign policy towards Iraq during the 1990s was a reflection of its overall foreign policy. Because of Iraq's economic potential, the Chinese government supported the lifting or easing of sanctions against Iraq. Because of its principle opposition to foreign intervention in a sovereign state's internal affairs, the Chinese government politically supported Iraq against US military attacks. This support was out of fear that the United States would redefine a state's sovereignty in terms that serve US interests around the world, which would enable the United States to impose destructive wars on countries that obstruct its interests. This worried China, which was faced with separatist tendencies and struggle in Tibet, Xinjiang, and also Taiwan. For this reason, China remained a strong opponent to the US and Western military attacks and interventions in Iraq and remained a strong advocator of peaceful dialogue and cooperation in order to resolve differences between the UN and Iraq.

---

45 *Middle East International*, 24 December 1999, pp. 13–14.
46 *Beijing Review*, No. 52, 27 December 1999, p. 6.

CHINA AND IRAN

China and Iran in the 1950s

As previously suggested, the foreign policy of the PRC in the 1950s was attached to, and subservient to, the power blocs led by the Soviet Union and the United States. As a result, China–Iran relations were vitiated by the Chinese sharp focus on ideology, which led the Iranian government to show their unwillingness to start a relationship with the communist government in Mainland China. Both Mossadeq and the Shah's regimes were suspicious of China (Abidi 1982: 46). Two main factors had played a large role in Iran's opposition to a rapprochement with China. These factors were:

1. Iran's position stemmed from fear of China's communist ideology and its alignment with the Soviet Union. Soviet and Chinese support of the Iranian communist party (the Tudeh), which was operating unofficially in Iran, had increased the Iranian government's fears of communist-inspired subversion in Iran (Behbehani 1981: 217).
2. The emergence of the United States as the most influential foreign power in Iran following the coup of 1953 against Mossadeq[47] contributed to Iran's hostility towards China. After the coup, Iran had become an unambiguous client ally of the United States. The coup had not only restored a pro-Western government to power in Iran but had also restored control over Iran's oil production to the West. Within a year of the coup, a new consortium of Western oil interests was created to manage Iranian oil (Hyun Sang Yoo 1996: 230–59). To the United States, Iran was seen as a strategic partner to contain the threat of the Soviet Union and China. In May 1950, a Mutual Defence Assistance Agreement was signed between the United States and Iran for an average of US$23 million per year in military aid until 1956, and the agreement granted several economic loans to the Iranian government (Warne 1956: 18). It also provided the Iranian government with US$73 million in economic aid in the first week after the coup, and approximately US$1 billion in US military and economic aid in the first ten years after the coup (Hyun Sang Yoo 1996: 274).

Thus, China found itself unable to cultivate relations with Iran in the

---

47 When the Mossadeq government began to take control over the oilfields in Iran, Britain sent several warships to the Gulf; and, along with the United States, they started to build up political and economic pressures to weaken Mossadeq's regime and, reportedly, supported the 1953 coup. The US main goal in Iran was to keep that country from falling under Soviet domination.

1950s despite unofficial trade relations between the two countries. Iran supported the United States in Korea and condemned the PRC as an aggressor in the war. The Shah joined the West-oriented and sponsored collective security system known as the Baghdad Pact in 1954 as he wanted to preserve the monarchical system in Iran. Iran continued to oppose the question of China's admission to the UN throughout the 1950s and revived its diplomatic relations with the Nationalist government in Taiwan. Furthermore, the Chinese government sought to soften its image and present itself as a state that the rest of the Third World could exist with. This was evident in China's continued 'unofficial' trade relations with Iran in the 1950s. China's total trade of imports and exports with Iran from 1950 to 1959 was approximately $2.5 million (see Table A.2 in the Appendix). This strategy was also demonstrated by China's reluctance to attack the Iranian government policy of alliance with the West. In his statements to the Bandung Conference, Zhou Enlai denounced the US scheme of creating an anti-Communist alliance, and adopted a rational and softer tone towards Asian states, including Iran, that had associated themselves with the United States in opposition to the PRC. Zhou argued that differences between Third World countries could be solved through peaceful negotiations. According to Zhou, foreign intervention in the internal affairs of Third World countries must be stopped since it is the main cause of conflict and disagreement among the countries of the Third World and China.[48] However, the Iranian government, which participated in the conference, did not agree with the Chinese argument and continued its relationship with the United States and its opposition to the PRC. Therefore, China found itself unable to cultivate relations with Iran in the 1950s.

China, Iran, and changes in Chinese foreign policy

The 1960s witnessed tremendous changes in the foreign policy of both China and Iran. China's foreign policy had been fundamentally changed by its perception of the United States and the Soviet Union as the main enemies of China and the rest of the world. New foreign policy strategies were implemented to achieve China's new foreign policy objectives of opposing both the United States and the Soviet Union in the Third World. Iran's foreign policy also began to change. The emergence of the Shah as the prominent policy maker in Iran and his new 'independent national policy' influenced the direction of Iran's foreign policy. The Shah saw a decline in the importance of Iran to the United States following the US-Soviet détente. Furthermore, the US decision in 1964 to sell instead of handing out arms to Iran convinced the Shah to adopt an independent foreign policy that could

---

48 For Premier Zhou Enlai's statement, see *People's China*, 16 May 1955, pp. 7–10.

balance Iran's relations with the superpowers. The Chinese government interpreted the new Iranian foreign policy posture and the establishment of the Regional Co-operation for Development[49] as steps in the region toward challenging the West and as a new effort toward fostering Third World solidarity. China's interpretation was coupled with changes in Iran's voting behaviour concerning the question of China's admission to the UN. In the past, Iran had voted against China's admission to the UN. However, since 1965, Iran began to abstain from voting on the issue (Abidi 1982: 87–92). Iran's abstention on this issue was a fundamental departure from its former pattern of voting for US draft resolutions. However, it is important to note that Iran remained a member of the US-sponsored Baghdad Pact (later known as the Central Treaty Organization, CENTO, August 1959). Iran also remained suspicious of continued Chinese support for the Tudeh party and China's continued attacks on CENTO (Behbehani 1981: 217).

After the Arab defeat in the June 1967 war and the subsequent shift in the power balance from the Arabs toward Iran, the Iranian government felt comfortable to devote more attention to its relations with the PRC. The first direct Iranian statement on Iran–China relations was made by the Shah himself in 1967. In his statement, the Shah acknowledged *de facto* recognition of the PRC and argued for the admission of China to the UN (Abidi 1982: 47). In January 1969, the Shah declared for the first time that Iran would support China's application for membership of the UN (Abidi 1982: 51). These changes in Iran's foreign policy towards China suggest that the Iranian government hoped that initiating relations with the PRC would allow Iran to manoeuvre more easily between the two superpowers. The changes also suggest that Iran's fear of China was mainly because of its ideological and political connection with the Soviet Union. Once the Chinese had shifted their alliance with the Soviets and began their own massive propaganda campaign against them, the Iranian government felt much safer to deal with China. To the Iranian government, the Chinese could play the role of a counterpoise to Soviet penetration in Asia and the Gulf and Arabian Peninsula region. One could also argue that Iran was merely following the United States in its rapprochement with China.

To summarize, changes in the foreign policies of both China and Iran in the 1960s helped the Iranians in particular to view the Chinese in a positive manner for the first time since 1949. Despite the absence of political relations between the two sides, trade relations increased dramatically in the 1960s. China's total trade of exports and imports with Iran in the 1960s was about twenty times greater than in the 1950s (see Table A.2 in the Appendix).

---

49 Included Iran, Pakistan, and Turkey.

The establishment of diplomatic relations

As previously mentioned, China's foreign policy in the late 1960s and early 1970s altered to accommodate changes in its relations with both superpowers. China's interest in Iran during this time was reflected by the pattern of change in China's foreign policy. It was China's fear of Soviet attempts to refill the 'power vacuum' in the Gulf following the British withdrawal from the region, particularly after the signing of the Soviet–Indian treaty of friendship, that led the Chinese government to consolidate its relations with Iran. At the same time, Iran shared China's fear of the Soviet Union but waited for the Chinese to reduce and subsequently terminate China's political and military support for the national liberation movements and all other forces which opposed the ruling regimes in the Gulf region. Once the Chinese began to cease support for the PFLOAG in 1971, in order to cultivate relations with Iran and other Gulf states, Iran's government found itself in an unprecedentedly favourable position to consider establishing political relations with the Chinese government. Two major visits to China by Iranian Princess Ashraf Pahlavi on 14 April 1971 and Iranian Princess Fatamah Pahlavi on 30 April 1971 helped the Iranian government to hasten its decision to establish diplomatic relations with the PRC (Abidi 1982: 56–66). It is important to mention that Pakistan's mediation role had also played a large role in fostering the establishment of diplomatic relations between Iran and China.

The establishment of diplomatic relations between the two countries was announced on 17 August 1971 in the form of a joint communiqué simultaneously released in Beijing and Tehran. However, the document of recognition was signed in Islamabad a day earlier.[50] The Iranian government saw the establishment and development of diplomatic relations with China as a natural progression. At a press conference on 19 October 1971, the Shah emphasized this point in stating:

> The relations between our two countries, whether in the economic or cultural fields, have been long-standing. It is natural that these re-established relations not only should be resumed to the level reached in the past, but should also be further developed.
> (BBC, *SWB*, FE/3818, 21 October 1971: A4/1)

From China's perspective, the Chinese government viewed the new development in China–Iran relations as a victory against imperialism. In his speech during the Shah's birthday reception in Iran's embassy in Beijing, Chi Pengfei, Chinese Acting Foreign Minister, said:

---

50 BBC, *SWB*, FE/3765, 19 August 1971, p. A4/1.

China's relations with Iraq, Iran, and Yemen

We are very glad that the ties between China and Iran which were weakened and even once interrupted as a result of imperialist aggression have now been restored and developed on new basis.

(BBC, *SWB, FE/3824*, 28 October 1971: A4/1-2)

Regardless of their perceptions, the establishment of diplomatic relations between China and Iran appeared to serve both countries' national interests. Iran was an important state to China for the following reasons:

1. Iran's political and military strengths could serve as a counterpoise to Soviet advances in the Gulf region.
2. Iran shared China's fear of the Soviet presence and influence in India and later in Iraq, which both China and Iran interpreted as a Soviet move to contain China, Iran, and Pakistan.
3. Both China and Iran were interested in maintaining the independence and integrity of Pakistan. China and Iran accused the Soviet Union of attempting to trigger off the disintegration of Pakistan and the establishment of the independent states of Pakhtoonistan in north Pakistan and Baluchistan in the south.
4. Iran's large market could serve as a potential market for Chinese goods.
5. China could collaborate with Iran in such fields as petroleum technology and chemical fertilizers.
6. Establishing diplomatic relations with Iran could create a positive image for China to help foster the development of its relations with other Gulf and Arabian Peninsula countries.

To Iran, China was an important state for the following reasons:

1. The establishment of diplomatic relations with China, which graduated to the status of a nuclear power after the successful test of a nuclear device in 1964, could enhance Iran's bargaining position in world affairs, particularly in its relations with the United States and the Soviet Union.
2. China shared Iran's fear of the Soviet Union's advance into the Gulf region, in particular, and Asia, in general.
3. The Iranian government hoped that, by establishing diplomatic relations and befriending China, Iran would be able to stop Chinese support for revolutionary communist and nationalist movements in the Gulf region.
4. Iran had no reason to remain unfriendly with China, particularly after the US government had already begun improving relations with China.
5. The establishment of diplomatic relations between China and Canada (October 1970), Equatorial Guinea (October 1970), Italy (November 1970), Ethiopia (December 1970), Chile (January 1971), Nigeria (February 1971), Cameroon and Kuwait (March 1971) suggested to

the Iranian leadership that China could coexist with states of different socio-economic-political systems.

Following the establishment of diplomatic relations, many official and non-official political, economic, and cultural delegations visited the two countries in the 1970s. These included a visit to Iran in April 1972 by a Chinese government trade delegation headed by Chen Chieh, the Chinese Vice-Minister of Foreign Trade. This was the first Chinese government delegation sent to Iran since the establishment of diplomatic relations between the two countries. During the visit, a Chinese–Iranian trade agreement and a payment agreement were signed (Shih Tsan-Yen 1975: 67). The following April, an Iranian government economic delegation visited China, led by Hushang Ansari, the Iranian Minister of Economy. The first long-term trade and payment agreements were signed by both governments.[51] The main feature of these agreements was that the Iranian rial would be the sole unit of accounting currency. China's Foreign Minister Chi Pengfei visited Iran in June 1973[52] and Chinese Vice-Premier Li Hsiennien visited Iran in April 1975. China reportedly began to buy Iranian crude oil in 1974. The arrangement is believed to have been made during a visit to Tehran in late 1974 by Li Chiang, the Chinese Minister of Foreign Trade (Calabrese 1991: 87). China also purchased 200,000 tons of crude oil from Iran in 1976 and 300,000 tons in 1977. All Chinese purchases of Iranian crude oil were paid for in hard cash and at OPEC prices (Abidi 1982: 262). In August 1978, Chairman Hua Guofeng visited Tehran. The Chinese Chairman's visit marked the first visit made by a high-ranking Chinese official to Iran since the establishment of diplomatic relations. However, the Chinese Chairman's visit came during a very sensitive and crucial time for Iran, as the Shah's regime was facing large-scale resistance from the opposition. In June 1972, the Chinese Red Cross Society donated blankets, tinned food, and medicine valued at 200,000 yuan for the victims of the earthquakes in southern Iran.[53] China welcomed the Shah of Iran's announcement on 31 July 1973 of a new agreement between the National Iranian Oil Company (NIOC) and the Western oil consortium, in which Iran recovered all rights concerning production, management, and ownership of oil installations from the consortium. An article in *Peking Review* in August 1973 stated:

> The 72-year long struggle by the Iranian people to safeguard their country's oil rights and interests has resulted in a resounding victory. It has turned a new page in the annals of Iran's oil industry.
>
> (*Peking Review*, No. 33, 17 August 1973: 17)

51 *Peking Review*, No. 16, 29 June 1973, p. 5.
52 *Peking Review*, No. 25, 22 June 1973, pp. 3–5.
53 BBC, *SWB, FE/4019*, 20 June 1972, p. A4/1.

China also welcomed the bilateral agreement signed between Iran and the Soviet Union on 17 August 1974 to raise the price of Iranian gas exported to the Soviet Union from 30 to 57 US cents per 1,000 cubic feet.[54] Since the establishment of diplomatic relations, the total volume of trade between the two countries increased sharply. The 1972 figure was approximately six times greater than in 1971; the 1973 figure was more than ten times greater than in 1971; the 1975 figure was a little over fourteen times greater than in 1971; and the 1978 figure was about twenty times greater than in 1971 (see Table A.2 in the Appendix). From the beginning of 1970 until the end of 1973, the balance of trade was in favour of Iran. However, this began to change in 1974 with China enjoying a small surplus in its trade with Iran.

China and new developments in Iran

As China's political and economic relations with Iran started to augment after the establishment of diplomatic relations between the two countries, two major developments in Iran caught the Chinese government by surprise: the Islamic Revolution in Iran in 1979 followed by the breakout of the Iraq–Iran war in 1980.

The Islamic Revolution overthrew the Shah's regime, ended the monarchical system in Iran, and presented Ayatollah Khomeini's regime to the world as the new ruling authority in Iran. China had enjoyed a promising relationship with the Shah throughout most of the 1970s and did not know what to expect from the new regime in Iran. China feared that Khomeini's regime would offset the newly-developed relationship between China and Iran because of its support for the Shah in the 1970s and particularly after the ill-timed Chinese Chairman Hua Guofeng's visit to the Shah in August 1978, when the Iranian crisis was reaching its peak. China was also concerned that the Khomeini regime's anti-US stand would lead Iran toward a closer relationship with the Soviet Union. The Chinese were strongly opposed to such a development. So, they publicly criticized Soviet attempts to take advantage of the new development in Iran and to exploit it to Soviet interests in the region.[55] The Chinese government encouraged the United States to resist Moscow's 'expansionist' efforts in Iran and protect its (US) interest in that country.[56]

China itself did not publicly express its support for or opposition to the Islamic Revolution in Iran. Chinese media coverage of the 'turmoil' or the 'turbulence' in Iran, as they referred to it, was expressed by quoting Iranian sources. Some have argued that, in order to stay out of Iran's internal

---

54 *Peking Review*, No. 35, 30 August 1974, pp. 35–6.
55 See *Beijing Review*, Vol. 22.1, No. 15, 13 April 1979, pp. 19–20.
56 *Ibid.*

affairs, the Chinese media specifically adopted the practice of quoting the worst aspects of the revolution leadership from Iranian sources (Abidi 1982: 176). Thus, the Chinese, in their first reaction to the new development in Iran, did not applaud the establishment of a revolutionary regime in Iran, nor were they impressed by the anti-imperialist and non-aligned postures of the revolutionary regime in Iran. Most importantly, in March 1979 the Lebanese weekly *Al-Kifah al-Arabi* alleged long cooperation between China, the Israeli secret services, and the Iranian secret services in exchanging information about the Iranian Islamic Revolution. The Chinese government, however, denied such allegations in an official statement on Tehran Radio.[57]

Eventually, the Chinese government found itself with no choice but to recognize the new government in Iran. Chairman Hua Guofeng sent his congratulations and expressed the hope that 'traditional friendship' would continue between the two states (Freeze 1979: 4–6). On 21 January 1979, Jiao Ruoyu, the Chinese Ambassador to Iran, met with the Iranian Prime Minister Mehdi Bazargan, and the two expressed their desire to develop relations between the two countries further.[58] It was reported that Chairman Hua Guofeng conveyed, in July 1979, an apology to Khomeini, through a Pakistani mediator, for his visit to Iran the previous year (Abidi 1982: 174–5). China had started to celebrate Iran's Revolution and Iranian National Days as gestures toward improving its image with the Iranian government. However, political exchanges between the two countries were at minimum level. Culturally, China began to use Chinese Islamic Association members to foster its relations with Iran. Several Islamic delegations were sent to Iran and met with high-ranking Iranians leaders.[59] Economically, despite the signing of a memorandum between China and Iran during the Iranian Minister of Trade's visit to China in 1979,[60] total Chinese exports and imports with Iran reached their lowest point since 1975. Total trade dropped from US$118 million in 1978 to approximately US$68 million in 1979 (see Table A.2 in the Appendix).

The breakout of the Iraq–Iran war in September 1980 presented the Chinese government with a dilemma. To China, both Iran and Iraq were important countries to counterpoise Soviet advances in the Gulf region. A war between them could make them more vulnerable to Soviet penetration in the region. Iran was coming out of a fundamental revolutionary change. Its revolutionary militancy and its disengagement from the United States could trigger off a leaning toward the Soviet policy in Iran. While the

---

57 BBC, *SWB, Middle East (henceforth ME) 6081*, 31 March 1979, p. i.
58 *Xinhua News Agency News Bulletin*, No. 11056, 23 April 1979, pp. 1–2.
59 BBC, *SWB, FE/6349*, 19 February 1980, p. A4/1–2.
60 BBC, *SWB, FE/6275*, 19 November 1979, p. A4/3.

Chinese government was concerned with trying to restore its image in Iran, it adopted the same policy with Iran as it did with Iraq during the Iraq–Iran war. This policy was characterized by the following:

1   it avoided criticizing Iran's military and political actions against Iraq;
2   it stressed the need for a peaceful settlement of Iran's disputes with Iraq;
3   it praised the Iranian leadership's opposition to hegemony and intervention by foreign powers in Iran's internal affairs;[61]
4   it welcomed the Iranian government's opposition to the Soviet invasion of Afghanistan;
5   it portrayed the Soviet Union as the ultimate beneficiary of the continued conflict between Iran and Iraq;[62]
6   it encouraged the rapprochement of relations between Iran and the United States.

In addition, the Chinese government's foreign policy towards Iran's conflict with Iraq was characterised by its attempts to prevent the Iranian government from leaning toward the Soviet Union. Recognizing the limitation of the US ability to influence Iran, the Chinese government refused to support the UN-imposed arms embargo against Iran under Security Council Resolution 598. China's interpretation of the situation argued for reaching a political solution before imposing an embargo (Hunter 1990: 161). The Chinese government did not want the Soviet Union to appear to be Iran's only supporter in the council. Furthermore, the Chinese government did not take part in voting on the US draft resolution to the UN Security Council on 13 January 1980 for economic sanctions against Iran. The Chinese representative Chen Chu, explaining why China did not vote on the draft, stated:

> At present, the application of economic sanctions against Iran may not necessarily lead to the relaxation of tension and the release of hostages. It can also be seen from developments over the past few days that the possibility still exists for a solution to be found through patient consultations and negotiations and that this possibility merits further exploration.

Chen also pointed out the reason behind the Soviet decision to veto the resolution and said:

---

61   For instance, the Chinese government and media praised the Iranian leadership's refusal to accept Soviet military aid and sales on the grounds that Iran opposed foreign intervention in its internal affairs.
62   *Beijing Review*, No. 4, 25 January 1984, pp. 14–15.

The performance of the Soviet Union over the question now under consideration shows that it intends to take advantage of the crisis in the US–Iranian relations to disguise itself as the 'guardian' of Iran and 'natural ally' of the Islamic countries, so as to make cheap political capital out of it. We believe that the peoples of Iran and the rest of the Islamic world will certainly see through the intrigues of the Soviet Union and not allow it to succeed in its plot to sow discord and fish in muddied waters.

(*Beijing Review*, No. 3, 21 January 1980: 11)

China's decision not to veto the US draft resolution was a Chinese foreign policy strategy to avoid harming its relationship with the United States and, simultaneously, demonstrate China's willingness to befriend the Iranian government. The Chinese government welcomed Iran's refusal to accept Soviet military aid and sales. An article in *Beijing Review*, entitled 'The Iranians did right', stated:

Iranian vigilance and effective measures taken to guard against the Soviet Union are of immense importance for Iran in safeguarding its security and independence as well as in safeguarding peace and stability in the Persian Gulf area.

(*Beijing Review*, No. 36, 8 September 1980: 14–15)

The Chinese government criticized Moscow when it proposed to provide Iran with a radar system in exchange for permission to allow the Soviet Union to study electronic devices on the wreckage of US aircraft. The Chinese argued that, had Iran accepted the deal, Moscow would gain not only technological information of US aircraft and helicopters, but also Iranian telecommunication secrets. Instead, the Chinese emphasized that, if Soviet intentions to assist Iran were serious, it should pull its forces out of Afghanistan so that there would be no excuse for the US military presence in the region.[63] The Chinese also criticized the Soviet stand on the hostage crisis. The editorial in Hong Kong's pro-communist *Wen Wei Po* on 1 May 1980 stated:

It [Soviet Union] is using the American military action to rescue the hostages to divert the attention of world opinion to plan its suppression of guerrilla activities in Afghanistan with ease. The Soviet strategy of southward expansion to secure a warm water port was defeated when it got itself into the Afghan quagmire. However, now it has been given an

---

63 Joint Publications Research Services (hereafter JPRS)-75732-China Report, No. 84, 20 May 1980, p. 47.

opportunity to expand into Iran by the deepening of the hostage crisis. In the whole course of the hostage crisis, the Soviet Union is the real beneficiary.

(*JPRS 75672-China Report*, No. 82, 9 May 1980: 20–1)

During Iran's period of domestic political instability in 1981, following the dismissal of President Bensadir and the election of Mohammad Ali Rajai as new president, China tried to exclude itself from Iran's internal affairs. The Chinese media reported the situation in general in Iran, and an article in *Beijing Review* stated:

> What road Iran will choose is completely a matter to be decided by the Iranian people themselves. However, it is painful to see Iran embroiled in internal strife. Iran did not win independence easily. Its people had been long subject to imperialist and colonialist oppression and exploitation. The Third World peoples, who have had the same experience as the Iranian people, naturally wish to see the Iranian people restore internal peace in their country and embark on the road to happiness and prosperity as soon as possible.
>
> (*Beijing Review*, No. 38, 21 September 1981: 10–11)

China–Iran relations started to develop rapidly after political stability was restored in Iran. Dr Ali Akbar Velayati, Iranian Foreign Minister, visited China in 1982, and the Chinese Foreign Minister, Wu Xueqian, travelled to Iran in November 1983.[64] The two visits helped to expand cooperation in cultural and economic endeavours between the two countries. A Chinese delegation headed by Zhang Jinfu, Chinese State Councillor, visited Iran in February–March 1985. Iranian President Seyyed Ali Khamenei said, while meeting the visiting delegation, that in national development Third World countries cannot expect help from the superpowers, it can only be done by relying on unity and cooperation among themselves.[65] The two sides set up a ministerial joint committee for cooperation on economic, trade, science, and technology. The establishment of the committee was said to lay down the foundation for stable and long-lasting cooperation between the two countries.[66] In June, Ali Akbar Hashemi Rafsanjani, speaker of the Iranian Islamic Consultative Assembly, visited China. Premier Zhao Ziyang said, while meeting Rafsanjani, that Chinese–Iranian friendship and cooperation 'are based on their common independence and anti-hegemonism'.[67] Ali Akbar Velayati visited Beijing in June 1987. His visit coincided with

64 *Beijing Review*, No. 50, 10 December 1984, pp. 6–7.
65 *FBIS-CHI-85-043*, 5 March 1985, p. I1.
66 *FBIS-CHI-85-044*, 6 March 1985, p. I1.
67 *FBIS-CHI-85-124*, 28 June 1985, p. I1.

Chinese consideration of a Kuwaiti request that Beijing cooperate with Washington and Moscow in protecting Kuwait's oil tankers against Iranian attacks in the Gulf.[68] The following month, China's Vice-Minister of Foreign Affairs Qi Huaiyuan travelled to Kuwait and delivered his government's refusal to take part in protecting Kuwaiti vessels in the Gulf.[69]

China condemned the US action that brought down an Iran Airlines passenger plane flying over the southern part of the Gulf on 3 July 1988. *China Daily* said:

> Now the fatal incident of the Airbus crash has once again underlined the urgency for the removal of big powers' military meddling in the region and for the peaceful settlement between the warring nations.
> (*FBIS-CHI-88-128*, 5 July 1988: 14)

When Iran acknowledged UN Security Council Resolution 598 on 18 July 1988, China welcomed the development. China's Vice-Foreign Minister visited Tehran in August and expressed his country's support for the Iranian decision and stressed China's willingness to take part in the post-war economic reconstruction in Iran.[70] Iran's President Khamenei visited China for a six-day visit in May 1989. His visit to China was the first by an Iranian head of state since the revolution. During his meeting with the Chinese President Yang Shangkun, Khamenei said that, Iran in its reconstruction efforts following the end of the war, 'seeks co-operation with countries that had left no unpleasant memories on the Iranian mind during the war'. For this reason, he added, 'we have chosen friendship and co-operation with China and we are ready to conduct further co-operation'.[71] While meeting with Deng Xiaoping, Khamenei ensured the Chinese leader that 'Iran sticks to its policy of neither East, nor West' in its foreign policy and that 'it is one of the fundamental bases of the Islamic revolution'.[72] This reassuring statement came after China's concern that Iran was moving towards the Soviet Union, particularly after the visit to Tehran by the Soviet Foreign Minister Eduard Shevardnadze in late February 1989. During Khamenei's visit, the two sides emphasized the need to develop economic, trade, technological and cultural relations further. In a meeting with the visiting Chinese Foreign Minister Qian Qichen, on 9 October 1989, the Iranian Foreign Minister expressed his country's 'understanding of China's firm stand' towards the demonstrators

---

68 *FBIS-CHI-87-114*, 15 June 1987, p. F2.
69 *FBIS-CHI-87-145*, 29 July 1987, p. F1–F2.
70 *FBIS-CHI-88-158*, 16 August 1988, p. 18.
71 *FBIS-CHI-89-089*, 10 May 1989, pp. 8–10.
72 *FBIS-CHI-89-090*, 11 May 1989, p. 10.

in Tiananmen Square and voiced support for China's drive to restore order and realize stability.[73]

Regarding trade relations, total Chinese exports and imports with Iran increased substantially after 1980. Trade rose from US$67.9 million in 1979 to US$179 million in 1980, an increase of about $111 million. Total trade between China and Iran in the 1980s reached US$1,627 million compared with only US$627 million in the 1970s (see Table A.2 in the Appendix). This shows that, despite the prolonged war between Iran and Iraq, China–Iran economic relations continued to progress. Throughout the 1980s, China exported to Iran various kinds of manufactured goods and raw materials such as machinery, tools, steel wires, yarns, textile fabrics, chemicals, aluminium, fishing equipment, and ships. In return, China received crude oil from Iran.[74] China's oil imports from Iran increased sharply from 300,000 tons/year in 1977[75] to approximately 1 million tons/year (25,000 bbl./day) in 1982[76] and then to 2 million tons/year (40,000 bbl./day) between 1989 and 1990.[77] Throughout the 1980s, China also assisted Iran in constructing power stations, upgrading airport facilities, operating offshore drilling, constructing a dam on the Karoum River in south-east Iran, and establishing factories for silk weaving, light industries, and fishery products.[78] From 1984 to 1989, China signed up for nineteen projects with Iran totalling US$66.74 million.[79] Cultural relations between the two sides were advanced. The two countries developed student exchange and scholarship programmes, scientific research programmes, art cooperation programmes, joint training programmes in fishing and tourism, as well as cooperation in archaeology and various fields of sports, in addition to mutual exemption of visas.[80] The first Iranian women delegation since the revolution visited China in April 1989.[81] Several religious delegations travelled between the two countries.[82]

This improvement in the economic and cultural fields was coupled with an increase in China's arms transfers to Iran. In the 1980s, Iran became China's second-largest arms customer in the world with total purchases valued at

---

73 *FBIS-CHI-89-194*, 10 October 1989, pp. 14–17.
74 *Petroleum News Letter* (Iran), Vol. 56, March/April 1990, p. 12.
75 Chinese purchase of Iranian oil in 1976 totalled 200,000 tons. *Middle East Economic Survey*, Vol. 20, No. 46, 5 September 1977, p. 3.
76 *Middle East Economic Survey*, Vol. 25, No. 30, 10 May 1982, p. 3.
77 *Middle East Economic Survey*, Vol. 32, No. 32, 15 May 1989, p. A7; China signed an agreement with Iran on 4 August 1987 for the purchase of 1 million tons of crude oil from Iran. *FBIS-CNI-87-152*, 7 August 1987, p. F1.
78 *Petroleum News Letter*, pp. 12–13.
79 *FBIS-CHI-89-226*, 27 November 1989, p. 11.
80 *Beijing Review*, No. 2, 22–23 May 1989, p. 7.
81 *FBIS-CHI-89-065*, 6 April 1989, p. 16.
82 *FBIS-CHI-89-176*, 13 September 1989, p. 7.

US$3,800 million between 1982 and 1991. China was Iran's largest single arms supplier during the Iran–Iraq war. The low cost of Chinese weapons made China an attractive arms source for Iran. While Chinese officials continued to deny Chinese arms transfers to Iran, Western reports argued that China had transferred arms to Iran throughout the 1980s. This transfer included F-6 (MiG-19 equivalent) interceptors and F-7 (MiG-21) fighters, Type-59 main battle tanks, Type-501 armoured personnel carriers, surface-to-air missiles, rocket launchers, anti-ship missiles, and field artillery and shells.[83] It was alleged that, by the end of the war with Iraq, Iran owned 12 F-6's and over 50 F-7's as well as some 260 T-59's (Ehteshami 1995: 176). Despite China and Iran's denial of any direct Chinese arms transfer to Iran, some Iranian officials did not deny Western reports that China was one of Iran's principal arms suppliers in the 1980s. For instance, Iran's Deputy Foreign Minister for political affairs Hosey Sheykh al-Eslam said:

> We buy weapons from any country, with the exception of South Africa, Japan and Israel.
>
> (*FBIS-CHI-87-101*, 27 May 1987: I1–I2)

China's foreign policy toward Iran in the 1980s was dominated by China's fear of Soviet penetration in the region. The editorial in *Hong Kong Standard* on 3 June 1987 described China–Iran relations as a 'new alignment' that 'appeared to be emerging' as a result of the arms deals. The editorial went on to say that China's interest in Iran was not due to its oil requirements; instead, it was China's desire to 'blunt the Soviet Union's increasing ties with Iran', particularly after Soviet First Deputy Foreign Minister's, Georgiy M. Korinyenko, visit to Tehran in 1986.[84] An article written in 1989 in *Xinhua News Agency News Bulletin*, entitled 'Iran Chooses the East rather than the West', analysed the new trend in Iran's foreign policy towards the superpowers. It reported that Iran was moving toward the Soviet Union while its relations with the West were deteriorating. This shift, according to the article, was evident in Shevardnadze's visit to Tehran in late February 1989 and his meeting with Ayatollah Khomeini. China was particularly concerned because Khomeini's meeting with the Soviet Foreign Minister was his first ever with a foreign minister of a major power since the revolution. Shevardnadze was also the highest-ranked Soviet official to visit the Islamic Republic. As a result, the Chinese sensed a shift in Iran's foreign policy toward Moscow. Therefore, they sought to encourage Iran to

---

83 See *Business Week*, 29 December 1986, p. 47; and Schichor 1988: 323.
84 *FBIS-CHI-87-107*, 4 June 1987, pp. I1–I2.

maintain its neutral policy in terms of its relations with both powers.[85] Shortly after, the Chinese Vice-Premier Tian Jiyun visited Tehran on 7 March for a five-day visit. He met with Rafsanjani who assured the visiting official that Iran's decision to develop relations with China 'is a result of careful consideration' and that the relations are not only of great significance for the time being, but also of far-reaching strategic importance.[86]

China and Iran in the 1990s

The end of the Iraq–Iran war led many to believe that China's earnings from arms sales could fall in the 1990s (Tai Ming Cheung 1992: 42). This prediction proved to be correct, particularly after the UN arms embargo was imposed on Iraq, China's principal arms customer in the 1980s. China, therefore, began to focus its attention on Iran as a potential partner in the Gulf region after Iraq. The Chinese government regarded Iran as:

1 a potential energy supplier and a source of investment;
2 a potential large market for Chinese commercial goods;
3 a potential buyer of Chinese arms and military technology;
4 a potential investment avenue for Chinese companies to participate in the reconstruction of Iran;
5 a potential ally against the 'New World system' dominated by the United States.

Iran's interest in China in the 1990s emerged because of its aim:

1 to secure a valuable arms, advanced technology, and weapons supplier;
2 to increase its exports of crude oil and strengthen its economic relations with China;
3 to obtain mutual cooperation with China in the agricultural, industrial, economic, and technological fields, in which the Chinese have achieved remarkable success, in order to counter the US blockade of Iran;
4 to strengthen its relations with countries that share Iran's view of the 'New World system' and oppose the domination of the United States in the new system;
5 to use China's good relations with Pakistan to lobby Islamabad to curb the anti-Iranian Taliban movement in Afghanistan.

Mindful of the reasons above, the Chinese and the Iranian governments continued their emphasis on the need for improving their political,

---

85 *FBIS-CHI-89-041*, 3 March 1989, p. 15.
86 *FBIS-CHI-89-044*, 8 March 1989, p. 3.

economic, and cultural relations. Several official visits by high-ranking officials of both countries took place in the 1990s. Among them was the visit to Iran by the Chinese Premier Li Peng in July 1991. While meeting with Iranian President Akbar Hashemi Rafsanjani and after praising the relationship between the two countries, Li Peng said:

> We are not in favour of the world being dominated by America or any minority, and the establishment of a new order by America in international relations. We are in agreement with Iran on that score.
> (*FBIS-NES-91-131*, 9 July 1999: 66)

It was reported by *Sawt al-Kuwayt* that, during the Chinese premier visit, the two sides reached an agreement in which China would replace West Germany and France in constructing the Iranian nuclear reactor. France and Germany had began constructing the reactor before the outbreak of the Islamic Revolution, until the new Iranian government abandoned its financial commitment to German and French companies. According to the report, Li agreed in his talks with Rafsanjani to provide the necessary expertise and technology for completion of the Iranian nuclear reactor in accordance with a comprehensive agreement confirming China as Iran's largest trading partner and arms supplier. The report also stated that China would launch into space a satellite for Iran to help it in the fields of radio and television transmission and in reconnaissance and observation.[87] In November 1991, Chinese President Yang Shangkun visited Iran. His visit marked the first visit to Iran by a Chinese head of state since the Islamic Revolution. The goal of Yang's visit was, reportedly, to encourage the expansion of China–Iran relations. The presence of the Chinese president in Iran, combined with his previous visit to Pakistan, was considered by many an opportunity for the three countries to review their policies toward recent developments in the international system, especially the United States taking the leading role in international affairs. It was argued that the expansion of cooperation and relations between these countries would lead to the establishment of a new system for the maintenance of regional security without the presence of the world powers, in the form of defence and military cooperation between China, Iran, and Pakistan.[88] Iranian President Rafsanjani visited China in September 1992 and an agreement was reached by China and Iran on the establishment of two 300-MW nuclear power plants for Iran.[89] Concerning the objectives of the agreement, it had been said that peaceful use of nuclear energy was intended. The agreement called

---

87 *FBIS-NES-91-138*, 18 July 1991, p. 38.
88 *FBIS-NES-91-214*, 5 November 1991, p. 80.
89 *FBIS-NES-92-178*, 14 September 1992, pp. 47–8.

Table 5.1 Iranian arms transfers by major suppliers 1983–1997 (in US$ million) (source: Cordesman 1998: 15)

Agreements	1983–6	1987–90	1991–7
Soviet Union/Russia	10	2,500	1,400
China	1,845	3,400	1,300
United States	0	0	0
Major West European	865	200	200
All other European	3,835	2,100	200
All others	2,385	2,000	1,200
Total	8,940	10,200	4,300

Deliveries	1983–6	1987–90	1991–7
Soviet Union/Russia	100	1,100	3,100
China	1,165	2,500	1,900
United States	0	0	0
Major West European	460	500	200
All other European	3,285	1,900	100
All others	2,250	1,800	500
Total	7,260	7,800	5,800

for cooperation between the two sides in wide-ranging fields such as basic and applicable research for peaceful utilization of nuclear energy, designing, building, and operating of nuclear power plants, research on reactors, extraction and exploration of uranium ore, radiation safeguards, and ecological protection.[90] Chinese Vice-Premier Li Lanqing visited Iran in May 1997. President Rafsanjani, while meeting with the visiting Chinese Vice-Premier, described Iran, China, and Russia as three important and strategic countries of the world, and stressed that many opportunities existed in the political, economic, industrial, and trade areas in those three countries. He added that trilateral cooperation between the three countries would not only satisfy the needs of these countries, but would contribute significantly to the development of regional cooperation.[91]

In the military field, China's arms supplies to Iran declined sharply in the 1990s due to competition from Russia, whose arms sales to Iran had increased, and other sources (see Table 5.1). This new competition convinced the Chinese government that, in order for China to remain influential in Iran, it would have to upgrade its services to Iran, in spite of US opposition. It was reported by an Iraqi newspaper that the Chinese

90 *FBIS-NES-93-070*, 14 April 1993, pp. 48–9.
91 BBC, *SWB, FE/2911*, 6 May 1997, p. G/5.

President Yang Shangkun promised, during his visit to Iran, to supply technology for enriching uranium to Iran.[92] It was also reported that in September 1992, during President Rafsanjani's visit, China agreed to help Iran in strengthening and expanding its armed forces under a strategic agreement worth billions of US dollars. According to the report from the London-based newspaper *Al-Sharq al-Awsat*, China would sell Iran nuclear technology and participate in building no less than four nuclear power stations and one centre for advanced nuclear research. According to the report, China would also supply Iran with 100–150 Soviet-designed fighter bombers.[93] There was also an agreement to supply two 300-MW nuclear reactors to Iran that have remained on hold due to several points of disagreement between the two sides.[94] In his visit to Beijing in January 1993, General Mohsen Reza'i, the Commander of the Islamic Revolution Guard Corps, negotiated the purchase of new weapons with the Chinese Defence Minister and the Joint Chief of Staff, in particular new battleships for the Iranian navy.[95] The Paris-based newspaper *Al-Watan al-Arabi* reported that China had sold three kinds of Silkworm missiles to Iran: surface to sea, air to sea, and air to surface. According to this report, China had also helped Iran build a military plant in Kermān Province in south-east Iran, which started assembling cruise missiles and M-11 missiles with a range of 300 km.[96] It was also reported that China had supplied Iran with a CSS-8 ballistic surface-to-surface missile in 1992[97] and a C-802 anti-ship cruise missile to Iran in March 1996,[98] and helped Iran build a Silkworm and M-9 plant. It was also reported that China is assisting Iran in developing the solid-propellant unguided Mushak-120, the Mushak-160, and the Mushak-200.[99] Different Western reports also contended that China helped the Iranians manufacture chemical weapons (see previous chapter). *Al-Sharq al-Awsat* reported on 24 August 1996 that China and Iran were expected to sign a new draft military agreement to be completed in December in Tehran. The new agreement concerned US$4.5 billion worth of Chinese aircraft, missiles, rocket launchers, high-speed launchers,

---

92 *FBIS-NES-91-219*, 13 November 1991, pp. 54–5.
93 *FBIS-NES-92-180*, 16 September 1992, p. 46.
94 The points of disagreement are not believed to be due to US pressure on China; instead: (1) China was not sure of its ability to provide all the technology and equipment necessary for the plant because of other countries' involvement in such technology (e.g.Germany, The Netherlands, and the Czech Republic may not be willing to supply Iran with such parts); and (2) Iran was unable to produce detailed financial plans necessary for starting the work on the first two stations. *FBIS-NES-95-099*, 23 May 1995, p. 54.
95 *FBIS-NES-93-023*, 5 February 1993, p. 53.
96 *FBIS-NES-95-064*, 4 April 1995, p. 55.
97 *The New York Times*, 22 June 1995, p. A1.
98 *The Washington Times*, 7 March 1996, p. A12.
99 Ibid., http://www.fas.org/irp/threat/missile/iran.htm, p. 2.

auxiliary vessels, and armoured personnel carriers. The deal also included a further Chinese contribution to developing Iranian military industries and to build missiles and helicopters and manufacture artillery. Iran would repay China over the next five years in cash and oil. The report discussed China's past military supplies to Iran. It stated that under previous agreements China provided Iran with military equipment worth approximately US$3 billion, including Shenyang F-7 and F-8 aircraft, Silkworm missiles, HQ anti-aircraft missiles, and C-801 and C-802 advanced missiles, as well as the latest Type-69 tanks, artillery, rocket launchers, and the medium- and long-range 155-mm, 156-mm, and 230-mm guns.[100]

China–Iran economic relations improved in the 1990s. Trade relations between the two countries from 1990 to 1996 reached US$3,537 million compared with US$1,627 million in the 1980s (see Table A.2 in the Appendix). Several economic cooperation agreements were signed by China and Iran to promote economic relations between them. This included an agreement in November 1991 to construct a copper-production factory in Iran with an annual production capacity of 200,000 tonnes, and a cement factory with an annual production capacity of 1,000 tons.[101] An agreement in June 1992 concerned the progress of joint projects, particularly the Yazd zinc project; the iron alloys project; the construction of a copper smelting factory with a capacity of 50,000 tonnes; manpower training; a new project for producing concentrated metals, graphic electrodes, and fire-resistant materials; cooperation in geology; and the construction of a cement manufacturing plant on Qeshm Island with a daily capacity of 700 tons.[102] A memorandum of understanding on railway cooperation was agreed between the two countries' railway officials in December 1992.[103] China granted Iran two loans of US$120 million and US$150 million to build a cement factory and procure equipment for the Tehran Metro.[104] The two countries also reached an agreement for Iran to purchase four multi-purpose cargo ships, each with a loading capacity of 22,000 tons.[105] On 30 May 1995, the Iranian News Agency (IRNA) reported that Iran would increase the volume of its crude oil sales to China from the current 20,000 bbl./day to 60,000 bbl./day. The agreement was reached during the eighth China–Iran joint economic commission meeting held in Beijing during the last week of May. It was reported that Iran had agreed to invest approximately US$25 million in China's oil refining industry in order for Iran to expand further its oil exports to China. Hamid Mirzadeh, head

100 BBC, *SWB*, *FE/2704*, 30 August 1996, p. G/3.
101 *FBIS-NES-91-226*, 22 November 1991, p. 53.
102 *FBIS-NES-92-123*, 25 June 1992, p. 53.
103 *FBIS-NES-92-245*, 21 December 1992, p. 69.
104 *FBIS-NES-93-138*, 21 July 1993, p. 50.
105 *FBIS-NES-93-090*, 12 May 1993, p. 67.

of the Iranian delegation, signed economic agreements with China worth more than US$2 billion, including a US$586 million[106] contract with China to build a subway in Tehran, US$425 million in crude oil sales and refinery investment, US$120 million worth of investment in cement, glass, zinc, and copper production and processing, US$264 million for the construction of a hydroelectric dam in Iran, US$100 million for shipbuilding and US$269 million for the construction of a steel mill.[107] Shanghai's Electronic General company signed a contract with Iran to export two generating units, each with a capacity of 325,000 kW. This contract marked the first export of this type of power equipment to a country in the Gulf and Arabian Peninsula region.[108] While visiting Iran in May 1997 to participate in the ninth session of the Sino-Iran Joint Commission on Economic, Trade, Science and Technology, Li Lanqing, Chinese Vice-Premier, signed a protocol for China to increase imports of Iranian oil from 70,000 bbl./day to 100,000 bbl.day over the following two years, with imports estimated to reach 200,000 bbl./day in 1999. The protocol also stipulated details concerning the completion of a project to build a cement factory with a 700-ton capacity in Iran, the transfer of satellite communication technology and technology needed to implement fluted-glass projects in Iran and the increase of trade exchanges. The two countries also reached agreements on joint investment and expanding cooperation in the spheres of shipbuilding, fisheries, roads, and transport.[109] In May 1997, Iranian oil Minister, Gholamreza Aqazadeh, signed an oil, gas, and petrochemicals agreement in Beijing. The agreement covers Iranian investments in the reconstruction of China's refineries in order to facilitate the processing of Iranian crude oil at these refineries. According to the Iranian Minister, this would increase Iranian crude oil exports to China to more than 170,000 bbl./day the following year (beginning 21 March 1998), and they would reach approximately 270,000 bbl./day after the year 2000.[110] China and Iran are also interested in building pipelines for the export of landlocked Central Asian-energy resources, which are dominated so far by American oil companies. China is interested in building a 1,000-km pipeline from the Uzen oilfield in south-western Kazakhstan across Turkmenistan to Iran. From there, oil could be shipped to China and the rest of the world (Rashid and Holland 2000: 26). If the project was completed, it would be a major blow to US ambitions to build pipelines from Central Asia to Turkey.

106 Some said it was US$573. See *The Wall Street Journal*, 22 May 1995, p. A6; and *FBIS-NES-95-100*, 24 May 1995, p. 44.
107 *Middle East Economic Survey*, Vol. 38, No. 36, 5 June 1995, p. A9.
108 BBC, *SWB, FE/2873*, 21 March 1997, p. G/4.
109 BBC, *SWB, FE/2912*, 7 May 1997, p. G/3.
110 BBC, *SWB, FE/2930*, 28 May 1997, p. G/2.

In sum, China's efforts to foster political and economic relations with Iran coincided with Iran's own interests in pursuing political and economic relations with China. China's attention toward Iran increased as Iran began to pursue a firm policy in the face of America's strategy in the region. Iran's criticism of US policy in the Gulf and Arabian Peninsula region, and the Middle East in general, persuaded Beijing to pay greater attention to its relations with Tehran in order to counter US and Russian expansionist efforts in the region. China's interest in Iran also stemmed from its need for oil and its efforts to cooperate and stabilize relations with Iran's neighbouring countries and prevent them from being dominated by a hostile power.

CHINA AND YEMEN

China and Yemen, 1950–1965

The Republic of Yemen, as it is known today, is a product of two political entities that merged on 22 May 1990: the Yemen Arab Republic (YAR) in the north and the People's Democratic Republic of Yemen (PDRY) in the south. Prior to September 1962, the northern part of Yemen was governed by the Imamat regime while the south was mainly under British control. China's early interest in Yemen was mainly facilitated by Chinese–Soviet alignment and the Soviet Union's initial involvement in Yemen. For China, Yemen in the mid-1950s constituted a region of strategic opportunity that could enable the socialist camp to seize the initiative from the capitalist camp. Therefore, the Chinese collaborated with the Soviets in exploiting anti-Western sentiments and providing economic assistance to the Imamat regime in Yemen. Imam Ahmad's dislike of the British and his policy of leaning towards the Soviet Union, Saudi Arabia, Egypt, and China captured the latter's interest in Yemen. The two countries established formal diplomatic relations in August 1956. The establishment of formal relations with Yemen was China's most significant political development in the Gulf and Arabian Peninsula region at that time. Its significance is that Yemen was the first country in the Arabian Peninsula, and the third country in the Arab world, to acknowledge the PRC as the legitimate representative of all China, when most other countries in the world recognized the nationalist government in Taiwan as the legitimate representative of China.

As China's perception of the Soviet Union was starting to take a new direction after Moscow's new policy of peaceful coexistence with the capitalist camp, the Chinese found it useful to extend their assistance to the Yemeni government. Therefore, they continued to support the Yemen's claim to Aden and its opposition to Britain (Schichor 1979: 75). Yemeni Crown Prince Mohamed al-Badr visited China in 1958 as the first Arab leader to visit the PRC. The two countries signed a treaty of friendship, which marked China's first friendship treaty in the Arab world (Harris 1993:

90–1). They also signed, in January 1958, an agreement on scientific, technical, and cultural cooperation, under which China granted Yemen an interest-free loan of US$16 million repayable over ten years (Bartke 1989: 139–40). While hundreds of Soviet technicians worked to construct Hodeida harbour and Hodeida hospital, the Chinese signed a protocol on 23 January 1959 for the construction of the Hodeida–Sana'a road, a textile mill, and for China to provide an interest-free loan of US$140,000 (Bartke 1989: 140). China's aid to Yemen did not slow down after the September 1962 pro-Soviet coup by Colonel Abdullah as-Sallal, who proclaimed the Yemen Arab Republic. President as-Sallal visited China in June 1964 where he signed a new treaty of friendship to replace the treaty signed with the Imamat regime in 1958, and further agreements on economic, technical, and cultural cooperation. China granted the YAR a loan of US$4.8 in November 1962 and another US$28.2 million in June 1964 (Bartke 1989: 140). Many Chinese worked for many years in building highways in the YAR. Thus, China's early involvement in Yemen was reflected by China's overall foreign policy in the 1950s and early 1960s. Its alignment with the Soviets against the West compelled the Chinese to adopt the Soviet's policy in Yemen. But as China–Soviet relations started to deteriorate, the Chinese began adopting a policy that could challenge the Soviet position in Yemen. Although the Chinese provided more visible and successful aid to Imam Ahmad and to the YAR than the Soviets, they did not exert influence over the regime. However, China–Yemen relations yielded significant advantages for both sides. While the Yemenis received economic and financial assistance from China, the Chinese gained valuable political recognition from an Arabian Peninsula country that later became a member in the UN, at a time when China was isolated diplomatically.

China's interest in South Yemen

Southern Yemen had been controlled by Great Britain since 1839, when the forces of the British East India Co. occupied Aden. In 1937, the area, which by then consisted of 24 sultanates, emirates, and sheikhdoms, was designated the Aden protectorate and was divided for administrative purposes into the East Aden protectorate and the West Aden protectorate. In 1959, six small states of the West Aden protectorate formed the Federation of the Emirates of the South; it was later enlarged to ten members. Despite considerable opposition from its population, in 1963 the Aden colony became part of the federation, subsequently renamed the Federation of South Arabia. By 1965, sixteen tribal states had joined the federation. However, nationalist groups in Aden remained adamantly opposed to the federation and began a violent campaign against the British. Two rival nationalist groups emerged: the National Liberation Front (NLF) and the Front for the Liberation of Occupied South Yemen (FLOSY). Although Britain had promised to withdraw from the region by 1968, the Marxist oriented NLF, which had emerged as the dominant group by 1967, forced the collapse of the federation after taking control of the governments of all the component states. Britain accelerated its withdrawal, and Southern Yemen became independent in November 1967 with Qahtan al-Shaabi of the NLF as its first president. The new state adopted the name the People's Republic of South Yemen (PRSY), which in November 1970 was changed to the People's Democratic Republic of Yemen (PDRY) (O'Ballance 1971; Stookey 1982; Bidwell 1983; Holiday 1990).

In the 1960s, Chinese–Soviet disputes mounted into intense rivalry for leadership of the world socialist revolution, in general, and championship of Third World national liberation movements, in particular. Therefore, South Yemen captured China's attention as it could play a valuable role for the Chinese in their rivalry with the Soviets. In addition to that, South Yemen is strategically located at the junction of the Arabian and Red Seas and it dominates the sea lines of communications both from the Gulf oilfields and between the Mediterranean Sea and the Pacific Ocean via the Suez Canal. This location was of significant importance for the Chinese who sought to prevent the domination of the Soviet Union or the United States over such an important part of the world. Thus, the Chinese government provided political and economic support for the government of the PRSY. Formal diplomatic relations were established between the PRC and PRSY on 31 January 1968. The agreement on the establishment of diplomatic relations was reached in Cairo between Huang Hua, the only high-ranking Chinese ambassador outside the country, and Muhammad Hadi 'Awad, plenipotentiary of the government of the PRSY. The establishment of formal relations with the PRSY was another breakthrough for the Chinese in the Arabian Peninsula. The Chinese government supported the armed struggle of the South Yemen and emphasized:

> Southern Yemen won its independence because its people persevered in a prolonged armed struggle and dealt the British imperialists very severe blows.

But, according to the Chinese analysis, independence was not the end of the struggle for South Yemeni. It believes that:

> The US imperialists and Soviet modern revisionists too will try to get a foothold there. For the Southern Yemeni people, independence is not the end of their struggle, but a continuation of it in new conditions.
> (*Peking Review*, No. 6, 1968: 9)

Eight months after the establishment of diplomatic relations, in September 1968, an official high-ranking delegation from the PRSY visited China. The delegation was headed by Foreign Minister Saif Ahmad al-'Dal'i. In their meetings and statements with the visiting delegation, the

Chinese criticized and attacked US imperialism and 'Soviet socialist imperialism and revisionism'. The Chinese also tried to convince the South Yemeni government to side with China against the Soviet Union. However, the South Yemeni delegation was not in a position to promise a policy of leaning toward China that would upset the Soviets. Therefore, unlike the Chinese, the South Yemeni delegation's statements did not attack the Soviets. Instead, they focused their attacks on the West and on what they called the 'reactionary' regimes in the Gulf region and Arabian Peninsula region, particularly Saudi Arabia (Behbehani 1985). Thus, the South Yemeni government did not want to align itself with either power against the other. The Yemenis wanted to learn from the Chinese experience in building socialism, but they also wanted to remain close to the Soviets. They preferred an independent foreign policy where they could balance between the two giant socialist states. At the end of the visit, the two sides signed an agreement on economic and technical cooperation under which China granted a loan of US$9.6 million.[111] The most significant aspect of the visit and its outcome was that it took place in the midst of the Chinese Cultural Revolution. There are very few examples of the Chinese involving themselves in agreements with foreign countries during the Cultural Revolution. Therefore, analysis of China's involvement with South Yemen suggests that the Chinese could not forgo the significant opportunity to tie themselves closer to the new socialist-born state in the heart of the Arab world. Salim Rubay Ali, Chairman of the Presidential Council of the PRSY, visited China in August 1970. Recognizing PRSY's strong ties with the Soviet Union, the Chinese officials, this time, refrained from using the phrases 'Soviet social imperialism' or 'Soviet social revisionism' in their statements and speeches. In a banquet speech, Tung Piwu, Vice-Chairman of the PRC, praised the South Yemenis' long struggle against imperialism and their support for revolutionary armed struggle against imperialism around the world. He said:

> The government and the people of Southern Yemen, under the leadership of the National Front and Chairman Salim Rubay Ali, have continuously won victories in eliminating imperialist forces, strengthening national defence and carrying out national construction. In international affairs, the government and people of Southern Yemen support the Palestinian and other Arab peoples in their struggle against US–Israeli aggression, support the people of the Arabian Gulf in their revolutionary armed struggle against imperialism, and support the three peoples of Vietnam, Cambodia and Laos in their struggle against US aggression and for national salvation. Southern Yemen is among the

---

111 BBC, *SWB, FE/2889*, 3 October 1968, p. A4/1.

earliest Arab countries which have recognised the Royal Government of National United Front of Kampuchea with Head of State Samdech Sihanouk as its Chairman. The Chinese government and people highly admire this noble stand of the government of Southern Yemen. We sincerely wish the government and people of Southern Yemen continuous new victories on their road of opposing imperialism and colonialism and of independent development.[112]

(BBC, *SWB*, *FE/3447*, 4 August 1970: A4/4-5)

In his banquet speech, Salim Rubay Ali praised the Chinese people's struggle against imperialist powers and said:

We the people of Southern Yemen have benefited from the advanced experience of the Chinese people in defeating our enemies, the colonialists and reactionaries, and frustrating the aggressive schemes against the revolution and the progressive revolutionary regime of Southern Yemen under the leadership of the political organisation of the National Front ... The essence of the imperialist challenge to the fighting peoples in the third world demands that the genuine revolutionary forces unite in one front which enjoys the support of the socialist camp.

(BBC, *SWB*, *FE/3447*, 4 August 1970: A4/6)

The Chinese government recognized the sensitivity, particularly inside South Yemen, of criticizing the Soviets in China's statements with South Yemen and of encouraging South Yemen to side with China against the Soviets as the Chinese had done two years earlier. South Yemeni leadership was divided into two major political schools of thought regarding South Yemeni relations with Moscow and Beijing. Rubay's school of thought was pro-China and sympathetic to the Chinese line of Marxism; however, Abd al-fattah Ismail's, NFL General Secretary, school of thought was in favour of the Soviets and their line of Marxism. Each of these two leaders had used visits to China and the Soviet Union to cultivate support for the PRSY. Prior to Rubay's visit to China, Ismail visited Moscow in the same year. While the latter's visit yielded no significant new aid commitments, the former's visit elicited a Chinese aid offer of UK£43 million, and a promise to release another UK£12 million originally pledged in 1967 (Calabrese 1991: 57-8). Thus, it appeared that China preferred to pay more attention to improving its ties with the government of the PRSY by trying to impress it with substantial economic aid. China signed several economic, trade, and

---

112 His only mention of 'social imperialism' came with reference to the issue of Palestine: 'Not long ago, with the co-ordination of social imperialism, US imperialism again dished up a 'political initiative for a so-called peaceful settlement of the Middle East question'.

technical cooperation agreements with the renamed PDRY; it also helped with constructing roads, bridges, and factories. The value of China's trade with the PDRY also increased after the establishment of formal relations in 1968. The value of bilateral trade jumped from US$1.5 million in 1967 to approximately US$3.9 million in 1969 and approximately US$11.20 million in 1972 (see Table A.4 in the Appendix).

China and Yemen in the 1970s

As China's fear of Soviet penetration of the world, in general, and the Gulf and Arabian Peninsula region, in particular, rose in the early 1970s, China's foreign policy towards the YAR and the PDRY reflected its concern. China continued its economic aid to both Yemens, providing both sides with textile plants; road, building and hospital constructions; and financial, medical, and agricultural assistance. It even provided the PDRY with a small-scale supply of arms (Creekman 1979: 76). It increased its trade volume with the YAR from US$1.25 million in 1970 to US$30.74 million in 1974 and US$66.30 million in 1979; and with the PDRY from US$3.84 million in 1970 to US$12.59 million in 1974 and US$20.37 million in 1979 (see Tables A.3 and A.4 in the Appendix). However, China's continued commitment to aid and support for the PDRY did not lead to the establishment of Chinese influence over the South Yemeni regime, nor the disengagement of the Soviets from that country. Instead, the pro-Soviet group gained the upper hand in South Yemen. Salim Rubay Ali was ousted in June 1978 by Ismail, who signed a twenty-year friendship treaty with the Soviet Union in October 1979 (Page 1985: 94). Soviet influence, including the presence of naval bases, became predominant in the PDRY (Creekman 1979: 77). These developments cooled relations between China and South Yemen. This was evident in China's reaction to North Yemeni President al-Ghashmi's assassination. China showed its sympathy for the YAR by publishing the Sana'a government's version of the assassination instead of Aden's version in the media.[113]

The PDRY government was leaning towards the Soviet Union because it perceived that the presence of the United States in the Gulf and Arabian Peninsula region, which had been developing in the early and mid-1970s, posed an increasing threat to the South Yemeni regime during the late 1970s and early 1980s. The South Yemeni government believed that China could not offer the PDRY the much-needed sophisticated weapons and naval protection that the Soviet Union could provide to protect the South Yemeni regime. Although China continued its assistance to the PDRY in constructing roads and textile mills as well as in extending a loan of US$12.5 million,

113 *FBIS-CHI-78-123*, 26 June 1978, p. A26.

its activities decreased after the Maoist-oriented Salim Rubay Ali faction lost in its struggle with supporters of the Soviet model of socialism.

As in the South, China's economic assistance to the North did not lead to the establishment of significant Chinese influence on the regime. In November 1979, the North Yemeni government of Col. Ali Abdullah Saleh began purchasing arms from the Soviet Union. When Saudi Arabia offered Saleh US$300 million in aid to keep the Soviets out, the Soviets responded with a US$1 billion arms programme over the next half-decade for the North Yemeni military (Kaplan 1986: 1). Thus, as the Soviets had already established themselves in the PDRY by providing military and economic aid to secure the survival of the new regime in South Yemen, and as they had started to gain some ground in North Yemen, the Chinese government renewed its interest in the China–US strategic relationship. The Chinese began to support the American presence in the region. They also moved towards strengthening their ties with neighbouring countries of the Gulf and Arabian Peninsula region by terminating their commitment to and support for the revolutionary group in Oman and the communist party in Iran. Such changes were mandated by China's desire to counter Soviet presence and influence in and around the region by encouraging the United States and the countries of the region to resist Soviet penetration.

China and Yemen in the 1980s

The strategic threat to the survival of the South Yemeni regime was perceived by Aden to be on the rise in the early 1980s. The establishment of the GCC was interpreted in Aden as a reinforcement of the pro-Western stance in the region through cooperation and mutual protection and as opposition to the leftist groups in the region. In addition, the PDRY was concerned about increasing US activity in the Indian Ocean and the Red Sea basin, as a result of President Jimmy Carter's new determination to defend Western interests in the region. In 1981 and 1982, the United States in cooperation with Sudan, Somalia, Egypt, and Oman conducted the 'Bright Star' manoeuvres, which were perceived by South Yemen as a direct American threat to the South Yemeni regime (Kostiner 1990: 92–3). Therefore, the South Yemeni government continued its alignment with the Soviets and its support for Soviet penetration around the world.[114] Soviet arms continued to reach South Yemen in the 1980s, the number of Soviet military advisors doubled, and Soviet Union naval forces were stationed in the Gulf of Aden (Page 1985: 97). As a result, PDRY relations

---

114 For example, the PDRY was the only Arab state to vote with the USSR when the UN General Assembly voted on 14 January 1980 to condemn the Soviet invasion of Afghanistan.

180 *China's foreign policy toward the Gulf and Arabian Peninsula region*

with its neighbouring countries continued to deteriorate in the early 1980s. Despite South Yemen's economic difficulties, Saudi Arabia was not willing to promise aid as long as Aden was so close to Moscow and so hostile to the Sultan of Oman. Meanwhile, North Yemen wanted to maintain good relations with the Soviet Union in order to obtain Soviet arms and exert pressure on Aden. As a result, YAR relations with certain neighbouring countries, including Saudi Arabia, also declined (Editorial Board 1998: 1101). Against this background, the Chinese government found itself limited to exert influence on both Yemens. As China attempted to cultivate better relations with the United States and the states of the Gulf region, relations with the South Yemeni government were limited to a few economic assistance programmes and gradually-developing trade relations in the early 1980s (see Table A.4 in the Appendix). However, China's economic relations with North Yemen continued to develop on a grand scale. Principally because China believed that, unlike the South, North Yemen was not a Soviet satellite.

One of the most important features of China's foreign policy toward the two Yemens in the 1980s was China's insistence that both Yemens improve their relations with neighbouring Gulf and Arabian Peninsula countries in order to strengthen their unity against foreign intervention. China encouraged and welcomed the rapprochement of relations between Saudi Arabia and the two Yemens. Saudi Arabia resumed its aid to the YAR throughout the 1980s to help the country cover its budget deficit, and in 1989 the Kingdom lifted almost all restrictions imposed on Yemeni migrant workers. The Kingdom also moved positively to ease its strained relations with the PDRY. China also welcomed the normalization of relations between the PDRY and Oman, South Yemen's main rival, in October 1982. An article in *Beijing Review* stated:

> The US and Soviet military presence in Oman and Democratic Yemen is a major cause of their long-standing hostility. This presence will continue for some time to come, but Oman and Democratic Yemen have agreed that this should not be an obstacle to the normalisation of their relations.
>
> (*Beijing Review*, No. 49, 6 December 1982: 13–14)

The Chinese viewed such developments as a positive strategy towards strengthening the security of the Peninsula region against Soviet and US manoeuvres to dominate the region.[115]

In March 1987, PDRY Premier Yasin Sa'id Nu'man paid an official visit to China. The Chinese government agreed to offer more economic,

---

115 *Beijing Review*, number 16, 1980, pp. 11–12.

technical, and cultural aid to South Yemen and agreed to reschedule the repayment of Chinese loans to Aden.[116] It also agreed to assist South Yemen in building a 44.5-km highway, with a Chinese loan of UK$30 million.[117] The Chinese government also continued to send delegations to participate in South Yemen's National Days. Meanwhile, China–YAR relations were strengthened even further. YAR President Ali Abdullah Saleh visited Beijing in December 1987. This was Saleh's first visit to China since he became president nine years previously. In their meetings with the visiting President, the Chinese officials focused their statements and speeches on praising North Yemen's non-aligned foreign policy and its distance from the Soviet Union. In a banquet speech to the visiting President, Chinese President Li Xiannian said:

> In international affairs, the Chinese government admires the Yemen Arab Republic's foreign policy. The Yemen Arab Republic has followed a policy of neutrality, nonalignment and good-neighbourliness and made an active contribution to strengthen the unity among Arab countries and to safeguard regional peace and stability.

He added:

> We have treasured our friendship and co-operation with the Yemen Arab Republic ... and we are willing to strengthen friendly relations and economic and technical co-operation between the two countries under the principles of equality and mutual benefit, stressing practical results, adopting various forms and achieving common development.
> (*FBIS-CHI-87-248*, 28 December 1987: 14)

The Chinese agreed to provide North Yemen with a long-term interest-free loan of US$40.32 million and to construct the 127-km Heghana–Mareb road.[118]

In summary, China's relations with both South and North Yemen in the 1980s were conducted on the basis of China's determination not to leave either country completely at the will of the Soviet Union. Therefore, China provided economic and technical assistance to both sides. However, China supplied more assistance to the North than to the South. This could be explained in terms of China's satisfaction with North Yemen's foreign policy of non-alignment, particularly with the Soviet Union, and its dissatisfaction with South Yemen's alignment with the Soviet Union.

---

116 *FBIS-CHI-88-020*, 1 February 1988, p. 7.
117 *FBIS-CHI-88-191*, 3 October 1988, p. 14.
118 *FBIS-CHI-88-242*, 16 December 1988, pp. 17–18.

China and the Republic of Yemen

The two Yemens were officially united on 22 May 1990. North Yemen's President Ali Abdullah Saleh became the president of the Republic of Yemen, and South Yemen's Ali Salim al-Baid became the vice-president. Sana'a was chosen as the nation's political capital while Aden became the nation's economic capital. China was among the first nations to extend its recognition to the newly-established republic in Yemen. Yang Shangkun, Chinese president, sent a congratulatory message to Saleh, Chairman of the Presidential Council of the Republic of Yemen, on the following day of its proclamation. Yang said:

> On the occasion of the deceleration of the establishment of the Republic of Yemen, I, on behalf of the Chinese people and on my own behalf, wish to extend my warmest congratulations to Your Excellency Mr Chairman and through Your Excellency Mr Chairman to the people of Yemen. Through friendly consultations the Yemeni leaders have fulfilled the great task of unification. This is an event of great significance in the history of Yemen. China has had very close relations of friendship and co-operation with both South and North Yemen and has always supported Yemen's unity, stability, and peace. The Chinese government and people respect this historical choice made by the people of Yemen. We wholeheartedly hope the unification of Yemen will help Yemen develop and help bring peace and stability to the local region. We wish the Republic of Yemen prosperity and its people happiness. May Sino-Yemeni relations of friendship and co-operation continuously consolidate and develop.
> (*FBIS-CHI-90-101*, 24 May 1990: 12)

The Republic of Yemen's President Saleh expressed his appreciation for China's support for the reunification of Yemen and China's assistance in Yemen's economic development. Saleh made the remarks at a meeting with a visiting Chinese government delegation led by Minister of Energy Resources Huang Yi Cheng, which had arrived to participate in the celebration marking the first anniversary of the Republic of Yemen.[119]

During the Kuwait crisis, the Yemeni government sent a special envoy to China in the hope of gathering support to stop the US-led military offensive against Iraq. Yemen's Minister of State for Parliamentary Affairs met with China's Vice-Premier Wu Xueqian and gave him a letter from the Yemeni President to be forwarded to President Yang Shangkun. The Yemeni minister briefed Wu about the Yemeni government's position on the Gulf

---

119 *FBIS-CHI-91-101*, 24 May 1991, pp. 7–8.

crisis and its efforts to push for a peaceful settlement of the war as soon as possible.[120] Throughout the crisis, both China and Yemen continued to advocate the need to stop the war and allow political means an opportunity to solve the crisis. Unlike the Yemeni government, the Chinese government was not willing to commit itself to challenging the Western powers over this issue.

China's support for Yemeni unification emanated from its concern over Soviet and US penetration in the region. To the Chinese government, a divided Yemen could easily bring more foreign intervention in Yemen's affairs, especially from the two superpowers. However, a united Yemen could prevent such a possibility. Therefore, the Chinese government continued to pay attention to Yemen's domestic developments, following the early 1994 disputes between the different parties over power in Yemen. As the disputes started to escalate, three Chinese workers were kidnapped in February 1994 while working on a road project financed by China to link Hajana and Mareb. They were released on 3 April.[121] China proceeded to evacuate about 505 Chinese medical personnel and contract workers from Yemen by May.[122] China–Yemen's relations, however, did not deteriorate as a result of the kidnapping. Chinese officials were satisfied with the Yemeni government efforts to release the kidnapped Chinese, but their concern was over the continuing conflict in Yemen. When meeting with the visiting Yemeni Vice-Foreign Minister Abdul Kadir in March, Chinese Vice-Premier and Foreign Minister Qian Qichen said:

> We are very much concerned about Yemen's domestic situation, hoping that the country will realise its social stability and enjoy a good environment for its construction ... *we believe that the Yemeni people will solve their own problems themselves* [emphasis added].
> (*FBIS-NES-94-032*, 16 February 1994: 20)

Fear of foreign intervention, particularly from the Soviets, concerned the Chinese government over the impact of continued conflicts on the unified state. When Abd al-Aziz Abd al-Ghani, Presidential Council member of Yemen, visited Beijing in June, the Chinese officials again stressed the importance of solving the differences through dialogue and preventing foreign intervention, and al-Ghani assured the Chinese that Yemen rejected any external attempt to intervene in its domestic affairs.[123] China's support

---

120 *FBIS-CHI-91-024*, 5 February 1991, p. 14.
121 *FBIS-CHI-94-074*, 18 April 1994, p. 22.
122 *FBIS-CHI-94-094*, 16 May 1994, p. 10.
123 *FBIS-CHI-94-117*, 17 June 1994, p. 12.

for the unity of Yemen was appreciated by various Yemeni officials. President Ali Saleh, upon his arrival in Beijing on 14 February 1998, said:

> I would like to seize this opportunity to express my heartfelt appreciation for Chinese stands that are supportive of Arab rights, and also of the Yemeni people and their revolution, unity, and development efforts.
> (BBC, *SWB*, *FE/3152*, 16 February 1998: G/13)

Chinese officials continued to speak highly of Yemen foreign policy throughout the second half of the 1990s. They stressed China's appreciation of Yemen's 'peaceful, neutral, good-neighbouring foreign policy' and its efforts to boost relations with neighbours and other Arab states. They also looked at Yemen as a major force to maintain solidarity among Arab states and safeguard peace and stability in the Red Sea and Gulf region.

In the economic realm, China and Yemen continued their meetings to review aspects of cooperation between the two countries in the economic and oil and gas sectors, the exchange of technical expertise in developing the free zone area, trade exchange and means of improving this cooperation. China and Yemen signed a memorandum of understanding in Sana'a on 16 May 1996, during Chinese Vice-Premier Wu Bangguo's visit to Yemen, for the development of cooperation in the fields of oil prospecting, production, marketing, and refining. An economic and technical cooperation agreement was also signed. According to the agreement, China would grant Yemen 30 million yuan in aid to implement the economic and technical cooperation projects agreed upon by the two sides.[124] During the meetings of the Joint Chinese–Yemeni Trade and Technical Co-operation Committee in Sana'a in June, the two countries signed the minutes of meetings and an agreement on economic and technical cooperation and implementation of the Friendship Bridge project in the city of Sana'a.[125] They also formally signed a new cooperation agreement in Sana'a on 11 September, in which both sides signalled their intention to increase cooperation in the field of news services further. This was the first-ever news cooperation agreement between the two countries.[126] On 15 November, a summary of talks between China and Yemen on oil cooperation was also signed. It stressed that both sides would make more effort to strengthen their cooperation in the oil sector. Under the summary, China would conduct oil exploration in Yemen and purchase crude oil direct from Yemen.[127] In 1996, China's Zhenhai refinery began to

---

124 BBC, *SWB*, *FE/2617*, 21 May 1996, p. G/4.
125 BBC, *SWB*, *Weekly Economic Report (henceforth MEW) 0436 WME*, 2 July 1996, p. 12.
126 BBC, *SWB*, *FE/2718*, 14 September 1996, p. G/4.
127 BBC, *SWB*, *MEW/0454 WME*, 24 September 1996, p. 13.

purchase all the Yemeni government's 30,000-bbl./day share of Mareb crude.[128] Several economic, trade, medical, and cultural agreements were signed between the two countries when President Ali Saleh visited Beijing in February 1998.[129] Throughout the 1990s, the volume of trade continued to increase in an impressive fashion. From 1990 to 1996, the value of trade reached US$2,024 million, which was approximately 1.5 times higher than China's trade with both Yemens in the 1980s (see Table A.5 in the Appendix).

CONCLUSION

The above discussion suggests that the foreign policy of the PRC toward Iraq, Iran, and Yemen from October 1949 to the late 1980s had been guided by the direction of China's relations with the United States and the Soviet Union. In the 1990s, however, the data suggest that China's relations with these three countries were more a reflection of China's own economic and political interests.

In Iraq, Baghdad's close alignment with Washington and London prevented Beijing from furthering close relations with that country. Thus, China classified Iraq as part of the imperialist camp. However, China's interest in Iraq shifted in 1958 toward supporting the Qasim regime. China, which began to look for support from Third World countries in its ideological and political struggle against the United States and later on the Soviet Union, regarded Baghdad as a potential strategic ally, particularly after Iraq's withdrawal from the Baghdad Pact. China's hope was short-lived. From 1967, Moscow enjoyed strong ties with Baghdad, which shortly became very dependent on Moscow for military and political support. China's interest then shifted towards revolutionary groups. After the signing of a treaty of friendship between Moscow and Baghdad in the early 1970s, China started to develop strategic alignment with the United States and to pursue political ties with some other countries of the region. Its aim was to undermine the Soviet presence in Iraq. Once China perceived a decline in Moscow–Baghdad relations in the second half of the 1970s, it began to further political and economic ties with Iraq. Its interest in Iraq continued throughout the 1980s. China's policies towards Iraq in the 1980s were aimed at strengthening its relations with that country in order to prevent the Soviet Union from establishing a presence for itself in Iraq, so China provided military and economic assistance to Baghdad throughout its prolonged war with Iran. In the 1990s, China's foreign policy toward Iraq

---

128 *Middle East Economic Survey*, Vol. 39, No. 41, 8 July 1996, p. A8.
129 See BBC, *SWB, MEW/0526 WME*, 24 February 1998, p. 17.

was limited by UN resolutions against Iraq. China supported the UN resolution against Iraq and remained faithful to the imposed sanctions against Baghdad. China could not challenge the UN actions against Iraq because of its need for good ties with the oil-producing countries of the Gulf and Arabian Peninsula region. Thus, China did not want to be seen siding with Iraq, whom the oil producing countries of the region saw as a threat to their stability. However, Chinese foreign policy continued to call for the removal of sanctions against Iraq since, on one hand, Iraq held one of the largest proven oil reserves in the world and, on the other hand, it could provide Chinese companies with great opportunities for investment. Therefore, China's foreign policy toward Iraq in the 1990s was guided more by China's economic interests in the region than by its relations with either Washington or Moscow.

In Iran, China's foreign policy in the 1950s was attached to the power blocs. The strong Western influence in Iran and China's close alignment with Moscow prevented China from establishing ties with Tehran. Throughout the 1960s, China remained isolated from Iran. This was mainly due to China's support for revolutionary groups in the region, including the communist party in Iran. However, as China's foreign policy toward Washington and Moscow changed in the 1970s, China's foreign policy toward Iran also changed. China stopped its support for revolutionary groups in the Gulf and Arabian Peninsula region, including those in Iran, in favour of accumulating better relations with the governments of the region to undermine Soviet influence. Such a change won China political recognition from Iran in August 1971. Since then, China had continued to expand its bilateral ties with Iran on all levels. The Soviet presence in Afghanistan urged the Chinese to accept the revolutionary changes that took place in Iran in 1979. It also encouraged China to neutralize its policy toward both Iran and Iraq during their lengthy war. Political, economic, and military cooperation between China and Iran reached its highest point in the two countries relations in the 1980s. Cooperation with Iran was aimed at keeping Tehran away from leaning toward Moscow for help and assistance, particularly since Washington was engaged in full-scale support of Iraq. In the 1990s, China's foreign policy toward Iran began to reflect China's own modernization programme. Iran assumed a new significance to China as China's need for oil continued to increase throughout the 1990s.

In Yemen in the 1950s, China's interest was initiated by Moscow's initial involvement there. China supported the Soviet Union's efforts to exploit anti-Western sentiment in Yemen and provided economic assistance to the North Yemen regime. China also supported North Yemen's claim over British-controlled South Yemen. But as Beijing–Moscow relations began to diverge, the Chinese started to compete with the Soviets in Yemen. They offered a substantial amount of financial and economic assistance, which even exceeded Soviet assistance. As Beijing–Moscow relations continued to deteriorate, South Yemen assumed a greater significance in China's foreign policy strategy to take the leading role not only in the socialist camp, but also in the Third World. China, which was interested in the revolutionary activities of the South Yemeni forces, provided South Yemen with political, technical, financial, and military support. But, as the Soviets increased their presence in the South, the Chinese opted for a strategic alignment with the United States and the countries of the Gulf and Arabian Peninsula region, including North Yemen, to counter Soviet influence in South Yemen. Thus, China's support and assistance to South Yemen decreased rapidly in the 1980s while its relations with North Yemen developed quickly. In the 1990s, China gave its backing to the creation of a unified Republic of Yemen. Its interest in Yemen was deepened by the fact that the republic assumed a leading role as one of the major oil suppliers to China in the 1990s.

6 China's relations with the countries of the Gulf Co-operation Council

CHINA AND KUWAIT

China and Kuwait before recognition

In the 1950s and most of the 1960s, Kuwait was an important British concern and an area of considerable interest to the United States. This was mainly due to its oil potential. Kuwait had the world's largest oil reserves and was ranked fourth in world oil production. Kuwait's oil production assumed a substantial significance in the early 1950s. The nationalization of Iranian oil in 1951 and the subsequent Western boycott of Iranian oil created heavy demand for Kuwait's oil. Therefore, British firms and personnel dominated development planning in Kuwait (Joyce 1998). The al-Sabah family favoured the presence of both the British and the Americans in Kuwait in the 1950s. Meanwhile, China was leaning toward the Soviet policy against the United States and the rest of the capitalist camp. Against this background, Beijing's policy toward Kuwait was a reflection of its alignment with Moscow. Thus, recognizing the socialist camp's weakness to exert any influence on Kuwait, the Chinese leadership classified the Kuwaiti regime as part of the capitalist camp headed by the United States. Even after the Bandung conference, China did not consider Kuwait to have the potential to wage a struggle against the West in the Arab world. The Kuwaiti regime remained loyal to the British and did not oppose the establishment of the Baghdad Pact, which China criticized heavily. Despite its support for Nasser's nationalist policies in the Arab world, the Kuwaiti regime did not advocate Nasser's anti-British propaganda in Kuwait.[1] While Egypt–Britain relations continued to deteriorate, Kuwait–Britain relations remained unharmed.

However, one could argue that, while the Chinese lacked direct political

---

1 When Anwar Sadat, Nasser's closest associate, visited Kuwait in December in 1955, the Kuwaiti officials kept him busy so that he would not have a chance to promote anti-British sentiment to the Kuwaiti government.

relations with Kuwait in the 1950s, they did not eliminate Kuwait from their foreign policy in the Arab world. Instead, they hoped to use their support for Nasser's nationalist policy and popularity to influence nationalist movements in the Gulf and Peninsula region. As Egyptian teachers travelled to Kuwait, pro-Nasser nationalist ideas started to spread among young Kuwaitis. Therefore, China's policy toward Kuwait in the 1950s can be explained in the context of China's foreign policy toward Egypt and Nasser's nationalist policy.

When Kuwait gained its independence from Britain on 19 June 1961, the Chinese Premier Zhou Enlai sent a congratulatory message on 30 June to Sheikh Abdullah al-Salim saying:

> On the occasion of the proclamation of independence of Kuwait, I have the honour, on behalf of the Government of the People's Republic of China, to extend hearty congratulations to the Government and people of Kuwait. May the people of Kuwait achieve further successes in the cause of opposing imperialism and colonialism, safeguarding national independence and building their country. May your country attain prosperity and its people enjoy happiness.
>
> (Behbehani 1981: 193)

When Kuwait proclaimed its independence from Britain, China was prompted to support Kuwait. Therefore, the Chinese welcomed the independence of Kuwait and extended its recognition to the new state despite the fact that Iraq, China's closest Arab ally, was against the independence of Kuwait and was threatening military action. China's interest in supporting Kuwait's independence stemmed from the fact that China wanted to see the British military leave Kuwait as a first step towards a complete withdrawal of all foreign presence from the Gulf region. However, events did not go the way that the Chinese had hoped for. Soon after gaining its independence, Kuwait, driven by the fear of an Iraqi attack, requested British military protection and assistance. On 31 June, British troops began to arrive in Kuwait. The Chinese press began to attack the reinforcement of British military forces in Kuwait, but never criticized the Kuwaiti government. They described the British military presence as a 'British occupation of Kuwait' (Behehani 1981: 193-4); and they began to be more sympathetic to Iraqi claims. However, Chinese criticism subsided after the Arab League welcomed Kuwait as a new member on 20 July and decided to send Arab military forces to Kuwait to replace the British troops to keep peace and to prevent Iraqi invasion. The Chinese government welcomed the Kuwaiti decision to replace the British troops with Arab peacekeeping forces (Behbehani 1981: 196-7), but its criticism this time was shifted towards the transfer of British troops from Kuwait to other British military bases in the Gulf and Arabian Peninsula region.

China's relations with Kuwait were very low in the 1960s. Several developments had contributed to the cooling of relations. First, Sheikh Jabir al-Ahmad al-Sabah's, Kuwaiti Minister of Finance, Industry and Commerce, visit to China in February 1965 yielded no significant improvement in China–Kuwait political relations. Second, China became frustrated with Kuwait's closer alignment with the West and its unwillingness to reciprocate China's recognition of Kuwait in June 1961. Kuwait preferred not to rush to recognize the PRC. This was mainly due to the Kuwaiti government's unwillingness to sever its political relations with Taiwan, which supported Kuwait in the UN Security Council throughout its dispute with Iraq. And, third, China began to support revolutionary movements in the region. Kuwait did not appreciate China's support for such groups in the region; therefore, bilateral relations throughout the 1960s never exceeded trade relations.

The establishment of diplomatic relations

China's insistence on the termination of relations with Taiwan and its support for revolutionary movements prevented the Kuwaiti government from pursuing political ties with China in the 1960s. However, this was about to change in the 1970s. China's foreign policy toward the government of Kuwait was reflected by changes in China's view of the international system. In the late 1960s and early 1970s, the Soviet Union had become China's principle enemy and, to China, the Soviet Union replaced the United States as the world's most dangerous source of instability. The Chinese feared that the Soviet Union would penetrate the Gulf and Arabian Peninsula region to refill the power vacuum following the British withdrawal. Meanwhile, Kuwait was following a more neutral foreign policy and shared the Chinese fear of the Soviets. The Kuwaiti government invited the Chinese ambassador to Iraq, Kung Tafei, to Kuwait where he held talks with Kuwaiti officials from 8 to 22 March 1971. Behbehani (1981) states that the Kuwaiti government tried to convince the Chinese official of their preference to keep political relations with both China and Taiwan. Although the Chinese official rejected the Kuwaiti demand, the Kuwaiti government decided on 22 March 1971 to establish formal relations with the PRC. A joint communiqué said:

> The Government of the PRC and the Government of the state of Kuwait, in accordance with the principle of developing the common interests of the two countries and the desire of promoting the relations between the two countries in all fields, in view of the noble stand of the PRC in supporting the Arab struggle against imperialism and Zionism, in view of the stand of the Government of the state of Kuwait in recognising the Government of the PRC as the sole legal Government of China, have decided to establish diplomatic relations at

the ambassadorial level and exchange ambassadors within the shortest possible period.

(BBC, *SWB*, *FE/3648*, 31 March 1971: A4/1)

Kuwait's decision to establish diplomatic relations with China originated in Kuwait's assessment that China's replacement of Taiwan in the UN Security Council was imminent. The Kuwaiti government recognized that the political importance of China as a permanent member of the UN Security Council exceeded the economic importance of Taiwan. To the Kuwaitis, China could not only enhance its support for Arab causes, but could also support Kuwait's causes against Iraq. To the Chinese, the establishment of formal relations with Kuwait meant clearing the way for the Gulf and Arabian Peninsula region states to follow suit.

On the establishment of formal relations, the official *People's Daily* paid tribute in an editorial to the Kuwaiti government's decision and praised its efforts to protect its national resources:

> The Chinese Government and the Government of the state of Kuwait have decided after friendly talks to establish diplomatic relations between the two countries. We welcome this heartily and extend our warm congratulations. Since their independence in 1961 the Kuwaiti people together with the people of other Arab countries have been opposing the US and Israeli aggressors and supporting the Palestinian people's just struggle. To safeguard their state sovereignty and national resources, the Kuwaiti government and people together with other petroleum exporting countries carried out recently a powerful struggle against the imperialist oil monopolist groups headed by the United States. The Chinese people resolutely support the just struggle of the Kuwaiti Government and people and regard this support as our bounded internationalist duty.
>
> (BBC, *SWB*, *FE/3649*, 1 April 1971: A4/1)

On 25 October 1971, Kuwait was among the few Arab states that voted in favour of China's admission to the UN. China's first ambassador to Kuwait, Sun Shengwei, arrived in Kuwait on 5 August.

The Chinese welcomed Kuwaiti press criticism of the Soviet Union for allowing Soviet Jews to emigrate to Israel. They published many of the Kuwaiti press articles that attacked the Soviet Union's policies in the Arab world. For example, *Peking Review* published an editorial issued on 9 March 1973 by the Kuwaiti newspaper *Al-Rai al-Amm*, which criticized the Soviet Union's 'friendship' with the Arab world. The editorial said:

> We do not believe that the purpose of the Soviet investment of dozens of billions of US dollars in this area is only for God's sake ... How can we believe Soviet friendship with us Arabs as 'gratuitous' when the Soviet

Union has opened the door for the emigration of Jews to Palestine? Even if we were foolish enough we cannot believe that a friend who brought our enemies for us is a friend indeed.

(*Peking Review*, No. 11, 16 March 1973: 19–20)

The Chinese also praised Kuwait's oil policy and its efforts to protect its national resources. When the Kuwaiti government gained a 60 per cent share in the Kuwait Oil Company (KOC) in January 1974, the Chinese government perceived this development as a blow to Western monopoly in the region. It stated:

This was a new victory for the government and people in defending state sovereignty and national resources and another heavy blow to Western monopoly capital.

On the Soviet penetration, the Chinese said:

While continuing the struggle against Western oil monopoly capital, the Kuwaiti people are on guard against the other superpower's predatory designs on the oil riches in the region. In recent years the Kuwaiti press has exposed the scandalous acts of the Soviet Union in making fabulous profits by reselling oil obtained from the Arab region to Western Europe. It has also sternly refuted Soviet nonsense about the oil in the Gulf being 'international property', pointing out that this fallacy is the 'latest imperialist logic' aimed at legalising Soviet plunder of Gulf oil.

(*Peking Review*, No. 14, 5 April 1974)

The Chinese were also satisfied with the outcome of Sheikh Sabah al-Ahmad al-Jabir al-Sabah's, Kuwaiti Minister of Foreign Affairs, visit to Beijing in May 1977 where he assured the Chinese government that:

We are committed to preventing our Gulf from being an arena of political and military rivalry between the powers.

(*Peking Review*, No. 20, 13 May 1977: 20)

Despite the fact that Kuwait did not dispatch its first ambassador to Beijing until August 1975, trade relations between the two sides continued to grow throughout the 1970s. The volume of China's trade with Kuwait jumped from US$20.44 million in 1970 to US$33.88 million in 1972, then to US$78.48 million in 1974, reaching US$174.97 million in 1979 (see Table A.6 in the Appendix). Chinese imports consisted mainly of chemical fertilizers. The two sides reached agreement on 26 December 1977 on economic and technological cooperation. From that time, the Chinese began to send Chinese medical groups to work in Kuwait (Bartke 1989: 77).

The establishment of diplomatic relations with Kuwait was China's other significant political achievement in the Gulf and Arabian Peninsula region. China was emerging from political isolation during the Cultural Revolution, and was more than happy to find that there were some countries in the region willing to establish mutual diplomatic relations. China could not resist the opportunity to establish diplomatic relations with Kuwait in order to benefit from potential political and economic gains. Politically, the Chinese government would be able to find further recognition for their authority as the legitimate government of all China. Economically, China would gain a new market for its goods and a potential supplier of energy and chemical fertilizers. However, China's relations with Kuwait in the 1970s did not witness a substantial political or strategic improvement. This might be due to Kuwait's neutral foreign policy. Kuwait was able to balance its relations between the United States and the Soviet Union. For instance, when Kuwait rejected an American arms sales proposal, it moved to purchase Soviet weapons. Such a move was not appreciated by the Chinese government which, at the time, perceived the Soviet Union as the most dangerous power to the security of the Gulf region.

China and Kuwait in the 1980s

The 1980s witnessed two important developments in China's foreign policy. First, China proclaimed its independent foreign policy. This new foreign policy was similar to Kuwait's neutral foreign policy. This similarity created few divergences in the foreign policies of both China and Kuwait toward many world issues. Second, the Chinese government started to commit itself to the Four Modernizations programme, which raised the level of Kuwait's economic significance to China. Kuwait, resolutely, became an important source of loans and investments to China and was an influential contributor to South–South cooperation in the Chinese view.[2] From the Kuwaiti point of view, China could bring another investment destination in order to diversify Kuwait's investments and expand its geographical presence. In an interview with the Kuwaiti daily *Al Qabas* on 18 May 1986, the Kuwaiti Minister of Finance and Economy Jasim al Khurafi said that Kuwait's investments in China were driven by the desire to expand the area in which Kuwaiti funds were invested in order to reduce risks and to seek a better return.[3] The Kuwait Fund for Arab Economic Development (KFAED) provided China with over US$150 million in loans from 1982 to 1983. A US$30 million low-interest loan was extended in 1984 for the construction

---

2 *Beijing Review*, No. 11, 14 March 1982, p. 14.
3 *FBIS-CHI-86-100*, 23 May 1986, p. 12.

of a hydroelectric power station in Fujian (Calabrese 1991: 142). Another loan was granted in July 1985 in which the KFAED would provide China with US$13.2 million to finance construction of a small vehicle plant in Tianjin in north China.[4] As a result, China–Kuwait economic relations were expanded throughout the 1980s. The Kuwait Petroleum Corporation (KPC) acquired joint exploration rights in offshore China (Brady 1984: 108), including an agreement to build a production platform and an underwater pipeline costing an estimated US$400 million from which 15 per cent was to be paid by Santa Fe Minerals (Asia) Inc., a unit of the KPC-owned Santa Fe International.[5] In October 1985, KPC acquired a 15 per cent equity interest in the development of a gasfield off South-west China's Hainan Island. An Arab–Chinese joint-venture firm was established, the Sino-Arab Chemical Fertiliser Company (SACF), to construct a fertilizer plant near the port of Quinhuandao for the production of 480,000 tons/year of diammonium phosphate and 600,000 tons/year of nitrogen potassium phosphate. The plant would utilize phosphoric acid feedstock produced by the Kuwaiti–Tunisian joint-venture company Société Industrielle d'Acide Phosphorique et d'Engrais (SIAPE) and ammonia produced locally. Sixty per cent (US$15 million) of the capital would be held equally by Kuwait Petrochemical Industries Company (KPIC) and SIAPE, and the remaining 40 per cent would be owned by the Chinese National Chemical Construction Company (CNCCC).[6] On 23 November 1985, China and Kuwait signed an investment guarantee agreement providing for the promotion and protection of joint investment in the two countries.[7] On 9 March 1988, the KFAED director-general, Badr Mishari al-Humaydi, signed the KFAED's tenth loan agreement with China to finance the Jinzhou Harbour project in North-east China. This project, together with another nine, involved a total of US$240 million.[8] On 13 December 1988, the two countries signed an agreement to build Yaoqiang Airport in Jinan with a US$10 million loan provided by Kuwait.[9] In September 1989, the KFAED agreed to provide a loan of US$21 million to help China finance a ductile cast-iron pipe project in north-eastern China.[10] It also agreed to grant China a preferential loan of US$28 million to buy navigation instruments and equipment for Shenzhen Airport.[11] By 1989, China had received a total of US$300 million of long-term and low-interest loans from Kuwait for the construction of thirteen

---

4 *FBIS-CHI-85-130*, 8 July 1985, p. 12.
5 *The Wall Street Journal*, Eastern edition, 30 September 1985, p. 1.
6 *Middle East Economic Survey*, Vol. 30, No. 7, 24 November 1986, p. A6.
7 *Middle East Economic Survey*, Vol. 29, No. 8, 2 December 1985, p. A5.
8 *FBIS-CHI-88-047*, 10 March 1988, p. 9.
9 *FBIS-CHI-88-241*, 15 December 1988, p. 11.
10 *FBIS-CHI-89-184*, 25 September 1989, p. 17.
11 *FBIS-CHI-89-203*, 23 October 1989, p. 9.

projects in China.[12] China and Kuwait also signed a civil aviation accord, a trade agreement, a cultural exchange accord, and an economic and technical cooperation accord. The two countries were also engaged in cooperation regarding the provision of labour services. By the end of 1989, Kuwait had signed a total of 175 contracts for labour with China (Footnote 12: 5). According to the Chinese Ministry of Foreign Economic Relations and Trade, at the peak there were as many as 20,000 Chinese, mostly construction workers, in Kuwait prior to the Iraqi invasion. China constructed projects in Kuwait at a value of more than US$530 million prior to the Iraqi invasion.[13] Trade relations between the two countries increased impressively in the 1980s. The value of trade in the 1980s was almost twice that of the 1970s. China's imports mainly consisted of chemical fertilizer from Kuwait. In 1985, China bought 200,000 tons of urea fertilizer from Kuwait and 400,000 tons in 1987. This was the largest Chinese import of fertilizers from Kuwait since KPIC began fertilizer exports to China in 1969.[14] The first Chinese regular full-container cargo ship arrived in Kuwait in November 1985 marking the start of the service of full-container transportation between China and the Gulf region.[15]

In addition to the increase in economic cooperation between the two countries, social relations had also improved. Both Chinese and Kuwaiti Muslim delegations exchanged visits throughout the 1980s.[16] Journalist delegations visited each other's capital.[17] News exchanges were established between China's news agency, Xinhua, and Kuwait's news agency, Kuna.[18] The two countries also shared expertise in controlling desertification and developing agriculture in land recovered from desert.[19]

Throughout the 1980s, China–Kuwait relations remained unharmed despite China's decline of a Kuwaiti request to join Moscow and Washington in protecting its oil tankers in the Gulf against Iranian attacks. Qi Huaiyuan, China's Vice-Foreign Minister, when visiting Kuwait in July 1987, explained his country's decision by stating that 'the problem is that China does not maintain a large shipping fleet and has no spare tankers to lease'; he then added that China 'does not agree with the military presence and involvement of the big powers in the Gulf and Gulf affairs'. On the other hand, he said that China was sympathetic to and understands

12 *Beijing Review*, No. 52, 25–31 December 1989, p. 4.
13 *Beijing Review*, No. 10, 11 March 1991, p. 8.
14 *Middle East Economic Survey*, Vol. 30, No. 7, 24 November 1986, p. A6.
15 *FBIS-CHI-85-229*, 27 November 1985, p. 1.
16 *FBIS-CHI-84-188*, 26 September 1984, p. I4; and *FBIS-CHI-85-130*, 8 July 1985, p. I2.
17 *FBIS-CHI-85-095*, 16 May 1985, p. I1.
18 *FBIS-CHI-85-180*, 17 September 1985, p. I3.
19 *FBIS-CHI-86-141*, 23 July 1986, p. I3.

Kuwait's situation and the measures taken by Kuwait in safeguarding its security.[20] Thus, the stability in political relations between the two countries throughout the 1980s can be explained in terms of China's political weight regarding its relations with both Iran and Iraq. The Kuwaiti government understood that China was the only UN Security Council member to have good relations with both Iran and Iraq. Therefore, Kuwait hoped that China would make some efforts to mediate between Iran and Iraq to bring about a peaceful settlement to their dispute. In fact, during meetings with Chinese officials, Kuwaiti officials always stressed their hope to see China become more involved in the peace process between Iran and Iraq. Qi Huaiyuan, for example, promised the Kuwaiti government that China would actively mediate between the two sides.[21]

Chinese President Yang Shangkun visited Kuwait on 24 December 1989, for a forty-five-hour official goodwill visit at the invitation of the Kuwaiti government. His visit was mainly to assure the Kuwaiti government that the situation in China was stable, despite the Tiananmen Square episode. The Kuwaiti government voiced understanding to the measures that were taken by the Chinese government to restore stability in China. In its 1 October 1989 issue, the Kuwaiti English daily *Kuwait Times* presented the Kuwaiti official reaction that criticized the economic sanctions imposed by the West upon China and asked Western countries to take a second look at their policies toward China.[22] The Chinese President again stressed his government's willingness to mediate between Iran and Iraq in order to solve their disputes peacefully. In its 25 December issue, the Kuwait Times said:

> At a time when the US and the Soviet Union are concentrating their entire attention on East European changes, the Arabs would expect China to enhance its role in the conflict-ridden Middle East.
> (*FBIS-CHI-89-246*, 26 October 1989: 1)

The 1980s were a very productive decade for China–Kuwait relations. Kuwait was the only Third World country that has ever extended loans to China. Joint ventures between the two countries were expanded and trade relations were increased substantially. Throughout the 1980s, Chinese officials praised the development of relations with Kuwait and described it as a model for south–south cooperation. In support of Kuwait's position in OPEC, China did not increase its oil exports in 1987 (Calabrese 1991: 142). It did not even criticize Kuwait's purchase of Soviet arms in 1984 and its admission of Soviet technicians. Therefore, China remained pragmatic in

---

20 *FBIS-CHI-87-145*, 29 July 1987, pp. F1–F2.
21 *Ibid.*
22 *FBIS-CHI-89-193*, 6 October 1989, p. 12.

its relations with Kuwait in the 1980s, particularly as China did not perceive Kuwait as aligning itself with Moscow. Kuwait's neutral foreign policy kept China satisfied with Kuwait's policy of balancing itself between the two superpowers. However, the Kuwaiti government perceived China as having political importance to the Iran–Iraq dispute because of China's good relations with both countries.

China and the Iraqi invasion of Kuwait

As discussed above, China–Kuwait relations developed steadily during the 1980s. China accumulated economic benefits from its developing relations with Kuwait. Even when China's relations with the West and Japan started to deteriorate following the Chinese government crackdown of the peaceful demonstrations in Tiananmen Square, China–Kuwait relations remained unharmed. Unlike the West and Japan, Kuwait emphasized that what was happening in China was China's internal affairs and Kuwait abided by the principle of non-interference in the internal affairs of other countries.[23] China was completely shocked by the Iraqi invasion of Kuwait on 2 August 1990. The Iraqi invasion was against China's long-held belief that there is no conflict of fundamental interests among Third World countries, and also against its principles of peaceful coexistence that should govern relations among nations. The Chinese ambassador to the UN, Li Daoyu, presented his country's position on the Iraqi action and said that Iraq should cease its action of invasion immediately and withdraw its forces to the positions where they were located on 1 August 1990.[24] China continued to emphasis that the independence, sovereignty, and territorial integrity of Kuwait should be respected.[25] China's immediate support for the restoration of Kuwait's independence and legitimate government can be explained by the following three points:

1   China's foreign policy principle that no party should resort to force of arms in resolving its disputes with others obligated the Chinese government to stand against the Iraqi invasion of Kuwait. The Chinese have always believed that relations among nations should be governed by the five principles of peaceful coexistence.
2   China had been enjoying fruitful economic relations with Kuwait, and faced the possibility of losing, even temporarily, most of its economic benefits. China had planned to use Kuwaiti funds for the development of Shenzhen airport, Phase 2 of Xiamen airport, Jinzhou harbour in

---

23 BBC, *SWB, FE/0443*, 27 June 1989, p. A4/1.
24 *FBIS-CHI-90-150*, 3 August 1990, p. 4.
25 *FBIS-CHI-90-151*, 6 August 1990, pp. 12–13.

Liaoning, and Jinan airport in the eastern province of Shandong. Therefore, the continuation of Iraqi occupation of Kuwait meant China was unable to draw down loans from Kuwait.[26]

3 The continuation of the Iraqi occupation of Kuwait could also mean that thousands of Chinese nationals in Kuwait, who were engaged in economic, trade, and other activities, could lose their jobs and be evacuated from Kuwait,[27] and that many Chinese companies with investments in Kuwait would lose millions of US dollars (Lake 1991: 36–8).

The Chinese government's financial and economic cooperation with the West and Japan had terminated following the Tiananmen crackdown, so China was eager to work with the international community on the Gulf issue in order to restore economic relations with the West and Japan. China also wanted to avoid jeopardizing its relations with most of the Arab governments, which had preferred military action against Iraqi troops in Kuwait. China therefore voted for all the UN Security Council resolutions concerning the Gulf crisis except Resolution 678 when it abstained on the grounds that China stood for peaceful resolution of the conflict. China's non-opposition to the UN Security Council efforts to give Western powers the right to use force in the Gulf was confirmed during Kuwaiti Deputy Prime Minister and Foreign Minister's, Sabah al-Ahmad al-Jabir al-Sabah, visit to Beijing in August 1990. Chinese Premier Li Peng emphasized in a meeting with the visiting Kuwaiti official that his country firmly opposed Iraq's invasion and annexation of Kuwait and opposed military involvement by the big powers; moreover, the Chinese official indicated that his country will neither vote for nor against the UN Security Council proposal for the use of force against Iraq.[28] Three weeks prior to 15 January (the UN Security Council's deadline for Iraq to withdraw from Kuwait), Kuwaiti Emir Jaber al-Ahmad al-Sabah visited Beijing. His visit was to ensure that:

1 China would not change its position on the Iraqi invasion of Kuwait when the US-led coalition forces begin the military operation to liberate Kuwait; and
2 that China would not supply Iraq with arms once the military operations started.

The Kuwaiti Emir's visit achieved these two objectives. The Chinese government assured the visiting Emir that China would never change its

26 *FBIS-CHI-90-155*, 10 August 1990, p. 8.
27 *FBIS-CHI-90-163*, 22 August 1990, pp. 12–13.
28 *FBIS-CHI-90-163*, pp. 12–13.

principled stand against the Iraqi invasion of Kuwait and that China would not sell arms to Iraq under such circumstances.[29] When Kuwait was liberated, the Chinese immediately congratulated the Kuwaiti government on the restoration of Kuwait's independence, sovereignty, territorial integrity, and its legitimate government. They also assured the Kuwaiti government that China would continue to work in the UN Security Council to solve the unsettled issues between Kuwait and Iraq.

China and Kuwait after the Kuwait war

Once the Kuwait war ended, China began to involve itself in international efforts to rebuild war-damaged structures in Kuwait. The Chinese Ministry of Foreign Economic Relation and Trade (MFERT) indicated that Kuwait had already invited China to play an active role in its reconstruction. A MFERT official said 'we plan to supply workers, technicians and engineers to help rebuild Kuwait'.[30] In March, China sent a ten-member team of experts in oil fires and environmental control to help put out oil fires in Kuwait.[31] Another Chinese firefighting team arrived in Kuwait in August. The team consisted of sixty-three members to work in the Burgan field, the second largest oilfield in the world.[32] China also donated equipment to help oil spill clean-up efforts in the Gulf.[33]

In every official meeting between the two countries following the liberation of Kuwait, Chinese officials had always expressed their country's willingness to conduct multi-level and multi-form cooperation with Kuwait. This was evident in Kuwaiti Minister of State for Cabinet Affairs A. R. al-Awadhi's visit to Beijing in March 1991,[34] in Chinese Premier Li Peng's visit to Kuwait in July,[35] and in Kuwaiti Emir Jaber al-Sabah's visit to China in November.[36] During all these visits, Chinese officials stressed that their government would continue its support for Kuwait to secure its independence, state sovereignty, and integrity of its territory. Kuwaiti officials stressed their country's appreciation for China's stand in opposing Iraqi aggression against Kuwait. The Kuwait government worked to reach a military agreement with China similar to those signed with the United States, Britain, and France. In March 1995, the two governments reached a memorandum of understanding on military cooperation in Beijing. The

29 *Beijing Review*, Vol. 34, No. 1, 7–13 January 1991, pp. 7–8.
30 *Beijing Review*, No. 10, 11 March 1991, p. 8.
31 *FBIS-CHI-91-064*, 3 April 1991, p. 9.
32 *FBIS-CHI-91-164*, 23 August 1991, p. 13.
33 *Ibid.*
34 *Beijing Review*, No. 13, 1–7 April 1991, p. 8.
35 *FBIS-CHI-91-135*, 15 July 1991, pp. 17–18.
36 *Beijing Review*, No. 47, 25 November 1991, p. 5.

agreement called for the two countries to cooperate in the military domain and it also called on China to develop the Kuwaiti armed forces.[37] This agreement is China's first military cooperation agreement with a GCC country. Such an agreement was a new achievement not only in China–Kuwait relations but also in China's policy in the Gulf region. With this kind of agreement, China's military experts would become directly involved in training and maintaining the armed forces of Kuwait, an involvement that used to be carried out secretly with many of the countries of the region. In March 1998, China reached its first arms deal with Kuwait. The Kuwait Defence Ministry announced, according to the *Al Wafd* Egyptian newspaper, that the Kuwaiti government had approved an arms deal with China. The deal included the supply of one battery of 155-mm Chinese artillery guns, and ammunition worth US$186.5 million. The paper said that the Kuwaiti government favoured the Chinese offer over several other offers from the United States, Britain, and South Africa for technical, military, and financial reasons.[38]

In the post-Kuwait war era, Kuwait continued to present its economic significance to China. China's Petrochemical Corporation (SINOPEC) won the contract to renovate the Kuwaiti al-Ahmadi refinery.[39] In late 1992, KFAED agreed to provide China with a US$18 million loan to expand Xiamen airport, which was built in 1982–1983 with a Kuwaiti loan of US$22 million.[40] When Kuwaiti Crown Prince and Prime Minister Sheikh Saad Abdullah al-Salem al-Sabah visited China in April 1995, the two sides signed an agreement, according to which Kuwait would grant China loans worth US$24 million for the construction of a new airport in Zhengzhou, capital of Henan Province in central China.[41] On 30 December 1995, KOC signed a US$398 million contract with the Chinese state-owned firm China Petroleum Engineering Construction Company (CPECC) for the construction of two large oil tank farms in West Kuwait and the laying of ten oil pipelines with a total length of over 270 km. Construction was scheduled for completion in October 1998. CPECC was also awarded a US$390 million contract by KOC for the construction of two new gathering centres, Nos 27 and 28, with capacity of 410,000 bbl./day to service the Minagish and Umm Gudair oilfields in west Kuwait.[42] Chinese Deputy Prime Minister and Foreign Affairs Minister Qian Qichen said, when visiting Kuwait in March

---

37 BBC, *SWB, FE/2262*, 27 March 1995, p. G/2; and *SWB, MEW/0430 WME*, 9 April 1996, p. 8.
38 Note that China offered 10 per cent discount on its offer. *Al Wafd*, Cairo, 31 March 1998, in BBC, *SWB, FE/3200*, 14 April 1998, p. G/2.
39 *FBIS-CHI-94-209*, 28 October 1994, p. 9.
40 *The Wall Street Journal*, Eastern edition, 2 November 1992.
41 *Beijing Review*, No. 17, 24 April 1995, pp. 4–5.
42 *Middle East Economic Survey*, Vol. 39, No. 18, 29 January 1996, p. A12.

1996, that loans granted to China by Kuwait following the Kuwait war amounted to over US$600 million for financing approximately twenty construction projects in China.[43] On 10 August 1996, the Chinese Maritime Engineering Company signed a sixteen-month contract with Kuwait for the construction and reparation of the Shu'aybah refinery loading quay. The Shu'aybah refinery's capability was about 150,000 bbl./day in 1996 compared to 195,000 bbl./day prior to the Iraqi invasion.[44] China National Petroleum Company's (CNPC) officials reported that, in Kuwait, China had passed a preliminary qualification examination for undertaking five petroleum and petrochemical projects in 1997, with a total investment topping US$3 billion.[45]

Trade relations between the two countries also increased substantially after the liberation of Kuwait. The amount of trade between the two countries jumped from US$19 million in 1991 to US$100 million in 1993, and to US$130 million in 1995 (see Table A.6 in the Appendix).

To summarize, both China and Kuwait needed each other following the Kuwait war. China needed Kuwait's investments, loans, and economic cooperation to continue to foster its own modernization programme. Kuwait needed China's political support in the UN Security Council against Iraq and needed to ensure that China continued to fulfil its obligations as a responsible member of the UN Security Council and prevent China from supplying arms to Iraq.

CHINA AND OMAN

China's early involvement in Oman

During its first decade as an independent state, communist China was politically isolated from most of the governments of the Gulf and Arabian Peninsula region, including Oman. China's interest in Oman during the 1950s and 1960s was a reflection of the direction of its foreign policy at that time. When China was in close alignment with the Soviet Union, the Chinese government regarded Oman as a 'puppet' of the West. This prevented China from establishing relations or pursuing connections with Oman. However, this began to change toward the end of the 1950s. As China's alliance with the Soviet Union began to break down, the Gulf and Peninsula region started to assume a new significance in China's foreign policy. The Chinese began to view the Gulf and Peninsula region as a

---

43 BBC, *SWB, FE/2568*, 23 March 1996, p. G/2.
44 BBC, *SWB, MEW10449 WME*, 20 August 1996, p. 11.
45 BBC, *SWB, FE/2832*, 1 February 1997, p. S1.

potential theatre to wage a revolutionary campaign against Western imperialism and as an arena of Sino-Soviet rivalry (Calabrese 1990: 862–76).

This new analysis in China's foreign policy toward the two superpowers prompted the Chinese government to extend relations to the Omani nationalist movement. The Chinese supported Imam Ghalib Bin Ali's movement against the Sultan of Oman, whom the Chinese had always associated with British and US imperialism. They even offered Bin Ali military aid (Behbehani 1981: 165). Many meetings between Chinese officials and the Omani movement's leaders took place in Cairo and Aden; several delegations from the Dhofar Liberation Front (DLF), and later the Popular Front for the Liberation of the Occupied Arabian Gulf (PFLOAG), visited Beijing. Throughout the 1950s and 1960s, China provided political, economic, and military support to the revolutionary movement in Oman. By 1970, the PFLOAG was believed to be almost completely dependent on China for political, military, and ideological support. This support had led the Chinese to enjoy an ideological and political influence within the movement, which was evident in regional and international perceptions of the movement as a Maoist movement (Behbehani 1981: 178). This influence was also manifested in the movement's leader's statements, which emphasized the Chinese ideological strategies to wage a struggle against colonialism. Muhammed Ahmad Ghasani, a responsible member of the executive committee of the general command of the movement, stated:

> In accordance with the experience of the Chinese revolution under the leadership of the great leader Chairman Mao, our People's Front has formulated a line of self-reliance, depending on the broad masses of poor people to carry out a protracted people's war, and using the countryside to encircle the cities and seize the cities ultimately, thus developing the revolution to the whole of the Arabian Gulf to defeat and drive out the British colonialists ... The colonialists can no longer succeed in stamping out the flame of the '9th June' [1965] revolution, because we have the weapon of Mao Zedong's thought. The great truth that 'political power grows out of the barrel of a gun' has taken deep root in the hearts of our people. We the people of the Arabian Gulf don't believe in the fallacies of 'parliamentary road' and 'peaceful transition'. Our unshakeable belief is: the counter-revolutionary violence of colonialism can be liquidated only with the revolutionary violence of the people; the independence of the motherland can be achieved only through the barrel of a gun; and the liberation of the people can be obtained only through battles of bloodshed.
>
> (BBC, *SWB, FE/3402*, 12 June 1970: A4/2–3)

Speaking about the movement's friendly relationship with China, Ghasani praised China's support for the armed revolution and said:

> This support will give an impetus to the development on a still larger scale of our armed revolution in the crucial year of 1970.
> (BBC, *SWB, FE/3402*, 12 June 1970: A4/5)

As a result of this Chinese connection with the opposition movement in Oman, in April 1972 the Sultan of Oman, Sultan Qaboos bin Sa'id al-Sa'id, declared that, despite the establishment of formal relations between China and Kuwait and Iran, his country would have nothing to do with China (Abidi 1982: 252). Therefore, relations between the Sultanate of Oman and China, prior to the establishment of diplomatic relations, were limited to indirect trade consisting mainly of imports of Chinese goods. Thus, China's early involvement with Oman and its support for the revolutionary movement in that country originated at a time when the Chinese government advocated a certain international militancy aimed at discrediting the Soviet Union and countering the United States. Due to this Chinese connection with the Omani revolutionary movement, China–Oman diplomatic relations did not exist until 1978.

The establishment of diplomatic relations

China and Oman established diplomatic relations several years after the end of the Dhofar war. A joint communiqué on the establishment of diplomatic relations between the Sultanate of Oman and the PRC was signed in London and issued in May 1978. It said:

> The Government of the People's Republic of China and the Government of the Sultanate of Oman have decided to establish diplomatic relations at ambassadorial level as from May 25, 1978, and to exchange ambassadors. The Government of the People's Republic of China firmly supports the Government of the Sultanate of Oman in its just cause of safeguarding national independence and developing the national economy. The Government of the Sultanate of Oman recognises the Government of the People's Republic of China as the sole legal government representing the entire Chinese people. The two governments have agreed to develop friendly relations and cooperation between the two countries on the basis of the principles of mutual respecting for state sovereignty and territorial integrity, mutual non-aggression, non-interference in each other's internal affairs, equality and mutual benefit, and peaceful co-existence.
> (*FBIS-CHI-78-103*, 26 May 1978: A37)

Although the communiqué recognized Beijing as the sole legitimate representative of all China, a Taiwanese trade mission was allowed to remain in the Omani capital of Muscat.[46] Welcoming the new ties with the Omani government, an editorial in the *People's Daily* underlined the strategic and political significance of Oman by stating:

> Oman situated in the southern part of the Arabian Peninsula occupies a position of strategic importance as it is the threshold linking the Gulf with the Indian Ocean. It suffered historically from aggression and oppression by imperialism and colonialism, and its people have waged heroic struggle against imperialism and colonialism in order to achieve national independence. Today, the Omani Government is dedicating its efforts to the struggle in defence of national independence and for the development of the national economy. Following in foreign affairs the principles of neutrality and non-alignment, Oman advocates unity and co-operation among the countries in the Gulf and Red Sea and opposes big power contention there. All this earns the firm support of the Chinese Government and people.

And, in a statement directed toward easing the other Gulf and Peninsula countries' fear of China, the editorial went on to emphasize that:

> The Chinese Government always maintains that all countries, whether big or small, should be equal. The people of each country have the right to choose their own road in accordance with their own aspirations. It is our hope to establish and develop friendly relations with all other countries on the basis of the principles of mutual respect for state sovereignty and territorial integrity, mutual non-aggression, non-interference in each other's internal affairs, equity and mutual benefit, and peaceful co-existence. The establishment of diplomatic relations between China and Oman has opened excellent prospects for friendly co-operation in many fields between our two countries and it will be conducive to the further development of our friendly ties with the Arab countries and people.
>
> (*FBIS-CHI-78-105*, 31 May 1978: A30)

There were several decisive factors that played major roles in the two governments' decision to establish diplomatic relations. To the Chinese government, the establishment of formal relations with Oman was driven mainly by the following factors:

---

46 *FBIS-CHI-78-123*, 26 June 1978, p. A26.

1   China feared Soviet penetration in South Yemen, Iraq, India, and Zaire and it presumed that Soviet penetration in these countries, under its southward policy, was aimed at dominating the Gulf and Peninsula region. Moscow itself criticized the establishment of diplomatic relations between the two countries because it perceived it as an effort to form an anti-Soviet alliance in the region (Kechichian 1995: 190).
2   China was not willing to harm its established political relations with Kuwait and Iran. China, which supported the revolutionary group in Oman, did not want to appear against Iran's policy in Oman, where Iran was supporting the Sultan against the revolutionaries. So, by establishing diplomatic relations with the government of Oman, China would be able to improve its relations with Iran and halt the Kuwaiti government's fear of the revolutionary movement in the region.
3   China hoped that the establishment of formal relations with Oman would open the doors for the other remaining Gulf and Peninsula states to establish relations with China and eliminate their ties with the government of Taiwan.

To the Omani government, the establishment of diplomatic relations with China was driven by the following factors:

1   The Omani government shared China's fear of Soviet penetration in and around the region and wanted, therefore, to improve its relations with China as a counterpoise to the Soviets, particularly after China's relations with the United States, Oman's close ally, had already improved. Sultan Qaboos said:

> The Soviet Union is pushing forward a scheduled and fixed policy of expansionism in this region. This policy is no way different from the savage acts of the old colonialists during their time. This has been obvious for some time, undoubtedly, the Soviet Union has two intentions: ultimately gaining control of the Middle East, in particular, the oil region; and second, carry out expansion towards the Indian Ocean in order to control the African countries and then the entire Far East.
> (Interview with Xinhua in JPRC-76-746-China Report, 3 November 1980: 16)

2   The Omani government hoped that, by establishing a formal relationship with China, it would be able to completely stop China, the primary source of political, ideological, and military support to the Omani rebels, from continuing its commitment to support the revolutionary movement in Oman.

Shortly after the establishment of diplomatic relations between the two countries, Qais 'Abd al-Munim al-Zawawi, Minister of State for Foreign

Affairs of Oman, visited China in June 1978. During his visit, he met with the CCP's Chairman Hua Guofeng, who expressed the view that Oman could be directly threatened by Soviet ambitions to control the oil route. The Chinese leader encouraged Oman to work with the Gulf and Peninsula Region countries, to put aside their differences, and strengthen their unity in order to prevent Soviet intervention in the region.[47] A similar argument was made earlier by the Chinese Foreign Minister Huang Hua. In a banquet given in honour of the Omani guests, Huang said:

> The distinguished guests come from the coast of the Gulf and the Red Sea, an area of strategic importance with rich strategic resources. The two superpowers are fiercely intensifying their contention in this area in order to seize petroleum resources and control navigation channels and strategic positions. Bloated with wild ambition, the superpower flaunting the signboard of 'socialism' is making trouble everywhere and stepping up all-round expansion in an attempt to place the area under its control.
>
> (*FBIS-CHI-78-121*, 22 June 1978: A22–A23)

China's first Ambassador to Oman, Yuan Lulin, arrived in Muscat in April 1979, and Oman appointed Ibrahim Hamud al-Subayhi as Envoy to the PRC.[48]

China and Oman in the 1980s

China's relations with the Sultanate in the 1980s continued to reflect China's overall foreign policy in the region. China's fear of the Soviet Union, particularly after the latter's invasion of Afghanistan, led the Chinese government to welcome the conclusion of an agreement between Oman and the United States to provide military facilities to the Americans in the event of a crisis in the region and, in return, the United States would help reequip Oman's armed forces. It also welcomed the signing of the Oman–Britain agreement to provide Oman with more arms, including jet fighters, missiles, and minesweepers.

These Omani defence measures were viewed by the Chinese government as Omani efforts to safeguard the security of the Gulf region against Soviet penetration in and around the region:

> The Soviet invasion of Afghanistan and its southward thrust to the Persian Gulf have underlined the need for Oman to strengthen its defence and diplomatic efforts to safeguard its security and that of the region.

---

47 *FBIS-CHI-78-123*, 26 June 1978, p. A26.
48 *FBIS-MEA-79-081*, 24 April 1979.

The Chinese applauded the Omani government's stand on Soviet penetration in the region:

> Oman has taken a clear-cut stand against hegemonism. It has openly denounced Moscow's aggression and expansion, maintaining that the Soviet strategic southward drive gravely threatens Oman and other Gulf states as well as the rest of the world.
> (*Beijing Review*, No. 29, 21 July 1980: 10)

China, which had began in the early 1980s to stress the importance of improving relations among the Gulf and Peninsula Region countries as a step toward preventing Soviet intervention, welcomed the Sultanate's decision to normalize relations with South Yemen in October 1982. The Chinese viewed this development as a positive step toward strengthening the unity among the Gulf and Peninsula region countries.[49]

During the 1980s, political relations between the two countries developed rapidly. Both sides saw a great significance in each other's political role in the Gulf's affairs. With regard to the Soviet Union, which was trying to use the situation in the region to its own advantage, China and Oman shared the same objective, which was to prevent the Soviets from achieving their goals in the region. Another reason was the Iran–Iraq war and China's good relations with both belligerents. Oman saw China as having a great deal of influence in the region because:

1 It was the only great power that enjoyed close relations with both Tehran and Baghdad during their war; and
2 large quantities of Chinese weapons were deployed on the battlefield.

As a result, several official visits took place between the two governments. The Chinese Vice-Premier Chi Pengfei visited Oman in October 1980. Fahr bin Taimur, Omani Deputy Prime Minister for Defence and Security visited China in November 1982 (Footnote 49: 10). Among many of the issues that he discussed with Chinese officials was Oman's concern that China was providing Iran and Iraq with Scud and Silkworm missiles, capable of destroying fixed petroleum facilities or supertankers moving through the Strait of Hormuz. Fahr promised to seek GCC support in fostering formal relations with China, in exchange for China's promise to halt any missile transfers to either Iran or Iraq (Kechichian 1995: 192). Wu Xueqian, Chinese State Councillor and Foreign Minister, visited Oman in October 1983 to formally invite Sultan Qaboos to visit China. The visit never occurred; however, Sa'id Thuwainu ibn Shehab, special representative of

---

49 *Beijing Review*, No. 49, 6 December 1982, p. 14.

the Sultan, toured China in July 1984 where he was received by high-ranking Chinese officials eager to foster closer bilateral relations.[50] In November, a Chinese justice delegation headed by Minister of Justice Zou Yu visited Oman.[51] In December, a Chinese military delegation headed by the Deputy Chief of Staff of the PLA, General He Zhengwen, visited Oman.[52] He Zhenqwen met with several high-ranking Omani military officials including the Omani Assistant of the Chief of Staff, Major General Hassan bin Ihsan bin Nasib, Commander of the Sultan's Ground Forces, Major General Nasib bin Hamad al-Rawahi, Director of Operation at the Sultan's Air Force Staff, Colonel Muhammad bin Mubarak al-Amiri, Commander of the Training Battalion of the Sultan's armed forces, Colonel Jum'ah bin Salim Al-Khatiri, and Major Muhammad bin 'Umar al-Zubaydi from the Sultan's navy. This was the first meeting of its kind between military officials of both countries. Joseph Kechichian (1995) argues that these meetings did not lead to a shift in Oman's sourcing of weapons supplies from the West to China. However, according to Kechichian, the meetings allowed Omani officers to familiarize themselves with what was available in China and to broaden their knowledge. However, it allowed Muscat to better assess China's position in the Iran–Iraq war, given that China provided large quantities of its weapons to both countries (Kechichian 1985: 194). Chinese Vice-Premier Yao Yilin visited Oman in November 1985 and attended the Fifteenth National Day celebration of the Sultanate.[53] In July 1986, Yusuf al-'Alawi 'Abdallah, Omani Minister for Foreign Affairs, visited and headed a delegation to Beijing.[54] Omani Minister of Social Affairs and Labour, Mustahil bin Ahmad al-Maashini visited China in March–April 1987.[55] Haitham ibn-Tariq al-Sa'id, Omani Foreign Minister Undersecretary for Political Affairs, visited China in September 1988.[56] Haitham's visit to Beijing was to express Oman's formal appreciation for Beijing's positive role in bringing the Iran–Iraq war to an end (Kechichian 1995: 195). President Yang Shangkun visited Oman in December 1989. He was received with a highly-visible public welcome with thousands of Omanis lining city streets waving Chinese and Omani flags. Yang was received by Qaboos who thanked China for its support of Security Council Resolution 598.[57]

Throughout all these meetings, the Chinese praised Oman's foreign policy and emphasized that China and Oman shared identical views on a wide

---

50 *FBIS-CHI-84-135*, 12 July 1984, p. 11.
51 *FBIS-CHI-84-232*, 30 November 1984, p. 14.
52 *FBIS-CHI-84-251*, 28 December 1984, p. 11.
53 *FBIS-CHI-85-226*, 22 November 1985, p. 11.
54 *FBIS-CHI-86-136*, 16 July 1986, p. 11.
55 *FBIS-CHI-87-064*, 3 April 1987, p. 11.
56 *FBIS-CHI-88-183*, 21 September 1988, p. 18.
57 *Beijing Review*, No. 52, 25 December 1989, pp. 4–5.

range of international issues. Although China had officially invited Sultan Qaboos to visit China several times, the Sultan, who did not reject the invitations, did not visit China in the 1980s.

Culturally, the two countries signed an agreement in 1981 on cooperation in such cultural fields as the exchange of visits by artists and folklore troupes.[58] The Omani traditional vessel *Sohar* arrived in Guangzhou in the same year.[59] In May 1980, a delegation of the Oman Ministry of Religious Trusts and Islamic Affairs, led by Minister Walid ibn Zahir al-Hinnawi, visited China. A few months later, a Chinese Islamic delegation led by Shen Xiaai, Vice-President of the Chinese Islamic Association, reciprocated the visit. Prior to these visits, Haj Mohamed Ali Zhang Jie, Vice-President of the Chinese Islamic Association, led a delegation of Chinese Muslims to Oman in November 1979 to participate in the celebration of Oman's National Day (Abidi 1982: 290–1). In June 1980, an Omani information delegation including representatives from the Oman Publishing House an-Nahda magazine, *al-Watan al-Arabi* newspaper, and the *Times* of Oman paid a visit to China (Abidi 1982: 285). An Omani youth delegation visited China in June 1982 and the two countries signed an accord on youth visits, exchanges, and cooperation.[60] A civil aviation agreement was signed by the two governments in Muscat in May 1983.[61] A sport exchange agreement was signed in January 1985.[62]

Economically, Chinese exports to Oman dominated trade relations between the two countries in the 1980s. After the establishment of diplomatic relations in May 1978, China's exports to Oman jumped from US$5.85 million in 1976 to US$9.06 million in 1983 and to US$10 million in 1986 (see Table A.7 in the appendix). However, China's trade relations with Oman, despite the increase in trade volume in the 1980s to approximately six times that of the 1970s, represented only 3 per cent of China's total trade relations with the Gulf and Arabian Peninsula region countries. This does not imply that China was not interested economically in Oman. Instead, one could argue that Oman had very little economic benefits to offer China in the 1980s. China had sufficient energy to pursue its economic modernization programme and was not in need of Omani oil. On the other hand, Oman's long trade relations with Japan and the West made the Omani market less dependent on Chinese products.

58 *FBIS-CHI-91-197*, 10 October 1991, p. I1.
59 *FBIS-CHI-91-135*, 15 July 1991, pp. 20–1.
60 *FBIS-CHI-82-108*, 4 June 1982, p. I1.
61 *FBIS-CHI-83-087*, 4 May 1983, p. I2.
62 *FBIS-CHI-85-017*, 25 January 1985, p. I1.

China and Oman in the 1990s

In addition to its strategic importance, Oman assumed a new significance to China in the 1990s. China, particularly since 1993, began to turn to Oman and other Gulf states to secure long-term energy supplies in order to obviate the sharp increases in its energy consumption resulting from its rapid economic growth. China, therefore, started to pay more attention to developing its economic relations with Oman. In June 1993, Qiu Zhongjiang, Vice-President of China's National Petroleum (CNP), visited Muscat to seek Omani investments for the Tarim Basin oilfields.[63] The CNP's President visited Muscat in 1993 and expressed his company's willingness to have CNP employees trained by Omani workers (EIU 1993: 20).

Thus, oil was high on the agenda. As China became a net importer of oil in 1993, it began to import large amounts of Omani crude oil (see Table 6.1). Since then, China became one of the major recipients of Oman's crude oil. After China first started to import Oman's crude oil in large quantities in 1993, it immediately assumed a leading position. China was in third place behind Japan and South Korea. Its imports of Oman's crude oil continued to increase every year after 1995, which allowed China to become the third leading recipient of crude oil from Oman in 1997. China ranked only behind Japan who remained Oman's top crude oil customer by 1997 and Thailand who assumed second place. In 1995, China signed a contract with the Omani government to increase its purchases of Oman's crude oil from less than 20,000 bbl./day in 1995 to 100,000 bbl./day in 1996.[64] In the first four months of 1998, China imported 40.5 million barrels of oil from Oman and dropped to fourth place behind Japan, Thailand, and South Korea, respectively (EIU 1999: 33).

The suitability of Oman's crude oil to China's existing refining technology and ability means Oman has become a very successful trading partner with China. This is significant because, if China wants to be a major importer of crude oil from other major exporters of oil in the Gulf and Peninsula region, it will have to spend billions of dollars to upgrade its refining technology to suit the type of crude oil that these other exporters in the Gulf region. Therefore, as China's economic growth continues to mount in the next century, China's imports of Oman's crude oil are expected to increase as long as Oman continues its production of oil.

In 1997, the Chinese government began to import Oman's liquefied natural gas (LNG). It was also in the process of selecting three coastal locations for the construction of LNG-receiving terminals. At least one of

---

63 *Middle East Economic Digest*, Vol. 37, No 23, 11 June 1993, p. 29.
64 http://www.uae.internetact.com/newsreport/19970612.htm, p. 2.

Table 6.1 Oman's exports of crude oil by country

	1992 (%)	1992 (million bbl.)	1993 (%)	1993 (million bbl.)	1994 (%)	1994 (million bbl.)	1995 (%)	1995 (million bbl.)	1996 (%)	1996 (million bbl.)	1997 (%)	1997 (million bbl.)
Japan	40.4	102.0	33.6	89.9	42.1	113.9	34.7	99.4	30.4	90.5	28.2	85.9
USA	0.6	1.5	4.1	10.9	5.9	16.0	2.5	7.2	4.6	13.6	0.5	1.5
France	0.4	0.9	0.3	0.7	–	–	–	–	0.6	1.8	–	–
S. Korea	28.0	70.8	25.7	68.7	17.1	46.3	18.8	53.8	19.2	57.0	16.5	50.3
Singapore	4.6	11.6	6.2	16.5	2.3	6.1	3.0	8.7	2.6	7.8	0.2	0.5
Thailand	5.3	13.5	6.5	17.5	9.9	26.8	13.5	38.8	18.3	54.4	23.5	71.6
Philippines	–	–	–	–	1.0	2.6	2.2	6.3	3.7	11.1	4.8	14.5
Taiwan	7.9	20.0	7.9	21.0	7.1	19.2	5.8	16.7	3.0	9.0	2.0	6.2
India	–	–	0.2	0.5	–	–	–	–	–	–	–	–
Australia	–	–	0.2	0.6	1.4	3.9	1.0	2.9	1.3	3.9	0.9	2.7
China	–	–	10.4	27.9	9.8	26.5	11.4	32.8	14.2	42.4	22.7	69.2
Other	12.8	32.2	4.9	13.2	3.4	9.1	7.0	20.0	2.0	6.1	0.8	2.3
Total	*100.0*	*252.5*	*100.0*	*267.4*	*100.0*	*270.4*	*100.0*	*286.6*	*100.0*	*297.6*	*100.0*	*304.7*

Source: Oman Ministry of Development, *Statistical Yearbook 1994* (Oman: Information and Documentation Centre, 1995), p. 189; *Statistical Yearbook 1995*, p. 193; and *Statistical Yearbook 1997*, p. 173.

Table 6.2 Oman's main trading partners (US$ million) (source: EIU 1999: 33)

Export to:	1993	1994	1995	1996	1997
Japan	1,416	1,689	1,694	1,774	1,665
China	510	376	438	753	1,223
Thailand	273	361	621	957	1,212
S. Korea	1,016	716	844	1,103	921
USA	277	452	292	407	237
Total (including others)	5,370	5,545	5,962	7,339	7,630
Import from:					
UAE	1,156	1,139	1,012	1,053	1,116
Japan	860	779	670	721	813
UK	343	346	445	711	668
USA	332	264	276	237	376
Germany	182	192	216	249	262
Total (including others)	4,114	3,915	4,248	4,578	5,026

these was reportedly to be in Guandong province, whose municipal government signed a letter of intent with Oman LNG in 1994.[65] In May 1999, the Chinese government also offered its willingness to conduct a joint study with Oman in the protection, exploration, and use of water resources.[66]

China's trade with Oman also increased from being only 3 per cent of China's total trade with the Gulf and Peninsula region countries in the 1980s to 15 per cent in the first six years of the 1990s. Chinese imports constituted over 95 per cent of total trade with Oman in the first six years of the 1990s (see Table A.7 in the Appendix). Oman became the principal exporter to China from the Gulf and Arabian Peninsula region (see Table 6.2). The Chinese market's total value with Oman was US$3,256 million, approximately US$1,000 million ahead of Saudi Arabia, which was in second place. This sharp increase in China's imports from Oman is due to its increasing crude oil imports from Oman. Realizing the importance of Oman, Chinese President Jiang Zemin met Thuwayni Bin Shihab al Sa'id, a special representative of Sultan Qaboos, and emphasized China's willingness to forge a long-term, stable, and comprehensive cooperative relationship with Oman for the new century, on the existing basis of bilateral links. The Chinese President praised Oman's efforts in promoting unity among Arab states and working toward peace and stability in the Gulf region.[67]

65 *Middle East Economic Survey*, Vol. 41, No. 13, 30 March 1998, p. A8.
66 BBC, *SWB, FE/3540*, 21 May 1999, p. G/5.
67 BBC, *SWB, FE/2943*, 12 June 1997, p. G/4.

CHINA AND SAUDI ARABIA

China and Saudi relations in the 1950s and 1960s

China's communist ideology had created an unfavourable opinion of China in Saudi Arabia. King Faisal bin Sa'ud of the Kingdom of Saudi Arabia was outspoken in his strong opposition to communist ideology as an alien ideology that encourages instability and revolutionary change and is in fundamental conflict with Islam (Quandt 1981: 64). China's close alignment with the Soviet Union, its revolutionary policy, as well as its policy towards its Muslim minority, contributed toward the Saudi negative view of China in the PRC's first two decades as an independent state. Saudi Arabia was greatly concerned about the possible indirect Soviet–Chinese threat to the region through radical ideologies such as Nasserism, Baathism, socialism, and communism. From the Saudi point of view, Chinese and Soviet support for the Marxist regime in Aden and the Dhofari insurgents in Oman, and China's continued revolutionary propaganda throughout the world generated a further threatening situation to the security of the Gulf and Arabian Peninsula region. In addition to that, China's harsh treatment of its own Muslim population in the early 1950s and during the Cultural Revolution had added to unfavourable Saudi sentiments toward China.

Although China perceived Saudi Arabia as a reactionary state, hostile to communism, and closely aligned with the capitalist camp, Beijing's leaders still hoped to win its goodwill for a number of reasons:

1 Saudi Arabia abstained consistently on UN votes concerning the PRC;
2 Saudi Arabia, unlike some other Arab states, did not condemn China as an aggressor in Korea;
3 Saudi Arabia did not support the US-sponsored resolution to postpone consideration of any proposal to exclude Taiwan from the UN;
4 Saudi Arabia refused to join regional alliances with the West (Baghdad Pact November 1955) and disputed the British over the Buraymi Oasis;
5 Saudi Arabia concluded a mutual defence treaty with Egypt in October 1955 and cooperated with Nasser in efforts to contain Iraq and prevent others, including Syria and Jordan, from joining the Pact (Safran 1988: 78).
6 Saudi Arabia supported Nasser's move in September 1955 to conclude an arms deal with the Soviet Union, in which the Chinese played a large role (Safran 1988: 79).
7 Saudi Arabia supported Nasser's nationalization of the Suez Canal, broke off its diplomatic relations with Britain and France, and declared an embargo on oil shipments to the two European powers when they invaded Egypt in 1956;

8   Saudi Arabia supported the Imam of Yemen's claim to the British colony of Aden and assisted, for a while, the Omani rebels against the British-backed sultan (Safran 1988: 79).

All the above developments made the Chinese government perceive Saudi Arabia as pursuing a foreign policy independently of the West (Shichor 1979: 29–31). China appreciated such developments, particularly after Beijing's efforts since the mid-1950s to enhance its image in the Third World as a reliable Third World country. As its relations with the Islamic World became more and more important in its foreign policy, Islam in China acquired a new significance. In addition to its belief that Muslims all over the world, who were oppressed by imperialism, shared the same common interests with China and, therefore, should unite to fight against imperialism (Schichor 1984: 310), China had used Islam and Muslim figures to lay the groundwork for formal relations with the Islamic World including Saudi Arabia.

The Chinese use of the Islam card with Saudi Arabia was first orchestrated by China's Premier Zhou Enlai at the Bandung conference. Zhou brought with him two prominent Chinese Muslim figures to the conference, Ta P'u-sheng and Yusuf Ma Yuhuai. This was a strong indication that the Chinese government was willing to use China's Muslims as stepping stones to reach the Muslim World. Zhou and his Muslim delegation met with Prince Faysal ibn Sa'ud, the Saudi Foreign Minister. For the first time, they raised the issue of permitting Chinese Muslims to enter the Kingdom to perform the *hajj* (pilgrimage) (Shichor 1989: 3). Up to that time, Chinese Muslims were not allowed by the Saudi government to enter the Kingdom for pilgrimage. The Saudi government agreed thereafter to allow twenty Chinese Muslims to visit Mecca every year (Shichor 1989: 3). The use of Islam in China's foreign policy toward Saudi Arabia was also evident in meetings between Burhan Shahidi, Chairman of the CCP-established China Islamic Association and head of the Chinese pilgrimage mission to Mecca in 1956, and King Sa'ud, the Saudi Prime Minister, and the Saudi Finance Minister.[68] Yitzhak Shichor (1979: 44) argues that Burhan's meetings with such significant top Saudi leaders were an indication that Burhan was not merely a religious figure but also an important figure in China's Foreign Ministry.

As Islam in China became a valuable instrument for the Chinese government not only to foster its relations with the countries of the Muslim World, but also to spread Mao's thought to the millions of

---

68 Burhan also met, when he led the Chinese pilgrims to Mecca in 1956, with King Hussein of Jordan, the Prime Minister of Lebanon, the Prime Minister of Syria, the Prime Minister of Egypt, and Prince al-Badr of Yemen.

Muslims in Asia and Africa (Adie 1967: 222), Chinese Muslims gained considerable religious freedom. Mosques were reopened, lands were retained by Muslims, and Muslim leaders assumed high-ranking positions in the government (Winters 1979: 47). Muslims in China played a major role in fostering China's political relations with countries such as Indonesia, Pakistan, Egypt, Syria, Yemen, and Afghanistan.

Since 1955, the China Islamic Association sent a pilgrimage mission to Mecca every year until the beginning of the Cultural Revolution in 1964 when the missions were terminated. The Cultural Revolution was a bitter struggle for supremacy within the CCP, between the radical faction of Mao and the more pragmatic group led by Liu Shaoqi and Deng Xiaoping. The premise of the Cultural Revolution was to attack the 'four olds' – old thinking, old culture, old morality, and old custom. As a result, the CCP carried out harsh practices against Muslim minorities, as well as against other religious minorities such as the Tibetans and Mongols, in order to solve the 'nationality problem' and achieve ethnic uniformity in China. Most mosques and Muslim schools were forced to close down and many were destroyed, the use of minority language scripts was restricted, copies of the Koran and other religious texts were burned, Muslims were killed or arrested for their resistance, and Muslims lost their high position in the government (Dillon 1999: 164–6).

Meanwhile, the Saudi government's perception of the threat to its own security had changed in the late 1960s (Safran 1988: 123). The Saudis saw the following two major developments in the region as the two most threatening developments to the security of the kingdom:

1 the establishment of the PRSY (PDRY) under the control of the Marxist National Liberation Front and the proclamation of its dedication to overthrow all traditional regimes in the region; and
2 the revolutionary movement in Oman, which was originally supported by the Saudis, adopted a Marxist–Leninist–Mao Zedong thought ideological orientation in 1968 and proclaimed its duty as the liberator of the entire occupied Arab Gulf region.

However, China escalated support for the above movements, and, so, its valuable political, ideological, and material support to both in the late 1960s and most of the 1970s intensified Saudi Arabia's unfavourable attitude toward China.

Against this background, China's only direct contact with Saudi Arabia was interrupted by the Cultural Revolution and China's support for liberation movements in the region. Thus, the Saudi government, once again, came to view China as a hostile force against Islam and a source of instability and revolutionary change in the region (Quandt 1981: 64–5). Therefore, the Chinese use of the Islam card to foster political relations with the Saudi government was unsuccessful. Had the Chinese government

216 *China's foreign policy toward the Gulf and Arabian Peninsula region*

continued its tolerance of its Muslim population and discharged itself from supporting the revolutionary movements in the Gulf and Arabian Peninsula region, the Saudi government might have felt more comfortable dealing with the Chinese in more formal political relations. But China's continued negative treatment of its Muslims and, more importantly, its continued support for the Marxist revolutionary movement in South Yemen and Oman prevented the Saudi government from pursuing better relations with the Chinese government.

China's changing policy

As discussed above, China's treatment of its Muslims and its involvement with the revolutionary movements in the Gulf and Arabian Peninsula region prevented China from achieving direct relations with the Kingdom. This was about to change. In the 1970s, China began to pursue a much more favourable foreign policy toward the countries of the Gulf and Arabian Peninsula region. It started to lean toward the United States and began to court the governments of the Gulf and Peninsula region. This shift was due to China's fear of Soviet expansionism. Recognizing the significance of Saudi Arabia's dominant position and political weight in the region and its ability to play a major role in efforts to contain Soviet penetration, China stepped up its efforts to establish contacts with the Kingdom. Since the late 1970s, it has followed the following strategies to foster contacts with the Kingdom:

Abandoning its revolutionary stance

China terminated its support for the revolutionary movement in Oman and established diplomatic relations with the government of Oman. It also limited its support to the government of South Yemen and accelerated its political and economic relations with North Yemen. Paving the way, therefore, for the governments of the region to establish diplomatic relations with Beijing.

Adopting similar policies

China paid considerable attention to the opinions of Saudi leaders, endorsing many Saudi policies, particularly with regard to the Arab–Israeli conflict and the security of the Gulf and Peninsula region. The Chinese media carried several articles informing the public of Saudi attitudes. For example, *Peking Review* republished Prince Fahd ibn 'Abd al-Aziz's, Second Deputy Prime Minister of the Kingdom, interview with the Lebanon daily *Al Anwar*, where he commented on the policy of the oil embargo.[69] The Chinese government hailed Saudi government efforts to build up unity among the Gulf countries,[70] to bring about a ceasefire in Lebanon,[71] to foster peaceful settlement of the Middle East problem by forwarding an eight-point proposal (Fahd Plan),[72] to achieve peace between Iran and Iraq, and to solve the Soviet presence in Afghanistan.[73] China supported the Saudi desire to buy the airborne warning and control system aeroplanes (AWACS) from the United States and criticized the US delayed decision to sell the aeroplanes to the Kingdom.[74] The Chinese believed that the Soviet threat to the region, through South Yemen, East Africa and Afghanistan, was increasing and that the United States should support the Kingdom in order to defend the region from Soviet penetration.

Appealing for good offices

China tried to use certain Gulf countries, which had already established diplomatic relations with the PRC, to use their good offices to mediate between China and Saudi Arabia. Hashim Behbehani (1981: 224) argues that China tried unsuccessfully to use Kuwait as a 'stepping stone' in its effort to win Saudi recognition. China, according to Behbehani, continued pressing the Kuwaiti government to use its good offices to bring about Saudi recognition. China's Ambassador in Kuwait, Ting Hao, told the Kuwaiti daily *As-Siyassah* on 2 May 1979 that his country would like to establish formal relations with Saudi Arabia. He added that China and Saudi Arabia maintain identical viewpoints on different international issues (Abidi 1982: 231–2). The Vice-Director of China's National Sports Commission, Xu Yunsheng, met the Saudi Minister of Social Affairs and Vice-President of the Saudi Arabian Football Federation in Malaysia on 15 November 1981. Both expressed their hopes for improving relations with each other.[75]

69 *Peking Review*, No. 2, 10 January 1975, p. 20.
70 See 'Why does the West rely so heavily on Saudi Arabia', in *FBIS-CHI-81-96*, 19 May 1981, p. 11; and BBC, *SWB*, *FE/6853*, 7 October 1981.
71 *FBIS-CHI-83-004*, 6 January 1983, p. 18.
72 *Beijing Review*, No. 34, 24 August 1981, pp. 10–11; *JPRS 79457-China Report*, No. 238, 17 November 1981, pp. 6–13; the Chinese said that the Plan 'provided a comprehensive and fair solution to the conflict between Israel and Arab nations', in *FBIS-CHI-81-219*, 13 November 1981, p. 11.
73 *Beijing Review*, No. 4, 12 October 1981, p. 12; and *Beijing Review*, No. 16, 21 April 1980, p. 12.
74 *Beijing Review*, No. 41, 12 October 1981, pp. 11–12.
75 *The China Quarterly*, No. 89, March 1982, p. 146.

Setting the pattern

China also used its improving relations with the countries of the Gulf and Peninsula region to demonstrate to the Saudis that countries of different social and ideological beliefs can coexist with China. It was reported by Chinese sources in June 1978 that, following the establishment of diplomatic relations with Oman, China had started talks with Saudi Arabia on the opening of formal relations between the two countries.[76] The daily *South China Morning Post* reported on 31 October 1978 that negotiations were quietly under way for the establishment of diplomatic relations between the two countries. The paper observed that, in the past six months, there had been numerous indications that the two countries were preparing to normalize their relations. It indicated that Saudi nationals had been visiting China as private individuals, 'but obviously with the tacit approval of the Saudi government'. The paper went on to say that the establishment of diplomatic relations with Oman was a definite sign because the Sultan of Oman, according to the paper, could not have acted without consulting the Saudi government.[77] Despite these reports, Saudi Arabia remained strongly against establishing diplomatic relations with Beijing, although Riyadh allowed small indirect amounts of trade with China (see Table A.8 in the Appendix and Harrison 1995: 35).

On 17 November 1981, Premier Zhao shook hands with Crown Prince Fahd at the Cancun North–South summit (Tanzer 1982: 28–9). Although it was not an official meeting, this was the first highest-level meeting between officials from both countries. There was very little publicity from both countries about this meeting, but it did concern Taiwan, which already had diplomatic relations with the Kingdom. Shortly after, the Kingdom reassured Taiwan that Riyadh had no intention whatsoever to change its policy toward Beijing. During his visit to the UAE in 1985, Chinese Vice-Premier Yao Yilin mentioned, while speaking at the airport, that it is China's consistent policy to develop friendly relations with the Gulf countries, and said: 'we are also willing to develop relations with Saudi Arabia'.[78] While visiting Oman in November 1985 to attend the Sultanate's Fifteenth National Day celebrations, Yao Yilin met with Saudi Arabia's Crown Prince and First Deputy Prime Minister 'Abdullah ibn 'Abd al-Aziz al-Sa'ud at the Al-Bustan Palace. The Chinese official used the Palestinian issue to initiate dialogue with Saudi Arabia. At the meeting, Yao reiterated China's support of the Palestinian cause and the unity of the Arab world. He expressed his country's appreciation of what the Kingdom had done to support the Palestinian cause and in the affairs

---

76 *FBIS-CHI-78-123*, 26 June 1978, p. A26.
77 *FBIS-CHI-78-211*, 31 October 1978, p. A26.
78 *FBIS-CHI-85-219*, 13 November 1985, p. I1.

of the region.[79] This meeting marked the second meeting between a Chinese leader and a Saudi Arabian leader. Beijing Radio described the meeting as a 'new page in the annals of a relationship between China and Saudi Arabia'.[80]

While visiting the UAE, Chinese Councillor and Foreign Minister, Wu Xueqian said, in an interview with the UAE daily *Al Khaleej* on 23 December 1985, that his country was interested in establishing diplomatic relations with Saudi Arabia, Qatar, and Bahrain. However, as there were no diplomatic relations with these countries and China, he said China could wait. He added that although China had no diplomatic relations with the Kingdom, the two countries had contacts in many fields. He also said that China had no conflict of interests with Saudi Arabia, Qatar, and Bahrain but had identical viewpoints with them on the issues of the Middle East, the Iran–Iraq war, and Afghanistan. He stressed that, with the strengthening of mutual understanding, the day would come for China to establish diplomatic relations with these countries.[81]

Using Islam

China, once again, turned to the use of Islam as an important instrument to achieve its foreign policy objective regarding Saudi Arabia. The use of Islam to develop relations with other countries had been one of the major tasks of the China Islamic Association. During the Second Session of the Fourth Committee of the Association from 13 to 20 August 1982, which was attended by several CCP leaders, China pledged to continue to develop friendly relations and to conduct academic and cultural exchanges with other Muslim countries in order to promote mutual understanding and friendship.[82] The year 1979 was the turning point in China's policy toward its own Muslim population. Since that year, the Chinese government started to return to its old practices that were stopped by the Cultural Revolution policies against Muslims in China. Mosques and Muslim schools were reopened, copies of the Koran and other Islamic classics were printed and distributed to Muslims in China, and by 1990 the number of Muslims making the pilgrimage to Mecca increased to over 2,000 annually.[83] China consistently sent its Muslim delegations to participate in international Islamic academic symposia, commemorative meetings, and celebration activities.[84] China also received Muslim delegations, including a delegation from the Saudi-based World Islamic Organization (Rabetat al 'Alam al

---

79 *FBIS-CHI-85-223*, 19 November 1985, p. I1.
80 *FBIS-CHI-85-229*, 27 November 1985, p. I1.
81 *FBIS-CHI-85-247*, 24 December 1985, pp. I1–I2.
82 *FBIS-CHI-82-164*, 24 August 1982, p. K23.
83 *Beijing Review*, No. 28, 9–15 July 1990, p. 25.
84 *Ibid.*

Islami), which visited China in May–June 1981 (Bowring 1982: 10–11). The delegation visited China's Muslim communities and met with Yang Jingren, a high-ranking Muslim official in the Chinese government. A donation of US$500,000 was made by the visiting delegation to the China Islamic Association (Wang 1993: 68). Although Chinese organizations, including the China Islamic Association, were prohibited by law from accepting foreign contributions, the Chinese government made an exception allowing the Association to accept the Saudi gift (Shichor 1989: 8). By allowing the Saudi contribution, the Chinese government wanted to represent itself favourably to the visiting delegation and to show that the Chinese communist regime was not against China's Muslim minority.

Several reasons could have contributed to the change in China's policies toward its Muslim population in 1979. Primarily, China had started to take a more pragmatic and open policy with the outside world, with the arrival of the Deng Xiaoping leadership, and began introducing integral changes in its internal policies, including the treatment of its minorities. Second, Iran, China's main partner in the Gulf region, had achieved a revolutionary change by introducing an Islamic government in 1979. China, therefore, found it necessary to treat its own Muslims in a means that would not harm its relations with Iran. Finally, the Soviet invasion of Afghanistan and the mujahedin military operation against Russian troops demonstrated the significance of Muslims to China's policy of undermining Soviet influence in Afghanistan, in particular, and the surrounding region, in general.

China encouraged the practice of combining pilgrimage with politics. Chinese Muslim pilgrims to Mecca served as ambassadors helping to foster relations with Saudi Arabia. The Chinese Muslim pilgrimage delegation to Mecca, led by Ilyas Shen Xiaxi, Vice-President of the China Islamic Association, attended a state banquet in September 1984 given by Saudi Arabia's King, Fahd ibn 'Abd al-Aziz. The delegation reportedly extended congratulations on the occasion of the Qorban Muslim Festival to the King, Crown Prince, and First Deputy Minister 'Abdallah, Second Deputy Prime Minister Sultan ibn 'Abd al-Aziz, the royal family, and principal government officials. It was said that the King welcomed Chinese pilgrims to Mecca and wished happiness for all Muslims in China.[85] A Chinese Muslim delegation headed by Ismail Amat, Chairman of the Xinjiang Uygur Autonomous Region, visited Riyadh in December 1985 and met with the Saudi Grand Mufti 'Abd al-Aziz ibn al-Baz.[86] The delegation also met with the Saudi Vice-Minister of Defence and Aviation, Prince 'Abd al-Rahman ibn 'Abd al-Aziz.[87] Upon its return to China, Ismail said that during their

---

85 *FBIS-CHI-84-182*, 18 September 1984, p. I4.
86 *FBIS-CHI-85-231*, 2 December 1985, p. I1.
87 *FBIS-CHI-85-235*, 6 December 1985, p. I1.

meetings both sides expressed their desire to further economic, cultural, and religious cooperation and exchange. The Saudi official, according to Ismail, expressed admiration for the Chinese policy of freedom of religious belief and the economic policy, and hoped that more Chinese Muslims would visit the Kingdom.[88] Marouf al-Dawalibi, Chairman of the Muslim World Congress and advisor about foreign affairs and religious affairs to the King, visited China and met with Muslim leaders including Mohammed Ali Zhang Jie and Ilyas Shen Xiaxi. The Chinese Muslim leaders briefed the guest on the position and the role of Chinese Muslims in the country's political and economic life and the role of the China Islamic Association in promoting Islam in China. Al-Dawalibi reportedly left with a very positive image of Islam in China.[89] Jamil 'Abd al-Rahman, deputy director of the China Hajj Affairs Office of the Saudi Pilgrimage Company visited China in March 1987. His visit came at the invitation of the China Islamic Association to discuss matters related to a Chinese *hajj* mission to Mecca proposed for 1987.[90] Throughout the 1980s, the Muslim World Organization financed many Chinese Muslim students studying in Al Azhar University in Cairo (Gladney 1992: 12).

All these Chinese and Saudi religious visits were seen as important developments in fostering China's relations with Saudi Arabia. China's use of Islam as a foreign policy instrument succeeded this time in creating direct contact between the two peoples. 'People to people' contact was seen as the first step toward establishing mutual understanding of each other. Such contacts created, for the first time, a favourable opinion of China among both religious and political leaders in Saudi Arabia. Therefore, in a country where religious leaders have influential status, Islam cannot be ruled out as having had a powerful influence in Saudi Arabia's decision to foster political relations with China in the early 1990s.

Conducting business

China had also used businessmen to develop China's economic links and to promote friendship with Saudi Arabia.[91] Saudi businessmen visited China and attended the Canton trade fair in the early 1980s (Tanzer 1982: 28). In April–May 1985, Haji Husayn Hei Boli, Chairman of the Ningxia regional government visited Saudi Arabia; and later a Saudi trade delegation visited Yinchuan in November to 'explore ways of promoting economic and

---

88 *FBIS-CHI-85-245*, 20 December 1985, p. I2.
89 *FBIS-CHI-86-201*, 17 October 1986, p. I2.
90 *FBIS-CHI-87-055*, 23 March 1987, p. I1.
91 In regard to China's official line on using economic cooperation to further friendly relations see, for example, *FBIS-CHI-82-145*, 28 July 1982, p. K11.

technological co-operation' with the Ningxia Autonomous Region. The delegation held talks on cooperation projects in various fields including agriculture and the chemical industry.[92] Another delegation of Saudi businessmen–bankers visited Ningxia in December 1985–January 1986 and expressed interests in establishing a financial institute in Ningxia.[93] In November 1986, a group of Saudi entrepreneurs, led by former Governor of the Saudi Monetary Agency (the Central Bank of Saudi Arabia) 'Abd al-Aziz al-Qurayshi, visited China and met with Chinese Premier Zhao. Zhao expressed his belief that the visit of the Saudi entrepreneurs, whom he called 'envoys', would lead to 'promoting the Sino-Saudi friendship and economic co-operation'. He said that he would welcome more Saudis to visit China in order to pave the way for creating a better understanding, establishing friendship, and promoting economic and trade relations between the two countries. He hailed Saudi's 'neutral and non-alignment foreign policy', its role in safeguarding Arab unity and its support for the cause of the Palestinian people, and the struggle of the Afghan and Cambodian peoples. Zhao reiterated that China and the Kingdom hold the same policies on many of the world's issues. Al-Qurayshi conveyed thanks from the Saudi government to the Chinese government for its stand on the Middle East issue. He also said that Saudi leaders were grateful to China for its efforts in promoting peace and stability in the Gulf and Peninsula region and an early end to the Iran–Iraq war.[94]

A year later, a Chinese delegation of entrepreneurs visited Saudi Arabia for a goodwill visit at the invitation of al-Qurayshi. The delegation was headed by the President of the China Council for Promotion of International Trade, Jia Shi. This was the first Chinese delegation that consisted solely of entrepreneurs ever to visit the Kingdom.[95] The delegation was received by Saudi Second Deputy Prime Minister and Defence and Aviation Minister, Prince Sultan ibn 'Abd al-Aziz al-Sa'ud.[96] During its meeting with Saudi officials, the delegation expressed China's interest in strengthening cooperation with Saudi Arabia in the fields of trade, joint ventures, fairs, investment, and labour exports. He also hoped that Chinese companies could qualify for project loans and assistance from the Saudi Development Fund.[97]

In November 1988, China and Saudi Arabia decided to establish commercial representative offices in their capital cities to 'further develop

---

92 *FBIS-CHI-85-219*, 13 November 1985, p. 11; and *FBIS-CHI-85-223*, 19 November 1985, p. 12.
93 *FBIS-CHI-86-002*, 3 January 1986, p. 11.
94 *FBIS-CHI-86-221*, 17 November 1986, p. 11.
95 *FBIS-CHI-87-223*, 19 November 1987, p. 5.
96 *FBIS-CHI-87-229*, 30 November 1987, p. 9.
97 *FBIS-CHI-87-223*, p. 5.

the friendly relations and co-operation' between the two countries 'in economic and commercial fields'. The decision was signed in Washington by Han Xu, Chinese Ambassador to the United States, and Prince Bandar bin Sultan, Saudi Ambassador to the United States. The decision was the result of Prince Bandar's mid-October visit to China.[98] The Chinese press reported the Prince as stating that the commercial representative offices were only the first step, and the following year relations would develop toward establishment of diplomatic relations.[99] However, this was not mentioned during the signing of the memorandum. In an interview with Saudi newspaper *Al-Riyadh*, Han Xu said:

> The establishment of commercial representative offices in each other's territory by China and Saudi Arabia is an important indicator of the positive and steady development of friendship and co-operation between the two countries. The purpose of all of this is to achieve the normalisation of their relations.

He added that:

> The Chinese Government is happy with the steady development of the friendship and co-operation between China and Saudi Arabia in the trade, political and other fields over the past few years. It thinks that there is a solid foundation for the development of friendship and co-operation between the two countries and that this is in the fundamental interest of their peoples and beneficial to world peace and stability. It hopes that by making joint efforts, the two countries can make the relations between China and Saudi Arabia a model of friendship and co-operation between countries with different social systems and beliefs.
> (*FBIS-CHI-88-248*, 27 December 1988: 13–14)

The Japanese press reported a disagreement between China and the Kingdom over the location of the Chinese trade office in Riyadh. According to the report, China demanded that its trade office be located in the same Western outskirts of Riyadh where other diplomatic missions are located and for its representatives to enjoy diplomatic privileges instead of the Saudi proposal to locate the office inside the local industry and commerce chamber in Riyadh.[100] By insisting on its demands, Beijing wanted its trade office to look like other diplomatic missions. After accepting China's demand, the Chinese trade office in Riyadh became

---

98 *FBIS-CHI-88-219*, 14 November 1988, p. 19.
99 *Ibid.*
100 *FBIS-CHI-89-042*, 6 March 1989, p. 11.

operational in April 1989.[101] It was headed by Deng Shaoqin, known among Saudi businessmen as 'Najib', who had a good command of Arabic, both spoken and written. In an interview with the Saudi daily *Al-Riyadh* on 5 April 1989, Deng Shaoqin said:

> We will work and make efforts to increase mutual understanding, strengthen co-operation, and develop Saudi–Chinese relations in all fields, so that our relations can reach a higher level in the interest of both countries and both peoples.
>
> (*FBIS-CHI-89-068*, 11 April 1989: 12)

The Saudi trade office was subsequently opened in Beijing and Tawfiq Khalid al-Madar, the Saudi first commercial representative to China, presented his certificate of appointment to the Chinese Foreign Minister Qian Qichen on 28 August 1989.[102]

Meanwhile, the Ningxia Islamic International Trust and Investment Corporation of China signed a contract on 13 April 1989 with the Al-Barakah group of Saudi Arabia to jointly set up an international trust and investment company – the Al-Barakah–Ningxia Islamic International Trust and Investment Company. The Company is based in Yinchuan, capital of the Ningxia (Hui) Muslim Autonomous Region with a registered capital of US$80 million. Its aim was reported to be the promotion of financial and economic cooperation among Muslim regions.[103] In December 1989, the International Chamber of Commerce of China opened a Chinese export exhibition in Riyadh, which was the first of its kind ever held in the Kingdom. Fifty-six Chinese companies participated in the exhibition from fields such as light industry, textiles, machinery, modern building materials, handicrafts, and others. It was reported that Chinese companies had concluded deals worth more than US$30 million.[104]

As a result of all these business contacts between China and the Kingdom, trade relations between the two countries increased substantially in the 1980s. Prior to the 1981 lifting of the ban on direct imports to the Kingdom from China, trade relations were limited to indirect trade through other countries, mainly Hong Kong, Kuwait, Oman, and the UAE. However, following the lifting of the ban, the Kingdom established a direct maritime line between China and Saudi Arabia (Shichor 1989: 15). China's indirect trade relations with the Kingdom in the 1970s were valued at US$149 million or about 4 per cent of China's total trade relations with the countries

---

101 *FBIS-CHI-89-065*, 6 April 1989, p. 15.
102 *FBIS-CHI-89-165*, 28 August 1989, p. 12.
103 *FBIS-CHI-89-065*, 6 April 1989, pp. 15–16.
104 *FBIS-CHI-89-243*, 20 December 1989, p. 15.

of the Gulf and Arabian Peninsula region. This value, however, jumped to US$2,212 million or just over 22.5 per cent of China's total trade with the countries of the region in the 1980s (see Table A.8 in the Appendix). China's exports to the Kingdom were dominated by textile yarn, fabrics, clothing and clothing accessories, metals, vegetables, fruit, and food products. China's imports from the Kingdom consisted primarily of chemicals, fertilizers, and food products. In 1987, the Saudi Arabian Basic Industries Corporation (SABIC) exported 320,000 tons of urea and other petrochemicals worth US$43 million to a Hong Kong company for resale to China (Schichor 1989: 17). It was reported that SABIC was to sell China a total of 340,000 tons of plastic, fertilizers, and other chemicals worth US$60 million following a visit to the Kingdom by a Chinese trade delegation headed by Jia Shi.[105] In December 1987, the Kingdom exported approximately 300,000 tons of Saudi wheat to China.[106]

Selling missiles

China and Saudi Arabia concluded a secret missile deal in March 1988 in which the Saudis received an unspecified number of Chinese made DF-3 (known to the West as CSS-2) intermediate-range ballistic missiles (IRBM), capable of reaching any location in the Middle East.[107] The missile is able to carry nuclear and chemical warheads, as well as conventional ones. The real cost was not revealed but it was suggested that the Kingdom probably paid US$3 billion to US$3.5 billion for the missile package (Seib 1988: 1). The Chinese Foreign Minster Wu Xueqian confirmed on 6 April 1988 that China had sold a number of ground-to-ground missiles to Saudi Arabia. He added that the Saudi government had promised that it would not transfer, or be first to use, the missile and it would use them only for defence purposes. He argued that the sale of Chinese missiles to the Kingdom would help stabilize the situation in the region.[108] Later on, it was reported in *The Sunday Telegraph* on 29 March 1992 that the US Defence Department had become convinced that the Kingdom had given secrets about the US Patriot anti-missile system to China as part of the DF-3 missile deal (Porter 1992: 2). The Saudis, however, denied the allegation.[109]

The discussions that led to the acquisition of the Chinese CSS-2 missiles go back to July 1985 when Prince Bandar visited China after the Saudi

---

105 *Middle East Economic Survey*, Vol. 31, No. 8, 30 November 1987, p. A8.
106 *FBIS-CHI-87-250*, 30 December 1987, p. 8.
107 'Beijing Surprise: Missiles for the Saudis', in *Time*, 11 April 1988, p. 40.
108 *FBIS-CHI-88-066*, 6 April 1988, p. 8.
109 *FBIS-NES-92-064*, 8 April 1992, p. 11.

government's decision to obtain arms from sources other than the United States (Seib 1988: 1). Since then, several meetings had taken place between officials from both governments, but nothing was reported to suggest that they had discussed the missile deal. When Vice-Premier Yao Yilin met with the Crown Prince 'Abdullah ibn 'Abd al-Aziz in Oman, the meeting was described as 'a new page' in China–Saudi Arabia relations. When the Chinese entrepreneur delegation visited the Kingdom, it met with the Saudi Defence and Aviation Minister. Saudi Minister of Agriculture, 'Abd al-Rahman al-Shaykh, visited Beijing in January 1988, and it was reported that the two sides discussed the situation in the Gulf region.[110] Qi Huaiyuan, special envoy of the Chinese President Li Xiannian and Vice-Minister of Foreign Affairs, visited Riyadh in April 1988 as the first senior official of the PRC to visit the Kingdom.[111] There were no public statements or even indications that the two sides were negotiating a missile deal in all these meetings. Both Beijing and Riyadh wanted to keep the missile deal secret. The two sides arranged for the deal through several secret visits by officials from both sides. In 1986, China sent Lieutenant General Gao Gangchuan, Deputy Chief of the General Staff of the PLA, to Saudi Arabia to discuss the deal in detail. His visit was kept secret from the eyes of the West and Taiwan. Later, General Khaled Bin Sultan, Commander of the Saudi Air Defence, was assigned to take charge of the missile deal project with China. He visited China secretly four times to discuss with Chinese officials the details of their deal. In his book *Desert Warrior* (1995), he outlined his visits to China and his discussion with the Chinese officials on the purchase of the DF-3. His visits were conducted by travelling through other Asian countries such as Malaysia and Hong Kong. Khaled was the first foreigner to visit the site where DF-3s are manufactured. Saudis were trained in China and the Kingdom to maintain and operate the missiles (Sultan and Seale 1995: 137–52).

It was even reported in *The Sunday Times*, 7 August 1994, that Saudi Arabia tried to buy experimental nuclear reactors from China as part of a secret twenty-year programme to become a nuclear power. According to the paper, Prince 'Abd al-Rahman Bin Muhammad, the nephew of King Fahd, travelled secretly to China, toured facilities, and opened negotiations on the purchase of a miniature neutron source reactor in 1989. Muhammad Khilaywi, a Saudi diplomat seeking asylum in the United States, claimed that the Kingdom bought at least two mini-reactors (Colvin and Sawyer).

Why China sold such weapons to a country like Saudi Arabia, which was known as an anti-communist state, can be explained in terms of the following points:

---

110 *FBIS-CHI-88-015*, 25 January 1988, p. 7.
111 *FBIS-CHI-88-064*, 4 April 1988, p. 10.

1 Saudi Arabia was one of just three major countries that had full diplomatic relations with Taiwan and the only major Arab state that had no diplomatic relations with the PRC. Therefore, the deal was intended as a sweetener for Riyadh to recognize Beijing. Wu Xueqian said, when he confirmed the deal, 'we want to see the earliest possible establishment of diplomatic relations with Saudi Arabia' (Tai Ming Cheung 1988: 26–7).
2 The timing was most favourable to achieving the above objective and for the Chinese government to create a favourable opinion of China among Saudi leaders. The Saudi government was in need of a more sophisticated missile system, keeping in mind that both Israel and Iran already possessed such a system, to deter any possible Iranian attack on the Kingdom as the missile war between Iran and Iraq reached its highest point (Editorial 1988: 1). However, the Saudi request for the purchase of forty-eight US F-15 fighters and related ground-strike equipment were turned down by its close ally, the United States (Yang and Greenberger 1988). Therefore, the deal was well timed by the Chinese government both to demonstrate its willingness to work with the Kingdom, and to present itself as a valuable alternative for the Kingdom should the West, mainly the United States, be unwilling to accommodate Saudi military's needs.
3 The deal would generate much-needed foreign exchange income for China's military modernization programme.

Thus, China's adoption of all the above foreign policy strategies throughout the 1980s stemmed from:

1 fear of Soviet penetration in the Gulf and Arabian Peninsula region and support for the Saudi government's strong opposition to the Soviet presence in Afghanistan and South Yemen; and
2 the need to eliminate the established political relations between Saudi Arabia and Taiwan.

So, the Chinese paid much more attention to its Saudi policies. They adjusted their own policies regarding their own Muslim population. They also worked to develop their relations within the Gulf and Peninsula region in order to set examples to the Saudi leaders and to create a new pattern within which two different social systems and ideologies can coexist. They also worked hard to develop their economic relations with businessmen from the Kingdom. China was also even willing to provide advanced military technology to Saudi Arabia. Despite all of the above efforts by the Chinese, diplomatic relations between the two countries remained absent. However, the effort did create mutual understanding between the two governments, which the Chinese perceived as a necessary step that could lead to the establishment of formal relations in the near future.

The establishment of diplomatic relations

The delayed establishment of diplomatic relations between China and Saudi Arabia was caused by the issue of Taiwan. The Kingdom wanted to use diplomacy to foster diplomatic relations with both China and Taiwan. But the Chinese government's insistence that the Saudis abolish diplomatic relations with the Taiwanese regime, as the first step toward fostering political relations with China, delayed the process. Eventually, the Saudi government realized that the political and military significance of China was much more important than the economic significance of Taiwan. Prince Bandar, who indicated Saudi's willingness to purchase Chinese missiles, flew to Beijing on 9 July 1990 to discuss the possibility of establishing formal relations with Beijing (Seib 1990: 12). The Chinese press did not reveal much about the visit and covered it briefly. It was reported that meetings between the Prince and Chinese officials covered 'matters of mutual concern to the two countries'.[112] However, it was the Taiwanese press, the Taipei Central News Agency in particular, that revealed that the Prince's visit to Beijing was to negotiate the establishment of official ties (Footnote 112: A4(1). Taiwan was very concerned about the development and tried to maintain diplomatic relations with the Kingdom. Premier Hao Po-tsun instructed his Ministry of Foreign Affairs to do 'everything possible' to maintain Taiwan's diplomatic relations with the Kingdom.[113] But all efforts failed to deter the Saudi government from its decision to establish formal relations with China.

Following Prince Bandar's visit to Beijing, Riyadh sent 'Abd al-Aziz bin 'Abdullah al-Zamil, Minister of Industry and Electricity, to Taipei as a special envoy of the Saudi government. Al-Zamil delivered to President Lee Teng-hui a written message from the King in which he said that his government had decided to set up official ties with China, and asked that the two countries' embassies change into 'representative offices'.[114]

Following the Kingdom's move to eliminate official ties with Taiwan, Chinese Foreign Minister Qian Qichen visited Saudi Arabia on 20 July on an official three-day visit at the invitation of his Saudi counterpart. This was the first visit to Saudi Arabia by a Chinese foreign minister. Qian's visit was intended to put the finishing touches to an agreement to establish diplomatic relations between the two countries.[115] On the second day of his visit, the two countries signed a communiqué in Riyadh on the establishment of diplomatic relations between the Kingdom of Saudi Arabia and the People's Republic of China. It said:

---

112 BBC, *SWB*, *FE/0815*, 13 July 1990, p. A4/2.
113 BBC, *SWB*, *FE/0819*, 18 July 1990, p. A4/1.
114 BBC, *SWB*, *FE/0822*, 21 July 1990, p. A4/1.
115 BBC, *SWB*, *ME/0822*, 21 July 1990, p. I.

> The Governments of the People's Republic of China and the Kingdom of Saudi Arabia have decided to establish diplomatic relations between the two countries at the ambassadorial level as of 29th Dhu al-Hujjah 1410 AH, corresponding to 21st July 1990 AD. The Government of the People's Republic of China supports the policy of the Government of the Kingdom of Saudi Arabia in pursuing of achieving its security, stability and national interests. The Government of the Kingdom of Saudi Arabia recognises that the government of the People's Republic of China is the sole legitimate government that represents the entire Chinese people. The two governments have agreed to develop co-operation and friendly relations between the two countries on the basis of the principles of mutual respect for sovereignty and territorial integrity, mutual non-aggression, non-interference in each other's internal affairs, equity and mutual benefit, and peaceful coexistence.
> (BBC, *SWB*, *FE/0823*, 23 July 1990: A4/1)

On 22 July, Qian met King Fahd and delivered to him a letter from the Chinese President Yang Shangkun. Yang's letter expressed the Chinese government's happiness over the establishment of diplomatic relations between the two countries and stressed that this development 'does not only respond to the fundamental interests of the two peoples but also serves peace and stability in Asia, and in fact the world over'.[116]

Press in the two countries hailed the establishment of diplomatic relations. An editorial in *Renmin Ribao*, 23 July, said:

> China and Saudi Arabia differ in [their] social system and ideology. But both are willing to forge and push forward friendly and co-operative ties on the basis of the five principles of peaceful co-existence.

The editorial praised Saudi foreign policy stating:

> In foreign affairs, Saudi Arabia pursues a policy of neutrality, non-alignment and peace. It upholds that countries should act on mutual respect, good neighbourliness and non-interference in each other's internal affairs, and should co-operate to bring about stability and prosperity.
> (BBC, *SWB*, *FE/0824*, 24 July 1990: A4/1)

The editorial in the government-controlled *Al Riyadh*, 23 July, not only applauded the new development but also explained why the Kingdom should pursue diplomatic relations with China. It said:

---

116 BBC, *SWB*, *ME/0824*, 24 July 1990, p. A/2

We do not believe that there is anything exciting or glamorous about the mutual recognition between the Kingdom and the PRC or about raising representation between them to ambassador level. Especially when we consider that China has a notable international status and is moving towards becoming as influential and strong as the superpowers, which influence international decisions. China has moved towards Muslims and allowed them to perform their rites without any pressure or ideological rigidity; and it maintains distinctive stances towards the Arabs and their causes ... the Kingdom was prompted to regard these practices as a realistic factor for establishing these relations between the two countries with a view of placing them in their sound and positive context. The two countries' need for one another will be beneficial in terms of industrial and agricultural products as well as the other joint business over which government and private sectors co-operate.

(*FBIS – Near East & South Asia (NES)-90-145*, 27 July 1990: 25–6)

The first Saudi ambassador to Beijing, Tawfiq al-Almadar, who was in charge of the Saudi trade representative office in Beijing, presented on 7 August his letter of credence to the Chinese president.[117] The appointment of al-Almadar, a soldier turned diplomat, as the Kingdom's Ambassador to Beijing revealed Riyadh's ambitions to increase its arms trade with Beijing in the future, particularly when we know that Prince Khaled recommended him for the job (Sultan and Seale 1995: 142). The first Chinese ambassador to the Kingdom, Sun Bigan, was appointed in September 1990.[118]

China and the Kingdom after the establishment of formal relations

Less than a month after the establishment of diplomatic relations between China and the Kingdom, Iraq invaded Kuwait. The invasion and the subsequent developments presented the first real test for the Chinese government to show how far the Chinese government was willing to accommodate its relations with Saudi Arabia and the GCC countries. Saudi Foreign Minister Prince Sa'ud bin Faysal travelled to Beijing on 19 September. He met with Premier Li Peng and President Yang Shangkun, respectively. Prince Sa'ud reportedly briefed both leaders on the Saudi position toward the crisis and said that the Saudi leadership appreciated China's stand of, so far, supporting and favouring the relevant UN resolutions and called upon China to 'play a larger role in the future resolutions' of the crisis. The Chinese leaders stressed China's stand on

---

117 BBC, *SWB, FE/0837*, 8 August 1990, p. A4/2.
118 BBC, *SWB, FE/0871*, 17 September 1990, p. A4/1.

the crisis and expressed their country's understanding of the measures adopted by the Kingdom and other Gulf countries to safeguard their own security. The visit was said to have achieved satisfactory results.[119] Later, in October, the Chinese Foreign Minister Qian Qichen met with his Saudi counterpart in New York.[120] The Gulf crisis dominated their discussion. In December, King Fahd sent a letter to the Chinese president through his special envoy 'Abd al-Aziz al-Thunayyan. The letter, reportedly, expressed the King's appreciation to the Chinese government for its position on the crisis.[121] Nothing else was reported concerning these contacts. But one could argue that the main themes of these contacts were:

1   to present the Saudi position regarding to the Iraqi invasion and its own defence measures;
2   to ensure the support of the Chinese government to the UN resolution relevant to the crisis; and
3   to ensure that the Chinese did not provide military support to the Iraqi regime.

Chinese Premier Li Peng visited Saudi Arabia from 9 to 11 July 1991. His visit marked the first visit to the Kingdom by a Chinese leader since China and the Kingdom established relations. His visit was intended to 'boost the further advancement of the friendly and co-operative relations between the two countries'. He called Saudi Arabia 'an important country in the Middle East and the Gulf region, and an important factor for regional peace and stability'.[122] The Chinese leader discussed with King Fahd and his government officials the Gulf crisis, the Palestinian issue, and other international issues, as well as ways to expand bilateral political and economic relations.[123] Li described his visit as 'successful' and 'fruitful'.[124]

China donated, in mid-August 1991, equipment to the Kingdom to help the oil spill clean-up efforts in the Gulf. The equipment included a 3,000-m railing that could entrap oil.[125] A Muslim delegation visited the Kingdom in December for a friendly visit. It was the first of its kind since the establishment of diplomatic relations. The delegation was headed by Mohamad Hanafy Wan Yaobin, deputy director of the Bureau of Religious Affairs under the State Council.[126] The Saudi Arabian retired general Prince

---

119   BBC, *SWB, FE/0876*, 22 September 1990, p. A4/1.
120   BBC, *SWB, FE/0888*, 6 October 1990, p. A4/1.
121   BBC, *SWB, FE/0950*, 18 December 1990, p. A4/1.
122   *FBIS-NES-91-133*, 11 July 1991, pp. 12–18.
123   See the joint communiqué in *FBIS-NES-91-134*, 12 July 1991, p. 14.
124   *Beijing Review*, No. 29, 22–28 July 1991, pp. 10–11.
125   *FBIS-CHI-91-139*, 19 July 1991, p. 17.
126   *FBIS-CHI-91-247*, 24 December 1991, p. 11.

Khaled Bin Sultan Bin Abd al-Aziz visited China in March 1995. He met with President Jiang Zemin and the Vice-Chairman of China's Central Military Commission and Minister of Defence General, Chi Haotian. Khaled said: 'a strong China would contribute to the peace and development of Asia and the world'.[127] However, what he meant by 'a strong China' is not clear. But one could assume that, as a military man himself, his judgement of a state's strength could only mean strength in military terms. This assumption is supported by the fact that his visit did not yield any economic or social agreements and his meetings were limited to high-level military officials. He visited China again in May of the following year and again met with General Chi Haotian.[128] A few days later, Chi arrived in the Kingdom and on 1 June visited the Saudi Western Fleet.[129] No further details were reported about this visit. A delegation from the Chinese People's Political Consultative Conference visited the Kingdom in November 1996 and met with the Saudi Crown Prince and First Deputy Prime Minister and National Guard Commander 'Abdullah.

Prince 'Abdullah visited China between 14 and 21 October 1998, the first highest-ranked Saudi official to visit the PRC. His talks with Jian Zemin embraced various bilateral, regional, and international issues and revealed a consensus on bilateral relations. In a joint communiqué, the two sides expressed satisfaction with the development of bilateral ties, and stressed their concern that little progress had been made towards a political settlement of the Middle East question. They emphasized the importance of the Jerusalem issue and the necessity of not undertaking any unilateral measures that could prejudice final-status negotiations over the city. They called on Syria and Israel to resume negotiations and they also urged the implementation of UN Resolution 4216 on Lebanon.[130] In April 1999, Prince Salman ibn 'Abd al-Aziz, the governor of Riyadh Province, visited China. He was received by the Beijing Mayor and discussed bilateral cooperation in such fields as urban infrastructure, real estate, transportation, and entertainment facilities. He was also received by the Chinese Defence Minister, Chi Haotian, and President Jiang Zemin.[131] President Jiang Zemin paid a four-day visit to the Kingdom on 31 October 1999. His visit marked the first visit ever by a Chinese president and the first visit ever by Jiang to any country in the Gulf and Arabian Peninsula region. He met with King Fahd, stating that China, as a permanent member of the UN Security Council, would continue with its efforts to promote peace and

---

127 BBC, *SWB, FE/2267*, 1 April 1995, p. G/2.
128 BBC, *SWB, FE/2617*, 21 May 1996, p. G/4.
129 BBC, *SWB, FE/2628*, 3 June 1996, p. G/2; and *FE/2630*, 5 June 1996, G/1.
130 *Saudi Economic Survey*, Vol. 32, No. 1589, 21 October 1998, p. 2; and *China Quarterly*, Vol. 157, March 1999, p. 272.
131 BBC, *SWB, FE/3514*, 21 April 1999, p. G/5.

stability in the Gulf region and the entire Middle East.[132] It was said that the two sides had decided to form 'a political and economic partnership'.[133] Despite no elaboration on the so-called 'partnership', one can argue that both countries recognized the political and economic weights of one another. China's political importance as a permanent member of the UN Security Council and its relatively advanced military arsenal elevated China's significance to the Saudi leaders. On the other side, Saudi economic power and its political status in the region strengthened China's interest in the Kingdom. The groundwork for this 'partnership' had already been laid down by the two governments. Economically, the two countries had achieved a substantial improvement in relations. Politically, the Chinese worked to fulfil their commitments to the UN Security Council toward issues related to the Gulf and Peninsula region and the Middle East. They continued to support or at least not oppose UN resolutions related to Iraq, and continued their support for the Palestinian as well as other Arab causes. Most importantly, China has become a very valuable source of advanced weapons to the Kingdom. In addition to the missile deal of 1988 and the alleged nuclear reactors deal of 1989, Western reports alleged that China–Saudi military cooperation had not been halted in the 1990s. It was reported in January 1991 that China had shipped twelve nuclear warheads to Saudi Arabia.[134] Both sides denied the allegation and called it 'groundless'. *The New York Times Current Events Edition* in its 5 March 1992 issue called for an investigation into why Chinese missile technologists keep visiting a plant in Hama. The paper claimed there was enough evidence to suggest the Chinese were attempting to circumvent agreements made in a missile non-proliferation pact (Safire 1992: A27).

China–Saudi economic relations

Economic relations between China and the Kingdom have continued to increase since the establishment of diplomatic relations between the two countries. In August 1993, a high-level delegation from the China Council for the Promotion of International Trade visited the Kingdom. Later, the two sides signed a trade and economic cooperation agreement in Beijing (Parker 1993: 29). Another trade delegation visited the Kingdom in August from the Muslim city of Jinan in Shandong Province to look into cooperation between the city and the Kingdom in the export of Chinese labour to the Kingdom, joint exploitation of Jinan's mineral resources, joint ventures in the building materials, contracting, foodstuffs, consultancy, and

---

132 *China Daily*, Hong Kong Edition, Vol. 3, No. 22, 2 November 1999, p. 1.
133 *Beijing Review*, No. 46, 15 November 1999, p. 6.
134 BBC, *SWB*, FE/0970, 15 January 1991, p. I1.

livestock sectors (Parker 1993: 29). In May, Saudi Arabia's Al-Zamil Steel Building Company won its first order from China for a US$2 million steel structure for an air-conditioning plant in Shenzhen (Parker 1993: 29).

In November 1993, the Kingdom approved China's status as the preferential state in terms of trade.[135] A Chinese–Saudi Arabian economic conference was held in Beijing on 21 March 1994. It was attended by some 100 Chinese and Saudi businessmen and government officials.[136] In February 1996, the first meeting of the Sino-Saudi Arabian Mixed Trade and Economic Committee was held in Beijing. The meeting was co-chaired by Chinese Minister of Foreign Trade and Economic Cooperation, Wu Yli and the Saudi Minister of Finance, Ibrahim al-Assaf.[137] The value of China's trade relations with the Kingdom jumped from US$71 million in 1989 to US$525 million in 1991, US$1,027 million in 1994, and US$1,588 in 1996. This substantial increase led the Kingdom to become China's leading trade partner in the Gulf and Arabian Peninsula region by 1996, accounting for more than 30.5 per cent of China's exports and 23.2 per cent of China's imports from the region from 1990 to 1996. China's exports to the Kingdom consisted mainly of refined sugar crystals, textiles, cassette-type magnetic tapes, furniture, silk carpets, machinery, foodstuffs, while the Kingdom's main exports to China were petrochemicals, fertilizers, and wheat (SMFNE 1997). In May 1995, the National Shipping Co. of Saudi Arabia (NSCSA) started a service to the Chinese port of Tianjin, after launching operations at the port of Shanghai the previous year. NSCSA was the first Arab shipping firm to do business with China.[138]

As for oil, China is not yet a major recipient of Saudi oil mainly because the quality of the Saudi crude oil is not suitable for existing Chinese refineries. However, Chinese officials have always stressed their country's willingness to conduct oil agreements and ventures with the Kingdom in order to meet China's short- and long-term needs for oil.[139] When Vice-Premier for Foreign Economic Relations and Trade, Li Lanqing, visited the Kingdom in July 1993, he signed on behalf of the China National Oil Company (CNOC) an oil deal with Saudi Aramco to import 3 million tons of crude oil from the Kingdom (Parker 1993: 29), although it was not stated when the imports would start. In March 1996, Wu Yi, China's Minister of Foreign Trade and Economic Cooperation, expressed her country's desire to increase its import of Saudi crude oil, petrochemicals, and fertilizers– China was already the largest market for fertilizers from Saudi Arabia.[140]

135 *FBIS-NES-93-211*, 3 November 1993, p. 33.
136 *FBIS-CHI-94-056*, 23 March 1994, p. 7.
137 BBC, *SWB, FE/2548*, 29 February 1996, p. G1.
138 *FBIS-CHI-95-068*, 10 April 1995, p. 16.
139 BBC, *SWB, MEW/0416*, 2 January 1996, p. 10.
140 *China Economic Review*, May 1995, pp. 22–30.

She added that, despite the fact that China lacks the ability to process certain Saudi Arabian crude oil, China imported 300,000 tons of crude oil from the Kingdom in 1995 (or 3 per cent of its total oil import in that year), in addition to 440,000 tons of urea in 1994. She pointed out that China was building a refinery to process this type of crude oil,[141] the completion of which would result in increased crude oil imports from Saudi Arabia.

The Chinese also continued to urge Saudi Arabia to invest in the development of Chinese refineries. Several meetings between officials from the two countries met in each other's capitals and discussed plans for a joint venture for refining in China. There were in fact two joint venture refining projects in China in which Saudi Aramco had negotiated with Chinese officials. One was a project for which Saudi Aramco and its South Korean partner Ssangyong would join China's Sinochem to build, in 1997, a new refinery designed to run mainly Saudi crude at the north-eastern port city of Qingdao, in Shandong province. Its capacity was said to be in the range of 200,000–300,000 bbl./day and a total cost of US$1.5 billion. Aramco would hold a 45 per cent stake in the project. The refinery, once completed, would allow China to import 3.5 million tons of Saudi oil annually.[142] The other project that the Saudis negotiated with the Chinese was the expansion of an existing 170,000-bbl./day refinery at Maoming in Guandong province in south China to reach 270,000 bbl./day. The project was estimated to cost US$1 billion.[143] On 13 October 1997, Aramco, American Exxon, and Chinese companies based in Wuhan signed an agreement for a joint petrochemical project in Wuhan province, in South-east China. The project included increasing the capacity of a refinery in the region from 80,000 to 240,000 bbl./day. The project also included the setting up of new distillation and breaking units, which could produce some light oil and petrochemical products. It also included marketing and distribution operations in the province.[144]

A delegation from China Petrochemical Corporation (SINOPEC) signed, in June 1997, a crude oil export deal with Saudi Aramco to increase Saudi Arabia crude supplies to China from its 1997 level of 30,000 to 60,000 bbl./day.[145] During President Jiang Zemin's October–November 1999 visit to the Kingdom, the two sides signed several cooperation agreements including one covering oil. No further details have been given about the oil agreement. Jiang was said to have discussed the construction of a US$1 billion refinery

---

141 BBC, *SWB*, *FE/2549*, 1 March 1996, G/3.
142 'World Wire: Refinery Venture set in China', *The Wall Street Journal*, 6 August 1996, p. 4; and *Middle East Economic Survey*, Vol. 39, No. 12, 18 December 1995, p. A3.
143 *Ibid.*
144 BBC, *SWB*, *MEW/0509 WME*, 21 October 1997, p. 14.
145 *OPEC Bulletin*, Vol. 28, No. 7, July 1997, p. 20; and *Middle East Economic Digest*, Vol. 41, No. 44, 31 October 1997, p. 3.

and petrochemicals complex in China's southern province of Guandong with Saudi assistance that would use Saudi oil.[146]

CHINA AND THE UAE

China and the UAE prior to the establishment of diplomatic relations

Due to their dependence on Britain, China's view of the Sheikhdoms prior to the establishment of the UAE was highly critical. This was evident in China's increasing political, ideological, and material support for the South Yemenis and the PFLOAG's efforts to carry on its policy of liberating the whole region from Britain and its so-called 'lackeys', namely the governments of the Gulf countries. However, as China's foreign policy began to shift toward pragmatism in the region, it began by 1971 to hail the Sheikhdoms' efforts to pursue unity among themselves and to manage their own affairs following the British withdrawal from the region.

Sheikh Zayed Bin Sultan al-Nahayyan, President of the newly proclaimed UAE, sent a message to the Chinese Premier Zhou Enlai on 3 December 1971 on the founding of the UAE. The message said:

> It gives me great pleasure to bring to Your Excellency's notice that the Emirates of Abu Dhabi, Dubai, Sharjah, Ajman, Umm Al-Qawain and Fujairah, following the termination of the treaties previously held between them and the United Kingdom, have decided, on this day, 2nd December 1971, to unite and form among themselves the State of the United Arab Emirates and to declare it as an independent State with complete sovereignty. The State declares its adherence to the Charter of the United Nations and that of the Arab League. It also expresses its belief in the necessity of peaceful coexistence between all nations and international co-operation in all fields and confirms its intention to preserve the international peace. While expressing the willingness of my people and Government to strengthen all relations with your Excellency's people and Government, I send to Your Excellency my best wishes for Your Excellency's health, happiness and for your people's prosperity.
> (BBC, *SWB, FE/3861*, 10 December 1971: A4/1)

Premier Zhou responded on 8 December with a message to Sheikh Zayed informing him of the Chinese government's decision to recognize the UAE. The message said:

---

146 *www.lasvegassun.com/sunbin* ... /s/w-me/1999/nov/03/110300614.htm, p. 1.

I thank your Highness for your friendly message addressed to me on the occasion of the independence of your country. I wish to take this opportunity to inform your Highness that the Chinese Government has decided to recognise your country. May the United Arab Emirates enjoy prosperity and its people happiness. May the friendship between the people of China and the United Arab Emirates develop continuously.

(BBC, *SWB, FE/3681*, 10 December 1971: A4/1)

In both letters, the two sides expressed willingness to further political and economic relations between the two countries. However, the furthering of mainly political relations did not take place immediately. From the Chinese view, China preferred to wait for several days before it extended its recognition to the UAE. This was mainly due to China's newly-established diplomatic relations with Iran. China wanted to wait and see the Iranian reaction first before it publicized its own decision. Iran and the UAE emirates of Sharjah and Ras al Khaimah, which later joined the union, had territorial disputes over the Iranian occupation on 30 November 1971 of Sharjah's island of Abu Musa and Ras al-Khaimah's islands of the Greater and Lesser Tunbs (al-Alkim 1989: 140–5). China avoided, at least publicly, to take sides on the islands issue. When Iran recognized the UAE on 4 December, China felt at ease to extend its recognition to the new federation.

In his message to Premier Zhou, Sheikh Zayed avoided mentioning the issue of UAE's recognition of the PRC. Thus, the UAE did not reciprocate China's recognition. So, why then did the UAE send a message to the Chinese government expressing its willingness for strengthening 'all relations' with China? Abidi (1982: 226) argues that Sheikh Zayed's message might have been aimed at strengthening his state position vis-à-vis Saudi Arabia in the context of the border dispute over the Buraimi oasis and against Iran in the wake of the latter's occupation of the islands. But if that is the case, then why did the UAE still refuse to establish diplomatic relations with China? This was said to be partly due to the overbearing influence of Saudi Arabia and partly because of Chinese support for revolutionary movements in South Yemen and Oman (Abidi 1982: 226; al-Alkin 1989: 13, 79). While there is no true evidence to suggest that the Kingdom prevented the UAE from recognizing China, one could argue that the newly-established state of the UAE did not want to conflict with the Kingdom's policy towards China. The UAE's government recognized the Kingdom's political weight in the region, particularly when it gave in to the Saudi territorial claims of its territory in the early 1970s in order to receive political recognition. It also followed the Saudi policy lines in Yemen and Oman. This indicates that the UAE was interested, in its early days, in avoiding contradicting the Kingdom's foreign policies, which in turn might have prevented the UAE from establishing diplomatic relations with China.

Until the establishment of diplomatic ties between the two countries in November 1984, relations remained limited to economic spheres. A delegation from the Abu Dhabi Chamber of Commerce and Industry visited China in October 1978, at the invitation of the China Council for the Promotion of International Trade. The delegation was led by Sa'id Ahmad al-'Utayba. The delegation visited the Canton Fair and held business talks with Chinese companies.[147] At the beginning of 1980, the Civil Aviation Administration of China signed an agreement for on air service with the Sharjah Civil Aviation Administration. From then on, most of China's civil airlines flying to Europe stopped at Sharjah.[148] The Ruwais Fertiliser Industries Company (FERTIL), which is owned by the Abu Dhabi National Oil Company (ADNOC) and Compagnie Française des Pétroles (CFP), agreed, in 1984, long-term contracts for the export of up to 100,000 tons/year of ammonia and urea fertilizers to Japan's Mitsubishi company for re-export to China.[149] Trade relations, mainly Chinese exports, had increased between the two countries despite the absence of political relations. The value of Chinese exports to the UAE rose from US$3.81 million in 1969 to US$34.86 million in 1974, then to US$80.71 million in 1979, and to US$100.67 million in 1981 (see Table A.9 in the Appendix). China's exports to the UAE were dominated by textiles, light industrial goods, meat, and vegetables. The increase in trade relations between the two countries could be related to the following two main points:

1   the increasing role of Dubai as a trade centre in the Gulf and Arabian Peninsula region; and
2   the lack of any foreign political pressure on the UAE, due to the absence of political relations with Taiwan.

The establishment of diplomatic relations

China and the UAE established diplomatic relations on 1 November 1984. A joint communiqué said:

> Out of a common desire to strengthen and develop the friendly relations and co-operation between the two countries, the Government of the People's Republic of China and the Government of the United Arab Emirates have decided to establish diplomatic relations between the two countries at ambassadorial level.

---

147   *FBIS-CHI-208*, 26 October 1978, p. A28.
148   *Beijing Review*, No. 52, 21–31 December 1989, p. 5.
149   *Middle East Economic Survey*, Vol. 27, No. 22, 12 March 1984, p. A6.

On the establishment of diplomatic relations with the UAE, *Renmin Ribao* wrote:

> The establishment of diplomatic relations between China and the UAE entirely conforms with the common interest and aspiration of the peoples of the two countries. This indicates that the friendship between the Chinese people and the peoples in the Persian Gulf area has been developing profoundly. The Chinese people express their warm congratulations on this.

The paper went on to hail the UAE's foreign policy and said:

> In international affairs the UAE government has pursued a neutral and non-aligned policy. It has supported the just struggle of the Palestinian people and opposed the aggressive and expansionist acts of Israel. It has advocated that the Persian Gulf countries strengthen their unity, iron out their differences, and solve their disputes through peaceful means and consultations. It has opposed interference in the internal affairs of the Persian Gulf area by foreign forces. The just stand of the UAE has been highly praised by the Third World countries and their peoples.
> (*Beijing Review*, No. 46, 12 November 1985: 10–11)

The UAE newspaper *Al Khaleej* said that the decision made by the government of the UAE to establish diplomatic ties with China was in line with the UAE's policy on non-alignment and its rejection of international polarization in the Gulf region. The paper stressed that the UAE's foreign policy was based on keeping balanced relations with the big powers so as to help avoid polarization in the region.[150] The UAE *Al Wahdah* newspaper in its 26 December 1985 said that the UAE wants to develop its relations with China because China has long advocated Arab causes and taken a positive stand over the Arab–Israeli dispute and the issue of international security and peace. The paper added that:

> China's attitude deserves respect as its foreign policy is based on mutual respect and non-interference in the domestic affairs of other countries, quality and peaceful coexistence.
> (*FBIS-CHI-85-249*, 27 December 1985: I1–I2)

China's success in establishing relations with the UAE was significant, politically and economically. Politically, the UAE was among four countries in the region that did not recognize Beijing and maintained ties with Taipei.

---

150 *FBIS-CHI-84-216*, 6 November 1984, p. I2.

Economically, the UAE could present a potential market for Chinese goods and a long-term supplier of oil to meet China's growing demand for oil in the twenty-first century. The two UAE newspapers summarize the reasons behind the UAE's decision to establish diplomatic relations with China. It could be argued, therefore, that the political and strategic importance of China contributed to the UAE's decision. The UAE saw China as a valuable power to enable the UAE government to balance its relations with Iran, while exerting some influence on Beijing's military cooperation with Tehran. Thus, the UAE government came to realize the significance of engaging China rather than isolating it in order to achieve its foreign policy objectives. Here, however, we should mention that the Kingdom remained an important factor in allowing the UAE to step toward establishing diplomatic relations with China. As mentioned earlier, the absence of political and any other forms of contact between the Kingdom and China prevented the UAE from establishing diplomatic relations with the PRC in the early 1970s. However, this had changed. The Kingdom itself had started to pursue some cultural and economic contacts with China since the late 1970s. This development could have been the catalyst for countries such as the UAE and Oman to forge cultural, economic, and even political links with China.

China and the UAE after the establishment of diplomatic relations

Relations between China and the UAE were strengthened through intergovernmental contact. The first official visit between the two countries after the establishment of diplomatic relations came from China's Vice-Chairman of the Standing Committee of the National People's Congress (NPC) and Chairman of the China International Trust and Investment Corporation (CITIC), Ron Yiren, in December 1984.[151] Ron's visit was said to formally establish and further improve economic relations between the two countries.[152] On 26 February 1985, China's Minister of Urban and Rural Construction and Environmental Protection, Rui Xingwen, headed a delegation to Abu Dhabi for an official visit to the UAE. Rui was the highest Chinese official to visit the UAE since the two countries established diplomatic relations. It was reported that the Chinese official discussed the Iran–Iraq war with UAE officials. He reiterated his country's belief that a peaceful solution was the only way to end the war. It was said that Rui assured the UAE government that his country would not establish diplomatic relations with Israel unless 'the Palestinian people's inalienable rights

---

151 *FBIS-CHI-84-236*, 6 December 1984, p. 12.
152 *FBIS-CHI-84-242*, 14 December 1984, p. 14.

are restored and Israel stops its expansion in the Middle East'.[153] President Sheikh Zayed received a letter from the Chinese President inviting him to visit China. The UAE president reportedly accepted the invitation.[154] In November, Chinese Vice-Premier Yao Yilin visited the UAE and met with President Sheikh Zayed. Yao was the first high-ranked Chinese government official ever to visit the UAE. At a meeting with the UAE president, Yao told Sheikh Zayed that China appreciated the non-aligned foreign policy of the UAE. He spoke highly of the role played by the UAE in promoting Arab unity and peace in the region and its support for the Palestinian struggle. Sheikh Zayed praised China's policy of not interfering in the internal affairs of other countries. In reference to China's position on the superpowers, he pointed out that other big powers interfered in the internal affairs of other countries and said 'we must keep vigilance against these powers'. He also appreciated China's policy towards its own Muslim population.[155] During his visit the two countries signed an agreement on economic, trade, and technological cooperation.[156] The agreement covered the establishment of a committee of deputy trade ministers, which would meet regularly to expand economic ties and explore joint ventures in such fields as oil and tourism. Commenting on the agreement, the Chinese official said:

> We welcome investment not only from the government but also from the private sector, and our country has the capacity to provide manpower and technology and you could contribute by financing these projects.

He also said that Beijing would increase its imports from the UAE and was considering oil, aluminium, and petrochemicals.[157] In 1985, China was the third top buyer of aluminium from the Dubai Aluminium Company (Dubal) with 19,280 tons, following the United States with 34,314 tons in second place and Japan with 42,456 tons in first place.[158] A month later, Chinese State Councillor and Foreign Minister, Wu Xueqian, went to Abu Dhabi for a two-day visit to the UAE. He was the first Chinese foreign minister and the second high-ranked Chinese official to pay an official visit to the UAE since the establishment of diplomatic relations. Just like other Chinese officials who visited the UAE, Wu praised, in a meeting with the UAE Minister of State for Foreign Affairs, Rashid 'Abdullah al-Nu'aymi,

---

153 *FBIS-CHI-85-039*, 27 February 1985, p. I1.
154 *FBIS-CHI-85-143*, 25 July 1985, p. I1.
155 *FBIS-CHI-85-220*, 14 November 1985, p. I1.
156 *FBIS-CHI-85-222*, 18 November 1985, p. I1.
157 *Middle East Economic Survey*, Vol. 29, No. 6, 18 November 1985, pp. A5–A6.
158 *Middle East Economic Survey*, Vol. 29, No. 17, 3 February 1986, p. A11.

the UAE foreign policy in trying to bring a peaceful end to the Iran–Iraq war. He noted that China highly appreciated the 'good-neighbour policy' of the UAE and its position for settling disputes in the region through peaceful means and dialogue.[159] Most importantly, Wu's visit came twenty days after the announcement of the establishment of diplomatic relations between the UAE and the Soviet Union on 28 November 1985. During their meetings, the UAE official echoed Chinese foreign policy interests. He assured him that the rapprochement with the Soviet Union would not be at the expense of relations with China, which was up to that time refusing to normalize its relations with Moscow, and would not change the UAE's position regarding the Soviet presence in Afghanistan.[160] In January 1986, a protocol on trade and cooperation was signed in Abu Dhabi under which China's first centre for promoting China's international trade was opened in Abu Dhabi.[161] China's National Metal and Minerals Export and Import Company and China's Ever-bright Company contracted Um al-Quwain Aluminium Company (UMALCO) to purchase 65 per cent or 120,000 ton/year of its output for a period of twelve years starting in 1986.[162]

A delegation from China's Xinjiang Uyghur Autonomous Regional People's Government, headed by Tomur Dawamat, visited the UAE and met with the ruler of Sharjah Emirate, Sheikh Sultan Bin Muhammad al-Qasimi in December 1986. The delegation held talks with the Sharjah Chamber of Commerce and Industry to improve economic and trade links between the two regions.[163] Rashid 'Abdullah al-Nu'aymi visited China in April 1987. His visit was the first by a UAE minister to China. He discussed the Iran–Iraq war, the situation in the Gulf, the Strait of Hormuz, and the Palestinian question with his counterpart. Al-Nu'aymi explained his country's concern over the escalation of the war in the Gulf. The Chinese side, reportedly, shared UAE's concern over these issues. Premier Zhao, in a separate meeting with the visiting minister, said that China was concerned about the Strait of Hormuz where navigation was under threat and:

> We disapprove jeopardising navigation of this international channel by any country under whatever name or using whatever methods.

He reaffirmed China's position of 'strict neutrality' towards Iran and Iraq. Nothing else was reported about this visit. The delegation expressed its

---

159 *FBIS-CHI-85-249*, 27 December 1985, p. 11.
160 *Al Ittihad*, 24 November 1985, p. 1 and p. 8.
161 *FBIS-CHI-86-005*, 8 January 1986, p. 11.
162 *Middle East Economic Survey*, Vol. 29, No. 39, 7 July 1986, pp. A6–A7.
163 *FBIS-CHI-86-237*, 10 December 1986, p. 12.

government's desire to see China use its good relations with Iran to seek a peaceful settlement of the war, which claimed Abu Dhabi's Abu-Bakush offshore oil platform as its latest victim in November 1986.[164]

The first economic delegation from the UAE to visit China after the establishment of diplomatic relations was a delegation from the Dubai Chamber of Commerce and Industry in June 1987. It was led by President of the Chamber, Sa'id Juma al-Nabudah and was received by Yao Yilin.[165] In 1987, the al-Aotaba Group of the UAE started to discuss with the Chinese government the possibility of investing in building an oil refinery with an annual handling capacity of 3 million tons of oil in the Shenzhen special economic zone in Guandong province (the investment would involve some US$324–360 million).[166] The UAE firm would undertake to provide the crude feedstock from the UAE for the refinery and to market the products overseas.[167] Final agreement on the project was reached in June 1988. The refinery was said to be the largest foreign investment project approved by China in 1988. It was also the first Chinese project the UAE invested in.[168] A UAE economic and trade delegation headed by Economic and Commerce Minister, Sayf Bin 'Ali al-Jarwan, visited China in November 1988. The two sides signed agreed minutes of the First Session of the Joint Commission for Trade and Economic and Technical Cooperation. The agreed minutes focused on bilateral cooperation in the fields of trade, labour contracts, and techniques.[169] In 1988, China imported 24,000 metric tons of LNG from the UAE (UAE 1992: 145).

Vice-Premier Tian Jiyun visited the UAE in March 1989 and met with Sheikh Zayed and delivering a letter from the Chinese President. It was said that the letter contained an official invitation for Sheikh Zayed to visit China. Tian was the first Chinese leader to visit the UAE since November 1985, when Vice-Premier Yao Yilin paid a visit. He held talks with Defence Minister Sheikh Muhammad Bin Rashid al-Maktum, who was also in charge of the free zone affairs, on the possibility of utilizing UAE natural gas. He also met with Sheikh Sultan, ruler of Sharjah.[170] Seven months later, the Chinese President Yang Shangkun paid a one-day official goodwill visit to the UAE at the invitation of the UAE government. He arrived on 23 December 1989 after visiting Cairo. President Yang was the first Chinese president to visit the UAE. During his meeting with Sheikh Zayed, he reaffirmed his country's position on the Gulf conflict and said:

164 *FBIS-CHI-87-080*, 27
165 *FBIS-CHI-87-121*, 24 June 1987, p. F4.
166 *FBIS-CHI-87-133*, 13 July 1987, p. F2.
167 *Middle East Economic Survey*, Vol. 39, No. 52, 5 October 1987, p. A6.
168 *FBIS-CHI-88-168*, 30 August 1988, p. 17.
169 *FBIS-CHI-88-222*, 17 November 1988, p. 17.
170 *FBIS-CHI-89-052*, 20 March 1989, pp. 11–12.

As a permanent member of the UN Security Council, China will play its due role in helping push forward the Iran–Iraq peace talks together with the international community.

On China's relations with the UAE, Yang said:

The Sino-UAE relations are based on the Five Principles of Peaceful Coexistence and completely comply with the mutual interests of the two countries.[171]

(*FBIS-CHI-89-246*, 26 December 1989: 8)

Ahmed al-Hosani, chargé d'affaires of the UAE Embassy in Beijing, described the Chinese President's visit to the UAE as 'an historical event in the relationship between the two countries'.[172] The significance of Yang's visit stems from the fact that it came as part of his tour to the Gulf countries and Egypt. He visited Egypt, the UAE, Kuwait, and Oman. His visit came after the Chinese government's military crackdown on the student demonstrations in Tiananmen Square and the subsequent Western and Japanese economic sanctions against China. Therefore, President Yang's visits were to reassure the Gulf governments that China's policies toward the Gulf region had not changed and that China would continue working to implement a peaceful settlement to the Iran–Iraq dispute. He also reassured the Gulf governments that China's open economic policy would continue. It is also important to note that, unlike the West and South-East Asian countries, Egypt and the Gulf countries did not criticize China's harsh treatment of the demonstrators and considered the matter as part of China's internal affairs. Therefore, his visit might also have been directed toward thanking the government of these countries for their refusal to comply with sanctions imposed by the West or criticize the Chinese government's action.

In May 1990, Sheikh Zayed visited China for a five-day official goodwill visit. His visit was the first by the UAE president and a GCC leader to China. He was received by President Yang on 8 May. The Chinese president pointed out in his banquet speech:

Since the establishment of diplomatic ties, the friendly, co-operative relations between the two countries have developed in a satisfactory manner, because the two countries hold identical or similar stands on major international issues and because the people of the two countries are peace-loving and dedicated to construction, upholding justice, and respecting each other.

---

171 See also 'Sino-UAE Ties Solid and Friendly', in *Beijing Review*, No. 21, 21 May 1990, p. 9.
172 *FBIS-CHI-89-241*, 18 December 1989, p. 10.

He added:

> We value the great importance attached by Your Excellency the President and the government of the UAE to developing friendly ties with China. The development of friendly, co-operative relations with the UAE and other Gulf nations also occupies a very important position in China's foreign policy.

Such rhetoric has always appeared in Chinese officials' statements to their counterparts from the Gulf and Arabian Peninsula region. They have always emphasized having common views with the countries of the region regarding many issues in and around the region. The fact remains, though, that China and the UAE have adopted different practices regarding many issues in the region. For example, despite China's neutrality in the Iran–Iraq war, China was the largest arms supplier to Iran and allegedly provided Iran with some advanced military capabilities. On the other hand, the UAE supported Iraq in the war and provided substantial assistance to the Iraqi regime. This difference, therefore, could have played a significant role in planning Sheikh Zayed's visit to China. The purpose of his visit, in addition to what had been reported as promoting political, economic, and cultural ties with China, could also be looked at from a security perspective. The UAE might have felt the need for high-level direct talks with Chinese officials about their military cooperation with Iran, and perhaps for joint co-operation between the two countries in the military field, similar to that of China and Saudi Arabia. It is worth noting that among the high-ranked UAE officials who accompanied him to China were his Minister of Defence, Sheikh Muhammad Bin Rashid al-Maktum, and his Commander of the Air Force and Air-Defence Corps, Sheikh Muhammad Bin Zayed al-Nahayyan.

Sheikh Zayed's speech praised China's foreign policy stance toward Palestine, the Gulf region, and the Pakistan–India dispute. He also hailed the Five Principles of Peaceful Coexistence that governed China's relations with the UAE.[173] Sheikh Zayed met separately with Chinese Premier Li Peng and the CCP General Secretary Jiang Zemin. He also visited Shanghai and met with its mayor Zhu Rongji.[174] It was reported that Sheikh Zayed regarded the results of his visit as 'much better than expected'.[175] Several economic, trade, and technical agreements were signed by the two sides.[176] But, most importantly, the visit was said to have achieved its intended aim, which was to strengthen the already-established relations between the two

---

173 *FBIS-CHI-90-090*, 9 May 1990, pp. 10–11.
174 *FBIS-CHI-90-091*, 10 May 1990, p. 12.
175 *Ibid.*
176 *FBIS-NES-93-128*, 7 July 1993, p. 26.

countries and to establish a common view toward international and regional issues.

China and the UAE in the 1990s

China–UAE relations improved substantially after the establishment of diplomatic relations between the two countries. Within just five years of their formal relations, both the Chinese president and the UAE president had visited each other's countries. Political and economic relations continued to grow between them throughout the 1990s. Sheikh Sultan of Sharjah visited China in May 1991 and met with the Chinese president. Sheikh Sultan was the first high-ranked UAE official to visit China since Sheikh Zayed's visit. President Yang welcomed the visiting ruler and reportedly said, 'Sultan is an old friend of the Chinese people and one of the founders of the Sino-UAE friendly ties'. Sheikh Sultan reaffirmed that he would continue his efforts to further consolidate and promote the friendly relations and cooperation between the two countries.[177] Later, in October 1991, Sheikh Sultan emphasized, while meeting with the visiting Deputy Director of the Chinese Civil Aviation Administration, that his emirate was ready to conduct long-term cooperation with China in the fields of air transportation, tourism, and trade, in order to further consolidate and develop friendly relations.[178] Sheikh Sultan's visit and his continued efforts to strengthen ties with China is something that must not be disregarded without some analysis. In the UAE federal system, it is the responsibility of the central government to establish most foreign contacts and ties on behalf of the other emirates. Therefore, it is unusual for rulers to pay official visits to other countries; but, if they do so, it must then have some political implications. So, what were the political implications for both Sheikh Sultan's visit and the expanding cooperation between his emirate and China? It could be said that the most important implication was the Iranian occupation of Abu Musa. The emirate of Sharjah has a long dispute with Iran over the island of Abu Musa, which was occupied by the Iranians in 1970. This dispute intensified when the Iranian authority took complete charge of the island in September 1992. Therefore, his visit could be understood in terms of his willingness to explain his emirate's position on the island issue to the Chinese side and to create an understanding about the issue, taking in mind that China is a key international player, with permanent membership of the Security Council, and has also enjoyed a history of good relations with Iran.

Chinese Vice-Premier Li Lanqing headed an economic delegation to the

---

177 *FBIS-CHI-91-100*, 23 May 1991, p. 17.
178 *FBIS-CHI-91-202*, 18 October 1991, pp. 12–13.

UAE in July 1993. His visit was said to bolster and promote bilateral economic and trade relations between the two countries and the possibility of opening new areas for this cooperation in the future.[179] At the end of his visit, Li described it as successful and had realized positive results that would strengthen economic relations.[180] In June 1994, Sheikh Zayed offered printing equipment worth US$350,000 as a gift to the China Islamic Association.[181] A delegation from the Chinese National People's Congress (NPC) visited the UAE in November 1994 and was headed by Vice-Chairman Li Peiyao. The delegation held talks with the UAE Federal National Council's chairman, al-Hajj Bin 'Abdallah al-Muhayribi.[182] Al-Muhayribi said that the UAE admired China's achievements and the 'correct' economic road it had chosen – namely, its open policy. He added that the UAE appreciated China's stand on international issues and its handling of the Iraqi invasion of Kuwait.[183]

Political relations did not deteriorate in April 1995, when Taiwan's President Lee Teng-hui visited the UAE at the invitation of the UAE Foreign Ministry.[184] Lee visited Jordan and the UAE and was going to stop-over in Israel, but the Israeli government refused him entry. His twenty-four-hour visit to the UAE led to a Chinese protest issued to the government of the UAE. A Chinese Foreign Ministry spokesman said that Lee's visit to Jordan and the UAE was planned to carry out 'political activities there' in order to promote the 'two Chinas' or the 'one China, one Taiwan' strategies. But, he added that those attempts were 'bound to end up in failure'. He also said, 'we stressed China's solemn and just position and lodged a protest with the governments of the countries involved'.[185] The UAE government, which did not want to sever its good relations with Beijing, assured the Chinese government that Lee's visit was private in nature and would not have any impact on UAE–China relations. In order to confirm the above position, President Lee was received at the airport by officials from the UAE Foreign Ministry instead of high-ranking governmental officials. He landed in the UAE using a special China Airline plane that does not bear the Taiwan flag. In addition, the entrance visa issued by the UAE to the Taiwanese officials reportedly read 'Taiwan Province of

---

179 *FBIS-NES-93-126*, 2 July 1993, p. 21.
180 Abu Dhabi United Arab Emirates Radio Network, 'PRC Vice-Premier Praises Bilateral Co-operation', 9 July 1993, in *FBIS-NES-93-131*, 12 July 1993, p. 17.
181 *FBIS-CHI-94-126*, 30 June 1994.
182 Abu Dhabi United Arab Emirates Radio Network, 'National Council Meet PRC Delegates', in *FBIS-NES-94-215*, 7 November 1994, p. 25.
183 *FBIS-CHI-940218*, 10 November 1994, p. 15.
184 *Free China Review*, Vol. 45, No. 7, July 1995, pp. 48-51.
185 *Xinhua News Agency News Bulletin*, Beijing, 'Foreign Ministry on Lee's Visit', 5 April 1995, in BBC, *SWB, FE/2272*, 7 April 1995, p. G/2.

China' in the nationality column. Further, he was not received by UAE President Sheikh Zayed, who was in the country at the time, and was only received by Abu Dhabi Crown Prince Sheikh Khalifah Bin Zayed and the UAE's Foreign Minister Sheikh Hamdan Bin Zayed.[186]

This incident demonstrated China's disapproval of the UAE, or any other country, trying to establish political contacts with the regime in Taiwan, an issue both countries have agreed upon as China's internal affairs. The manner in which the UAE government managed Lee's visit demonstrated the UAE attached great significance to China. Taiwan could be a significant supplier of technology to the UAE, but this economic importance was surpassed by China's political significance. China's permanent membership of the Security Council, coupled with its influence in world politics, ensured its status as a political asset for a country like the UAE, which was seeking to settle its territorial disputes with Iran peacefully. The latest developments facing the UAE in its relations with Iran, regarding the 1992 Iranian 'occupation' of the island of Abu Musa, demonstrates the UAE's need to create an international understanding to pressure Iran to submit to the International Court of Justice (for discussions about the 1992 Iranian move in Abu Musa, see el-Issa 1998 and Haseeb 1998). This could be sensed in the speaker of the UAE Federal National Council, Muhammad Khalifah Bin Habtur's, remark, while meeting the visiting Chinese delegation of the National Committee of the Chinese People's Political Consultative Conference headed by China's top advisor Li Ruihuan in May 1999, that 'the UAE paid much attention to its relationship with China since the Asian giant plays an important role in the international arena. As a permanent member of the UN Security Council, China could push forward the unsettled territorial dispute between the UAE and Iran'.[187]

The important question that remains to be answered is: Why did the UAE government invite the Taiwanese president to the UAE? The two sides cloak the answer with a great deal of secrecy. Initially, the author was unable to find an answer to this question either in Abu Dhabi or Taipei, provoking the author's interest further. Eventually, an answer was found but, due to its sensibility, permission was not granted for its publication. However, the author is able to confirm that President Lee's visit to the UAE was pushed forward by a third party who had an interest in convincing the UAE government to invite President Lee. However, there is yet another twist to the story. One of the highest-ranked military commanders of the UAE was very interested, even before the third party involvement, in establishing a high-level contact with Taiwan. This suggests that the UAE was interested

---

186 *Zhongguo Tongxue She*, Hong Kong, 'Lee's Visit to the Middle East', 1 April 1995, in BBC, *SWB, FE/2271*, 6 April 1995, p. F/2.
187 BBC, *SWB, FE/3537*, 18 May 1999, p. G/5.

in Taiwan either as a supplier of advanced technology in some military fields or as a political card against China to halt its military cooperation with Iran.

China–UAE economic relations

It was not just political relations that had flourished between the two countries in the 1990s. Economic relations were developing even faster. This was mainly due to China's willingness to further economic and trade relations with the UAE, which was considered by the Chinese to be the centre of trade in the Gulf region. Furthermore, the UAE's large oil reserves had convinced the Chinese government of the need to further economic relations with the UAE in order to ensure a long-term supply of oil to satisfy China's own short- and long-term oil needs.

Economic relations between the two countries expanded in the 1990s. China participated in the construction of a dry dock in the Fujairah emirate as well as in agriculture and fishery projects.[188] Its trade cooperation with the Dubai emirate was underscored by China's enhanced role as the second-largest trading partner of Dubai, behind Japan with US$1.4 billion in 1994 compared with US$560 million in 1990, registering an average annual growth of 37 per cent.[189] If cars and electronics were excluded, China would top the list of countries trading with Dubai. China's imports from Dubai consisted mainly of aluminium (DCCI 1995: 44). In 1995, China became the top exporter to Dubai. On the other hand, it was ranked twenty-fifth among countries importing from Dubai in 1995 (SODPC 1997: 232, 238). Trade relations with Fujairah also increased. Fujairah imports from China were figured at 67.5 per cent and the exports to China were 31 per cent of total Fujairah trade volume in 1998. This marked China as one of the ten leading countries trading with Fujairah in 1998 (FCCIA 1999: 31). The value of China's trade relations with the UAE, from 1990 to 1996, increased 4.5 times over that of the 1980s, reaching US$5,456 million and marking the UAE as the second leading trade partner of China in the Gulf and Peninsula region (see Table A.9 in the Appendix). China also assumed a top-ten position in terms of UAE's worldwide import partners. In 1994, China was in sixth place; later, it jumped to third place in 1996 (EIU 2000: 58). Chinese exports to the UAE in 1997 amounted to US$1.3 billion consisting of textiles, electronics, machines, and tyres. Its imports were US$85 million, mostly chemical fertilizers, aluminium, and crude oil.[190]

---

188 *FBIS-CHI-91-084*, 1 May 1991, p. 22.
189 *Xinhua News Agency News Bulletin*, 'UAE Trade Delegation In China', 12 April 1995, in *FBIS-CHI-95-070*, 12 April 1995, p. 8.
190 *Ak-bar al-bitrul Walsina'a*, No. 330, August 1998, pp. 1–4.

Chinese officials expressed repeatedly, in meetings with UAE officials, their country's desire to further oil cooperation between the two countries. It is important to note that the UAE was the second country in the Gulf, after Kuwait, to invest in China's refinery projects in the late 1980s. The president of SINOPEC (China Petrochemical Corporation) visited the UAE in May 1997 and expressed, in a meeting with the UAE Minister of Petroleum and Mineral Resources, a desire to establish joint cooperation with the UAE in the field of petroleum industries. He stressed China's interest in promoting ties with the UAE within the framework of diversifying its petroleum imports, and presented China's plan to build new projects in the petroleum sector.[191] Although the UAE was not as large an exporter of crude oil to China as Oman, the Chinese still wanted to ensure long-term suppliers to meet their future energy thirst. In August 1997, the Chinese began to hold talks with UAE officials to start buying a larger quantity of UAE oil to meet its rising consumption due to economic growth.[192] Later, China and the Abu Dhabi Chamber of Commerce and Industry agreed to establish a joint venture for building an oil refinery in China. This was Abu Dhabi's second refinery joint venture overseas and China's second refinery joint venture with a UAE company.

CHINA AND QATAR

China's relations with Qatar prior to the establishment of diplomatic relations

Like all other countries in the Gulf and Arabian Peninsula region, China's relations with Qatar was determined by China's relations with the superpowers and its perception of the international system. China was politically isolated from Qatar during the 1950s and 1960s. China criticized the regime in Qatar as being dominated by the British presence in the Gulf. It classified Qatar with the capitalist camp. Qatar's lack of any nationalist movement, such as the ones in Oman and South Yemen, convinced the Chinese that their chances to spread a people's war against imperialist powers were more likely to succeed in Oman and South Yemen than elsewhere in the region. The Chinese also had no chance to foster political relations with the Qatari regime because of the strong British influence on the small emirate. Therefore, China's only contact with the emirate was limited to indirect trade. The emirate had received Chinese goods through different destinations in the Gulf and Asia since the late 1950s. From 1958 to 1970, Qatar

---

191 BBC, SWB, *MEW/0489 WME*, 3 June 1997, p. 16.
192 *Al Khaleej*, 18 August 1997, p. 1.

received some US$4.7 million worth of Chinese goods (see Table A.10 in the Appendix).

The first direct political contact came when Qatar proclaimed its independence from Britain on 1 September 1971. Premier Zhou Enlai sent, on the 10 September 1971, the following message to the Emir of Qatar, Sheikh Ahmad Bin Ali al-Thani:

> On the occasion of the proclamation of the independence of Qatar, I wish, on behalf of the Government of the People's Republic of China and the Chinese people, to express congratulations to your Highness and the people of Qatar. The Chinese Government has decided to give recognition to your country. May your country enjoy prosperity and its people happiness. May the friendship between the peoples of China and Qatar develop continuously.
> (BBC, *SWB*, *FE/3786*, 14 September 1971: A4/1)

A day later, Sheikh Ahmad al-Thani sent a message to Zhou thanking him for China's recognition of the state of Qatar.[193] Despite China's recognition of Qatar's independence, the Qatari Emir's message did not contain anything about Qatar's recognition of the PRC. The Qatari leadership was most likely not in a position to recognize China, particularly when Saudi Arabia, Oman, and Bahrain had not done so. In addition to that, the Qatari leadership's main goal at that time was to safeguard the survival of the new political entity from any internal and external threats. China's relations with the South Yemeni Marxist regime and support for the PFLOAG posed a great obstacle in China's efforts to gain political recognition from Qatar. It is also worth mentioning that South Yemen was the only state to voice opposition to Qatar's admittance to the Arab League, maintaining that both Qatar and Bahrain were still dominated by 'political and military colonialism'. The PFLOAG called the League's decision a means of consolidating 'the frail entities set up by Britain in the territory of the Gulf' (Mostyn 1991: 119).

Therefore, China had no political relations with Qatar throughout the 1970s, despite the changes in China's foreign policy towards the Soviet Union, in general, and the Gulf and Peninsula region, in particular. China welcomed nationalization of the oil industry in Qatar in February 1977, when Qatar gained full sovereignty over its oil resources. An article in *Peking Review* hailed the development and said:

> Qatar is rich in oil resources, but prospecting and exploitation in the past had been controlled by the foreign-run Qatar Petroleum Company

---

193 BBC, *SWB*, *FE/3788*, 16 September 1971, p. A4/1.

and the Shell Company of Qatar ... the struggle to nationalise oil resources in the third world as a whole is surging forward vigorously. Up till now, Iran, Iraq, Kuwait and Venezuela in addition to Qatar have nationalised all their oil resources. This proves that the 'concession system' imposed on the oil producing countries by the imperialists over the past century is heading for collapse.

(*Peking Review*, No. 9, 25 February 1977: 28)

Despite the absence of political relations, trade relations had increased in the 1970s. The trade value between the two countries jumped from US$3.6 million by 1969 to US$73 million from 1970 to 1979 (see Table A.10 in the Appendix). It may sound positive, but Chinese trade volume with Qatar in the 1970s was second from bottom in China's trade with the Gulf and Peninsula region, just ahead of Bahrain's. Such volume cannot be compared with China's trade, for example, with Iraq, Iran, or even the UAE.

Political contact between China and Qatar remained very limited throughout the period prior to establishment of diplomatic relations in July 1988. Among the very few political contacts between officials of the two countries was a meeting between China's Vice-Premier Yao Yilin in Oman with the head of the Qatari delegation to Oman's Fifteenth National Day celebrations in November 1985.[194] Nothing resulted from these meetings to indicate any furthering of political relations. The Chinese government's observing delegation visited Doha in May 1987 to participate in the eighteenth anniversary of the Arab Red Crescent and Red Cross Societies.[195] Economic relations developed positively in the 1980s. The Chinese Council for the Promotion of International Trade sponsored, for the first time, an exhibition of Chinese export commodities in Doha in December 1987. The exhibition included light-industrial products, textiles, foodstuffs, silk fabrics, handicrafts, carpets, electronics, and jewellery.[196] Chinese officials stressed that the exhibition was conducted to further mutual understanding and friendship between the two countries.[197] China's trade with Qatar, from 1980 to 1987, at US$380 million, was over five times the amount of trade in the 1970s. Thus, their relations prior to the establishment of diplomatic relations were limited to economic contact and trade relations; political contact was non-existent.

---

194 *FBIS-CHI-85-229*, 27 November 1985, p. 11.
195 *FBIS-CHI-87-049*, 13 March 1987, p. 12.
196 *FBIS-CHI-87-231*, 2 December 1987, p. 11.
197 *FBIS-CHI-87-240*, 15 December 1987, p. 10.

The establishment of diplomatic relations

China and Qatar established full diplomatic relations on 9 July 1988. A joint communiqué was signed in Paris by Qatari Ambassador to France 'Abd al-Rahman al-'Attiyah and his Chinese counterpart Zhou Jue on the establishment of diplomatic relations between the two countries. The communiqué stated that the decision of the two governments was the result of their common desire to strengthen and develop relations of friendship and cooperation between them.[198] *Renmin Ribao* applauded, in its 10 July issue, the establishment of diplomatic relations with Qatar and said:

> Starting from the common will of strengthening and developing Sino-Qatari friendly co-operation, the PRC Government and Qatari Government have decided, through negotiations, to establish diplomatic relations at the ambassadorial level, effective 9th July 1988. Let us extend our warm congratulations to this great event of historical significance in the relations between the two nations.
>
> The friendship between the Chinese and the Qatari people has a long standing. On 10th September 1971, the late Premier Zhou Enlai sent a telegraph to Qatar addressed to Amir Khalifah ibn Hamad al-Thani to extend his congratulations on Qatar's independence, and to announce China's acknowledgement of the state of Qatar. Since then, trade, friendly visits and ties between the personalities of the two countries have continued to grow. The Qatari government has persisted in its one China position, and acknowledged that the PRC is the sole legitimate government representing China. The establishment of diplomatic relations between China and Qatar signals that the relations between the two nations have entered upon a new historical phase, and opened up new prospects for the development of the friendly relations between the two nations.
>
> (*FBIS-CHI-88-132*, 16 July 1988: 16)

The Qatari daily *Al Rayan* welcomed the new development in Qatar–China relations and said that the establishment of diplomatic relations served the common interest and contributed to boosting Chinese–Arab relations and reinforcing Chinese support of Arab causes. Another Qatari daily *Al Arab* said that China constituted at present a balancing force in international relations, and Qatari ties with China represented a gain for the Arab World and its struggle against Israel.[199]

---

198 *FBIS-CHI-88-132*, 16 July 1988, p. 16.
199 *FBIS-CHI-88-133*, 12 July 1988, pp. 15–16.

It is important to mention here that Qatar's decision to establish diplomatic relations with China did not merely originate from the Qatari government's desire to balance its foreign relations, but also from the changing attitudes of the Gulf and Arabian Peninsula countries toward China. Prior to July 1988, China had established full diplomatic relations with all the countries of the region except Qatar, Bahrain, and Saudi Arabia. Even China's relations with Saudi Arabia were moving toward political rapprochement, particularly after the missile deal between the two countries in early 1988. Therefore, Qatar could not remain isolated from the general regional attitude toward China.

China and Qatar after the establishment of diplomatic relations

Qatari Vice-Foreign Minister Sheikh Hamad ibn Suhaym al-Thani visited China from 23 to 26 August 1988. This visit was the first by a high-ranking Qatari official to Beijing after the establishment of formal relations. The two countries reportedly agreed to further their cooperation and relations in the fields of economy, culture, and sport. They also discussed the situation in the Gulf and the Middle East, and it was said that both shared the same views on regional and international issues.[200] The first Qatari Ambassador to China, Mohamed Sa'ad al-Fahid, arrived in Beijing for his post on 31 July 1989, and presented his credentials to the Chinese president on 23 August 1989.[201]

Trade relations increased substantially after the establishment of diplomatic relations. The trade value jumped from US$30 million in 1987 to US$49 million in 1989, then to US$86 million in 1991 (see Table A.10 in the Appendix). Chinese imports constituted the larger proportion of the trade volume. China imported Qatari mineral fuel, lubricants, natural and processed gas, chemical products, urea fertilizers, and polyethylene. While China mainly exported food, vegetables and live animals, textile fibres, rubber, chemical products, paper, iron, and steel (SQPCM 1994: 837, 985).

The highest-ranking Chinese official to visit Qatar after the establishment of formal relations was Vice-Premier Li Lanqing in June 1993. Li met with Qatari President, Sheikh Khalifah Bin Hamad al-Thani, on 30 June and discussed the Chinese desire to bolster bilateral ties and cooperation in all fields, particularly trade and economy, and exchanged views on regional and international issues.[202] In January 1995, the two countries signed an accord in which China would import 2.5 million tons/year of liquefied natural gas.[203] The agreement was finalized during the Qatari Minister of Energy

---

200 *FBIS-CHI-88-166*, 26 August 1988, p. 15.
201 *FBIS-CHI-89-163*, 24 August 1989, p. 5.
202 *FBIS-NES-93-126*, 2 July 1993, p. 20.
203 *Middle East Economic Survey*, Vol. 38, No. 18, 30 January 1995, p. A15.

and Industry, 'Abdullah Bin Hamad al-'Atiyah's, visit to Beijing in March 1995.[204] A delegation from the Chinese PLA, led by Deputy Chief of the PLA General Staff, Wu Quanxu, visited Qatar in April 1998 at the invitation of the Qatari armed forces. It was said that Qatar was seeking Chinese assistance in training its armed forces.[205] No further details were circulated on this matter.

Qatar's Emir Sheikh Hamad Bin Khalifah al-Thani visited China on 8 April 1999 at the invitation of Chinese President Jiang Zemin. His two-day visit marked the first visit ever to the PRC by a Qatari head of state. He held talks with Chinese officials such as President Jiang, Vice-President Hu Jintao, and Vice-Premier Qian Qichen. His talks with Chinese officials resulted in agreement that the two sides should establish a 'solid and stable relationship' and long-term cooperation. Agreements were signed related to protecting and encouraging mutual investments, air transportation, educational and cultural cooperation, as well as a memorandum of understanding between the foreign ministries of the two countries. They even agreed on respecting the universality of human rights, but stressed that protecting and safeguarding human rights should be combined with actual conditions in the country concerned. They opposed the politicization of the human rights issue and the practice of using related issues as a pretext for interfering in another country's internal affairs.[206] The Chinese vice-president appreciated Qatar's pursuit of the 'one China' policy on the issue of Taiwan, and praised Qatar's domestic and foreign policy; he also spoke highly of Qatar's 'independent foreign policy of peace, neutrality, and non-alliance, and its active role in safeguarding regional peace and stability'. The Emir stated his government's full awareness of China's role in world affairs and his appreciation of China's view that all countries, large or small, are equal (Footnote 206: G/4).

Against this background, we can argue that the importance of the establishment of formal relations with Qatar in China's foreign policy had achieved two goals – political and economic. Politically, China achieved another diplomatic partner for itself in the Gulf and Peninsula region and succeeded in eliminating Taiwan's position there. Economically, China succeeded in fostering economic and trade relations with Qatar as well as cooperation in the field of gas.

204 *FBIS-CHI-95-063*, 3 April 1995, p. 9.
205 BBC, *SWB, FE/3187*, 28 March 1998, p. G/3.
206 BBC, *SWB, FE/3507*, 13 April 1999, G/3.

CHINA AND BAHRAIN

China–Bahrain relations prior to the establishment of diplomatic relations

As with the other sheikhdoms, the Kingdom of Saudi Arabia, and Iran, China could not forge relations with the regime in Bahrain. This was due, as already mentioned, to the strong British presence in the region and to China's close alignment with the Soviet Union, as well as its strong revolutionary stance. China criticized the stationing of British's troops in Bahrain, particularly after they had moved out from Kuwait in the early 1960s. The first official contact between the two governments came with Bahrain's declaration of independence on 14 August 1971. On 23 August, Premier Zhou Enlai sent a message to the Emir of the State of Bahrain, Sheikh Isa Bin Salman al-Khalifah, congratulating him on behalf of the Chinese government and people. On 24 August, Isa Bin Salman replied to Zhou's message, thanking him for his congratulations and recognition.[207] The Emir's message did not reciprocate Chinese recognition. Instead, he preferred to remain aligned with the West and Saudi Arabia's position.

Therefore, Bahrain and China remained politically isolated from each other throughout the first three decades of the PRC's existence. The only contacts were Chinese statements supporting some of Bahrain's initiatives, like, for instance, the Bahraini government's decision in April 1978 to take the controlling interest in all foreign oil companies in the country;[208] as well as the visit to Bahrain in April 1988 at the invitation of the Bahraini Foreign Ministry of the Director of the Asian–African Department of the Chinese Foreign Ministry, Yang Fuchang.[209] Yang met with the Bahraini Emir Isa ibn Salman and both, reportedly, expressed the desire for better relations between the two countries. The Bahraini side stressed its appreciation for China's persistent support of Arab causes. Yang also met separately with Bahrain's Prime Minister Khalifah ibn Salman and the Foreign Minister Muhammad ibn Mubarak.[210] China's contact with Bahrain was also evident in social and economic fields. The Vice-President of the China Islamic Association, Hajj Mohammad Ali Zhang Jie, led a delegation of Chinese Muslims to participate in the Hijiri era celebration in Bahrain in November 1979. The delegation visited Saudi Arabia to make the pilgrimage and went on to Oman to participate in its National Day celebrations (Abidi 1982: 290). Bahraini businessmen from the Bahrain Chamber of Commerce visited

---

207 BBC, *SWB*, *FE/3773*, 28 August 1971, p. A4/1.
208 *FBIS-CHI-78-86*, 3 May 1978, p. A21.
209 *FBIS-CHI-88-067*, 7 April 1988, p. 11.
210 Ibid.

China in October 1984 and met with Rong Yiren, Vice-Chairman of the Standing Committee of the NPC and Chairman of China International Trust and Investment Corporation (CITIC). The visit was described as an attempt to increase mutual understanding and promote cooperation. 'Abd al-Rasul al-Jishi, head of the delegation, said:

> We are eager to develop economic, trade and cultural co-operation with China ... we expect to open new ways for co-operation through exchanging monetary businesses between the two countries.
> (*FBIS-CHI-84-205*, 22 October 1984: I2)

From 23-25 November 1988, China held a Chinese export commodity exhibition in Manama, its first in Bahrain. Tariq 'Abd al-Mu'ayyad, Bahrain's Information Minister, told the Xinhua News Agency that the Chinese exhibition 'is an indication of our respect for China as well as our willingness to co-operate through trade to the benefit of both countries'; he added that his country expected more cultural contacts with China: 'through cultural contacts we can develop more friendship on a personal level between institutions and government officials'.[211]

Trade contacts between the two sides date back to the late 1950s. Until 1974, China's trade relations with Bahrain was dominated by exports to Bahrain, textiles, food, and chemical products being the dominant Chinese exports. From 1956 to 1969, China exported goods worth US$15.73 million to Bahrain. Then, the value of trade between the two countries jumped to US$292 million in the 1970s, of which 86 per cent were Chinese exports to Bahrain. Prior to the establishment of diplomatic relations in 1988, the value of trade between 1980 and 1988 was US$198 million. Chinese exports still dominated the balance of trade between the two countries (see Table A.11 in the Appendix). But, it is important to note that the value of China's trade with Bahrain in the 1980s was much less than that of the 1970s. One reason was the fall in world oil prices in the early 1980s, which greatly curtailed Bahrain's ability to import foreign goods and was the main cause of the slowdown in the development of trade relations with China.

Thus, relations between China and Bahrain prior to the establishment of diplomatic relations in 1988 were limited to economic and social contacts. Official political contacts between the two countries were almost nonexistent. This could be related, from China's point of view, to the absence of a Taiwanese challenge in Bahrain, with which Taiwan had no diplomatic relations; also, arguably, because Bahrain had jumped on the Saudi bandwagon, the Chinese felt that once the Kingdom had established relations with Beijing, Bahrain would have no choice but to follow suit.

---

211 *FBIS-CHI-88-227*, 25 November 1988, p. 19.

The establishment of diplomatic relations

Bahrain decided in April 1989 to establish diplomatic relations with China. The Bahraini decision could be explained in the following terms:

1. The Bahraini government might have felt that it was the only GCC country, besides the Kingdom, that had no diplomatic relations with China, an important member in the UN Security Council. Plus, its relations with Taiwan did not extend beyond the economic field. Therefore, there was no real reason to prevent Bahrain from establishing diplomatic relations with China.
2. A factor that may have hindered the establishment of Bahraini–Chinese diplomatic relations would be the absence of diplomatic relations between the Kingdom and China. But, since the Kingdom itself started in the mid-1980s to lean toward establishing political contacts with China and since Bahrain was aware of this rapprochement (Sultan and Seale 1995: 140), the Bahraini government felt more comfortable establishing diplomatic relations with China.

Thus, the two governments decided to establish diplomatic relations at the ambassadorial level on 18 April 1989. The joint communiqué emphasized that diplomatic relations were established on the principles of peaceful coexistence, equality, and non-interference in each other's internal affairs. Both sides hoped that the establishment of formal relations would strengthen and develop friendly cooperation and maintain benefits, based on mutual respect for state sovereignty and territorial integrity for the people in both countries. In a message to Bahrain's Foreign Minister, Muhammad ibn Mubarak al-Khalifah, the Chinese Foreign Minister Qian Qichen said that the establishment of diplomatic relations 'entirely accords with the fundamental interests and aspirations of our two peoples and marks a new stage in the history of the friendly relations and co-operation between our two countries'.[212]

An editorial in *Renmin Ribao* applauded the new development in China–Bahrain relations and also hailed Bahrain's foreign policy saying:

> In developing its external relations, the State of Bahrain has all along followed a neutral and non-aligned foreign policy, made consistent efforts to safeguard the unity of the Arab world and the good-neighbour relations among various Gulf countries, and adhered to the principle of respecting other countries' state sovereignty, not interfering in other countries' internal affairs, not restoring to force, and settling

---

212 *FBIS-CHI-89-074*, 19 April 1989, p. 7.

disputes with other countries through peaceful means. Therefore, the foreign policy and stand adhered to by the State of Bahrain has been widely praised by the international community.

(*FBIS-CHI-89-075*, 20 April 1989: 10–11)

The first Bahraini Ambassador, Husain Rashid al-Sabbagh, presented his credentials to the Chinese president on 29 September 1989.[213] The first Chinese Ambassador Extraordinary and Plenipotentiary of the PRC to Kuwait and, concurrently, Ambassador Extraordinary and Plenipotentiary of the PRC to Bahrain, Guan Zihuai, presented his credentials to Bahrain's Emir on 11 December 1989.[214]

China and Bahrain after the establishment of formal relations

Political relations between the two countries developed steadily after the establishment of diplomatic relations. The Foreign Minister of Bahrain, Muhammad ibn Mubarak, visited China on 15 July 1989 for a week-long visit. He was the first senior Bahraini official to visit China, since the two forged diplomatic relations a year earlier. He held talks with China's Foreign Minister Qian Qichen. It was reported that the two sides discussed means of expanding their political and economic ties, and exchanged views on regional and international issues. They signed an agreement on economic, trade, and technical cooperation.[215] Later, in September, the Chinese Foreign Minister met with his Bahraini counterpart at the United Nations. Their talks were dominated by the Iraqi military invasion of Kuwait and the UN efforts to force Iraq to withdraw unconditionally from Kuwait.[216] Chinese Vice-Foreign Minister Yang Fuchang visited Manama in May 1993. During his visit, he met with the Bahraini Foreign Minister and discussed with him the promotion of bilateral ties of friendship and cooperation in trade, technical, and cultural fields. They examined means of facilitating air links as well as the exchange of visits as ways of enhancing these ties.[217] He was also received by the Bahraini Emir on 22 May and the Bahraini Prime Minister.[218] Chinese Vice-Premier Li Lanqing visited Bahrain in June 1993. He was the highest-ranking Chinese official ever to visit Bahrain. His visit was said to 'exchange views with Bahraini officials in order to promote bilateral co-operation and review issues of mutual concern'. He first held talks with Bahraini Minister of Commerce

---

213 *FBIS-CHI-89-192*, 5 October 1989, p. 21.
214 *FBIS-CHI-89-241*, 18 December 1989, p. 12.
215 BBC, *SWB*, *FE/0813*, 17 July 1990, p. A4/1.
216 *FBIS-NES-90-193*, 4 October 1990, p. 14.
217 *FBIS-NES-93-097*, 21 May 1993, p. 23.
218 *FBIS-NES-93-098*, 24 May 1993, p. 22.

and Agriculture Habib Ahmad al-Qasim. He was then received by the Emir and his prime minister.[219] A delegation from Bahrain's Consultative Council headed by its Chairman Ibrahim Humaydan visited Beijing in September 1994. The delegation met with Li Ruihuan, Chairman of the National Committee of the Chinese People's Political Consultative Conference. Li said to the delegation:

> During the course of establishing a socialist economic system, China needs to use the experience of certain foreign countries in relevant fields ... Bahrain enjoys advantages in financial and economic management and the prospects for exchanges and co-operation between China and Bahrain in this field would be very broad.

Humaydan said his trip to China was aimed at promoting cooperation in political, economic, financial, and other fields, at all levels between the two countries.[220] In April 1998, a delegation from the Chinese PLA, led by its Deputy Chief, visited Bahrain at the invitation of the Bahraini armed forces.[221]

In the economic field, China and Bahrain signed an agreement on economic, trade, and technical cooperation during the Bahraini foreign minister's visit to China in July 1990. The agreement called for the two countries to cooperate in construction, chemical industry, petroleum, light industry, public health, agriculture, and fishery. Forms of cooperation would include contract projects, labour services, exchange of technology, joint ventures, personnel training, and trade exhibitions. The Sino-Bahraini Committee for Economic, Trade, and Technological cooperation was also established.[222] Despite the two countries' continuing emphasis on the need to increase the level of trade, the volume of trade between them from 1990 to 1996 remained less than that of the 1970s. Chinese exports dominated the balance of trade between them. Chinese exports were mainly textiles, chemical products, and food, while China mainly imported aluminium.

CONCLUSION

China's foreign policy towards the six GCC countries was a reflection of China's perception of both Washington and Moscow and its need to ensure the supply of oil and access to markets in order to modernize its economy

---

219 *FBIS-NES-93-123*, 29 June 1993, p. 20.
220 *FBIS-CHI-94-180*, 16 September 1994, p. 15.
221 BBC, *SWB, FE/3187*, 28 March 1998, p. G/3.
222 BBC, *SWB, FE/0813*, 17 July 1990, p. A4/1.

and sustain a high level of growth. China's foreign policy toward these countries in the 1950s mirrored that of the Soviet Union. China's close alignment with Moscow, combined with the Gulf countries' close ties with Washington and the West, prevented Beijing from establishing relations with these countries despite its continued efforts to pursue ties with certain Gulf states following the Bandung meetings. As China began to devote much of its attention to revolutionary states in the world, the Dhofari rebels of Oman captured China's interest in the region in the 1960s. The result was continued political, financial, and arms support by China to the rebels. But, as China started to shift its perceptions of both Washington and Moscow toward favouring strategic alignment with Washington, Beijing began to adopt a more pragmatic foreign policy toward the countries of the Gulf region. It abolished its support for revolutionary groups in the region and established diplomatic relations with Kuwait and Oman. The perceived Soviet penetration in and around the region was the catalyst for change in China's foreign policy toward these countries. To undermine Soviet influence in the region, China upgraded its efforts to establish political, economic, and military cooperation with the GCC countries in the 1980s. During the 1990s, however, things started to change. China's policy towards the GCC countries was not conducted as a form of rivalry with both Moscow and Washington. Instead, it was China's own need of oil that directed its foreign policy toward the countries of the GCC in the 1990s. Thus, China worked throughout this period to secure a long-term supplier of energy from the region for China's thirsty economy and to increase its economic ties with the countries of the GCC in order to gain access to their markets.

Part IV
Conclusion

7 Summary, conclusions, and some remarks for future relations

The discussion suggests that the foreign policy of the PRC towards the Gulf and Arabian Peninsula region during the past half a century had exhibited a certain dynamism and an evolving trend. We have argued that China's foreign policy towards the Gulf and Arabian Peninsula region has changed according to changes in China's relations with Washington and Moscow and in China's own domestic economic needs – namely, increasing its demand for oil. Many changes in China's foreign policy toward the region have been introduced to accommodate changes in China's relations with the United States and the Soviet Union and in China's economic requirements. In the first forty years of China's interactions with the region – namely, from late 1949 to the end of the 1989 – China's foreign policy was closely connected to its relations with both superpowers and to its policy of excluding Taiwan politically from the region. Since 1990, China's relations with the countries of the region has been guided by China's interest in securing a long-term independent oil supplier in order to be able to continue to modernize its economy and sustain a high level of economic growth.

In the first thirty-two years, China lived in a dangerous, but somehow stable, triangular relationship with both superpowers. During the first half of the 1950s, China's national interest was seen to be compatible with that of the Soviet Union and the socialist camp. China saw the United States as the primary enemy that contradicted the newly-established Communist state in the mainland by, first, invading the neighbouring communist regime in North Korea and, second, by protecting the island of Taiwan from Communist China's ambition to gain control of the island. This perception encouraged the Chinese to lean further toward the Soviet Union and form an alliance in the struggle against the United States and the capitalist camp. Thus, China signed a treaty of friendship and an alliance with the Soviet Union that was directed mainly against the United States and its allies in Asia. China also sought to receive all kinds of assistance from the Soviet Union in order to fulfil its own military, economic, and technical needs. Throughout this period, China's foreign policy was directed toward creating a massive negative propaganda, mainly among the socialist states, against the United States, the West, and Japan's policies in Asia and around the world. However, the strong Western presence and influence in the Gulf and Arabian Peninsula region made it impossible for China to carry out its political and ideological ambitions into the region. The Chinese, therefore, associated the Gulf and Arabian Peninsula region with the capitalist camp headed by the United States. Conceived in this way, China did not pay attention to further ties and connections with the countries of the region. Not surprisingly, its foreign policy outlook toward the region during this period reflected that of the Soviet Union toward the region.

However, things started to change after the Bandung Conference. Starting in the mid-1950s, China's relations with both superpowers started to take a new direction. It was the change in the Soviet Union's foreign policy that triggered the change in China's foreign policy toward the United States and the Soviet Union, which in turn resulted in a change in China's foreign policy toward the rest of the world. Khrushchev's new foreign policy of peaceful coexistence with Washington was seen by Beijing as counter to Mao's thought of advocating struggle against the United States and the capitalist camp. The failure of the Chinese leadership to convince the Soviet leadership to pull away from the new policy marked the beginning of a long confrontational relationship between China and the Soviet Union. During this period, China–Soviet relations stumbled upon many other disagreements over many foreign, domestic, and ideological issues. Their disputes encouraged a major change in China's perception of the threat to its own security, in particular, and the stability of the world, in general. For the first time, the Soviet Union was perceived by the Chinese leadership to have joined the imperialist camp. China's foreign policy in this period took on itself the duty of contradicting both the 'imperialist power' of the United States and the 'revisionist government' of the Soviet Union. The countries of the Third World were seen as valuable partners in China's foreign policy strategy of contradicting both superpowers' efforts to 'dominate' the world. Thus, China from this period onward began to increase its efforts to woo the countries of the Third World and create a general understanding of the two superpowers' exploitative relation with them. As a result, China's relations with the superpowers remained low throughout this period. Meanwhile, its relations with the countries Third World entered a new phase, with China establishing new diplomatic contacts with many Third World countries soon after its participation in the Bandung Conference of 1955. Bandung was the turning point not only in China's relations with Third World countries, in general, but also in its relations with the countries of the Gulf and Arabian Peninsula region, in particular. Bandung was the first real chance for the Chinese government to interact directly with officials from countries of the Gulf and Arabian Peninsula region. The region was represented at the conference by delegations from Iran, Iraq, Saudi Arabia, and Yemen. In the hope of containing Washington's efforts to draw more of the countries of the region into the Baghdad Pact and challenging Moscow's authority in the Third World, China accelerated its efforts to pave the way for establishing political, economic, and social contacts with the participating countries of the region. It succeeded in establishing diplomatic relations with the YAR (August 1956) and Iraq (August 1958). It achieved higher economic relations with the countries of the region than in previous years. It also attained some desirable results by dispatching social, cultural, and religious delegations to Saudi Arabia, Iraq, and Yemen. Thus, it was the changes in China's relations with the superpowers in the second half of the 1950s that marked the beginning of China's interest in the countries of the region. Bandung, therefore, presented the Chinese government with a great opportunity to introduce itself and interact with the countries of the region.

After its failure to prevent the Soviet Union from establishing closer ties with the Iraqi regime and after its unsuccessful attempts to exclude Moscow from participating in the second Bandung Conference, China's foreign policy shifted its attention to those countries that appeared to have revolutionary potential in the region. Thus, South Yemen and the Dhofari rebels captured most of China's interest in the region in the 1960s. China offered political, financial, and even military support to the revolutionaries in South Yemen in their struggle to gain independence from Britain. It also provided the same to the Dhofari rebels in their fight against the British-backed Sultan of Oman.

From 1970, China's foreign policy witnessed yet another change as its relations with the United States and the Soviet Union entered a new phase. This time, the increasing Soviet penetration around the world and on their frontiers reinforced the shift in China's foreign policy from challenging both powers toward favouring one against the other. From 1970 to the early 1980s, Beijing's fear of Moscow's efforts to contain it encouraged China's policy to lean toward a strategic alignment with Washington. As the Chinese grew more and more suspicious of the Soviet penetration in the Third World, their relations with the United States assumed more significance. Both Beijing and Washington were very much concerned about the increasing Soviet influence around the world in the 1970s. The Soviets had already invaded Czechoslovakia, announced the Brezhnev Doctrine, escalated their border arms clashes with China, and later invaded Afghanistan – a neighbour of China. As a result, this led to two major changes in China's foreign policy, in general. First, China reached some important agreements with the United States on furthering bilateral relations, which led to the establishment of diplomatic relations between the two sides in the late 1970s. Second, China's perception of the threat to world stability changed from perceiving both superpowers as the principle threats to perceiving only the Soviet Union as the principle threat to world stability and the primary enemy of world security. During this period, China supported many of Washington's policies in Asia and around the world. It also encouraged and hailed US efforts to contain the Soviet Union and challenge its growing presence and influence around the world. Economic, political, social, and technological cooperation between Beijing and

268 *Conclusion*

Washington began to flourish. China's foreign policy outlook during this period, therefore, was a reflection of its relations with the United States and the Soviet Union.

This new shift in China's foreign policy left its mark on China's foreign policy toward the Gulf and Arabian Peninsula region. First, Beijing began to accept US policy in the Gulf and Arabian Peninsula region in order to offset Moscow's penetration in the region, particularly in Iraq and Yemen. Second, Beijing moved toward cultivating amicable relations with the governments of the region. These two changes in China's foreign policy towards the Gulf and Arabian Peninsula region produced some remarkable achievements in China's relations with the countries of the region. It succeeded in establishing diplomatic relations with Kuwait (March 1971), Iran (August 1971), and Oman (May 1978). It also achieved some economic gains including an increase in trade to around US$3.8 billion in the 1970s, of which 77 per cent was with those countries with which China had already established diplomatic relations – namely, Iraq, YAR, PDRY, Kuwait, Iran, and Oman. China also enjoyed a large favourable trade surplus in its trade relations with the countries of the region throughout the 1970s.

But the most significant change in China's foreign policy toward the region in the 1970s was the termination of its support for revolutionary groups in the region. Most notable of them all was the termination of its support for the Dhofari rebels' ambition to export their revolutionary ideas throughout the region and challenge the legitimacy of the ruling families of the states of the region. The Chinese government feared that the Soviet Union was attempting to fill the power vacuum left by the British withdrawal from the region. Therefore, it felt the need to halt its revolutionary rhetoric in the region in favour of accumulating better political, economic, and social relations with the ruling regimes of the region. This change was mainly directed toward preventing the Soviet Union from succeeding in filling the power vacuum.

Another change in China's foreign policy took place in 1982. That year witnessed the introduction and implementation of China's 'independent foreign policy'. The new Chinese policy came as a result of changes in China's perception of its relations with the United States and the Soviet Union. The continuing American arms supply to Taiwan and China's own drive for economic and military modernization in the context of implementing its Four Modernizations programme encouraged the adoption of an independent foreign policy in China's relations with both powers. The new policy was aimed at allowing China to achieve a greater degree of manoeuvrability within the Chinese–American–Soviet triangle and to avoid China from being drawn into conflicts between the two superpowers. As a result of the adoption of the new foreign policy, China's relations with both powers improved significantly. China–Soviet trade relations improved and many social and educational contacts took place between them. However, China's insistence on the removal of, what they perceived as, the three main obstacles (the Soviet presence in Afghanistan, Vietnamese invasion of Cambodia, the increasing Soviet military presence along their border) to better relations prevented the normalization of the relationship between the two countries until May 1989. Despite the cooling off of Beijing–Washington relations in the early 1980s, the second half of the decade saw the most productive era of cooperation in their bilateral relations. Political contacts, economic relations, military cooperation, and social and educational exchanges increased significantly. But the real souring of relations came at the end of the decade. China's harsh treatment of demonstrators in Tiananmen Square in June 1989 triggered sanctions against the Chinese government by the West, Japan, and ASEAN countries.

Despite improvements in its relations with the Soviet Union, China's fear of Moscow remained high throughout the 1980s. Moscow's presence in Afghanistan and South Yemen and the outbreak of the Iran–Iraq war elevated China's fear of the Soviet Union in this period. The Chinese government worried that the Soviet Union could use the prolonged war in the region to its own advantage by exploiting one side against the other. Therefore, China's foreign policy accelerated all its efforts to prevent Moscow from achieving that goal. It offered military and economic assistance to Iran, which China saw as the more vulnerable, of the two belligerents, to Soviet penetration, particularly since Iraq already received a substantial amount of assistance from the Soviet Union and the United States.

Taiwan's established political and economic relations with the countries of the region had also determined China's foreign policy toward the region in the 1980s. China worked to further its political ties with those countries that had remained politically isolated from China – Saudi Arabia, the UAE, Qatar, and Bahrain. Establishing diplomatic relations with these countries was one of China's most prominent goals in its foreign policy toward the region in the 1980s. China hoped not only to extend its political relations with all the countries of the region but also to isolate Taiwan. Saudi Arabia was one of only two major countries in the world to hold diplomatic relations with Taiwan and recognize the Taipei regime, instead of Beijing, as the sole representative of all China. In China's strategy, establishing diplomatic relations with the Kingdom would mean a huge blow to Taiwan's efforts to gain further international recognition. So, China wasted no time. It allocated massive political, economic, social, and military strategies to achieve this goal. This strategy bore fruit with the establishment of diplomatic relations with the UAE (1984), Qatar (1986), and Bahrain (1988). Economically, China increased its relations with the countries of the region. Its trade with the countries of the region jumped to around US$9.7 billion, of which Chinese exports amounted to US$7.3 billion and imports to US$2.4 billion. This increase was about US$6 billion higher than China's trade with the region in the 1970s. In addition to its arms sales to Iran and Iraq, China sold the Kingdom advanced ballistic missiles in the second half of the 1980s. This commercial and military cooperation was aimed at scoring political points to further its own interests. In the case of its relations with Iran and Iraq, China's interest was to undermine Soviet influence in the Gulf. In the case of China's relations with the GCC countries, China's interest was to exclude Taiwan from the region.

The 1990s introduced some other important changes in China's foreign policy. The collapse of the Soviet Union and also communism in Eastern Europe in general, the end of the Cold War, and the United States taking the leading role as the policeman of the world contributed to another shift in China's relations with both powers and, subsequently, in China's foreign policy toward the rest of the world. This time, China began strengthening its relations with Russia. The Chinese felt that they and the Russian leadership held a mutual interest in keeping their relations with the United States in balance. Both sides shared the same concerns over the US policy of using military means to force states to abandon some of their foreign and domestic policies. They also shared the same concerns over US efforts to expand NATO to include some of the neighbouring countries of Russia. Therefore, the Chinese felt the urge to reach a strategic understanding with Russia in order to combat US efforts to dominate the world, in general, and contain China and Russia, in particular. Thus, Beijing's relations with Moscow continued to develop at all levels during the post-Cold War era. However, this development of relations was not bound by an alliance in any strict sense of the term. At the same time, China's relations with the United States faced many obstacles that led to the slow development of relations. Issues such as the abuse of human rights in China, allegations of spying and buying influence in the United States, the bombing of the Chinese embassy in Belgrade, and the continuing debate and efforts in both Washington and Tokyo over deployment of the national theatre missile defence system in both countries contributed to the deterioration in Beijing–Washington relations in the 1990s. But the main issue in China–US relations that influenced China's foreign policy toward the region in this period was China's arms sales and military technology transfer to the Gulf and Arabian Peninsula region. The United States kept pushing China to halt its military transfer to the region. It twice imposed sanctions against military and technological cooperation with China, in the early and mid-1990s, respectively. China promised to halt its military transfer of advanced technological weaponry to the region in an effort to re-establish cooperation with the United States, which in the end resulted in the removal of sanctions. This could well explain the decline in China's arms sales to the region in the second half of the 1990s. Though not completely abolished, China's military cooperation with the countries of the region was very limited in the second half of the 1990s. Even Western sources reported very little information about Chinese military transfer to the region compared with that of the 1980s and early 1990s.

It was mainly China's present and future requirements for oil that directed most of its foreign policy strategy toward the region in the 1990s. In the early 1990s, the PRC became a net importer of oil for the first time in its forty-year history. With its increasing pace of economic development, China's net external oil requirements are expected to reach seven million barrels per day by 2015. Much of this oil will have to come from the Gulf and Arabian Peninsula region, which holds the world's largest proven oil reserves (Kemp 1998–9: 135–6). It was anticipated that 77 per cent of China's oil imports in 2000 would come from the Gulf and Arabian Peninsula region. The figure is expected to reach as high as 92 per cent in 2005. Because of its proven oil reserves and the fact that oil in the Caspian Basin (see Jaffe and Manning 1998–9: 112–31) might not be sufficient to make up for any possible loss of oil from the Gulf and Arabian Peninsula region, stability in the Gulf and Arabian Peninsula region had become the main concern of China in the 1990s. The Chinese believed that if the oil supply from the region was disrupted, the economies of most the leading countries including China would be disrupted. So, China began to acquire a fundamental interest in the stability of the region. This interest was evident in China's continued emphasis on the need to settle disputes between the countries of the region peacefully and without foreign intervention. China supported the UN policies on Iraq and condemned Iraq's invasion of Kuwait. No criticism was made of the security arrangements adopted by most of the countries of the region with the United States and the West, which gave foreign forces access to their military facilities. The Chinese government was, also, careful not to attack the foreign policy of the countries of the region. For instance, the government of the UAE was not criticized when it invited President Lee of Taiwan to visit in 1995. Any criticism was mainly limited to attacks on Taiwan's efforts to gather international recognition for the independence of Taiwan. Nor was there criticism of the Kingdom's policy in promoting the 're-islamization' of Central Asia. In addition, China continued to push for better economic ties with the countries of the region. Trade relations totalled US$22 billion for the first six years of the 1990s, twice the value of its trade relations with the region in the whole of the 1980s. Most importantly, China's imports from the region, mainly oil, amounted to US$9.5 billion (43 per cent of total trade), or four times that of China's imports from the region in the 1980s. Such an increase in China's imports from the region in only a few years demonstrates the importance of the region as a supplier of oil to China. Although China's oil imports from the region in the 1990s came mainly from Iran, Oman, and Yemen, China had sought to develop an economic partnership with Saudi Arabia. Saudi's large oil reserves encouraged Beijing to start building economic ties with the Kingdom. This was marked by President Jiang Zemin's first ever visit to the Kingdom in October–November 1999. His visit was not only his first to the Kingdom but also to any Gulf and Arabian Peninsula country. His choice of the Kingdom demonstrated the value Beijing placed on the Kingdom as China's main future oil supplier. While oil production in Oman, Yemen, and even Iran are believed to decrease in the early twenty-first century, the Kingdom's oil production is expected to continue throughout the century. China, therefore, has been investing in building and upgrading its refineries to suit the type of crude oil that the Kingdom produces and has been encouraging Saudi cooperation in the field. President Jiang's visit, therefore, was aimed at achieving greater economic relations in the field of oil between China and the Kingdom for the twenty-first century.

But one could ask why China continued to sell high-tech weaponry to countries such as Iran in the 1990s, if it really sought stability in the region. Arguably, the Chinese had hoped to achieve some strategic, political, and economic gains through increasing their military cooperation with the countries of the region. Strategically, China may have wanted to keep Iran, with which it enjoyed a fruitful relationship in the 1980s and the 1990s, militarily strong to deter any possible hostile country, like Iraq, from dominating the region. Like the West, China played the balance of power game in its relations with the countries of the region. Politically, the Chinese may have felt that furthering military cooperation with the countries of the region could upgrade the importance of China to the same level as that of Russia and the United States. The decision to sell advanced military technology to Iran may largely have been determined by the Chinese view of Iran's geopolitical importance. This view, which was predicated on the need to secure a long-term independent supply of oil, saw Iran as a vital gateway between China and both Gulf oil and Caspian oil. Therefore, China's military cooperation with Iran was one of China's foreign policy priorities, in order to obtain long-term economic gain, particularly in the supply of Iranian oil and gas to China. China's military cooperation may also be traced to China's hopes for generating hard currency to modernize its own military capabilities. On the other hand, China's arms sales to Iran may also be explained as a demonstration of Chinese dissatisfaction with US military cooperation with Taiwan. The Chinese may have wanted to use their supply of arms technology to Iran and others in the region as a political card to halt the US arms transfer to the island.

Throughout this book, we have sought to show that China's foreign policy toward the region changed simultaneously as the international system changed. Neo-realism as a theoretical framework, which attributes states' foreign policy to external rather than internal factors, worked nicely in explaining China's foreign policy toward the region during the PRC's fifty years of interactions with the region. As shown throughout the book, China's foreign policy toward the region in the Cold War era had been mainly determined by external factors – namely, China's relations with both the United States and the Soviet Union. In the post-Cold War era, however, China's efforts to upgrade its economic capability was the determining factor that shaped China's foreign policy toward the region. As mentioned earlier, neo-realists assume that states' foreign policies are shaped by their drive to increase or at least sustain their economic, political, and military capabilities relative to other regional and international powers. China exactly followed such a pattern. Its current and future requirements of oil forced China to further develop its relations with the countries of the region and be more concerned with the stability and security of the region. The Chinese leadership believes that its legitimacy depended on how it develops the country's economy and, therefore, sustains the well-being of its massive population. Thus, a strong economy requires a sufficient supply of raw materials including oil, the production of which started to decline in China in 1993. As China continues to develop economically, modernization will remain the most dominant factor in determining China's foreign policy toward the countries of the Gulf and Arabian Peninsula region for the next decade and beyond. With China becoming more and more dependent on Gulf and Arabian Peninsula oil, its policies toward the region will continue to focus on stability and solving disputes peacefully without foreign intervention. Internationally, China will continue to adopt policies that are favourable to the countries of the region, including supporting Arab initiatives over many issues like the Palestine–Israeli conflict; and it will avoid criticizing their domestic or foreign policies. Iraq's potential as a supplier of oil and a source of investment for Chinese companies will push China's foreign policy to support any proposal for the removal of economic sanctions against Iraq. China will also continue to sell weapons to the countries of the region and cooperate with them in the military field as long as it serves China's interests in the region. Clearly, much of it will remain secret, allowing Beijing to avoid any deterioration in its economic relations with the West. It will continue to stress its objections to any foreign or regional power's ambition to dominate the region. However, in the short term, China will not challenge the presence of the United States in the region. The Chinese see the American presence as the last-resort protector of the Gulf and Arabian Peninsula region against any possible threats, ensuring, therefore, the flow of oil from the region to the thirsty Chinese economy.

After the collapse of the communist party and the economy in the Soviet Union, the Chinese government became more and more aware of the fact that any threat to the flow of Gulf and Arabian Peninsula oil to China could have widespread political and security consequences. For this reason, China's foreign policy will continue to call for stability in the region. It will also continue to make sure that the oil routes from the region to the coastal areas of China are protected from domination by any hostile country. So, China will pay increasingly more attention to its relations with Iran and Oman, which jointly control the Strait of Hormuz. It will also work to strengthen its naval presence in the South China Sea where Gulf oil is shipped through to China. Consequently, China's relations with such large and growing military powers in the area as India, Japan, Indonesia, Vietnam, Thailand, Malaysia, the Philippines and South Korea will also be affected, because China will work to prevent any power from dominating the route, giving China an advantage over all other East and South-East Asian countries. In short, the Gulf and Arabian Peninsula region in the next decade and beyond will remain a very important region in China's foreign policy calculations.

Appendix

Table A.1 Value of China's trade with Iraq, 1950–1996 (in US$ million) (source: Editorial Board 1984: 840; IMF 1990: 134; IMF 1997: 158)

Year	Exports	Imports	Total
1950	N/A	N/A	N/A
1951	N/A	N/A	N/A
1952	N/A	N/A	N/A
1953	N/A	N/A	N/A
1954	N/A	N/A	N/A
1955	0.01	N/A	0.01
1956	0.03	N/A	0.03
1957	0.25	N/A	0.25
1958	1.16	N/A	1.16
1959	4.44	3.93	8.37
1960	5.64	1.21	6.85
1961	5.05	3.52	8.57
1962	10.16	4.62	14.78
1963	10.42	7.19	17.61
1964	13.06	3.98	17.04
1965	13.98	7.25	21.23
1966	18.09	5.55	23.64
1967	14.75	6.64	21.39
1968	16.61	4.22	20.83
1969	18.86	4.53	23.39
1970	17.52	4.54	22.06
1971	20.22	4.13	24.35
1972	18.74	7.27	26.01
1973	16.85	4.74	21.59
1974	54.60	69.24	123.84
1975	65.48	117.84	183.32
1976	55.44	83.49	138.93
1977	83.67	23.02	106.69
1978	69.12	56.75	125.87
1979	134.69	48.57	183.26
1980	124.35	127.96	252.31
1981	199.95	3.81	203.76
1982	130.57	11.26	141.83
1983	35.00	11.00	45.00
1984	55.00	8.00	63.00
1985	128.00	7.00	135.00
1986	151.00	5.00	156.00
1987	74.00	1.00	75.00
1988	75.00	14.00	89.00
1989	66.00	73.00	139.00
1990	33.00	71.00	104.00
1991	N/A	N/A	N/A
1992	1.00	1.00	2.00
1993	5.00	1.00	6.00
1994	2.00	1.00	3.00
1995	N/A	1.00	1.00
1996	1.00	N/A	1.00

276 Appendix

Table A.2 Value of China's trade with Iran, 1950–1996 (US$ million) (source: Editorial Board 1984: 839; IMF 1990: 135; IMF 1997: 158)

Year	Exports	Imports	Total
1950	N/A	0.56	0.56
1951	N/A	0.56	0.56
1952	N/A	N/A	N/A
1953	–	–	–
1954	N/A	N/A	N/A
1955	N/A	N/A	N/A
1956	0.01	–	0.01
1957	0.07	–	0.07
1958	0.44	–	0.44
1959	0.80	–	0.80
1960	0.92	–	0.92
1961	0.40	–	0.40
1962	1.58	–	1.58
1963	3.05	–	3.05
1964	5.44	–	5.44
1965	7.71	2.16	9.87
1966	10.45	1.44	11.89
1967	4.07	3.33	7.40
1968	1.62	1.03	2.65
1969	2.15	0.89	3.04
1970	1.69	4.95	6.64
1971	3.41	2.57	5.98
1972	14.06	21.28	35.34
1973	22.46	39.58	62.04
1974	47.52	3.84	51.36
1975	53.09	32.71	85.80
1976	53.73	39.60	93.33
1977	52.54	48.04	100.58
1978	64.97	53.45	118.42
1979	36.50	31.39	67.89
1980	120.56	58.55	179.11
1981	149.39	19.16	168.55
1982	44.56	155.51	200.07
1983	205.56	77.81	283.37
1984	167.00	50.00	217.00
1985	98.00	6.00	104.00
1986	130.00	–	130.00
1987	125.00	10.00	135.00
1988	166.00	9.00	74.00
1989	68.00	6.00	74.00
1990	292.00	43.00	335.00
1991	293.00	21.00	314.00
1992	336.00	101.00	437.00
1993	403.00	310.00	713.00
1994	266.00	182.00	448.00
1995	278.00	227.00	505.00
1996	399.00	386.00	785.00

– Not a significant amount.

Table A.3 Value of China's trade with the YAR, 1955–1989 (US$ million)

Year	Exports	Imports	Total
1955	N/A	N/A	N/A
1956	0.01	N/A	0.01
1957	–	N/A	–
1958	0.09	N/A	0.09
1959	3.62	N/A	3.62
1960	1.20	N/A	1.20
1961	1.30	N/A	1.30
1962	0.46	N/A	0.46
1963	0.21	N/A	0.21
1964	1.14	0.02	1.16
1965	4.25	0.71	4.96
1966	2.02	0.36	2.38
1967	0.97	0.49	1.46
1968	1.19	0.47	1.66
1969	1.92	–	1.92
1970	1.25	–	1.25
1971	3.94	0.92	4.86
1972	5.03	1.62	6.65
1973	12.79	2.74	15.53
1974	26.64	4.10	30.74
1975	18.21	3.99	22.20
1976	33.44	5.74	39.18
1977	34.99	7.26	42.25
1978	39.70	3.24	42.94
1979	63.31	2.99	66.30
1980	79.15	–	79.15
1981	58.99	2.72	61.71
1982	60.37	1.96	62.33
1983	81.00	N/A	81.00
1984	57.00	N/A	57.00
1985	39.00	N/A	39.00
1986	25.00	N/A	25.00
1987	17.00	N/A	17.00
1988	27.00	N/A	27.00
1989	35.00	N/A	35.00

– Not a significant amount.

Appendix

Table A.4 Value of China's trade with the PDRY, 1967–1989 (US$ million)

Year	Exports	Imports	Total
1967	1.54	N/A	1.54
1968	1.80	N/A	1.80
1969	3.69	N/A	3.69
1970	3.80	0.04	3.84
1971	4.56	0.88	5.44
1972	7.38	3.81	11.19
1973	15.29	3.81	19.10
1974	12.59	N/A	12.59
1975	18.55	0.01	18.56
1976	11.50	1.38	12.88
1977	13.86	0.02	13.88
1978	19.73	2.14	21.87
1979	20.37	N/A	20.37
1980	23.25	0.74	23.99
1981	30.81	3.69	34.50
1982	36.57	N/A	36.57
1983	53.00	N/A	53.00
1984	36.00	N/A	36.00
1985	28.00	2.00	30.00
1986	21.00	N/A	21.00
1987	25.00	1.00	26.00
1988	37.00	N/A	37.00
1989	22.00	1.00	23.00

Table A.5 Value of China's trade with the Republic of Yemen 1990–1996 (US$ million) (source: Editorial Board 1984: 850; IMF 1990: 158; IMF 1997: 135)

Year	Exports	Imports	Total
1990	74.00	2.00	76.00
1991	71.00	N/A	71.00
1992	74.00	74.00	148.00
1993	112.00	255.00	367.00
1994	85.00	149.00	234.00
1995	108.00	344.00	452.00
1996	106.00	570.00	676.00

Table A.6 Value of China's trade with Kuwait, 1955–1996 (US$ million) (source: Editorial Board 1984: 841; IMF 1990: 135; IMF 1997: 158)

Year	Exports	Imports	Total
1955	0.11	N/A	0.11
1956	0.43	N/A	0.43
1957	0.28	N/A	0.28
1958	1.10	N/A	1.10
1959	1.03	N/A	1.03
1960	0.67	N/A	0.67
1961	1.06	N/A	1.06
1962	1.83	N/A	1.83
1963	2.79	N/A	2.79
1964	5.35	N/A	5.35
1965	8.39	N/A	8.39
1966	10.55	N/A	10.55
1967	15.69	N/A	15.69
1968	18.05	N/A	18.05
1969	18.84	0.38	19.22
1970	16.76	3.68	20.44
1971	18.39	3.69	22.08
1972	24.10	9.78	33.88
1973	41.55	19.05	60.60
1974	54.33	24.15	78.48
1975	69.75	2.46	72.21
1976	99.91	10.39	110.30
1977	94.45	20.86	115.31
1978	92.98	33.11	126.09
1979	136.24	38.73	174.97
1980	156.98	42.13	199.11
1981	146.16	8.57	154.73
1982	124.50	26.69	151.19
1983	99.00	50.00	149.00
1984	85.00	26.00	111.00
1985	73.00	19.00	92.00
1986	73.00	26.00	99.00
1987	94.00	41.00	135.00
1988	131.00	75.00	206.00
1989	131.00	56.00	187.00
1990	65.00	43.00	108.00
1991	19.00	N/A	19.00
1992	60.00	3.00	63.00
1993	88.00	12.00	100.00
1994	191.00	36.00	227.00
1995	105.00	125.00	230.00
1996	102.00	111.00	213.00

Appendix

Table A.7 Value of China's trade with Oman, 1955–1996 (US$ million) (source: Editorial Board 1984: 844; IMF 1990: 135; IMF 1997: 158)

Year	Exports	Imports	Total
1955	0.01	N/A	0.01
1956	0.19	N/A	0.19
1957	0.18	N/A	0.18
1958	0.37	N/A	0.37
1959	0.11	N/A	0.11
1960	0.16	N/A	0.16
1961	0.12	N/A	0.12
1962	0.12	N/A	0.12
1963	0.18	N/A	0.18
1964	0.29	N/A	0.29
1965	0.38	N/A	0.38
1966	0.73	N/A	0.73
1967	1.28	N/A	1.28
1968	2.79	N/A	2.79
1969	2.20	N/A	2.20
1970	2.61	N/A	2.61
1971	1.61	N/A	1.61
1972	2.58	N/A	2.58
1973	3.68	N/A	3.68
1974	5.07	N/A	5.07
1975	6.35	N/A	6.35
1976	5.85	N/A	5.85
1977	5.39	N/A	5.39
1978	7.38	N/A	7.38
1979	10.45	N/A	10.45
1980	12.76	–	12.76
1981	11.29	–	11.29
1982	10.48	–	10.48
1983	10.00	–	10.00
1984	11.00	2.00	13.00
1985	9.00	–	9.00
1986	10.00	–	10.00
1987	8.00	–	8.00
1988	7.00	67.00	74.00
1989	7.00	132.00	139.00
1990	8.00	125.00	133.00
1991	10.00	400.00	410.00
1992	8.00	447.00	455.00
1993	11.00	561.00	572.00
1994	18.00	413.00	431.00
1995	15.00	482.00	497.00
1996	14.00	828.00	842.00

– Not a significant amount.

Table A.8 Value of China's trade with Saudi Arabia, 1954–1996 (US$ million) (source: Editorial Board 1984: 846; IMF 1990: 135; IMF 1997: 158)

Year	Exports	Imports	Total
1955	0.12	N/A	0.12
1956	0.04	N/A	0.04
1957	0.17	N/A	0.17
1958	0.19	N/A	0.19
1959	0.21	N/A	0.21
1960	1.26	N/A	1.26
1961	0.73	N/A	0.73
1962	0.77	N/A	0.77
1963	1.45	N/A	1.45
1964	2.63	N/A	2.63
1965	4.20	N/A	4.20
1966	7.66	N/A	7.66
1967	8.84	N/A	8.84
1968	4.38	N/A	4.38
1969	0.75	N/A	0.75
1970	1.06	N/A	1.06
1971	2.10	N/A	2.10
1972	1.42	N/A	1.42
1973	1.64	N/A	1.64
1974	3.06	N/A	3.06
1975	3.89	N/A	3.89
1976	6.75	N/A	6.75
1977	14.79	N/A	14.79
1978	36.99	N/A	36.99
1979	68.01	8.38	76.39
1980	136.15	15.54	151.69
1981	168.29	12.30	180.59
1982	143.74	10.42	154.16
1983	149.00	19.00	178.00
1984	133.00	28.00	161.00
1985	133.00	22.00	155.00
1986	134.00	52.00	186.00
1987	247.00	107.00	354.00
1988	230.00	195.00	425.00
1989	235.00	66.00	301.00
1990	337.00	80.00	417.00
1991	387.00	138.00	525.00
1992	444.00	127.00	571.00
1993	579.00	119.00	698.00
1994	674.00	353.00	1027.00
1995	734.00	553.00	1287.00
1996	748.00	840.00	1588.00

Appendix

Table A.9 Value of China's trade with the UAE, 1964–1996 (US$ million) (source: Editorial Board 1984: 849; IMF 1990: 135; IMF 1997: 158)

Year	Exports	Imports	Total
1964	0.70	N/A	0.70
1965	0.85	N/A	0.85
1966	1.23	N/A	1.23
1967	2.33	N/A	2.33
1968	3.34	N/A	3.34
1969	3.81	N/A	3.81
1970	3.92	N/A	3.92
1971	5.44	N/A	5.44
1972	9.03	N/A	9.03
1973	20.28	N/A	20.28
1974	34.86	N/A	34.86
1975	42.60	N/A	42.60
1976	49.15	N/A	49.15
1977	47.22	N/A	47.22
1978	58.51	N/A	58.51
1979	80.71	N/A	80.71
1980	91.66	N/A	91.66
1981	100.67	N/A	100.67
1982	85.31	N/A	85.31
1983	68.00	N/A	68.00
1984	63.00	13.00	76.00
1985	64.00	21.00	85.00
1986	90.00	10.00	100.00
1987	123.00	28.00	151.00
1988	185.00	71.00	256.00
1989	239.00	52.00	291.00
1990	246.00	41.00	287.00
1991	408.00	69.00	477.00
1992	543.00	66.00	609.00
1993	711.00	106.00	817.00
1994	862.00	37.00	899.00
1995	1101.00	120.00	1221.00
1996	1078.00	68.00	1146.00

Table A.10 Value of China's trade with Qatar, 1958–1996 (US$ million) (source: Editorial Board 1984: 845; IMF 1990: 135; IMF 1997: 158)

Year	Exports	Imports	Total
1958	–	N/A	–
1959	0.02	N/A	0.02
1960	0.02	N/A	0.02
1961	–	N/A	–
1962	0.02	N/A	0.02
1963	0.04	N/A	0.04
1964	0.11	N/A	0.11
1965	0.34	N/A	0.34
1966	0.52	N/A	0.52
1967	0.66	N/A	0.66
1968	0.69	N/A	0.69
1969	1.12	N/A	1.12
1970	1.15	N/A	1.15
1971	1.45	N/A	1.45
1972	2.41	N/A	2.41
1973	3.81	N/A	3.81
1974	4.79	N/A	4.79
1975	6.28	N/A	6.28
1976	6.82	12.95	19.77
1977	7.58	1.36	8.94
1978	5.65	–	5.65
1979	7.42	11.66	19.08
1980	11.13	41.47	52.60
1981	8.30	22.15	30.45
1982	8.26	36.65	44.91
1983	6.00	43.00	49.00
1984	6.00	63.00	69.00
1985	4.00	36.00	40.00
1986	5.00	27.00	32.00
1987	9.00	21.00	30.00
1988	7.00	48.00	55.00
1989	5.00	44.00	49.00
1990	6.00	25.00	31.00
1991	6.00	80.00	86.00
1992	8.00	69.00	77.00
1993	11.00	42.00	53.00
1994	10.00	48.00	58.00
1995	10.00	90.00	100.00
1996	21.00	49.00	70.00

– Not a significant amount.

284 Appendix

Table A.11 Value of China's trade with Bahrain, 1956–1996 (US$ million) (source: Editorial Board 1984: 835; IMF 1990: 135; IMF 1997: 158)

Year	Exports	Imports	Total
1956	–	N/A	–
1957	0.08	N/A	0.08
1958	0.11	N/A	0.11
1959	0.07	N/A	0.07
1960	0.06	N/A	0.06
1961	0.07	N/A	0.07
1962	0.14	N/A	0.14
1963	0.18	N/A	0.18
1964	0.38	N/A	0.38
1965	0.76	N/A	0.76
1966	1.78	N/A	1.78
1967	2.46	N/A	2.46
1968	3.18	N/A	3.18
1969	6.53	N/A	6.53
1970	7.53	N/A	7.53
1971	9.36	N/A	9.36
1972	11.76	N/A	12.76
1973	19.43	N/A	19.43
1974	26.57	1.96	28.53
1975	32.63	9.20	41.83
1976	48.21	17.59	65.80
1977	40.89	13.15	54.04
1978	32.45	N/A	32.45
1979	25.89	N/A	25.89
1980	23.60	N/A	23.60
1981	21.15	N/A	21.15
1982	19.40	N/A	19.40
1983	11.00	23.00	34.00
1984	8.00	18.00	26.00
1985	7.00	19.00	26.00
1986	8.00	3.00	11.00
1987	10.00	4.00	14.00
1988	9.00	3.00	12.00
1989	9.00	3.00	12.00
1990	9.00	N/A	9.00
1991	11.00	1.00	12.00
1992	10.00	2.00	12.00
1993	39.00	6.00	45.00
1994	17.00	4.00	21.00
1995	14.00	19.00	23.00
1996	14.00	29.00	43.00

– Not a significant amount.

Bibliography

Abidi, A.H.H. (1982) *China, Iran, and the Persian Gulf*. New Delhi: Radiant Publishers.
ACDA (1987) *World Military Expenditures and Arms Transfers*, pp. 127–30. Washington, DC: US Arms Control and Disarmament Agency.
ACDA (1991–2) *World Military Expenditures and Arms Transfers*, pp. 131–4. Washington, DC: US Arms Control and Disarmament Agency.
Achminov, H. (1956) 'Social conflicts at the Twentieth Party Congress'. *The Bulletin* **3**(5) (5 May).
Adie, W.A.C. (1967) 'China's Middle East Strategy'. *The World Today* **23** (August), 317–26.
Al-Alkim, H.H. (1989) *The Foreign Policy of the United Arab Emirates*. London: Sagi Books.
Alger, C.F. (1977) 'Foreign policies of US publics'. *International Studies Quarterly* **21**(2).
Almond, G.A. and Coleman, J. (eds) (1960) *The Politics of the Developing Areas*. Princeton, NJ: Princeton University Press.
Almond, G.A. and Powell, G.B. Jr (1966) *Comparative Politics: A Development Approach*. Boston: Little, Brown.
Anselmo, J.C. (1997) 'China's military seeks great leap forward'. *Aviation Week and Space Technology* **146**(20) (12 May 1997), 324.
Ashley, R.K. (1986) 'The poverty of neorealism', in R.O. Keohane (ed). *Neorealism and Its Critics*. New York: Colombia University Press.
Avtorkhanov, A. (1956) 'The political outlook after the Twentieth Party Congress'. *The Bulletin* **3**(5) (May).
Azar, E.E. (1979) 'Soviet and Chinese roles in the Middle East'. *Problems of Communism* **28**(3) (May–June), 18–30.
Bachman, D. (1989) 'Domestic sources of Chinese foreign policy' in S.S. Kim (ed.) *China and the World: New Directions in Chinese Foreign Relations*. Boulder, CO: Westview Press.
Bachman, D. (1994) 'Domestic sources of Chinese foreign policy' in S.S. Kim (ed.) *China and the World: Chinese Foreign Relations in the Post-Cold War Era*. Boulder, CO: Westview Press.
Bachman, D. (1998) 'Structure and process in the making of Chinese foreign policy', in S.S. Kim (ed.) *China and the World: Chinese Foreign Policy Faces the New Millennium*. Boulder, CO: Westview Press.

Bibliography

Ball, N., Bergstrand, B.-G., Kosiak, S.M., Loose-Weintaub, E., Shambaugh, D. and Whitlock, E. (1994) 'World military expenditure'. *SIPRI Yearbook 1994: World Armaments, Disarmament and International Security*, pp. 441–8. Oxford: Oxford University Press.

Ban Yue Tan (1999) 'New imperialism in the post Cold War era'. *Fortnightly Review*, No. 7.

Ban Yue Tan (1999) 'New imperialist in the post Cold-War era'. *Fortnightly Review*, No. 7.

Barnett, A.D. (1977) *China and the Major Powers in East Asia*. Washington, DC: The Brookings Institution.

Barnett, A.D. (1985) *The Making of Foreign Policy in China: Structure and Process*. Boulder, CO: Westview Press.

Bartke, W. (1989) *The Economic Aid of the PR China to Developing and Socialist Countries*, p. 37. London: K.G. Saur.

Baum, R. (ed.) (1980) *China's Four Modernizations: The New Technological Revolution*. Boulder, CO: Westview Press.

Behbehani, H.S. (1981) *China's Foreign Policy in the Arab World 1955-1975: Three Case Studies*. London: KPI.

Behbehani, H.S. (ed.) (1985) *China and the People's Democratic Republic of Yemen: A Report*. London: KPI.

Benewick, R. and Donald, S. (1999) *The State of China Atlas*, pp. 11–17. London: Penguin Books.

Bernstein, R. and Munro, R.H. (1997) 'The coming conflict with America'. *Foreign Affairs* **76**(2) (March/April), 18–32.

Bernstein, R. and Munro, R.H. (1998) *The Coming Conflict with China*. New York: Vintage Books.

Bidwell, R. (1983) *The Two Yemens*. Boulder, CO: Westview Press.

Bilski, A. and Doder, L. (1989) 'Setting a bitter feud: Gorbachev's visit opens a new era'. *Maclean's* **102**(22) (29 May), 35–6.

Bin Sultan, K. and Seale, P. (1995) *Desert Warrior: A Personal View of the Gulf War by the Joint Forces Commander*. London: Harper Collins.

Bin Yu (1993) 'Sino-Russian military relations: Implications for Asian Pacific security'. *Asian Survey* **33**(3) (March), 302–6.

Black, J.L. (2000) *Russia Faces NATO Expansion: Bearing Gifts or Bearing Arms?*, pp. 130–3. Boston: Rowman and Littlefield.

Bowring, P. (1982) 'The Tithes that Bind'. *Far Eastern Economic Review* (15 January), 10–11.

Bracken, P. (1999) *Fire in the East: The Rise of Asian Military Power and the Second Nuclear Age*. New York: Perennial.

Brady, R. (1984) 'Moving downstream'. *Forbes* **133**(11) (7 May).

Brahm, L.J. (1996) *China As No. 1: The New Superpower Takes Centre Stage*. Singapore: Butterworth-Heinemann Asia.

Brown, C. (1997) *Understanding International Relations*. London: Macmillan Press.

Brown, L.R. (1995) *Who Will Feed China?* New York: W. W. Norton.

Brugger, B. and Kelly, D. (1990) *Chinese Marxism in the Post-Mao Era, 1978–84*. Stanford, CA: Stanford University Press.

Burr, W. (1999) *The Kissinger Transcripts: The Top Secret Talks with Beijing and Moscow*. New York: The New Press.

Calabrese, J. (1990) 'From flyswatters to Silkworms: The evolution of China's role in west Asia'. *Asian Survey* **30** (September), 862–76.
Calabrese, J. (1991) *China's Changing Relations with the Middle East*. New York: Pinter.
Calabrese, J. (1994) *Revolutionary Horizons: Regional Foreign Policy in Post-Khomeini Iran*. New York: St Martin's Press.
Calabrese, J. (1998) 'China and the Persian Gulf: Energy and security'. *Middle East Journal* **52**(3) (Summer), 351–66.
Calabrese, J. (1999) 'China and Iraq: A stake in stability' in P.R. Kumaraswamy (ed.) *China and the Middle East: The Quest For Influence*. London: Sage Publications.
Calder, K.E. (1996) 'Asia's empty tank'. *Foreign Affairs* (March/April), 55–69.
Cambone, S.A. (1997). 'The United States and theatre missile defence in north-east Asia'. *Survival* **39**(3) (Autumn), 66–84.
Chen Jian and Yang Kuisong (1998) 'Chinese politics and the collapse of the Sino-Soviet alliance' in O.A. Westad (ed.) *Brothers in Arms: The Rise and Fall of the Sino-Soviet Alliance, 1945–1963*, pp. 259–66. Stanford: Stanford University Press.
Chen, K.C. (1972) 'Traditional Chinese foreign relations' in K.C. Chen (ed.) *The Foreign Policy of China*. New Jersey: East-West Inc.
Chi Su (1984) 'China and the Soviet Union'. *Current History* **83**(494) (September) 245–8.
Chi Su (1993) 'The strategic triangle and China's Soviet policy' in R.S. Ross (ed.) *China and the United States, the Soviet Union and Tripolarity and Policy Making in the Cold War*. New York: M.E. Sharpe.
Chih-yu Shih (1990) *The Spirit of Chinese Foreign Policy*. New York: St Martin's Press.
Chou, S.H. (1984) 'China's foreign trade relations'. *Current History* **83**(494) (September), 261–4.
Christensen, T.J. (1996) 'Chinese Realpolitik'. *Foreign Affairs* **75**(5) (September/October), 37–51.
Chubin, S. (1982) 'Gains from Soviet policy in the Middle East'. *International Security* **6**(4) (Spring).
Chun-tu Hsueh and North, R.C. (1977) 'Peking's perceptions of Soviet-American relations' in Chun-tu Hsueh (ed.) *Dimensions of China's Foreign Relations*, pp. 49–53. New York: Praeger Publishers.
Clemens, W.C. Jr (1968) *The Arms Race and Sino-Soviet Relations*. Stanford University, CA: Hoover Institution.
Cloud, D.S. (1994) 'Renewal of China's MFN status angers some lawmakers'. *Congressional Quarterly* **52** (28 May).
Clubb, O.E. (1971) *China & Russia: 'the Great Game'*. New York: Columbia University Press.
Colvin, M. and Sawyer, P. (1994) 'Riyadh bargained with Chinese for nuclear reactors'. *Sunday Times*, 7 August, 7.
Conable B.B. Jr and Lampton, D.M. (1992) 'China: The coming power'. *Foreign Affairs* **71**(5) (Winter), 133–49.
Copper, J.F. (1979) 'China's Foreign Aid in 1978'. *Occasional Papers/Reprints Series in Contemporary Asian Studies*. Maryland: School of Law, University of Maryland.

Copper, J.F. (1992) *China Diplomacy: The Washington–Taipei–Beijing Triangle*. Boulder, CO: Westview Press.
Cordesman, A.H. (1998) *Military Balance in the Middle East*, Vol. IX, p. 15. Washington, DC: Centre for Strategic and International Studies.
Cox, R.W. (1986) 'Social forces, states and world orders: Beyond international relations theory' in R.O. Keohane (ed). *Neorealism and Its Critics*. New York: Columbia University Press.
Crankshaw, E. (1965) *The New Cold War: Moscow v. Peking*. Baltimore: Penguin Books.
Cranmer-Byng, J. (1973) 'The Chinese view of their place in the world'. *The China Quarterly* 53 (January/March), 67–79.
Creekman C.T. Jr (1979) 'Sino-Soviet competition in the Yemens'. *Naval War College Review* 32(4), 73–81.
CRS (1995) *Chinese Missile and Nuclear Proliferation*, p. 12. Washington, DC: Congressional Research Services.
Danspeckgruber, W.F. and Tripp, C.R.H. (eds) (1996) *The Iraqi Aggression against Kuwait, Strategic Lessons and Implications for Europe*. Boulder, CO: Westview Press.
Daugherty, J. and Pfaltzgraff, R. Jr (1990) *Contending Theories of International Relations: A Comprehensive Survey*. New York: Harper Collins.
Day, A.J. (1985) *China and the Soviet Union, 1949–84*. Essex: Longman Group.
DCCI (1995) *Trade and Industry*, Vol. 20, No. 238 (October), p. 12. Dubai Chamber of Commerce and Industry.
de Crespigny, R. (1995) 'Tradition and Chinese foreign policy' in S. Harris and G. Klintworth (eds) *China As a Great Power: Myths, Realities, and Challenges in the Asia-Pacific Region*. New York: St Martin's Press.
deGraffenreid, K. (ed.) (1999) *The Cox Report*, The unanimous and bipartisan report of the House Select Committee on US National Security and Military Commercial Concern with the People's Republic of China. Washington, DC: Regnery Publishing.
Delfs, R. (1990) 'The Gulf card'. *Far Eastern Economic Review* 149 (20 September), 19.
Deng Xiaoping (1994a) 'A new approach to stabilising the world situation' in *Selected Works of Deng Xiaoping*, Vol. 3, p. 59. Beijing: Foreign Language Press.
Deng Xiaoping (1994b) 'Sino-US relations must be improved' in *Selected Works of Deng Xiaoping 1982–1992*. Beijing: Foreign Language Press.
Denoon, D.B.H. and Frieman, W. (1996) 'China's security strategy: The view from Beijing, Asia, and Washington'. *Asian Survey* 36(4) (April).
Deutsch, K.W. (1964) *The Nerves of Government*. New York: Free Press.
Dibb, P. (1997–8) 'The revolution in military affairs and Asian security'. *Survival* 39(4) (Winter), 93–116.
Dillon, M. (1995) *Xinjiang: Ethnicity, Separatism and Control in Chinese Central Asia*, Durham East Asian Papers No. 1. University of Durham: Department of East Asian Studies.
Dillon, M. (1999) *China's Muslim Hui Community: Migration, Settlement and Sects*. Surrey: Curzon Press.
Dirlik, A. and Meisner, M. (eds) (1989) *Marxism and the Chinese Experience: Issues in Contemporary Chinese Socialism*. New York: M.E. Sharpe.

Bibliography   289

Disney, N. (1977) *China and the Middle East*, Middle East Research and Information Project Reports No. 63 (December), 3–17. Washington, DC: MERIP.

Dittmer, L. (1994) 'China and Russia: New beginnings' in S.S. Kim (ed.) *China and the World: Chinese Foreign Relations in the Post-Cold War Era*. Boulder, CO: Westview Press.

Doolin, D.J. (1965) *Territorial Claims in the Sino-Soviet Conflict, Documents and Analysis*. Stanford University: The Hoover Institution on War, Revolution, and Peace.

Easton, D. (1965a) *A Framework for Political Analysis*. Englewood Cliffs, NJ: Prentice-Hall.

Easton, D. (1965b) *A System Analysis of Political Life*. New York: Wiley.

Editorial (1988) 'Review & outlook: East Winds in the Mideast'. *Wall Street Journal*, Eastern edition, 22 March, 1.

Editorial Board (1984) *Almanac of China's Foreign Economic Relations and Trade*, pp. 817–71. Hong Kong: China Resources Trade Consultancy.

Editorial Board (1998) *The Middle East and North Africa*, 44th edn. London: Europa Publications.

Ehteshami, A. (ed.) (1994) *From the Gulf to Central Asia: Players in the New Great Game*. Exeter: University of Exeter Press.

Ehteshami, A. (1995) *After Khomeini: The Islamic Second Republic*. London: Routledge.

Ehteshami, A. (1998) *The Changing Balance of Power in Asia*. Abu Dhabi: The Emirates Centre for Strategic Studies and Research.

Ehteshami, A. (2000) 'Geopolitics beckons: Hydrocarbons and the politics of the Persian Gulf' in A. Mohammadi and A. Ehteshami (eds) *Iran and Eurasia*, p. 108. Reading, MA: Garnet Publishing.

EIU (1993) *The Country Report: Oman and Yemen*, No. 2, p. 20. London: Economist Intelligence Unit.

EIU (1998) *Country Profile: China and Mongolia, 1997–1998*, p. 52. London: Economist Intelligence Unit.

EIU (1999) *Country Profile: Oman 1999–2000*, p. 33. London: Economist Intelligence Unit.

EIU (2000) *Country Profile: UAE 1999–2000*, p. 58. London: Economic Intelligence Unit.

El-Issa, S. (1998) 'The dispute between the United Arab Emirates and Iran over three islands' in K. el-Din Haseeb (ed.) *Arab–Iranian Relations*, pp. 237–48. Beirut: Centre for Arab Unity Studies.

Ellison, H.J. (1993) 'Soviet Chinese relations: The experience of two decades' in R.S. Ross (ed.) *China and the United States, the Soviet Union and Tripolarity and Policy Making in the Cold War*. New York: M.E. Sharpe.

Fairbank, J.K. and Teng, S.Y. (1972) 'The traditional role of tribute' in K. Chen (ed.) *The Foreign Policy of China*. New Jersey: East-West Inc.

Faust, J.R. and others (1995) *China in World Politics*. Boulder, CO: Lynne Rienners.

FCCIA (1999) *Al-Ghorfa*, No. 64 (June), p. 9. Fujairah Chamber of Commerce.

Feeney, W.R. (1994) 'China and the multilateral economic institutions' in S.S. Kim (ed.) *China and the World: Chinese Foreign Relations in the Post-Cold War Era*. Boulder, CO: Westview Press.

Fei-Ling Wang (1988) 'To incorporate China: A policy for a new era'. *The Global and Mail* **21**(1) (Winter), 68.

Fieldhouse, R. (1991) 'China's mixed signals on nuclear weapons'. *Bulletin of Atomic Scientists* **47**(4) (May), 37–42.
Findlay, C. and Watson, A. (1997) 'Economic growth and trade dependency in China' in D.G. Goodman and G. Segal (eds) *China Rising: Nationalism and Interdependence*. London: Routledge.
Floyd, D. (1963) *Mao Against Khrushchev: A Short History of the Sino-Soviet Conflict*. New York: Frederick A. Praeger.
Foot, R. (1995a) *The Practice of Power: U.S. Relations with China Since 1949*. Oxford: Clarendon Press.
Foot, R. (1995b) 'China's foreign policy in the post-1989 era' in R. Benewick and P. Wingrove (eds) *China in the 1990s*. London: Macmillan.
Frank, W. (1967) *China and the West*, p. 4. Columbia: University of South Carolina Press.
Freedman, L. and Karsh, E. (1993) *The Gulf Conflict: Diplomacy and War in the New World Order*. Princeton, NJ: Princeton University Press.
Freeze, R. (1979). 'The Arab and China'. *Arab Report* (No. 3) (28 February).
Frolic, B.M. (1997) 'Re-engaging China: Striking a balance between trade and human rights' in *Canada Among Nations 1997, Asia Pacific Face Off*, Carleton Public Policy Series No. 21, p. 324. Ottawa: Carleton University.
Fulghum, D.A. (1995) 'China pursuing two fighter plan'. *Aviation Week and Space Technology* **142**(13) (27 March), 44–5.
Fulghum, D.A. (1995) 'New Chinese fighter nears prototyping'. *Aviation Week and Space Technology* **142**(11) (13 March), 26–7.
Garson, R. (1994) *The United States and China Since 1949*. Madison: Fairleigh Dickinson University Press.
Garver, J.W. (1982) *China's Decision for Rapprochement with the United States, 1968–1971*. Boulder, CO: Westview Press.
Garver, J.W. (1991) 'The Indian factor in recent Sino-Soviet relations'. *The China Quarterly* (No. 125) (March), 55–85.
Garver, J.W. (1993a) *Foreign Relations of the People's Republic of China*. Englewood Cliffs, NJ: Prentice-Hall.
Garver, J.W. (1993b) 'China and the new world order' in W.A. Joseph (ed.) *China Briefing 1992*. Boulder, CO: Westview Press.
Garver, J.W. (1993c) 'The Chinese Communist Party and the collapse of Soviet communism'. *The China Quarterly* (No. 133) (March), 1–26.
Garver, J.W. (1997) *Face Off: China, the United States, and Taiwan's Democratization*. Seattle: University of Washington Press.
Gertz, W. (1996a) 'Iran obtain patrol boats from China'. *Washington Times*, 7 March, A12.
Gertz, W. (1996b) 'China sold Iran missile technology'. *Washington Times*, 21 November, A1.
Gertz, W. (1996c) 'Beijing flouts nuke-sales ban'. *Washington Times*, 9 October, A1.
Gertz, W. (1997) 'Iran–China missile co-operation'. *Washington Times*, 18 June.
Gill, B. (1999) 'Chinese arms exports to Iran' in P.R. Kumaraswamy (ed.) *China and the Middle East: The Quest for Influence*. London: Sage Publications.
Gill, B. and Taeho Kim (1995) *SIPRI Report No. 11: China's Arms Acquisition from Abroad: A Quest for 'Superb Secret Weapons'*. Oxford: Oxford University Press.
Gilley, B. and Crispin, S.W. (1999) 'Limited engagement'. *Far Eastern Economic Review* **162**(16) (22 April), 12–14.

Gilpin, R. (1981) *War and Change in World Politics*. Cambridge: Cambridge University Press.
Gittings, J. (1968) *Survey of the Sino-Soviet Dispute: A Comentatory and Extracts from the Recent Polemics, 1963–1967*. Oxford: Oxford University Press.
Gladney, D. (1992) 'Trans-national Islam and Uighar National Identity: Salman Rushdi, Sino-Muslim Missile Deals, and Trans-Eurasian Railway'. *Central Asian Survey* **11**(3) (September), 1–19.
Glaser, B.S. (1993) 'China's security perceptions, interests and ambitions'. *Asian Survey* **32**(3) (March), 252–71.
Godwin, P.H.B. (1986) 'People's war revised: Military doctrine, strategy, and operations' in C.D. Lovejoy Jr and B.W. Watson (eds) *China's Military Reforms: International and Domestic Implications*. Boulder, CO: Westview Press.
Goldstone, J.A. (1995) 'The coming Chinese collapse'. *Foreign Policy*, No 99 (Summer), 35–52.
Griffith, W.E. (1967) *Sino-Soviet Relations 1964–1965*. MA: Massachusetts Institute of Technology Press.
Guocang Huan (1992a) 'China's foreign economic relations'. *Annals of the American Academy of Political and Social Sciences* **519** (January), 176–90.
Guocang Huan (1992b) 'The new relationship with the former Soviet Union'. *Current History* **91**(566) (September), 253–6.
Gupta, D.C. (1969) *The United States Attitudes towards China*. Bombay: S. Chen.
Haddad, W.W. and Foeldi-Hardy, M. (1999) 'Chinese-Palestinian relations', in P.R. Kumaraswamy (ed.) *China and the Middle East: The Quest for Influence*, pp. 42–51. London: Sage Publications.
Halliday, F. (1990) *Revolution and Foreign Policy: The Case of South Yemen 1967–1987*. Cambridge: Cambridge University Press.
Hanrrieder, W.F. (1978) 'Dissolving international politics: Reflections on the nation-state'. *American Political Science Review* **72**(4), 1276–87.
Harding, H. (1992) *A Fragile Relationship: The United States and China since 1972*. Washington, DC: Brookings Institution.
Harding, H. (1984) 'China's changing roles in the contemporary world' in H. Harding (ed.) *China's Foreign Relations in the 1980s*. New Haven: Yale University.
Harding, H. (1987) *China's Second Revolution: Reform after Mao*. Washington, DC: Brookings Institution.
Harding, H. (1988) *China and Northeast Asia: The Political Dimension*. London: University Press of America.
Harding, H. (1994) 'China's co-operative behaviour' in T.W. Robinson and D. Shambaugh (eds) *Chinese Foreign Policy: Theory and Practice*. Oxford: Clarendon Press.
Harris, L.C. (1978) 'Chinese politics in the Middle East'. *Current History* **74**(433) (January), 10–14.
Harris, L.C. (1993) *China Considers the Middle East*. New York: I.B. Tauris.
Harris, S. (1995) 'The economic aspects of security in the Asia–Pacific region'. *Journal of Strategic Studies* **18**(3) (September), 37.
Harrison, M. (1995) *Saudi Arabia Foreign Policy: Relations with the Superpowers*, CMEIS Occasional Papers No. 46. University of Durham: Centre for Middle Eastern and Islamic Studies.
Haseeb, K. el-Din (ed.) (1998) *Arab Iranian Relations*. Beirut: Centre for Arab Unity Studies.

Henley, L.D. (1988) 'China's military modernisation: A ten year assessment' in L.M. Wortzel (ed.) *China's Military Modernisation: International Implications.* London: Greenwood Press.

Hermann, M.G. (1976) 'When a leader's personality will affect foreign policy: Some propositions' in J.N. Rosenau (ed.) *In Search of Global Patterns.* London: Macmillan.

Hickey, D.v.V. (1994) *United States–Taiwan Security Ties: From Cold War to Beyond Containment.* London: Frederick A. Praeger.

Hinton, H.C. (1976) *Peking–Washington: Chinese Foreign Policy and the United States,* The Washington Papers No. IV. London: Sage Publications.

Holiday, F. (1990) *Revolution and Foreign Policy: the Case of South Yemen 1967–1987.* Cambridge: Cambridge University Press.

Hsiung, J.C. (1970) *Ideology and Practice the Evolution of Chinese Communism.* London: Pall Mall Press.

Hsu, I.C.Y. (1990) *The Rise of Modern China.* Oxford: Oxford University Press.

Hu Yaobang (1982) 'Create a new situation in all fields of socialist modernisation'. *Beijing Review* **25**(37) (13 September), 29–33.

Hu, R.W. (1999). 'India's nuclear bomb and future Sino-Indian relations'. *East Asia: An International Quarterly* **17**(1) (Spring), 40–68.

Hunt, M.H. (1996) *The Genesis of Chinese Communist Foreign Policy.* New York: Columbia University Press.

Hunter, S.T. (1990) *Iran and the World: Continuity in a Revolution Decade.* Indianapolis: Indiana University Press.

Huntington, S.P. (1973) 'Transnational organizations in world politics'. *World Politics* **25**(3) (April), 333–68.

Huntington, S.P. (1996) *The Clashes of Civilisations: Remaking of World Order.* New York: Touchstone.

Hwei-ling Huo (1992) 'Patterns of behavior in China's foreign policy, the Gulf crisis and beyond'. *Asian Survey* **32** (March), 263–76.

Hynes, H.A. 'China: The emerging superpower', in < http//:cfcsc.dnd.ca/irc/nh/nh9798/0046.html >, pp. 1–13.

Hyun Sang Yoo (1996) 'An analysis of United States security policy towards a Third World state during the Cold War rra: Case study of U.S.–Iran relations', PhD thesis, University Durham .

Ikenberry, G.J. (1986) 'The state and strategies of international adjustment'. *World Politics* **39**(1), 53–77.

IMF (1990) *Direction of Trade Statistics 1990 Yearbook,* p. 135. Washington, DC: International Monetary Fund.

IMF (1997) *Direction of Trade Statistics 1997 Yearbook,* p. 158. Washington, DC: International Monetary Fund.

Jacobsen, C.G (1981) *Sino-Soviet Relations since Mao: The Chairman's Legacy.* New York: Parger Publishers.

Jaffe, A.M. and Manning, R.A. (1998–9) 'The myth of the Caspian great game': The real geopolitics of energy'. *Survival* **40**(4) (Winter), 112–29.

Jervis, R. (1980) 'The impact of the Korean war on the Cold War'. *Journal of Conflict Resolution* **24**(4) (December).

Johnston, A.I. and Ross, R.S. (1999) 'Conclusion', in A.I. Johnston and R.S. Ross (eds) *Engaging China: The Management of an Emerging Power,* p. 283. New York: Routledge.

Jones, P. and Kevill, S. (1985). *China and the Soviet Union 1949–1984*. London: Longman Group.

Joyce, M. (1998) *Kuwait 1945–1996: An Anglo-American Perspective*. London: Frank Case.

Kan, S.A. (1997) *Chinese Proliferation of Weapons of Mass Destruction: Background and Analysis*, p. 33. Washington, DC: Congressional Research Services.

Kaplan, M.A. (1966) 'The new great debate: Traditionalism vs. science in international relations'. *World Politics* **19**(1) (October), 1–20.

Kaplan, M.A. (1976) *System and Process in International Politics*. New York: Krieger.

Kaplan, R.D. (1986) 'The battle for North Yemen'. *Wall Street Journal*, Eastern edition, 15 April, 1.

Kechichian, J.A. (1995) *Oman and the World: The Emergence of an Independent Foreign Policy*. Santa Monica, CA: Rand Publications.

Kemp, G. (1998–9). 'The Persian Gulf remains the strategic prize'. *Survival* **40**(4) (Winter), 132–49.

Keohane, R.O. and Nye, J.S. (1974) 'Transgovernmental relations and international organizations'. *World Politics* **27**(1), 39–62.

Kim, S.S. (1994) 'China's international organizational behaviour' in T.W. Robinson and D. Shambaugh (eds) *Chinese Foreign Policy: Theory and Practice*. Oxford: Clarendon Press.

Kim, S.S. (1996) 'Mainland China in changing Asia-Pacific regional order' in Bihjaw and J.T. Mayers (eds) *Contemporary China in the Post-Cold War Era*. Colombia, SC: University of South Carolina Press.

Klein, D.W. (1989) 'China and the Second World' in S.S. Kim (ed.) *China and the World: New Directions in Chinese Foreign Relations*, 2nd edn, p. 144. Boulder, CO: Westview Press.

Klintworth, G. (1995) 'China's evolving relationship with APEC'. *International Journal* **50**(3) (Summer), 488.

Kostiner, J. (1990) *South Yemen's Revolutionary Strategy, 1970–1985*. Boulder, CO: Westview Press.

Koyama, K. (1997) 'Growing energy demand in Asian countries: Opportunities and constraints for Gulf energy exports' in Emirates Centre for Strategic Studies and Research (ed.) *Gulf Energy and the World: Challenges and Threats*. Abu Dhabi: ECSSR.

Krasner, S.D. (1985) *Structural Conflict: The Third World against Global Liberalism*. Berkeley: University of California Press.

Kumaraswamy, P.R. (1999) 'China and Israel: Normalisation and after' in P.R. Kumaraswamy (ed.) *China and the Middle East: The Quest for Influence*, pp. 20–41. London: Sage Publications.

Lake, M.W. (1991) 'Casualties of war'. *Far Eastern Economic Review* **151**(8) (21 February), 38–9.

Landay, J.S. (1996) 'China to halt nuclear deal with Iran, US official says'. *Christian Science Monitor*, 19 December, 1.

Lardy, N.R. (1994) *China and the World Economy*. Washington, DC: Institute for International Economics.

Lardy, N.R. (1996) 'U.S.–China economic relations' in T.A. Metzger and R.H. Myer (eds) *Greater China and U.S. Foreign Policy: The Choice Between Confrontation and Mutual Respect*. Stanford, CA: Stanford University Press.

Laster, M. (1995) *The Changing of the Guard: President Clinton and the Security of Taiwan*. Boulder, CO: Westview Press.

Lawrence, A. (1975) *China's Foreign Relations since 1949*. London: Routledge and Kegan Paul.

Lawrence, S.V. and Holland, L. (1999) 'Deal of the century'. *Far Eastern Economic Review* **162**(47) (25 November), 80–4.

Legrold, R. (1993) 'Sino-Soviet relations: The American factor' in R. Ross (ed.) *China and the United States, the Soviet Union and Tripolarity and Policy Making in the Cold War*. New York: M.E. Sharpe.

Lenin, V.I. (1908) *The Essentials of Lenin*, Vol. 1. London: Lawrence-Wishart.

Levine, S.I. (1994) 'Perception and ideology in Chinese Foreign Policy' in T.W. Robinson and D. Shambaugh (eds) *Chinese Foreign Policy: Theory and Practice*. Oxford: Clarendon Press.

Li Daoyu (1993) 'Foreign policy and arms control: The view from China', *Arms Control Today* **23**(10) (December), 9–11.

Lin Qinggong (1992) 'The changing international military pattern from old to new: Development trends in the world military situation'. *Foreign Broadcast Information System*, No. 118 (June), 26–7.

Lu Ning (1997) *The Dynamics of Foreign-Policy Decision Making in China*. Boulder, CO: Westview Press.

Lu, C.H. (1986) *The Sino-Indian Border Dispute*. New York: Greenwood Press.

Lukin, A. (1991) 'The initial Soviet reaction to the events in China in 1989 and the prospects for Sino-Soviet relations'. *The China Quarterly* (No. 125) (March), 119–36.

Machiavelli, N. (1950) *The Prince and the Discourses*. New York: The Modern Library.

Mancall, M. (1963) 'The persistence of tradition in China's foreign policy'. *Annals of the American Academy of Political and Social Sciences* **349** (September).

Mandelbaum, M. (1997) 'Westernising Russia and China'. *Foreign Affairs* **76**(3) (1 May), 80–96.

Mao Zedong (1971) 'On contradiction' in *Selected Reading from the Works of Mao Tsetung*. Beijing: Foreign Language Press.

Mao Zedong (1971) 'On the People's Democratic Dictatorship' in *Selected Reading from the Works of Mao Tsetung*. Beijing: Foreign Language Press.

Mayer, P. (1962) *Sino-Soviet Relations since the Death of Stalin*. Kowloon, Hong Kong: Union Research Institution.

Medveded, R. (1986) *China and the Superpowers*. Oxford: Basil Blackwell.

Menon, R. (1997) 'The strategic convergence between Russia and China'. *Survival* **39**(2) (Summer), 101–25.

Meyer, P.F. (1992) 'Gorbachev and post-Gorbachev policy toward the Korean Peninsula: The impact of changing Russian perceptions'. *Asian Survey* **32**(8) (August), 757–72.

Mills, W. deB. (1986) 'Gorbachev and the future of Sino-Soviet relations'. *Political Science Quarterly* **101**(4) (Winter), 535–58.

Mojtahed-Zadeh, P. (1998) 'Arab–Iran territorial disputes: Co-operation in the region, not confrontation' in K. el-Din Haseeb (ed.) *Arab–Iranian Relations*, pp. 237–48. Beirut: Centre for Arab Unity Studies.

Morgenthau, H. (1967) *Politics Among Nations: The Struggle for Power and Peace*. New York: Alfred A Knopf.

Morse, E.L. (1970) 'The transformation of foreign policies: Modernization, interdependence and externalization'. *World Politics* **22**(3), 371–92.

Mosher, S.W. (2000) *Hegemon: China's Plan to Dominate Asia and the World*, pp. 106–7. San Francisco: Encounter Books.

Mostyn, T. (1991) *Major Political Events in Iran, Iraq and the Arabian Peninsula*. New York: Facts & File.

Mulvenon, J. (ed.) (1997) *China Facts & Figures: Annual Handbook*, Vol. 21. Florida: Academic International Press.

Munro, R.H. (1994) 'Central Asia and China' in M. Mandelbaum (ed.) *Central Asia and the World*. New York: Council of Foreign Relations Press.

Nelson, H.W. (1981) *The Chinese Military System: An Organizational Study of the Chinese People's Liberation Army*, pp. 200–1. Boulder, CO: Westview Press.

Neuhauser, C. (1968) *Third World Politics: China and the Afro-Asian People's Solidarity Organization, 1957–1967*. Cambridge, MA: East Asian Research Center, Harvard University.

Ngok Lee (1989) *China's Defence Modernisation and Military Leadership*. Oxford: Pergamon Press.

North, R.C. (1969). *The Foreign Relations of China*. Belmont, CA: Dickenson Publishing.

Nye, J.S. (1997–8) 'China's re-emergence and the future of the Asia-Pacific'. *Survival* **39**(4) (Winter), 65–79.

O'Ballance, E. (1971) *The War in the Yemen*. London: Faber.

Ogunsanwo, A. (1974) *China's Policy in Africa 1958–71*, pp. 52–3. Cambridge: Cambridge University Press.

Olcott, M.B. (1996) *Central Asia's New States: Independence, Foreign Policy, and Regional Security*. Washington, DC: United States Institute of Peace Press.

OPEC (1993) *Annual Statistical Bulletin 1992*. Austria, OPEC.

OPEC (1997) *Annual Statistical Bulletin 1997*. Austria: OPEC.

Orr, J. (1991–2) 'Evolution of U.S. trade with China'. *Federal Reserve Bank of New York Quarterly Review* **16**(4) (Winter), 47–54.

Page, S. (1985) *The Soviet Union and the Yemens: Influence in Symmetrical Relationships*. New York: Frederick A. Praeger.

Parker, M. (1993) 'Saudi–China: Chinese trade takes off'. *The Middle East* (October), 29.

Pentland, C. (1976) 'International organizations and their role' in J. Thompson, K.W. Rosenau and G. Boyd (eds) *World Politics*. New York: Free Press.

Pollack, J.D. (1984) 'China and the global strategic balance' in H. Harding (ed.) *China's Foreign Relations in the 1980s*, pp. 146–69. New Haven, CT: Yale University Press.

Pollack, J.D. (1991) 'The opening to America' in R. Macfarquhar and J.K. Fairbank (eds) *The Cambridge History of China*, Vol. 15. Cambridge: Cambridge University Press.

Porter, A. (1992) 'Patriot missile secrets leaked to China'. *Sunday Telegraph*, 29 March, 2.

Powles, A.J. (1991) 'What were the factors that contributed towards Qasim's overthrow in 1963', MA thesis, Durham University.

Purifoy, L. McC. (1976) *Harry Truman's China Policy: MacCarthysim and the Diplomacy of Hysteria, 1947–1951*. New York: New View Points.

Qimao Chen (1993) 'New approaches in China's foreign policy in the post-Cold War era'. *Asian Survey* **32**(3), 237–51.

QCSO (1994) 'State of Qatar Presidency of the Council of Ministers'. *Trade Exchange 1993*, pp. 837 and 985. Qatar: Qatari Central Statistical Organization.

Quandt, W.B. (1981) *Saudi Arabia in the 1980s: Foreign Policy, Security, and Oil*. Washington, DC: Brookings Institution.

Quested, R.K.I. (1984) *Sino-Russian Relations: A Short History*. London: George Allen & Unwin.

Rajan Menon, R. (1997) 'The strategic convergence between Russia and China. *Survival* **39**(2) (Summer), 101–25, 137.

Rashid, A. and Holland, L. (2000) 'Shifting sands'. *Far Eastern Economic Review* **163**(9) (2 March), 26–7.

Rea, K.W. (1975) 'Peking and the Brezhnev doctrine'. *Asian Affairs: An American Review* **3**(1), 22–30.

Rea, K.W. and Yawsoon Sim (n.d.) 'An attitudinal analysis of China's response to the Breznez doctrine and the Asian collective security system'. *Asian Forum* **7**(3–4), 1–10.

Rhode, G.F. and Whitlock, R.E. (1980) *Treaties of the People's Republic of China, 1949–1978: An Annotated Compilation*. Boulder, CO: Westview Press.

Robinson, T.W. (1991) 'China confronts the Soviet Union: Warfare and diplomacy on China's inner Asian frontiers' in D. Twitchett and J.K. Fairbank (eds) *The Cambridge History of China*, Vol. 15, Part 2. Cambridge: Cambridge University Press.

Robinson, T.W. (1994) 'Interdependence in China's foreign relations' in S.S. Kim (ed.) *China and the World: Chinese Foreign Relations in the Post-cold War Era*. Boulder, CO: Westview Press.

Rosecrance, R.N. (1963) *Action and Reaction in World Politics*. Boston: Little, Brown.

Ross, E.W. (1990) 'United States–Chinese military relations: Implications for Japan' in J. Radvany (ed.) *The Pacific in the 1990s: Economic and Strategic Changes*. New York: University Press of America.

Ross, R.S. (1997a). 'Beijing as a conservative power'. *Foreign Affairs* **76**(2) (1 March) 33–44.

Ross, R.S. (1997b). 'Why our hardliners are wrong'. *The National Interest*, No. 49 (Fall), 42–51.

Roy, D. (1998) *China's Foreign Relations*. New York: Rowman and Littlefield.

Ruggie, J.G. (1986) 'Continuity and transformation in world polity: Towards neorealist synthesis' in R. Keohane (ed.) *Neorealism and its Critics*. New York: Columbia University Press.

Safire, W. (1992) 'China's Hama Rules'. *New York Times*, Current Events edition, 5 March, A27.

Safran, N. (1988) *Saudi Arabia: The Ceaseless Quest for Security*. London: Cornell University Press.

Scalapino, R.A. (1962) 'Traditions and transition in the Asian policy of communist China' in E.F. Szczepanik (ed.) *Symposium on Economic and Social Problems of the Far East*. Hong Kong: Hong Kong University Press.

Shichor, Y. (1977) 'The Palestinians and China's foreign policy' in Chun-tu Hsueh (ed.) *Dimensions of China's Foreign Relations*. New York: Frederick A. Praeger.

Shichor, Y. (1979) *The Middle East in China's Foreign Policy 1949–1977*. Cambridge: Cambridge University Press.
Shichor, Y. (1984) 'The role of Islam in China's Middle-Eastern policy' in R. Israel and A.H. John (eds) *Islam in Asia: Southeast and East Asia*. Jerusalem: The Hebrew University, Magnes Press.
Shichor, Y. (1988) 'Unfolded arms: Beijing's recent military sales offensive'. *Pacific Review* **1**(3), 320–30.
Shichor, Y. (1989) *East Wind over Arabia: Origins and Implications of the Sino-Saudi Missile Deal*. Berkeley: University of California, Institute of East Asian Studies.
Shichor, Y. (1991a) 'China and the Gulf Crisis: Escape from predicament'. *Problem of Communism* **40** (November), 80–90.
Shichor, Y. (1991b) 'China and the role of the United Nations in the Middle East: Revised policy'. *Asian Survey* **31** (March), 255–69.
Shichor, Y. (1992) 'China and the Middle East since Tiananmen'. *Annals of the American Academy of Political and Social Sciences* **519** (January), 86–100.
Schram, S.R. (1984) 'Economics in command: Ideology and policy since the third plenum, 1978–84'. *China Quarterly*, No. 99 (September), 417–59.
Schram, S.S. (1993) 'Deng Xiaoping's quest for "Modernisation with Chinese characteristics" and the future of Marxism-Leninism' in M. Ying-Maohau and S.H. Marsh (eds) *China in the Era of Deng Xiaoping a Decade of Reform*. New York: An East Gate Book.
Schurmann, F. (1968) *Ideolgy and Organization in Communist China*, 2nd edn. Berkeley: University of California Press.
Sciolino, E. (1995a) 'China targeted on missile exports'. *International Herald Tribune*, 23 June, 1.
Sciolino, E. (1995b) 'CIA report says Chinese sent Iran arms components'. *New York Times*, 22 June, A1.
Segal, G. (1992) 'China and the disintegration of the Soviet Union'. *Asian Survey* **32**(9) (September), 848–68.
Seib, G.F. (1988) 'Saudi purchase of long-range missiles rekindles debate on U.S. arms to Arabs'. *Wall Street Journal*, Eastern edition, 4 April, 1.
Seib, G.F. (1990) 'Gulf Crisis casts Saudi Arabia's Prince Bandar in a high-visibility role on the global stage'. *Wall Street Journal*, Eastern edition, 26 November, 12.
Shih Tsan-Yen (1975) 'Development of Sino-Iranian trade relations'. *China Foreign Trade*, No. 4, 6–7.
Shinn, J. (ed.) (1996) *Weaving the Net: Conditional Engagement with China*. New York: Council on Foreign Relations Press.
Shulong Chu (1994) 'China and strategy: The PRC girds for limited high-tech war'. *Orbis* **38**(2) (Spring), 177–92.
SIPRI Yearbook 1989: World Armament and Disarmament, p. 252. London: Oxford University Press.
SIPRI Yearbook 1991: World Armaments and Disarmament, p. 157. Oxford: Oxford University Press.
SIPRI Yearbook 1992: Armament, Disarmament and International Security, p. 338. Oxford: Oxford University Press.
SIPRI Yearbook 1994: Armament, Disarmament and International Security, p. 526. Oxford: Oxford University Press.
SIPRI Yearbook 1995: Armament, Disarmament and International Security, p. 526. Oxford: Oxford University Press.

SIPRI Yearbook 1996: Armament, Disarmament and International Security, p. 502. Oxford: Oxford University Press.
SIPRI Yearbook 1997: Armament, Disarmament and International Security, p. 268. Oxford: Oxford University Press.
SIPRI Yearbook 1998: Armament, Disarmament and International Security, p. 339. Oxford: Oxford University Press.
SMFNE (1997) *Foreign Trade Statistics*. Saudi Arabia: Central Department of Statistics, Saudi Ministry of Finance and National Economy.
Smith, R.J. (1996) 'Chinese firms supply Iran with gas factories'. *Washington Post*, 8 March, A26.
SODPC (1997) *Dubai External Trade Statistics*, pp. 232 and 238. Dubai: Statistics Office of Department of Ports and Customs.
Spaeth, A. (1999) 'Wanna dance? Warming up for his Washington trip, Zhu Rongi tangoed and tangled – with Madeleine Albright on tough issues. Can China and the US get in step?'. See http://cnn.com/ASIANOW/time/asia/magazine/1999/990315/china1.html, p. 1.
State of Qatar Presidency of the Council of Ministers (1994) *Trade Exchange 1993*, pp. 837 and 985. Qatar: Central Statistical Organisation.
Steiner, H.A. (1961) 'Communist China in world community'. *International Conciliation*, No. 533 (May).
Stevenson, S. (1995) 'China's population: A dilemma for the future'. *Journal of Southeast Asia* **1**(1) (Summer), 12–30.
Stookey, R.W. (1982) *South Yemen: A Marxist Republic in Arabia*. London: Croom Helm.
Sutter, R.G. (1978a) *China-Watch: Toward Sino-American Reconciliation*. Baltimore: John Hopkins University Press.
Sutter, R.G. (1978b) *Chinese Foreign Policy after the Cultural Revolution, 1966–1977*. Boulder, CO: Westview Press.
Sutter, R.G. (1996) *Shaping China's Future in World Affairs: The Role of the United States*. Boulder, CO: Westview Press.
Sylvester, C. (1994) *Feminist Theory and International Relations in a Post-Modern Era*. Cambridge: Cambridge University Press.
Tai Ming Cheung (1988) 'Proliferation is good and there is money in it too'. *Far Eastern Economic Review* (2 June), 26–7.
Tai Ming Cheung (1992) 'Unguided missiles: China's arms exports stir consternation'. *Far Eastern Economic Review* **155**(5) (6 February), 42–3.
Tai Sung An (1976) *The Sino-Soviet Territorial Dispute*, pp. 160–1. Philadelphia: Westminster Press.
Tang Tsou and Halperin, N. (1965) 'Mao Tse-tung's revolutionary strategy and Peking's international behaviour'. *American Political Science Review* **59**(1) (March), 80–104.
Tanzer, A. (1982) 'The Saudi connection'. *Far Eastern Economic Review* (9 July), 28–9.
Timperlake, E. and Triplett, W. C. II (1998) *Year of the Rat*. Washington, DC: Regnery.
Timperlake, E. and Triplett, W.C. II (1999) *Red Dragon Rising: Communist China's Military Threat to America*. Washington, DC: Regnery.
Tucker, N.B. (1991) 'China and America: 1941–1991'. *Foreign Affairs* **70**(5) (Winter) 75–92.

UAE Statistical Yearbook 1992, p. 145. Abu Dhabi: Department of Planning, 1993.

Valencia, M.J. (1997) 'Energy and insecurity in Asia'. *Survival* **39**(3) (Autumn), 85–106.

van Kemenade, W. (1997) *China, Hong Kong, Taiwan Inc*. New York: Alfred A. Knopf.

van Ness, P. (1970) *Revolution and Chinese Foreign Policy: Peking Support for Wars of National Liberation*. Berkeley: University of California Press.

Viotti, P.R and Kauppi, M.V. (1993) *International Relations Theory: Realism, Pluralism, Globalism*, 2nd edn. Needham Heights, MA: Allyn and Bacon.

Waller, D. (1997) 'The secret missile deal'. *Time*, 30 June, 58.

Wallerstein, I. (1979) *The Capitalist World Economy*. Cambridge: Cambridge University Press.

Wallerstein, I. (1991) *Unthinking Social Science: The Limits of Nineteenth-Century Paradigms*. Cambridge: Polity Press.

Walsh, J.R. (1993) 'China and the new geopolitics of Central Asia'. *Asian Survey* **32**(3) (March) 271–84.

Waltz, K.N. (1954) *Man, the State, and War*. New York: Columbia University Press.

Waltz, K.N. (1979) *Theory of International Politics*. Reading, MA: Addison-Wesley.

Waltz, K.N. (1993) 'The emerging structure of international politics'. *International Security* **18**(2) (Fall) 44–79.

Wang Zhongren (1997) ' "China threat" theory groundless'. *Beijing Review* **40**(28) (14–20 July), 7–8.

Wang, T.Y. (1993) 'Competition for friendship: The two Chinas and Saudi Arabia'. *Arab Studies Quarterly* **15**(3) (Summer), 63–82.

Warne, W.E. (1956) *Mission for Peace: Point 4 in Iran*, p. 18. Indianapolis: Bobbs-Merrill.

Westad, O.A. (ed.) (1998) *Brothers in Arms: the Rise and Fall of the Sino-Soviet Alliance, 1945–1963*. Stanford, CA: Stanford University Press.

Whiting, A.S. (1987) 'The Sino-Soviet Split' in R. Macfarquhar and J.K. Fairbank (eds) *The Cambridge History of China*, Vol. 14, Part 1. Cambridge: Cambridge University Press.

Whiting, A.S. (1992) 'Foreign policy of China' in R.C. Macridis (ed.) *Foreign Policy in World Politics*, 8th edn. Upper Saddle River, NJ: Prentice-Hall International Editions.

Whiting, A.S. (1994) 'The future of China's foreign policy' in S.S. Kim (ed.) *China and the World: Chinese Foreign Relations in the Post-Cold War Era*. Boulder, CO: Westview Press.

Whiting, A.S. (1996) 'The PLA and China's threat perceptions'. *China Quarterly*, No. 146 (June), 597–615.

Willett, S. (1997) 'East Asia's changing defence industry'. *Survival* **39**(3) (Autumn) 107–34.

Williams, R.L. (1989) 'U.S. response to changes in China'. *Department of State Bulletin* **89**(151) (October), 27–30.

Winters, C.-A. (1979) *Mao or Muhammad: Islam in the People's Republic of China*. Hong Kong: Asian Research Service.

Wolf, J. (1999) 'Going ballistic'. *Far Eastern Economic Review* **162**(7) (18 February), 26.

Wolfe, B.D. (1957) *Khrushchev and Stalin's Ghost: Text, Background and Meaning of Khrushchev's Secret Report to the Twentieth Congress on the Night of February 24–25, 1956*. New York: Frederick A. Praeger.
Womack, B. and Guangzhi Zhao (1994) 'The many worlds of China's provinces: Foreign trade and diversification' in D.S.G. Goodman and G. Segal (eds) *China Deconstruct: Politics, Trade and Regionalism*. London: Routledge.
Wortzel, LM. (1994) 'Chinese pursues traditional great power status'. *Orbis* **38**(2) (Spring), 157–76.
Xie Yixian (1989) 'China's foreign policy: A 1980s tune-up'. *Beijing Review* **32**(7–8) (13–26 February), 12–17.
Xu Wei (1989) 'Sino-Iraq trade relations'. *China Foreign Trade*, No. 3, 12–13.
Yabuki, S. (1995) *China's New Political Economy: The Giant Awakes*. Boulder, CO: Westview Press.
Yahuda, M. (1981) 'Dilemmas and problems for China in the Middle East' in C. Legum (ed.) *Crisis and Conflicts in the Middle East: The Changing Strategy*. New York: Holmes & Meier.
Yahuda, M. (1983). *Towards the End of Isolationism: China's Foreign Policy After Mao*. London: Macmillan Press.
Yahuda, M. (1996) *The International Politics of the Asia-Pacific, 1945–1995*. London: Routledge.
Yang, J.E. and Greenberger, R.S. (1988) 'U.S. military sale to Saudis opposed by 58 senators'. *Wall Street Journal*, Eastern edition, 15 April.
Yodfat, A.Y. (1977) 'The People's Republic of China and the Middle East' in *Courrier de l'extreme-orient*, Bruxelles.
Zagoria, D.S. (1962) *The Sino-Soviet Conflict, 1956–1961*. Princeton: Princeton University Press.
Zagoria, D.S. (1989) 'The Soviet-Vietnamese alliance and its strategic implications' in T. Dreyer and I.J. Kim (eds) *Chinese Defence and Foreign Policy*. New York: Paragon House.
Zhao Quansheng (1992) 'Domestic factors of Chinese foreign policy: From vertical to horizontal authoritarianism'. *Annals of the American Academy of Political and Social Sciences* **519** (January), 158–75.

PERIODICAL SOURCES

Ak-bar al-bitrul Walsina'a (UAE)
Al Anwar
Al Arab
Al Ittihad (UAE Newspaper – Abu Dhabi)
Al Khaleej (UAE Newspaper – Sharjah)
Al Qabas
Al Rayan
Al Riyadh
Al Wafd
Al Wahdah (UAE Newspaper – Abu Dhabi)
Al-Ghorfa (UAE – Fujairah)
Al-Kifah al-Arabi

Al-Rai al-Amm
Al-Sharq al-Awsat
Al-Watan al-Arabi
An Nahda
As-Siyassah
Beijing Review (Peking Review)
British Broadcast Company, Summary of World Broadcasts
Business Week
China Daily (Hong Kong Edition)
China Economic Review
China News Digest
China Reconstructs
Current Digest of the Soviet Press
Dubai External Trade Statistics
Economist
Economist Intelligence Unit, Country Profile
Financial Times
Foreign Broadcast Information System
Foreign Trade Statistics (Saudi Arabia)
Free China Review
IMF Direction of Trade Statistics Yearbook
Jiefang Ribao
Joint Publications Research Services – China Report
Kuwait Times
Middle East
Middle East Economic Digest
Middle East Economic Survey
Middle East International
Military Balance
New York Times
New York Times Current Events Edition
OAPEC Bulletin
People's China
Petroleum News Letter (Iran)
Petroleum Times Energy Report
Renmin Ribao
Saudi Economic Survey
Sawt al-Kuwayt
SIPRI Yearbook: World Armament, Disarmament and International Security
South China Morning Post
Statistical Yearbook (Oman)
Sunday Telegraph
Sunday Times
Time Magazine
Times (Oman)
Trade and Industry (UAE – Dubai)
Trade Exchange 1993 (Qatar)
UAE Statistical Yearbook 1992
US News & World Report

Wall Street Journal
Washington Post
Washington Times
Wen Wei Po
World Military Expenditure and Arms Transfers
Xinhua News Agency News Bulletin
Zhengming
Zhongguo Tongzue She

ELECTRONIC SOURCES

www.cnd.org/CND-Global/CND-Global.95.2nd/CND-Global.95-06-27.html
www.cnd.org/CND-Global/CND-Global.96.3rd/CND-Global.96-08-06.html
www.cnn.com/ASIANOW/time/asia/magazine/1999/990315/china1.html
www.cns.miis.edu/research/iraq/uns_chro.html
www.fas.org/irp/threat/missile/iran.html
www.fas.org/news/iran/1998/980313-iran.html
www.fas.org/spp/starwars/congress/1997-h/s970410m.html
www.fas.org/spp/starwars/congress/1977-h/s971008m.htm.
www.fas.org/spp/starwars/congress/1998/s980313a.html
www.fas.org/spp/stawars/crs/92-056-1.html
www.fas.org/spp/starwars/crs/980717CRSWeapons.html
www.lasvegassun.com/sunbin.../s/w-me/1999/nov/03/110300614.htm
www.state.gov/www/regions/eap/fs-us-china-relations.html
www.uaeinteract.com/newsreport/19970612.html

Index

Afghanistan 70,106, 108, 111, 118–119, 134, 162, 186, 206, 215, 217, 222
Africa 8, 11, 60, 63, 98, 215
Algeria 14–16, 79, 130, 146
Angola 65
Arab League 136–137, 189, 236, 251
Arab world 3, 12, 15, 101, 137–138, 188, 191
Armenia 75–76
Asian Development Bank 35, 38
Australia 62
Azerbaijan 75

Baghdad Pact 97, 99, 100, 137–138, 154–155, 185
Bahrain 3, 17, 67, 107, 119, 134, 139, 219, 251, 253, 256–260, 269
  Isa Bin Salman al-Khalifah 256
Bandung Conference 7, 12–13, 16, 56, 96, 98, 102, 134, 137, 261, 266, 267
Britain 59, 134, 137, 150, 157, 173, 189, 199–200
Brunei 6
Bucharest Conference 59
Burma 62
Byelorussia 75

Cambodia 4, 9, 65, 70–71, 176–177
Canada 5, 50, 157
Central Asia 6, 11, 17, 76, 91, 172
Chen Chu 110, 161
Chen Yi 139
Chi Haotian 75, 79, 232
Chi Pengfei 105, 156, 158, 207
Chiang Kai-shek 29
China Council for Promotion of International Trade 233, 252

China Islamic Association 99, 103, 160, 209, 214–215, 219–221, 256
China Ministry of Foreign Economic Relations and Trade 37, 199
China National Petroleum Corporation 147, 201, 210
China Petrochemical Corporation 132, 200, 235, 250
China Precision Machinery Import–Export Corporation 126
China Road and Bridge Engineering Co. 146
China State Construction Engineering Corporation 143, 146
China Threat 9, 11
Chinese Communist Party (CCP) 33–34, 54, 56, 58–60, 73, 90, 215
Chinese defence budget, *see also* military expenditures 48–50
Chinese invasion of Vietnam 46, 166
Chinese Maritime Engineering Company 201
Chinese National Chemical Construction Company 194
Chinese People's Liberation Army 48–49
Cold War 3–4, 39, 46, 87
  Post-Cold War 9, 15–16, 47–48, 80, 91, 272
Confucianism 10, 29
Cox Report 85–86
Cultural Revolution 30, 61, 176, 193, 215, 219

Dalai Lama 81
Deng Xiaoping 9, 29, 33, 37, 47, 64–67, 70, 74, 76–77, 108, 141, 164, 215, 220
Dhofari rebels, *see* Oman

Index

Economic Modernization Programme (the Four Modernizations Programme) 4, 16, 34–35, 37, 46–47, 51, 68, 119, 193, 268
Egypt 4, 12–13, 67, 99, 101, 103, 108, 138, 173, 188, 215, 244
Ethiopia 65, 157
Europe 8, 16, 47, 67, 76
   Eastern 9, 74, 107
   Western 67, 112

Fatah 15–16
Five Principles of Peaceful Coexistence 32, 38, 57, 121, 123, 229, 244–245
Falun Gong 81
France 14, 50, 67, 139, 150, 152, 199, 213
Front Liberation National of Algeria 14

General Agreement on Tariff and Trade 35, 81, 86, 89
Georgia 75
Germany 12, 50
   West Germany 67
Great Leap Forward 57

Hao Po-tsun 228
Hong Kong 6, 224, 226
Hu Jintao 255
Hua Guofeng 67, 107, 158–160, 206
Huang Hua 206
Human rights 78, 81–82, 89

Independent foreign policy 34, 68–74
India 6, 38, 58, 67, 76, 84, 90, 205, 245, 273
Indonesia 6, 11, 62, 215, 273
International Bank for Reconstruction and Development, or World Bank 4, 35, 38
International Finance Corporation 35
International Monetary Fund 35, 38
Investments 35, 36
Iran 3–5, 13, 15–17, 67, 84, 96–98, 105–108, 133, 153–173, 186, 202, 205, 220, 227, 237, 245, 252, 256, 266, 268, 271–272
   arms sales to Iran 72, 79, 116–117, 125, 126–130, 165–166, 168–171, 207, 269
   hostage crisis 109–110

Iranian Revolution 17, 109–111, 159–160, 164, 168
Soviet policy in Iran 109–112, 159–162, 164, 166, 186
Iran–Iraq War 111–114, 144–145, 160–161, 167, 196, 207–208, 219, 222, 227, 240, 242, 244–245
Iraq 3, 5, 13, 17–18, 48, 51, 96–98, 100, 105–108, 133, 136–152, 165, 185–186, 198–199, 205, 213, 252, 266–268
   arms sales to Iraq 79, 116, 118, 129, 144, 146, 207
   Soviet influence in Iraq 139–142, 185
Islam (Muslims) 10, 16, 76, 97, 99, 130, 195, 209, 213–216, 219–221, 224, 227, 230–231, 241, 247
Israel 12–13, 15–18, 50, 72, 97, 113, 124, 160, 227, 232, 239–240, 247, 253, 273
Italy 50, 67, 157

Japan 6, 29, 35, 37, 47, 56, 67, 82, 90, 96, 108, 122, 150, 197–198, 209–210, 249, 266, 269, 273
Jiang Zemin 33, 75, 85, 87–88, 90, 212, 232, 235, 245, 255, 271, 272
Jordan 13, 58, 247

Kazakhstan 75, 80–81, 87, 89, 172
Korea 6, 9, 11, 38, 46, 154, 210, 266, 273
Korean crisis 4
Korean War 55–56, 96–97, 137, 154, 213
Kuwait 3, 13, 15–17, 97, 105–108, 134, 142, 146, 157, 164, 188–202, 205, 224, 244, 250, 252, 256, 261, 268
   arms sales to Kuwait 193, 196, 200
Kuwait crisis 120–125, 145
Kuwait Fund for Arab Economic Development 121, 193–194, 200
Kuwait oil policy 192, 194
Jaber al-Ahmed al-Sabah 121, 190, 198–199
Saad Abdullah al-Salem al-Sabah 189, 200
Sabah al-Ahmad al-Jabir 192, 198
UN resolutions on Kuwait 190, 198–199
Kyrgyzstan 75, 81, 87, 89

Laos 11, 62, 176
Latin America 8, 60, 63

Index   305

Leaning to one side policy 7, 13, 31–32
Lebanon 13, 58, 217, 232
Li Hsiennian 158
Li Lanqing 169, 172, 234, 246, 254, 259
Li Ruihuan 248, 260
Li Peng 71, 73, 80, 88, 123, 149, 168, 198, 199, 230, 231, 245
Li Xiannian 181, 226
Lin Biao 60, 103
Liu Huaging 73
Liu Shaoqi 29, 101, 215

Macao 6
Malaysia 6, 62, 152, 273
Mao Zedong 7, 29, 30, 33, 63–64, 103, 108
Mao Zedong thought 31–32, 53, 57, 202, 214–215
Marxism–Leninism 29–32, 53, 215
Mauritania 130, 146
Middle East 3–5, 11–18, 63, 67–68, 84, 98–99, 101, 107–108, 111, 113, 123, 125, 173, 196, 205, 217, 219, 222, 225, 231–233
Mischief Reef 46
Military capability 5, 10, 19, 44–45, 47–48, 50, 82
Military cooperation 50, 71–72, 86, 125, 160, 200, 269
Military transfer 5, 11, 79, 103, 115–116, 125–126, 166, 168, 170–171, 207
Moldova 75
Mongolia 11, 80, 215
Morocco 100
Most-favoured nation 77–78
Mujahideen 66, 108

NATO 56, 84, 86, 88
 operation in Yugoslavia 83–84, 88–89
Nepal 67

Oman 15, 17, 97, 106–107, 132, 134, 179–180, 201–212, 218, 224, 237, 244, 250, 252, 256, 261, 266, 271
 Dhofar Liberation Front, also Dhofaris and Dhofari rebels 14, 16, 102–104, 202, 213, 261, 267–268
 Popular Front for the Liberation of Oman 15–16, 103–104
 Popular Front for the Liberation of the Occupied Arabian Gulf 103–104, 106, 156, 202, 236, 251

Qaboos bin Sa'id al-Sa'id 203, 205, 207–208, 212

Palestine, also Palestinians 4, 13–15, 18, 113, 140, 192, 218, 222, 231, 233, 239, 241, 273
Pakistan 5, 11, 16, 66, 72, 79, 108, 156–157, 160, 167–168, 215, 245
Paracel Islands 46
People's war 12, 15, 101, 202
Peng Zhen 59
The Philippines 6, 11, 56, 273
Pot regime 46
Port Arthur 54

Qatar 3, 17, 107, 119, 134, 219, 251–255, 269
 Ahmad Bin Ali al-Thani 251
 Khalifah ibn Hamad al-Thani 253–254
Qi Huaiyuan 113, 164, 195
Qian Qichen 145–146, 164, 183, 200, 224, 228, 231, 255, 258–259
Quemoy Island 58

Red Sea 62, 184, 206
Romania 67
Ron Yiren 240, 257

Saudi Arabia 3, 5, 13, 17, 97–99, 107, 115, 119–120, 134, 173, 180, 213–237, 251, 253, 256, 266–267, 269, 271
 Abdullah ibn Abd al-Aziz al-Sa'ud 220, 226, 232
 Aramco 132, 234–235
 Arms sales to Saudi Arabia 79, 115, 130, 225–227
 Fahad ibn Abd al-Aziz 216, 218, 220, 226, 229, 231–232
 Fahd Plan 217
 Faisal bin Sa'ud 213–214
Shanghai Communiqué 64
Singapore 6, 62
Silk Road 16
South China Sea 10–11, 50, 122, 149, 274
Southeast Asia 6, 9, 11, 30, 38, 47, 63, 96, 132, 244
Soviet Union 6–9, 12–14, 16–17, 19, 28, 31–32, 44, 46–47, 50, 52–91, 95, 104–105, 107–108, 134–136, 138, 140, 143, 150, 152–153, 155,

159–160, 173, 179, 181, 190, 192–193, 195, 201–202, 205–207, 213, 217, 251, 261, 266–270, 272
Boris Yeltsin 74, 88–90
Eduard Shevardnadze 164, 166
Igor Nikolayevich Rodionov 86
Leonid Brezhnev 60, 69
Mikhail Gorbachev 69–70, 73–76
Nikita Khrushchev 8, 55–61, 90, 266
Soviet Communist Party 57, 59, 74
Soviet invasion of Afghanistan 66–67, 206, 227, 269
Soviet invasion of Czechoslovakia 61, 104
South Africa 50, 200
Strait of Hormuz 111, 207, 242, 273
Strategic arms limitation talks 62
Sudan 100
Sun Yat-sen 29
Syria 5, 12–13, 79, 100–101, 213, 215, 232

Tiananmen square, and Tiananmen massacre 37, 46, 73, 77, 122, 165, 196–198, 260
Taiwan, or Republic of China 6–7, 10–11, 46–47, 55, 58, 64–66, 72, 79–80, 83, 89–91, 98, 106, 119, 123, 136, 152, 154, 173, 190–191, 204–205, 218, 226–228, 238, 244, 247–248, 255, 257–258, 266, 269–272
arms sales to Taiwan 65–66, 68–69
Taiwan Relation Act 66
Lee Teng-hui 79, 83, 247–248, 271
Tajikistan 75, 81, 87, 89
Thailand 65, 210, 273
Theatre Missile Defence 6, 47, 82–83, 89
Third World, *and* Third World countries 7–9, 15, 30, 32, 46, 56, 60, 66, 74, 97–98, 100, 104, 106, 137, 154, 185, 187, 196–197, 214, 239, 266
Tibet 78, 82, 152, 215
Tian Jiyun 144, 167, 243
Tributary system 28
Turkey 141, 148, 172
Turkmenistan 75, 172
Two camps theory 7, 29

Ukraine 75
United Arab Emirates 3, 17, 107, 119–120, 134, 218, 224, 236–250, 269, 271

Khalifah Bin Zayed al-Nahayyan 248
Sultan Bin Muhammad al-Qasimi 242, 246
Zayed Bin Sultan al-Nahayyan 236–237, 241, 243–248
United Front 8, 56
United Nation 58, 97, 110, 113, 133, 137, 147, 149, 151–152
United Nation Development Program 38
United Nations resolutions on Iran–Iraq war 111–112, 114, 161, 164, 208
United Nation resolutions on Kuwait 37–38, 80, 120, 122, 145–146, 201
UN Special Commission 148–152
UN Monitoring Verification and Inspection Commission 152
United States 6–10, 12, 16, 19, 30–32, 37, 46, 50, 52–91, 95, 112–113, 135–137, 139, 151, 153, 193, 195, 199–200, 202, 206, 226–227, 266, 268–270, 272
Bill Clinton 77–79, 81, 85
George Bush 37, 73, 77, 79
Gerald Ford 65
Henry Kissinger 39, 41, 64, 108
Harry Truman 55
Jimmy Carter 65–66, 179
Richard Nixon 63–64, 108
Ronald Reagan 68–69
US and Iran 109–110, 159–160
Uzbekistan 75–76

Vietnam 9, 11, 56, 61–62, 65, 68, 76, 176, 273

World Trade Organisation *see also* GATT 81, 86, 89
Wu Bangguo 184
Wu Xueqian 145, 163, 182, 207, 219, 255, 241, 227

Xinjiang 83, 152, 220

Yao Yilin 218, 226, 241, 243, 252
Yang Fuchang 124, 256, 259
Yang Shangkun 164, 168, 170, 182, 196, 208, 229–230, 243–244, 246
Yemen 3, 12, 16–17, 97–100, 173–185, 186–187, 215, 266, 271
Abd-al-fattah Ismail 177

Ali Abdullah Saleh 176, 181, 184–185
Ali Salim al-Baid 182
The Front for the Liberation of
  Occupied South Yemen 174–178
National Liberation Front 101,
  174–178
People's Democratic Republic of
  Yemen 101–102, 104, 106–108, 134,
  174, 178–181, 187, 205, 207,
  215–216, 227, 236–237, 250,
  267–268
Soviet aid 102, 108, 179
Yemen Arab Republic 99, 106–107,
  173–174, 180–181, 186, 217, 267

Yugoslavia 59, 67, 84

Zaire 205
Zhang Jinfu 143, 163
Zhao Qizheng 86
Zhao Ziyang 36, 111, 163, 218, 222, 242,
  253
Zhou Enlai 29, 60, 61, 71, 98, 103, 108,
  139, 154, 188, 214, 236–237, 251,
  253, 256
Zhu Rongi 81, 245